White Power

White Power

& the Rise
and Fall
of the
National
Party

Christi van der Westhuizen

ZEBRA

Published by Zebra Press
an imprint of Struik Publishers
(a division of New Holland Publishing (South Africa) (Pty) Ltd)
PO Box 1144, Cape Town, 8000
New Holland Publishing is a member of Johnnic Communications Ltd

www.zebrapress.co.za

First published 2007

1 3 5 7 9 10 8 6 4 2

Publication © Zebra Press 2007
Text © Christi van der Westhuizen 2007

'City Johannesburg' © Mongane Serote, reproduced with permission; 'The child who was shot dead
by soldiers at Nyanga' © Ingrid Jonker, reproduced with permission of Human & Rousseau; lyrics
from 'Swart September', by Koos Kombuis © Shifty Music (ZA) 1989, reproduced with permission;
lyrics from 'Hou my vas korporaal', by Bernoldus Niemand © Shifty Music (ZA) 1984, reproduced
with permission; lyrics from 'Energie', by Johannes Kerkorrel © Shifty Music (ZA) 1989, reproduced
with permission; lyrics from 'Fortuinverteller', by Andries Bezuidenhout © Brixton Moord en Roof
Orkes, reproduced with permission; lyrics from 'De La Rey', written by Sean Else, Johan Vorster
and Bok van Blerk, as performed by Bok van Blerk © Mozi Records/Publishing reproduced with
permission; 'Patria' © Louis Esterhuizen, reproduced with permission of Protea Boekhuis, Pretoria;
'Waarheen?' © Herman Engelbrecht, reproduced with permission of Protea Boekhuis, Pretoria.

Every effort has been made to trace copyright holders and to obtain their permission for the use of
copyright material. The publisher apologises for any errors or omissions, and would be grateful if
notified of any corrections that should be incorporated in future reprints or editions of this book.

PUBLISHING MANAGER: Marlene Fryer
MANAGING EDITOR: Robert Plummer
EDITOR: Marléne Burger
PROOFREADER: Ronel Richter-Herbert
COVER DESIGN: Michiel Botha, Flame Design
TEXT DESIGN: Natascha Olivier
TYPESETTER: Monique van den Berg
INDEXER: Mary Lennox
PRODUCTION MANAGER: Valerie Kömmer

Set in 10 pt on 13.5 pt Minion

Reproduction by Hirt & Carter (Cape) (Pty) Ltd
Printed and bound by Paarl Print, Oosterland Street, Paarl, South Africa

ISBN 978 1 77007 305 0

In memory of my grandmother, Els Erasmus,
who broke through the shell

Dedicated to my mother, Alida van der Westhuizen

Contents

Author's note

A BOOK DOES NOT APPEAR WITHOUT THE HELP OF OTHER PEOPLE. I firstly thank my panel of academic reviewers, Professor David Moore, Professor Sheila Meintjes and Dr Siphamandla Zondi, for their incisive comments on certain chapters. Their critiques helped me to bring the book closer to its vision, which is to contribute to, if not stir, current debate. Any omission, however, is for my account.

I wrote the book as an honorary research fellow at the University of KwaZulu-Natal's School of Politics, for which I am grateful to both David Moore and Professor Raphael de Kadt, in their respective capacities as director of the economic history and development studies programme and head of the School of Politics.

I also wish to thank Dan O'Meara, William Mervin Gumede, Adriaan Basson, Paula Proudlock, Ilze le Roux, Jani van der Westhuizen, Thandi Lewin, Henry Jeffreys, Justice Malala, Karien van der Westhuizen, Verne Harris and Zelda la Grange at the Nelson Mandela Foundation, Riaan Aucamp, Brenda Steyn and Dave Steward at the FW de Klerk Foundation, the Campbell Collection archives at the University of KwaZulu-Natal, Esta Jones and Freddy Sentso at the Archive for Contemporary Affairs, University of the Free State, Marlene Fryer, Robert Plummer and Marléne Burger at Zebra Press. And, as always, Melanie Judge for inspiration and unfaltering support.

The book draws partly on interviews conducted with former National Party leaders. I am grateful to the following people for their time and input: Pik Botha, Annelizé van Wyk, Barend du Plessis, Rina Venter, Leon Wessels, Roelf Meyer, Tertius Delport, Sheila Camerer, James Selfe, Marthinus van Schalkwyk, Stan Simmons and Johan Kilian. Efforts to conduct interviews with ANC leaders Cyril Ramaphosa and Mosiuoa Lekota came to naught. In the case of the latter, I was informed by a functionary in his office that the reference to the 'fall of the NP' was problematic 'since they are our comrades now' – in itself illuminating.

To undermine the Afrikaner nationalist notion of a singular 'Afrikaner', I pay attention to the dissenters, revolutionaries and *dwarstrekkers* (those who go against the norm) in Afrikaner ranks. The focus on the roles of Afrikaners or white people should not be construed as an overemphasis of the part played by either the NP or whites in general in the eventual overturning of the unjust system of apartheid, but rather as a contribution to filling the silences in Afrikaner nationalist tracts.

As always, writing on race in the South African milieu is replete with language pitfalls. This book's subject matter necessitates the use of the apartheid classification of black, white, Indian and coloured. In some cases, depending on the context, 'black people' refers to coloured, Indian and African people.

This book aims to serve as a bridge between popular and academic works by opening academic discussions to a wider audience, while reflecting critically on both public and academic debate. It is intended not only to unmask the face of white power, but to expose at least some of its innards to scrutiny.

CHRISTI VAN DER WESTHUIZEN
Cape Town
May 2007

Abbreviations

AAC: Alexandra Advisory Committee
AHI: Afrikaanse Handelsinstituut
ANC: African National Congress
APK: Afrikaanse Protestante-Kerk
APLA: Azanian People's Liberation Army
APO: African People's Organisation
ARM: African Resistance Movement
ASB: Afrikaanse Studentebond
Assocom: Association of Chambers of Commerce
ATKV: Afrikaanse Taal- en Kultuurvereniging
AVF: Afrikaner-Volksfront
AWB: Afrikaner-Weerstandsbeweging
AZAPO: Azanian People's Organisation
BAABs: Bantu Affairs Administration Boards
BC: Black Consciousness
BEE: Black economic empowerment
BIG: Basic income grant
BOSS: Bureau of State Security
BWBB: Blanke Werkersbeskermingsbond
CCB: Civil Cooperation Bureau
COD: Congress of Democrats
Codesa: Convention for a Democratic South Africa
Cosag: Concerned South Africans Group
COSATU: Congress of South African Trade Unions
CP: Conservative Party
CPRC: Coloured Persons' Representative Council
DA: Democratic Alliance
DP: Democratic Party
DRC: Dutch Reformed Church
DTA: Democratic Turnhalle Alliance
ECC: End Conscription Campaign
EI: Ekonomiese Instituut/Economic Institute (attached to the FAK)
EPG: Eminent Persons Group
FAK: Federasie van Afrikaanse Kultuurverenigings

FF: Freedom Front
FF+: Freedom Front Plus
FRELIMO: Mozambique Liberation Front
GATT: General Agreement on Tariffs and Trade
GDP: Gross domestic product
GEAR: Growth, Employment and Redistribution plan
GNU: Government of national unity
GWU: Garment Workers' Union
HNP: Herstigte Nasionale Party
ICU: Industrial and Commercial Workers' Union
IFP: Inkatha Freedom Party
IMF: International Monetary Fund
JMCs: Joint management centres
MEC: Member of the Executive Council
MPLA: Popular Movement for the Liberation of Angola
MPNP: Multiparty negotiating process
NCM: National Coordinating Mechanism
NEF: National Economic Forum
NGK: Nederduits-Gereformeerde Kerk
NIS: National Intelligence Service
NP: National Party
NSMS: National Security Management System
NUSAS: National Union of South African Students
OAU: Organisation of African Unity
OB: Ossewa-Brandwag
PAC: Pan Africanist Congress
PFP: Progressive Federal Party
PP: Progressive Party
PRAAG: Pro-Afrikaanse Aksiegroep
RAU: Rand Afrikaans University
RDB: Reddingsdaadbond
RDP: Reconstruction and Development Programme
RENAMO: Mozambique National Resistance
ROU: Record of Understanding
SACBC: South African Catholic Bishops Conference
SACP: South African Communist Party
SADCC: Southern African Development Coordinating Conference
SADF: South African Defence Force
SANNC: South African National Native Congress

SAP: South African Party
SAP: South African Police
SAVF: Suid-Afrikaanse Vrouefederasie
SSC: State Security Council
SWAPO: South West Africa People's Organisation
TRC: Truth and Reconciliation Commission
UDF: United Democratic Front
UDM: United Democratic Movement
UNICEF: United Nations Children's Fund
UNITA: National Union for the Total Independence of Angola
UNTAG: United Nations Transition Assistance Group
UP: United Party
USSR: Union of Soviet Socialist Republics
UWUSA: United Workers Union of South Africa
Vekom: Volkseenheidkomitee
WARC: World Alliance of Reformed Churches
WEF: World Economic Forum
WHAM: Winning hearts and minds
ZAPU: Zimbabwe African People's Union
ZAR: Zuid-Afrikaansche Republiek
ZIPRA: Zimbabwe People's Revolutionary Army

You already know enough. So do I. It is not knowledge that we lack. What is missing is the courage to understand what we know and to draw conclusions.

— Sven Lindqvist, '*Exterminate all the Brutes*'

Introduction

An entanglement exists between what you know, what you don't know and what you want to know. —Leon Wessels, South African Human Rights Commissioner and former NP deputy minister of law and order, 2006[1]

I KNEW. FROM THE AGE OF FOURTEEN, I KNEW. AND THE AFRIKANERS around me knew.

In 1988, at the height of the National Party's frantic search for ways to maintain white power, Juffrou van Heerden instructed the Standard 10 pupils in her Afrikaans class at Boksburg's Dr EG Jansen High School to pen an essay on the topic 'Drome van Gister' (Yesterday's Dreams). I wrote about apartheid: its leaders, its laws, the damage. How job reservation and low wages forced underdevelopment on black people. How the 'homelands' were a pipe dream, partly because the lack of industry and infrastructure compelled black people to urbanise or join the annual pilgrimage of migrant labourers feeding the insatiable capitalist machine. How white people's denial of the franchise to black people blocked a basic channel to air grievances, which was compounded by the banning of political organisations. How poor housing and services in the townships, along with substandard education, caused further social erosion among urban black people. Because of all this, I wrote, violence had come to characterise South African society. 'Relentless uneasiness pervades the land,' I scrawled in the cursive script demanded by the education system of the era. I referred to the large-scale rejection of PW Botha's reforms as 'the second largest parliamentary crisis' after DF Malan had 'illegally and undemocratically' removed coloured people from the common voters' roll in the 1950s.

Juffrou van Heerden, expecting adolescent romanticism, was not impressed. In red ink, she drew my attention to 'third world and first world irreconcilability. Some blacks are ready for development, others not! ... You provoke reaction and this can be dangerous at the end of the year [matric examinations].' I received a lower mark, 'penalised because of interpretation'. Juffrou van Heerden knew, but she preferred to believe the official justifications. I was seventeen years old when I wrote that essay. I was determined to know.

Twenty years later, South Africa is a radically changed landscape. Knowing or not knowing had become a central theme of South African life in the late 1990s, when the Truth and Reconciliation Commission peered into the darkest

1

corners of Afrikaner power. Guilt and confusion overcame many Afrikaners as the forces of remembering momentarily overpowered the forces of forgetting, blowing apart the house of cards built from the justifications for apartheid. As a first step to dissociating themselves from *die gruwels van apartheid* (the horrors of apartheid), Afrikaners moved their votes away from the National Party (NP). This was a radical step. The NP had stood at the centre of Afrikaner political and cultural life for eight decades.

Democracy would not be kind to the party that had developed and applied the policy of apartheid. After starting out on a relatively high note in 1994 with 20 per cent of electoral support, the NP was cut down to a humiliating 1.6 per cent in South Africa's third democratic election in 2004. Within a single decade, the party's supporters had abandoned it. Many of them stopped voting altogether, while others cast their ballots for the Democratic Alliance. Stranger still, what was left of the NP found its final refuge in the African National Congress – its sworn foe for the greater part of the twentieth century.

In a poetic twist of history, Afrikaner nationalism was swallowed by African nationalism. This was confirmed in 2006 when the president of both the country and the ANC, Thabo Mbeki, went so far as to hail the deceased PW Botha, together with Oliver Tambo, as a 'partner in the peace of the brave', offering his family a state funeral and attending the subsequent private service for which they opted. Anton Rupert, who built a dynasty second only in wealth to the Oppenheimers, was praised after his death by Mbeki as 'an outstanding son of our people', 'a great South African'.[2] While general feelings of embitterment – among black *and* white – and the NP's never-ending blunders during the 1990s may make the ignominious swallowing of the NP by the ANC seem like nothing more than just desserts, closer inquiry is required. Why did this happen, and how?

Astonishingly, in its ascendance to power, the NP managed to attain a parliamentary majority only in the 1966 election, after nearly two decades in government. The effect of such a flimsy hold on power was to fuel its authoritarian impulses. It clung to the state vehemently. In the long run, controlling the state was essential to its survival. Under the virulent Afrikaner nationalism of DF Malan, the NP showed no hesitation in discarding whatever thin veneer of democracy existed in a country where 80 per cent of the population was denied the vote. Neither the principle of separation of powers nor the rule of law was allowed to stand in the way of the party's pursuit of white power.

By the 1960s, at the height of its power, the NP appeared to be an unstoppable force. Within the realm of Afrikanerdom, National Party politics was almost genetically imprinted – even after the Afrikaner nationalist class alliance finally collapsed in 1982. For more than ninety years, the party proved remarkably adaptable. It shifted between different forms of nationalism, typified by Barry

Hertzog, DF Malan, HF Verwoerd and PW Botha. It underwent a number of name changes before securing power for the second time in 1948, and shifted policy gears several times as apartheid's crisis grew from the 1970s onwards.

What was the driving force behind the NP's rise to power? Was it ethnic chauvinism based on some primordial instinct of 'being an Afrikaner', or a quest by the Afrikaner intellectual and business elite to gain political power and thereby control over the means of wealth accumulation? Scholars Heribert Adam and Hermann Giliomee argued in 1979 that '[w]hile there were obvious gains in the form of wealth and influence in exploiting the economically backward position of the Afrikaners [in the 1930s and 1940s], it would be a distortion to see the Afrikaner nationalist elite as driven by such motives. There seems to have been a sincerely held conviction among this group that only through a combination of ethnic mobilisation and *volkskapitalisme* could the position of the poor be fundamentally altered.'[3] They were suggesting that the Afrikaner nationalist elite was somehow different to elites the world over – that the promotion of their self-interest was tempered by a race and culture-specific altruism. The evidence suggested otherwise. Much later in his life, in 2005, Giliomee remarked that 'as someone with an Afrikaans background ... [m]y generation was never conscious of any "classes" ...'[4] This is a good example of conceiving the *volk* as 'a deep horizontal comradeship' despite 'the actual inequality and exploitation that may prevail'.[5]

Unlike Giliomee, I grew up seeing the effects of class among Afrikaners around me. There were the affluent, and there were 'the weak and faltering among us', as former chief negotiator, NP minister and Broederbond head Gerrit Viljoen called lower-class Afrikaners in 1979, using Social Darwinist parlance. By the 1970s, he and other *verligtes* in the NP sought to cut themselves off from those Afrikaners who had become a burden on the collective. He bemoaned the 'artificial self-protection and self-preservation' with which Afrikaners were making 'it easy and almost hazardless ... for the weak and the faltering among us to maintain their position'.[6] Shortly after Viljoen wrote this, the NP *verligtes* under PW Botha ejected the Treurnicht faction, which was more representative of the Afrikaner lower classes.

We cannot understand Afrikaner nationalism without factoring in socio-economic status or class. My own family history serves as an apt example of the socio-economic benefits that Afrikaners received under NP rule. Rewind to the early 1940s. My grandmother, Els Erasmus (née Viljoen), was a field cornet in the proto-fascist Ossewa-Brandwag. Just as she believed that the Afrikaner was oppressed by English-speaking white South Africans and threatened by black South Africans, she believed in the Afrikaner woman's 'duty' of self-sacrifice and the maintenance of racial purity.

She was among the thousands of Afrikaners who grew up on a farm in the 1920s and then made their way to the city to seek out a livelihood. As a working-class woman with a Standard 6–level education, she became a cleaner in state hospitals, laboured as a chicken farmer, baked cakes and prepared food in her husband's short-lived corner shop, before ending her working life in a state hospital's kitchen. Her husband, who had a Standard 7 education, failed at farming and small-scale retail and eventually became a railway worker. (When all else failed, the SA Railways & Harbours could always mop up un-employed Afrikaners.) Their four children all finished secondary school, with two going on to attain tertiary level qualifications – one up to postgraduate level. Their career choices reflected the enhanced variety of options available to Afrikaners in the 1960s, when the majority entered professional occupations in both the private sector and the public service. By the 1990s their economic status ranged from comfortably middle class to wealthy. Of the Erasmus grandchildren, one third acquired tertiary degrees and most were comfortably middle class.

This illustrates the tangible welfare benefits of apartheid across three gener-ations of one Afrikaner family. It also corresponds with official statistics showing a negligible incidence of poverty and unemployment among white South Africans in the 2000s.

While apartheid was not experienced as a policy of class, the NP set out to use political power to benefit big business and white workers, while harnessing state resources to improve the socio-economic status of Afrikaners by way of employment, training and capital disbursement. The effect was the upward mobility of Afrikaners in particular, and the further entrenchment of white privilege in general. The class dimension of apartheid, almost never discussed in popular Afrikaner discourses, is generally obscured by terms such as *verligte* and *verkrampte*, or *die regses* (the right-wingers).

Afrikaner society of the 1980s obsessed about the battle between the NP and *die regses* after Andries Treurnicht and his followers broke away to form the Conservative Party in 1982. At the time, Dr EG Jansen High School was a terrain of conflict that reflected the general NP preoccupation with *die regses*. As a Standard 9 pupil, my arguments for democratisation were challenged by a class-mate regarded as a 'moderate' because he was an NP supporter. He tried to convince me that all our energy should be focused on combating the CP and the extra-parliamentary neo-Nazi Afrikaner-Weerstandsbeweging (AWB). After all, wasn't the NP committed to 'reform', while these organisations still clung to … well, 'yesterday's dream' of apartheid? The far-right threat was real, of course, but it was especially so for NP supporters, because of the determination that their party should hold on to state power. The CP had gained control of the city council of Boksburg, and was enforcing petty apartheid at Boksburg Lake and other amenities. The authorities at my high school – named after Verwoerd's less 'innovative' predecessor in the ministry of Bantu affairs – were happily hosting a far-right-wing Afrikaanse Protestante-Kerk (APK) congregation in the school hall on Sundays. The APK had broken away from the Afrikaner nationalist Nederduits-Gereformeerde Kerk (NGK or Dutch Reformed Church) because it was considered too 'liberal'. The school had also refused to allow sport to be played against black teams.

Indeed, those were the days when many, if not most, white people in Boksburg were trying their best to reclaim their 'dream'. But it had become threadbare – so much so that dissidence, even from teenagers, could not be allowed. The school authorities threatened my sister, Karien van der Westhuizen, with expulsion for having written the words 'Apartheid Sucks' in big red letters across her white school bag. One afternoon, the maths teacher held me back after class. It had taken him a few weeks to discover that the 'I love Alex' sticker on my school case referred to a township in Johannesburg, and I was ordered to remove it. I got off with a scolding.

My classmates were more direct. They shared their thoughts about my political beliefs on a card for my sixteenth birthday, inscribed by all of them. Crudely drawn in blue ink was a stick figure within a round-ish circle and 'flames', evoking the 'necklacing' done with car tyres doused in petrol and ignited with a match. People were being killed in this manner in townships around the country at the time. To remove uncertainty about the meaning, the words '*tyre vir* [for] *Christi*' were scribbled next to the drawing, as well as 'WE HATE ALL BLACKS AND THEIR SUPPORTERS'. Elsewhere in the card, a vaguely recognisable swastika-like emblem, as employed by the AWB, was augmented by suggestions that I should move to the township of Soweto. One classmate wrote 'I love Soweto', with another adding 'just where it is'. 'Christi loves kaffers [*sic*]', another pointed out. The card didn't come as a surprise. In their eyes, I was a '*kafferboetie*' and 'feminist' (as though the latter were an expletive).

In the beleaguered white South Africa of the 1980s, even adolescent consciousness had become thoroughly corrupted by bigotry – a salient feature of the Afrikaner nationalist laager. But the anecdote cited above also shows how fierce the contestation of ideas had become as the apartheid edifice began to crack. It is but one example of everyday dissent and resistance within Afrikaner ranks against the accepted wisdom – dissent and resistance that refute notions of a monolithic Afrikanerdom. It shows how the policing of thoughts had been refined down to micro-level in Afrikaner society in order to extinguish even the faintest hint of opposition. And it shows what was 'known' and 'not known', and how much of that was allowed to be expressed. If no one 'knew', it was because they were determined not to – which implies that they did know. Why block out something that one is unaware of?

Even in the 'big city' of Johannesburg, I could not escape the Afrikaner nationalist affliction of silencing dissent. In 1989, about eight months before FW de Klerk unbanned the ANC and other pro-democracy organisations, a complaint from the CP-controlled Springs city council almost halted my tertiary education. The dean of student affairs at the Rand Afrikaans University (now University of Johannesburg) threatened to expel me. What could a first-year student have done to so upset the equilibrium of an institution literally cemented in huge concrete blocks? I had committed the odious crime of suggesting in an article entitled 'Wie was oom Hennie?' in the official student newspaper that Verwoerd was influenced by national socialist thinking during his studies in Europe. One more such transgression, the dean assured me, and I would be kicked out. This rather unsurprising titbit about Verwoerd was not something that RAU authorities could afford to have 'known'.

Almost a decade later, several years into the democratic transition, I *again* came up against the imperative to silence critical thinking, while working as the parliamentary correspondent of the Afrikaans daily newspaper, *Beeld*. The heady fluidity of thought and expression after the first democratic election had by the early 2000s been worn down by resentment and self-pity among many Afrikaners. The TRC revelations had led many to retreat into wilful amnesia. Less and less space was being allowed for questioning and confronting – the Afrikaner mind was closing again, to reinterpret Allan Bloom's phrase.[7] The popular Afrikaans media, so essential to maintaining the apartheid status quo and later in promoting Botha and De Klerk's reforms, were emitting worrying signals of a return to a stifling conformism, accompanied by the promotion of mind-numbing consumerism.

Thus, only shallow historical explorations would be tolerated. The issue of class among white *and* black had to be avoided, lest old or new anti-capitalist demons be awakened. In 2003, as part of my regular series of political columns in *Beeld*, I explored the reasons why the Afrikaner vote had moved from the NP to the DA. After all, the NP had contributed to the delivery of an elite compromise that assured its supporters of continuing privilege after 1994, so why did those very beneficiaries abscond? And why to the DA? Strictly speaking, if interests were measured according only to affluence, Afrikaners should have been voting for the ANC, as their standard of living had on average improved markedly since the dawn of democracy.

The column was scrapped at the last minute by the power(s) that be, an unprecedented move in my then seven years as a political journalist. The 'reason' was that 'our readers' would be alienated by an analysis of the class and race factors underlying Afrikaners' abandonment of the NP. Again I was confronted by a power broker's insistence on controlling the information – the 'known' and the 'unknown' – that reached Afrikaners. In this way, Afrikaner leaders in different spheres affirmed the lack of critical self-reflection among Afrikaners throughout the decades. One of the themes of this book is the reasons for the great Afrikaner trek from the NP to the DA.

From 1990 to 1994, an elite compromise was wrought. In the interest of political power, the ANC sacrificed redistribution and concomitant socio-economic upliftment of the majority of South Africans, while the NP exchanged political power for continuing white economic power. Consequently, patterns of wealth distribution changed only insofar as the top income levels were concerned. In continuation of a trend started under the NP government,[8] upper-income levels became more deracialised. Contrary to some expectations, socio-economic inequality *worsened* during the first decade of ANC rule. This was at least partly a result of the pre-1994 shift in government policy to neo-liberal capitalism; the NP positioning itself explicitly as promoter of capitalist interests during the 1980s and early 1990s; and how it used this position to contribute to the delivery of a transition that set limitations on socio-economic transformation. While the NP was not alone in nudging the ANC towards neo-liberal capitalism, it played a significant role. Indeed, the neo-liberal impulses evident in the South Africa of the 2000s were similar to those under NP rule. Since the 1970s, the NP had been seeking to create the conditions for some form of an elite compromise through the broadening of the middle classes to include more black people. While it got less than it bargained for, it did manage to maintain white privilege, paving the way for the circumscribed black economic empowerment of the 2000s.

While class interests explained much of the NP's manoeuvrings during its last sixteen years in power, they did not explain fully why the party's support base deserted it in the late 1990s. These reasons have to be sought in the issue of knowing/not knowing and taking responsibility, or not, for apartheid abuses. As I write, the *New York Times* has picked up on the rising public debate about Afrikaans pop singer Bok van Blerk's bestselling number, 'De La Rey'. The song seemingly calls for a twenty-first-century Afrikaner leader in the mould of South African War General Koos de la Rey to lead 'die Boere'. The NP has been discarded, but the nostalgia remains, mixed with resentment or outright anger. The song tugged at a collective *hartsnaar* (heartstring), conjuring up familiar images of Afrikaner victimhood, courage in the face of injustice and adversity, and an Africa-style 'big man' leader who will offer direction out of the miasma.

Why these excavations? The TRC's (partial) exposure of apartheid's real effects on the lives of ordinary black people shattered a self-serving conspiracy of silence about these realities among Afrikaners. It ripped through the paternalism, the racist obfuscation and the self-delusion that enabled apartheid and the increasingly extreme violations of human rights in the 1980s and early 1990s. The revelations caused many Afrikaners to sink into denial, disparagingly referring to the TRC as the 'Lieg- en Biegkommissie' (Lie and Confess Commission). This was not confined to private comment. For example, the Naspers publication *Die Burger*, under editor Ebbe Dommisse, used 'Biegbank' (Confession Bench or Rack) in headlines, news reports and editorial comment from 24 January 1996 onwards, and the phrase 'Wraak- en Vergeldingskommissie' (Revenge and Retribution Commission) in editorial comment on 8 December 1997.

In 2000, *volk* intellectual Willem de Klerk, both an opinion-maker and a reflector of developments in the collective Afrikaner psyche, diagnosed Afrikaners as 'depressed' and suffering from shock. He cited the following reasons: '[U]njustified, hopeless withdrawal ... Loss of power. Loss of influence. Loss of respect. Loss of security. Loss of privilege. Loss of credibility. Loss of language. Even loss of profession ... [and] a paucity of political, religious and cultural leaders ...'[9] But this was not true of all Afrikaners. Democratisation allowed many to escape the straitjacket of Afrikanerdom. Some used the freedom to demand that Afrikaner institutions such as the media or the NGK change to allow for the newly acknowledged diversity in Afrikaner ranks, including sexual orientation and racial diversity. Afrikaner women were moving into the public sphere (writer Antjie Krog, feminist theologian Christina Landman and various businesswomen) from which, despite their relative white privilege, they had hitherto been absent. In *Country of My Skull*, Krog confronted apartheid and the feelings of guilt permeating most corners of Afrikanerdom. Women were also speaking out in books (*Dis Ek, Anna*) and court cases (Esmé van Zijl's courageous action against her uncle, Imker Marais Hoogenhout) about the interpersonal and sexual violations fostered in insular Afrikaner families where the male head's dominance was decreed by God and government. Popular musicians such as Karen Zoid, the band Trike and the all-woman rock band Rokkeloos (literally 'without dresses', but also a play on the Afrikaans word *roekeloos*, or reckless) were challenging the feminine gender stereotype of docility and subservience. Author Marlene van Niekerk unflinchingly took a scalpel to gender and race relations in her book on poor urban Afrikaners in the 1990s (*Triomf*) and wealthy rural Afrikaners during and after apartheid (*Agaat*).

Shifting gender and race relations precipitated a crisis in Afrikaner masculinities, as confronted by playwright Deon Opperman in various dramas, by performance artist Peter van Heerden in *Bok* (Goat), journalist Chris Louw in his letter-turned-play *Boetman is die Bliksem in* and poets such as Louis Esterhuizen in his poem 'Patria'.[10]

These artists all sought to reinterpret Afrikaner identity in a post-apartheid, twentieth-century South Africa. In mainstream Afrikaner culture, however, the closing of the mind became more evident as the 2000s progressed. A pop musician singing the old national anthem 'Die Stem' caused a momentary stir. Singer Steve Hofmeyr scored a huge success by tapping into Afrikaner nostalgia with cover versions of traditional folk songs, marketed under the title *Toeka* (The Olden Days). Then Van Blerk, aged twenty-eight, came out of nowhere and sold more than 160 000 CDs featuring 'De La Rey' in 2006/7. He clocked up the best ever figures for a debut CD, sales trumping even those of the most popular black musicians.

The song followed the format of early twentieth-century nationalist compositions, opening with a drum roll that conjured up images of an army on the march. The lyrics paid homage to the 'valiant Boers' standing up against the overpowering might of the British Empire in the South African War (1899–1902); the concentration camps; and the scorched-earth policy of the British that destroyed Boer family farms. It promised that the 'fire' ignited by the war in the hearts of Afrikaners would burn on. The accompanying video showed Van Blerk in nineteenth-century Boer garb with rifle. It also resurrected the Afrikaner nationalist portrayal of the *volksmoeder* by featuring the hackneyed image of 'woman with child'. The song was soon played wherever Afrikaners came together (sport events, holiday resorts, on protest marches to the Union Buildings). Different sections of society either laid claim to the song or warned that 'the Afrikaner' was stirring. More than anything, the song and the associated public excitement reflected how some Afrikaner men were grasping at historically militarised masculinity as an anchor in the evolving social relations of a democratising country.

Given the decades spent on inculcating these nationalist myths and images in Afrikaners in order to mobilise them, their resurrection should not have been unexpected. The eager embracing of these symbols pointed to an inability among many Afrikaners to carve fresh identities out of the new material offered by a democracy in a globalising world. This partly stemmed from the persistence of the popular defence of 'we did not know'. Could these old myths and symbols be reinvented in ways that served the principles of democracy and human rights?

CHAPTER 1

From colonialism to apartheid

This is what an ideology achieves. Born in a context of suffering, it elevates certain ideals to an end that, in time, begins to exert an absolute attraction for people. It subtly draws a false image of reality before their eyes, an illusion from which images of ideological opponents [are] generated. It develops its own vocabulary. It thrives on the isolation of its supporters. It interprets self-criticism as disloyalty. It scoops out ethical values and endows them with a different content. By then, the end purifies the means and little hold can be exerted on the powers that have been let loose in society. South African history tells of this – from all sides ... —JJ Lubbe, Dutch Reformed Church minister, Bloemfontein, 2001[1]

THE NATIONAL PARTY WAS BORN IN BLOEMFONTEIN, IN THE VERY heart of South Africa, on 7 January 1914. A day less than two years earlier, the other major nationalist contender of twentieth-century South Africa – the African National Congress – was formed in the same city. These two parties were vehicles for ideologies created partly in response to each other and to a third nationalism, which was both British and imperial.[2] The scene was set for a struggle that would last eighty years, culminating in startling events.

In 1914, General JBM (Barry) Hertzog, founder of the NP, brought together wealthy wine and fruit farmers from the Cape and lower-class Afrikaners who were struggling to eke out a living on their land, or had lost it and were trying to find their way in the cities.

Lawyers, clergymen and small businessmen were also attracted to Hertzog's blend of segregation, republicanism and 'two-stream' approach to English-speaking whites. The latter recognised that both Afrikaners and English-speaking whites had the right to express their culture separately, while coming together on issues of 'national importance', such as segregation. The idea was that a unified white bloc could withstand the threat of black domination.

Hertzog had advocated segregation as a 'permanent solution' since before 1910. What 'horrified' him was that 'our children will more and more feel the weight of a lower civilisation dragging them down to the level of their native environment unless they abandon the country and emigrate elsewhere or unless they suffer themselves to be completely extirpated'.[3] These words encapsulate the usual justifications for the racist policies of twentieth-century South Africa. Such was the rationale for the decisions and actions of successive governments, starting with the 1909 Convention, where an exclusive group of white men agreed on a framework for the Union of South Africa.

The founding of the National Party represented the beginning of the political organisation of Afrikaner nationalism. Ethnicity and nationality gain meaning only if they are used to create awareness and mobilise people. Collective identities are thus not 'given facts of life', but rather ideological constructions frequently derived from a reinvention of history to create 'commonalities' (norms and customs; heroes). Consequently, as elites inevitably seek greater access to power and resources, they mobilise support for their claims on the basis of constructed identities.

Afrikaner nationalism passed through different phases during the twentieth century. In summary, it can be described as an ideology devised to recast Afrikaans- and Dutch-speaking whites as 'the Afrikaner *volk*'. The drivers behind this process were a self-conscious intelligentsia of *dominees*, academics, journalists, lawyers and others. The goal: self-determination for the *volk* – in other words, to capture political power. Language as communicator of the 'common' *volkskultuur* is integral to nationalist aspirations – thus Afrikaans was standardised and became a powerful ethnic and cultural mobiliser.

A deeply conservative variant of Calvinist religion formed an essential part of the ideology, as did a mythologised history that turned the Afrikaners into 'God's chosen people' and the Great Trek into the equivalent of the biblical exodus from Egypt to the 'Promised Land'. Historical events such as the nineteenth-century battle against the Zulus at Blood River and the Boers' experiences in the South African War between 1899 and 1902 were loaded with nationalist symbolism.

Racism was another essential part of the ideology with which the *volk* was demarcated from the rest of the population on the basis of their whiteness. Fears about *swart oorstroming* (black 'swamping') and *gelykstelling* (equalisation) were whipped up to justify white domination. At the heart of Afrikaner nationalism sat a gender hierarchy aimed at protecting racial 'purity' through a strictly circumscribed role for Afrikaner women.

Structures such as the NP, the Broederbond and its various civil society extensions set out to imbue an imagined Afrikaner community with nationalism. The ideology was adapted over several decades by cultural, political and business elites to capture political power and, with it, control over the accumulation of wealth. In order to do this, a cross-class cultural and racial alliance was cobbled together. Afrikaner nationalism was a response to industrialisation and urbanisation, and operated as a modernising force.

The NP adapted its name several times before ensconcing itself in the pillows of state power in 1948. It went from Gesuiwerde Nasionale Party to Herenigde Nasionale of Volksparty, ending up with Hertzog's original name. These changes partly reflected the ideological battles among Afrikaner nationalists. Afrikaner nationalism ebbed and flowed as historical conditions changed and as leaders tried to elbow each other out of the way in their thirst for state power.

Mobilising white Afrikaans-speakers was no easy task. Not all Afrikaans-speaking whites were anti British imperialism, as shown by those Boers who fought on the British side in the South African War.[4] While many Afrikaans-speakers shared a strong sense of patriotism, that did not necessarily make them Afrikaner nationalist. Many white Afrikaans-speakers were racist, but being Afrikaans and being racist were not synonymous. Racist rhetoric would not necessarily spur such people on in the service of Afrikaner nationalism. By no means were all white Afrikaans-speakers opposed to fighting on the British side in the two world wars. Many Afrikaners continued to vote for the South African Party and its successors. It took several decades and many different ideologues to meld a collection of white Afrikaans-speakers into an 'Afrikaner community'. Common enemies were identified, as well as what would constitute a '*regte* Afrikaner' (real Afrikaner). Myths were conjured up to produce a common past and destiny. 'Heroes' were unearthed; songs were written. And all the while, Afrikaner economic advance was being driven forward.

White Dutch- or Afrikaans-speaking ranks were historically disparate and without a collective consciousness. By the second half of the nineteenth century, little affinity existed between the Dutch/Afrikaans-speakers in the British-ruled Cape Colony and those of the two independent Boer republics. Indeed, many Afrikaners in the Cape had become assimilated into the English-speaking white community. Close political relations were maintained with the English-speaking inhabitants of the colony through an alliance between the Afrikaner Bond, a political party, and arch-imperialist and premier, Cecil John Rhodes. However, this changed when the threads of nascent Afrikaner nationalism in the colony and the republics were unintentionally drawn together by the 1895 Jameson Raid, a Rhodes-sponsored misadventure aimed at usurping control of the Zuid-Afrikaansche Republiek. This fundamentally broke the trust between the Bond and Rhodes.

Moves towards Afrikaner collectivism can be traced back to the 1870s.[5] Opinions differed on what constituted a truly national Afrikaner ideology. Living under the British crown, the Bond's 'Onze Jan' Hofmeyr expressed the pragmatic desire to unite Boer and Briton. On the other hand, Bond founder, cleric, author and newspaper editor SJ du Toit's neo-Calvinist variant promoted

Afrikaners as God's chosen people. Du Toit was the prime mover of the first Afrikaans language movement, founding the Genootskap vir Regte Afrikaners in 1875, as well as the first Afrikaans newspaper, *Die Patriot*.

In the ZAR, preacher-cum-president Paul Kruger propagated a variant that was similar to colonial rhetoric of the time and genuinely religious rather than neo-Calvinist or consciously directed at ethnic mobilisation.[6]

The Afrikaner nationalist stirrings of the late nineteenth century were spurred on by what the newly elected Liberal British premier, Sir Henry Campbell-Bannerman, in 1907 called the 'methods of barbarism' employed by the British against the Boers in the South African War. Historic events, coupled with contemporary hardships and British high commissioner Lord Alfred Milner's attempts to destroy an embryonic Afrikaner culture, were manipulated by emerging elites in the service of an ethnic-based class system. I wish to steer clear of a historical determinist position which propounds that Afrikaners were destined to become oppressors after enduring decimation at the hands of the British, but it is undeniable that the experiences of the Boers – the extreme methods of the British (the scorched-earth policy and concentration camps in which 27 000 women and children died) and Milner's subsequent anglicisation policies – reinforced and radicalised a self-aware Afrikaner cultural elite. The urbanisation forced upon Afrikaners by industrialisation and their impoverishment during the war exacerbated the situation. Post-war attempts by British officialdom to anglicise the Afrikaners added salt to the wounds, from whence surged resentment that could be ideologically manipulated. In short, the twentieth-century history of the Afrikaner demonstrates a truism: injustice breeds injustice.

The first elite transition

Contrary to the writings of early liberal scholars, the policy of segregation did not emanate directly from the Boer republics.[7] Indeed, levels of segregation were lower in the two republics than in the British-controlled Eastern Cape and Natal. South Africa's 'first example of structured segregation' was the allocation by Theophilus Shepstone, Natal's secretary of native affairs, of 'locations' to black people in the 1840s.[8] A system of indirect rule was enforced in which black people lived and cultivated their land under 'native law'. The law was applied by headmen and chiefs who were under the control of white magistrates and administrators. Hut taxes were levied to support the system. In contrast, while supporting white supremacist ideas, Boer leader General Louis Botha rejected tribal reserves as locking cheap black labour and land away from white farmers.

The first articulation of what segregation would look like in a newly forged South Africa came from Milner's Native Affairs Commission. As a result of hearings between 1903 and 1905, it recommended the following: racial separation of landownership; the establishment of 'native locations' in white towns; influx control with passes to regulate the movement of black people into the cities; differential wage levels; mission-based rather than state schooling for blacks; administration by separate native councils; and limiting the franchise for black people to the Cape. While some of these elements were already in force, Milner's administration combined them for the first time in an overarching policy.[9] It differed from the system of white supremacy in the US by enforcing separation of white and black people rather than just subordination, says historian Nigel Worden.

At the end of the nineteenth century, the British government, with its adherence to nominal racial non-discrimination, proffered Boer treatment of black people as one justification for interfering in the ZAR's affairs. However, while the British presented themselves as the liberal alternative to the Boers, the racism prevalent in the attitude and practice of both Briton and Boer differed in rhetoric but little in substance. Nor did it vary in regard to the actions that such racism was meant to justify, ranging from murder and land grabbing to forced labour and cattle theft.

Milner committed his government to protecting black people from oppression and injustice. He and British colonial secretary Joseph Chamberlain promised favourable consideration for extension of the black and coloured franchise to the ZAR and the Orange Free State, with citizenship based on 'civilisation' rather than race.[10] Sol Plaatje, author, journalist and founding member of the South African National Native Congress, attached great hopes to the promise of equality that the Union Jack held. In 1903 the Native Congress invoked Rhodes's 'equal rights for all civilised men'. The hope was that the Empire would protect blacks from local white exploitation by acknowledging equality before the law and democratic representation. Such anticipation frequently sprang from an education in British mission schools, leading to an idealised view of the Empire. Other leaders like Dr Abdullah Abdurahman of the African People's Organisation (APO) were more sober, but supported the Empire as the best that could be expected of the times.[11]

Milner held the paternalistic conviction that it was the Empire's duty to help black people rise to the 'civilised' standards of the whites. He regarded blacks as 'at best ... children, needing and appreciating a just paternal government'.[12] Milner also believed that the white settlers, whether Afrikaans- or English-speaking, would not tolerate concessions to the political demands of black people, and would in fact unite against the British government.[13] 'You have only to sacrifice "the nigger" and the game is easy,' he wrote.[14]

For the Boer leaders, an extension of the franchise to other races was unacceptable.[15] Two factors played a role here. Firstly, the Boers in particular were vulnerable to black competition after the socio-economic devastation of the war had pushed many unskilled, illiterate Boers off the land and into the cities to look for jobs. Secondly, the racial policies of the Boer republics illuminated the 'clear-cut racist ideology' and 'attitude of racial superiority'[16] inculcated in their people since before the Great Trek. Paul Kruger believed that black people were an inferior race (conveniently) destined by God to provide menial labour.[17] His policies prohibited them from owning land, marrying or voting. Racist ideologies have always served to justify such policies of exclusion and, in the case of the Boers, they also provided the rationale for other unjust practices, such as armed raids against black groups to demand tribute and the kidnapping of people who were then forced into labour.

The ideas underpinning this behaviour had not changed during the South African War – rather, they were reinforced, as many Boers emerged from the ruins of the conflagration with a stronger sense of ethnic solidarity. At war's end, the negotiators agreed to postpone a decision on the question of black franchise until after the newly occupied British colonies of Transvaal and Free State had been granted a form of self-government that would entrench white dominance, as stated by Milner.[18] Smuts presented the proposal, which was adopted as part of the 1902 Treaty of Vereeniging without protest by the British.[19] Political justice for black people was shelved in return for Boer acquiescence in the creation of a single political entity in service of British supremacy.[20] A black delegation to Britain later remarked that 1902 marked the moment when the British 'compromised with tyranny'.[21] Thus began a political pattern that would see Afrikaner interests continuously pitched against those of black people throughout the twentieth century.

The easily traded promises of black rights exposed the contradictions in British imperial policy, and showed that its claim to racial equality and justice was only skin deep. In Johannesburg, Milner urged an audience after the war to take a stand 'on the firm and unexpungable ground of civilisation against the rotten and indefensible ground of colour'.[22] But this 'civilisation' was determined by colour, as shown by this typically Social Darwinist statement from Milner in 1903: 'The white man must rule because he is elevated by many, many steps above the black man … which it will take the latter centuries to climb and which … the vast bulk of the black population may never be able to climb at all'.[23] The justification of 'civilisation' was false, not least because of the 'methods of barbarism' employed by the British to subdue black and white polities in the nineteenth century. Moreover, the numerous requests that members of the emerging black middle class directed at the British government through delegations and written requests after the war indicated the rise of a new generation of leaders alongside the remnants of traditional leadership. While black political activity was still weak, leaders who could have been engaged included Plaatje, Mohandas Gandhi, one of the founders of the Natal Indian Congress, and Abdurahman of the APO, which represented coloureds.

As confirmation of the British attitude towards black civil rights, the last black rebellion against proletarianisation[24] was brutally crushed when the Zulu rose against the British in the colony of Natal. In what is known as the Bambatha or Poll Tax rebellion of 1906 to 1908, this final spurt of resistance came in response to increasingly heavier tax and labour demands.[25] Twenty-four whites died, while up to 4 000 Zulus were killed. The devastation of the Zulu kingdom concluded a series of conquests of black polities in southern Africa as part of a more aggressive imperial approach, aimed at securing labour for the mines and plantations and thereby optimising colonial extraction for the Empire.[26]

Ultimately, the differing racial practices in the Cape and Natal illustrated the vagaries of imperial policy. In both colonies, formal equality between races was offered and limited franchise and property rights existed for black people. This situation made black leaders hopeful about the further extension of rights, hence the pleas directed at the British government. Nevertheless, in Natal the administration of 'native affairs' was poor and franchise requirements were biased against black people.[27] Ultimately, British imperialists such as Milner would not let rhetorical commitment to racial equality stand in the way of Empire.

Apart from Afrikaner leaders' racist attitudes, they were also divided from black leaders at the beginning of the twentieth century by the latter's strongly pro-Empire position. The early leaders of the South African Native National Congress (SANNC) placed their trust in the British liberal tradition, whereby blacks would be included in negotiations to hammer out the constitutional framework of a future South Africa. While not yet fully formulated, these black leaders were enunciating a liberal, non-racial nationalism – almost unique for its time. Several deputations of black leaders visited London to urge intervention. The hope was that, at the very least, the qualified Cape franchise would be extended nationally. This was not to be, despite some white participants, such as former premier John X Merriman, putting forward this position at the 1909 convention that resulted in the Union of South Africa. As with the Treaty of Vereeniging, black citizenship rights were sacrificed on the precarious altar of cooperation between white former foes. To appease Merriman *et al.*, black franchise was kept as it was, but with no further extension. Parliament remained reserved for whites. This was accepted by Britain, despite attempts to amend the law. Members of the British government expressed the hope that the whites of South Africa would graduate to a more liberal position, but were not willing to imperil the delicate truce.

This elite compromise led to a pact between the gold-mining industry and the government, precipitated by Jan Smuts's military suppression of the 1907 miners' strike. The alliance of 'gold and maize'[28] – the first elite pact of twentieth-century South Africa – held sway for most of the almost forty years before the NP came to power in 1948. It was an alliance based on a cheap and regimented black workforce being reproduced in reserves for the (English-speaking) mine bosses and the (Afrikaans-speaking) maize farmers, the export of primary products and the maintenance of socio-political stability.[29] As Merriman warned, the exclusion of black people would create a future volcano. By 1914, black leaders were still expressing their political aspirations in terms supportive of white paternalism, as in a petition referring to King George V as their 'father'.[30] By the 1920s, the African nationalist vision had become more sophisticated, as can be seen in Sol Plaatje's connection between legislated discrimination and economic competition:

> Native produce kept the mills busy at Ficksburg, Klerksdorp, Zeerust and other places and a Native export business was looming in the not very distant future; then public opinion (which in this country stands for white opinion) asserted itself: 'Where will we get servants,' it was asked, 'if Kaffirs are allowed to become skilled? A Kaffir with a thousand bags of wheat! What will he do with the money? If they are inclined to herd pedigree stock let them improve their master's cattle and cultivate for the landowner – not for themselves.' White farmers called for [the Natives Land Act of 1913] to stop that Native progress ...[31]

African nationalist politics was 'born in the optimism imbued by partial incorporation into an imperial world; their political edge came from the shattering of that optimism'.[32] The SANNC became the African National Congress, which challenged the political and economic marginalisation of black people more and more stridently.

'South Africa' first

Before 1938, the three dominant versions of Afrikaner nationalism were personified by Smuts, Hertzog and DF Malan. Louis Botha had founded *Het Volk* in 1906. The party's first task had been to heal the rifts in Afrikanerdom between 'hensoppers' (literally hands-uppers), 'bittereinders' (bitter-enders) and 'joiners', who had fought with the British.

In addressing the problem of white unemployment, the party managed to make a deal with mining companies to replace English strikers, who filled higher paid and skilled posts, with Afrikaner strike-breakers.[33] *Het Volk* also agitated for the repatriation of Chinese workers brought in by Milner in 1904 to address labour shortages on the mines, as these jobs could be offered instead to Afrikaners who had lost their farms in the war. Lastly, the party sought self-government for the colonised territories.

Het Volk merged with Hertzog's Orangia Unie and John X Merriman's South African Party, adopting the name of the latter for the new party. Botha's deputy, Jan Smuts, shared the racially discriminatory ideas of Britons such as Milner. He was strongly supportive of white people crossing the cultural divide and forging a united front against black competition. His was a more inclusive nationalism that saw the protection of white interests as paramount, regardless of language. The SAP orchestrated the coming together of the two white language groups in an alliance of 'gold and maize'. Smuts propounded the 'South Africanist' option, in which being South African meant being white, as demonstrated repeatedly in whites-only elections in which his SAP proved victorious.

Smuts did not believe that South Africa was ready for independence and supported close ties with Britain. He became an influential world politician, serving in the British war cabinet during the First World War and being involved in the abortive first attempt at a multilateral peace and security institution, the League of Nations. Ironically, he was also involved in drafting the United Nations Declaration of Human Rights, but South Africa was one of a handful of countries that abstained from voting for its adoption.

The SAP, pursuing white supremacy, passed a number of discriminatory laws. The regulation of white and black labour in the midst of rapid urbanisation was the party's main concern, so the first law to be passed was the 1911 Mines and Works Act, which imposed a colour bar and prohibited strikes by black workers. The notorious Land Act of 1913 forbade the purchasing and leasing of land outside the reserves by black people. The Native Affairs Act of 1920 created separate administrative structures in the reserves and advisory councils for black people in the urban areas, which would be extended under grand apartheid.

Of his generation of leaders, Hertzog – with his slogan 'South Africa First' – was the first to explicitly advocate a South African nationalism free from Britain's apron strings, but it was a whites-only nationalism. His slogan captured an enduring aspect of Afrikaner nationalism and was still being used by the NP in the 1980s. As a member of Botha's first union cabinet, Hertzog continually stated in various forums that his loyalties lay with South Africa and not with Britain. The country should not be ruled by strangers, and there was no place for fortune-seekers and adventurers, he declared with reference to English-speaking whites who continued to regard Britain as their home country. Botha, who had become rather partial to the Empire, asked Hertzog to resign, and, upon his refusal, did so himself. Botha was reinstated by the governor general and formed a new cabinet that excluded both Hertzog and the imperialist-minded George Leuchars, the latter as a sop to the anticipated loss of Afrikaner support over Hertzog's dismissal.

While white supremacy bound all the parties together, white politics remained deeply fractured. Hertzog's departure was followed by the 1914 rebellion, when Boer once again fought Boer, as had happened in the South African War. Barely a dozen years had passed and the ravages of the earlier conflict were still fresh in the memories of many – if not most – white Afrikaans- and Dutch-speakers. It was thus inconceivable for them to side with their oppressor against Germany and invade German South West Africa. Botha and Smuts managed to push through the British request with the slimmest of margins in cabinet (four against five, including their own votes). Given that Afrikaner nationalist Hertzog had already been ousted from the cabinet, the resistance shown by the naysayers was notable, and it spread.

About 12 000 men, headed by Boer war generals such as Christiaan de Wet and CF Beyers, took up arms against the government. However, the campaign was poorly conceived, badly organised and easily quashed by Botha, who personally led the government forces. An army officer, Jopie Fourie, was court-martialled and executed by firing squad, becoming a martyr to the cause of Afrikaner nationalism. When 6 000 women marched on the Union Buildings in Pretoria to demand the release of captured rebels, funds were raised to pay their fines.

The 1914 example of so-called *broedertwis* captivated Afrikaner nationalist imaginations a few decades later. *Bart Nel*, J van Melle's melancholic novel about the rebellion and the 'indomitable Boer spirit', refined in the 'fire of suffering', became a seminal text in Christian National Education under the NP. By the twenty-first century, many Afrikaners could still recite the closing lines of the book with its peculiar use of the third person:

> [The imperialists] now have everything … they have my land, my wife, my children. But they do not have me. Let them come, they can throw me in jail and take my land if they want to; they can even shoot me dead, but me they will not get … They will never get me … I have always been Bart Nel, and I am him still.[34]

In the 1915 election, almost as many Afrikaners voted for Hertzog's newly formed NP as for Botha's SAP. In the 1920 election the NP won the majority of votes. Talks between Smuts and Hertzog failed to produce results, and the SAP merged with the pro-British Unionist Party to become a new South African

Party, which won the 1921 election with ease. The 1920 strike by black mine-workers had led to a slight easing of the colour bar, which provoked the violent insurrection of white mineworkers in 1922. They were expressly opposed to attempts by mine bosses to use black workers (at lower wages) in positions formerly reserved for whites. The views of white workers were summed up in the incongruous slogan 'Workers of the world unite and fight for a white South Africa', which was paraded at meetings.[35] The strike was suppressed with disproportionate force – the aerial bombing of white working-class suburbs in Benoni and Germiston – which Smuts displayed several times during his many years of intermittent rule.

Afrikaner workers formed the majority of the strikers, leading Hertzog to decry Smuts as having hands dripping with the blood of his own people. It cost Smuts the 1924 election, won by Hertzog's NP in a seemingly unlikely pact with the Labour Party. While the latter supported a workers' republic – anathema to Afrikaner nationalists – they came together in their concern to protect the white worker from both the (English-speaking) capitalist and the black worker. The *Hertzogiete*'s brand of anti-imperialist, racist nationalism resonated with white workers' interests, while the SAP's pro-British capital stance did not.

The Pact government instituted the principle of 'civilised labour' in terms of which white wages would be prevented from falling below a standard of living 'tolerable from the European standpoint', while black wages for 'uncivilised labour' needed only to meet 'the bare … necessities of life as understood among barbarous and undeveloped people'.[36] As a result, black mining wages started to rise in real terms only in the 1970s. During the troubled 1920s, the NP-aligned *Die Burger* frequently published cartoons depicting a fictional anti-Semitic character called Hoggenheimer, who represented exploitative capitalists – always Jewish in the mind of cartoonist DC Boonzaier.

The NP and the Broederbond were tapping a rich vein. After the South African War, rural and working-class Afrikaners had found themselves impoverished and thrown into the unfamiliar fields of industrialisation and urbanisation. Less than 10 per cent of them were urbanised in 1900; by 1926, the figure was 41 per cent, while white unemployment stood at about 20 per cent at the start of the 1920s.[37] Poverty and lack of education placed Afrikaners in direct competition with black people, who had been forced into providing their labour – and therefore into urbanisation – by the 1913 Land Act in particular. Urban Afrikaners occupied an in-between position – below the frequently well-off English-speaking whites and just above the proletarianising blacks. Their 'upward' aspirations were displayed in the practice of adopting English nicknames in the 1920s.

Newly urbanised Afrikaners experienced a state of insecurity in which the imposition of a hierarchy of race ensured greater life opportunities. In these unpredictable conditions, Hertzog's nationalism provided an anchor. Under the Pact government, bilingualism was promoted in the civil service, and it was accepted that Afrikaans shared equal status with English. Until then, only Dutch was entrenched as a second language. This was also the time when professionals – *dominees*, teachers, journalists – whose positions depended on the status of Afrikaans, promoted the language intensively 'to build a nation from words'.[38] The flag provoked heated debates in 1926/7, with a compromise in the end incorporating the flags of both the Boer republics and the Union Jack.

Hertzog played an important role in preventing the Native (Urban Areas) Act of 1923 from allowing black property ownership. Instead, the 1921 Stallard Commission's dictum was adopted, according to which black people would be allowed outside the reserves only 'to minister to the needs of the white man' – similar to Botha's 1917 position. Botha had then declared that the government sought to avoid the mistaken approach of racial equality. Black people could reside outside 'their' areas only if they served white interests. But his bid to remove black property owners in the Cape from the voters' roll failed. Hertzog finished what Botha had started. The 1923 Act imposed passbooks and segregated 'locations', which would form the basis of government policy until the 1980s. The Pact government passed legislation to criminalise blacks who transgressed their conditions of employment. The Black Administration Act of 1927 laid the foundation for indirect rule on which apartheid architects would later build. It determined the 'retribalisation' of black people through a separate system of institutions and laws, thereby setting in motion the machinery that enabled the denial of black people's citizenship.

Worden notes the similarity with the Shepstonian system of indirect rule introduced in the British colony of Natal in the 1840s.[39] The Black Administration Act also retribalised black people on white terms and per white definitions that bore 'no resemblance to any pre-colonial structure'.[40] Shepstone claimed that the system was designed to protect 'indigenous culture' from corrosive European influences. (Later, Verwoerd seemed to have borrowed from Shepstone his justification for grand apartheid as 'decolonisation' and a means for black people to develop in accordance with their 'own customs'.)

In 1926, Hertzog did not have the requisite two-thirds majority in both houses of parliament to disenfranchise black people in the Cape province. The 1929 election was won with an enlarged majority for the NP on the back of Hertzog's *swart gevaar* (black peril) campaign. But the Great Depression struck and, unsure that he would win the next poll, Hertzog finally fused his party with that of Smuts in 1933/4. His anxieties about being too close to Britain had been resolved by the Balfour Declaration in 1926, which affirmed the autonomy and equality of Britain's dominions. He and Smuts both supported the Status Bill, which confirmed the union's sovereignty. But more than anything else, they were in accord on white supremacist principles, agreeing to continue with 'civilised labour' policies and segregation. In 1934, they created the Fusion government by bringing their parties together in the United South African National Party – shortened to United Party (UP).

With an enlarged and overwhelming majority (144 out of 150 parliamentary seats) behind him, Hertzog succeeded in scrapping the black Cape franchise in 1936, ostensibly in return for increasing the measly share of land allocated to black reserves – a step that had been overdue for almost two decades. Fusion drove the remaining pro-British SAP members under the leadership of Charles Stallard (of separate urban areas infamy) to form the predominantly Natal-based Dominion Party.

Fusion also led to the first split in the NP – and the second of its permutations. While Hertzog saw fusion as the only way to keep an Afrikaner nationalist government in power at that stage, Cape NP leader DF Malan feared a dilution of nationalist ideals. Consequently, he formed the Gesuiwerde (Purified) Nasionale Party in 1934, reflecting a further consolidation of reactionary trends. Malan's NP managed to woo only nineteen of the NP's seventy-five MPs to its ranks. Interestingly, most of the defectors came from the ostensibly moderate Cape (fourteen), with only four in the Free State and a paltry one in the Transvaal (the hardliner JG Strijdom). The rest of the MPs followed Hertzog into fusion.

Malan, the first NP leader to become prime minister under apartheid, leaned strongly on his background as a *dominee* (clergyman) to alchemise Afrikaner nationalism into a civil religion. This was encapsulated in his slogan 'Believe in your God, Believe in your Country, Believe in Yourself', compelling enough for Afrikaner nationalists for it to remain the NP's motto until the 1960s. Malan was a consummate ideologue who conjured up heady visions of the future in his rhetorical mix of religion, history and nationalism. Afrikaner nationalist mythology reinterpreted the motley groups of families that had left the Cape colony as a coherent nationalist action, the Great Trek, by ethnically similar people. Figures such as Piet Retief, Andries Pretorius and Sarel Cilliers were exhumed from the depths of history and paraded as leaders inspired by Afrikaner nationalism. To them, the Great Trek was more than a conquest of territory, proselytised Malan – it was 'an act of faith, and the acceptance of a God-given task'.[41] The Voortrekker victory over Zulu forces at the Battle of Blood River was immortalised in the Day of the Vow on 16 December, when Afrikaners were called upon to remember their promise to God to remain Afrikaner nationalists. The Afrikaners were 'a *volk* with a calling ... behind our South African volk existence and history sits a purpose. We as *volk* should be aware of it, and live it to the best of our ability.'[42] This awareness shone out of his famous ode to Afrikaner nationalism:

> Just as you cannot hold back the water of the Zambezi with your hand
> And just as you cannot still the East wind with a sieve
> Just as you cannot sweep away the rising flood of the ocean with a broom
> So you will never be able to stop Nationalism![43]

While Malan's immediate focus was on improving the Afrikaners' position relative to English-speaking whites, he had declared in a 1923[44] address on 'Vaderskap en Broederskap' (Fatherhood and Brotherhood) that the conflict between these groups was 'insignificant' compared to the 'colour problem'. The conflict between Afrikaner and English-speaker would disappear when equality in treatment by the state was achieved, he said. But the 'contradiction' between black and white went beyond 'difference in civilisation or language or history or general lifestyle'.

Malan insisted that the 'colour problem' had not been solved by political equality or education in the US, where 'the relationship between the white and the coloured races is today worse than during the time of slavery'. To him, the same was true in South Africa, as the 'expressed opinion of the educated section of the natives clearly shows that the present tolerable relations of the coloured races with the white is not improving but gradually worsening'. His pronouncements came at a time when black resistance was slowly becoming more radicalised.[45]

After the launch of the SANNC in 1912 and an address by Charlotte Maxeke, black women successfully blocked a planned extension of the pass system by Bloemfontein authorities in 1913. They collected 5 000 signatures on a petition, sent a deputation to Cape Town and, when that failed, tore up the passes at police stations. These demonstrations freed black women from having to carry passes for another forty years. By 1919, the SANNC was organising pass-burning campaigns.

In 1920, Pedi and Shangaan mineworkers staged a massive strike by 71 000 black miners that led mine owners to loosen the colour bar, precipitating the 1922 strike by white mineworkers. This was followed by Clements Kadalie's Industrial and Commercial Workers' Union (ICU) establishing itself as *the* mass-based pro-democracy organisation of the 1920s. It managed to mobilise white, coloured and black workers, moving beyond merely being an urban-based trade union movement to catalysing rural resistance. This shift was reflected in its demands, which changed to focus not only on better wages, but also on the franchise for blacks, the pass system, land and freedom of speech. At its peak, the ICU had up to 200 000 members.

In Malan's eyes, race relations worsened when black people claimed their rights to citizenship. In his 1923 speech, his 'solution' pointedly referred to black people as the 'weaker' race, towards whom white people had a responsibility. Blacks should be allowed to develop in accordance with their 'own nature'. He acknowledged the existence of educated black people, but the only blacks for whom there was space in Malan's scheme of things were those who 'needed' white people.

His *volk* also included English-speaking whites, as he explained in the 1961 book *Afrikaner-Volkseenheid en my ervarings op die pad daarheen*[46] (Afrikaner *volk* unity and my experiences on the way to it). The aim of 'the broad but authentic and healthy South African nationalism' was to bring *volkseenheid* by 'unifying everybody on the political front who belonged together through inner conviction'; in other words, the two *volksdele* (sections of the volk) that were 'Afrikaans-speaking and English-speaking Afrikaners'. As is typical of any nationalism, Malan's *volk* corresponded with a territorial area; his *volk* was the South African nation, but with one all-important proviso: membership was determined by race. It was a whites-only nation. Hence his book on national unity dealt with the quest to unite whites – first Afrikaans-speaking whites among themselves, and then English-speaking whites. It barely refers to black South Africans – his earlier comment in the 1920s, about how paramount the colour question was, thus really applied to what whites could do to maintain their monopoly on power.

South Africa had to be made 'safe for the white race and its civilisation in accordance with the [colonial] trusteeship principle', as Malan put it in a 1942 parliamentary motion.[47] The first thing they had to do was unite. Immediately after coming to power in 1948, Malan went out of his way to allay the fears of English-speaking whites. This conciliatory approach was carried forward by his successors and, by the mid-1960s, the NP had made significant inroads into English-speaking constituencies. By the late 1980s the bulk of the NP's supporters were English-speakers. By then, old, shared racist attitudes bound the majority of white South African voters together – regardless of culture, language or class. Such a 'breakthrough' in white politics was reserved for the NP, as it increasingly attracted support from the two white minority groups over a longer period than either Smuts or Hertzog could manage with their milder forms of nationalist and racist ideology.

Malan's pragmatic invitation to English-speakers set him apart from the cultural exclusivism of national socialist Afrikaner organisations. But Malanite nationalism still differed from that of Smuts, in that cooperation between the two groups could not be at the cost of 'national principles and Afrikaner *volk* ideals'. Indeed, as the 'Afrikaans-speaking section of the population [was] the creator and carrier of our own South African nationhood, [they have] the indisputable right to their continued existence as *volk* section and its unique unity ... Equally, a similar claim will not be withheld from the English-speaking section in terms of their language and culture. Therefore, we regard the preservation and the promotion of our own Afrikaans-speaking *volk* unity as an objective in itself.'[48]

The NP envisaged a republic in which Afrikaans-speaking whites would be able to exercise their language and cultural rights on an equal footing with English-speaking whites in the eyes of the state. What differentiated Malan and Hertzog from Smuts was the issue of the government's relationship with Britain. Hertzog's softening on British relations led to Malan's split from him in 1934.

Malan was profoundly opposed to British imperialism. His anti-imperialism could be so vehement as to be confused with anti-capitalism. What Malan and the NP under his leadership had in mind was 'sovereign independence ... the claiming of South Africa's right to make untrammelled decisions over its own destiny'. According to him, Smuts's position was that South Africa should not possess self-determination, and that this position was in the country's own best interest.[49] He was strongly opposed to the approach taken by Botha and Smuts towards Britain, particularly inasmuch as they expected unity between English- and Afrikaans-speaking whites on the basis of 'forgive and forget'. To his mind, the conciliation was 'one-sided and in the wrong direction, meaning that it should not emanate from the wronged and the vanquished but rather from the victor in the bitter but unfortunately also destructive struggle for freedom'.[50] The Botha–Smuts government's decision to support Britain in the First World War under the slogan 'honour and duty' was 'inhumane', given that it came a mere twelve years after 'the wandering commandos, the razed farm houses, the fleeing women and children, the concentration camps'. Malan thought the government's handling of the 1914 rebellion tragic, because it had created a rift in Afrikanerdom.

When it came to protecting the interests of white workers, as in the 1920s, Malan felt that Smuts had taken the side of the owners of capital too easily (they had been eager to lower the colour bar because black labour was cheaper). Malan also criticised Smuts's heavy-handed repression of the 1922 strike, when he sent in the army and banished leaders of the Labour Party without the endorsement of the courts. What was seen as Smuts's connivance with English capital influenced the NP to adopt anti-capitalist rhetoric up to 1948.

Meanwhile, relations in the uneasily fused UP degenerated sharply. Tensions among the *Smelters* (Fusionists) could no longer be contained when a decision had to be made about participation in the Second World War. Hertzog was not willing to fight on Britain's side. So strident was he in his opposition that he resigned as prime minister in 1939 when his proposal of neutrality was marginally defeated in parliament in favour of Smuts's push for participation on the Allied side. Hertzog formed the Volksparty, which joined Malan's Gesuiwerde Nasionale Party in early 1940.

But the Herenigde Nasionale of Volksparty (as the new party was then called) – with Hertzog as leader and Malan as his deputy – regarded Hertzogite nationalism as too pliable on the issue of English-speaking white interests. The Malanites were suspicious of Hertzog's nationalism, especially as he continued to promote the principle of equality between Afrikaners and English-speakers. At that point, the nationalists had their hopes pinned on a German victory and the establishment of 'a purely Afrikaner republic, excluding British and Jews'.[51] Hertzog's proposal for intra-white equality was rejected by his own Free State NP congress, leading an embittered Hertzog to resign. He died shortly thereafter, remembered as the one leader who, 'of all the leaders ... had made his countrymen conscious of the racial problem and the necessity of finding a permanent solution', as historian DW Krüger put it.[52]

The Hertzogites formed the Afrikaner Party, which in the end formed a pact with Malan's NP and entered government in 1948. Hertzogite nationalism was superseded by Malan's cultural nationalism, sharply focused on the Afrikaner.

Creating the cross-class alliance

After breaking away from Hertzog in 1934, Malan's NP used its time productively outside of government, neutralising other contenders for the Afrikaner nationalist crown and building extra-parliamentary alliances. A *volk* movement came into being, including the men-only secret society, the Afrikaner Broederbond (founded in 1918), and the Afrikaanse Handelsinstituut, representing big business and myriad other organisations that were NP-aligned. Several of these were segregated on the basis of gender, such as the Suid-Afrikaanse Vroue-Federasie and, years later, Jong Dames Dinamiek and Dameskring for women, and the Ruiterwag and Junior Rapportryers for men. Afrikaner children were organised in the Voortrekkers, based on the British Boy Scouts and Girl Guides.

In their writings before the 1970s, liberal and Afrikaner nationalist historians reduced the 'disparate, differentiated and highly fractious Dutch and Afrikaans-speaking populations ... to a static and monolithic ethnic entity'.[53] In this entity, all shared the same conservative values and were always available for mobilisation on the basis of their Afrikanerhood. As a result, the shifting and contradictory bases of the NP were lumped together as 'Afrikaners'. Afrikaner nationalist historians in particular posited a classless, monolithic entity called Afrikanerdom, hand-picked by God to overcome the hardships of Africa while fighting British imperialism and black encroachment.

A narrow class analysis cannot sufficiently explain the twists and turns of South African history and the NP's role in it. However, political and economic elite groupings are continuously seeking to maximise their power and status. In the context of a capitalist society, this means gaining access to or even control over the means to accumulate more capital. Ideology is an indispensable handmaiden in this enterprise. In the South African case, Afrikaner nationalism and the NP were at the centre of the socio-economic advancement of the group identified as Afrikaners.

Looking at the shifting class bases beyond the imagined horizontal comradeship of nationalism showed that the NP and its allies could not gain political power without Afrikaner workers on their side. The 1930s marked the redefinition of Afrikaner nationalism as the Afrikaner business and cultural elite launched its campaign of cross-class alliance building before battling it out for dominance in the early 1940s. The campaign culminated in the countrywide celebrations of the centenary of the Great Trek in 1938 and the Eerste Ekonomiese Volks-kongres (First Economic People's Congress) in 1939, respectively arranged by the Afrikaanse Taal- en Kultuurvereniging (ATKV) and the Federasie van Afrikaanse Kultuurverenigings (FAK), both front organisations for the Broederbond. The Great Trek centenary, which was dominated by the NP and the Ossewa-Brandwag, culminated in the laying of a foundation stone for the Voortrekker Monument in Pretoria. The Broederbond's planned 'economic renaissance' was 'mainly directed at promoting Afrikaner capitalism and the interests of the middle classes'.[54]

Dan O'Meara showed[55] convincingly how the Afrikaans *petit bourgeoisie* – those middle-class members who did not own the means of production and who were the predominant grouping in Afrikanerdom by the 1930s – mobilised a cross-class alliance. This alliance brought farmers and workers together with the *petit bourgeoisie* and capitalist fledglings. It resulted in the growth of Afrikaner capital and, eventually, the NP's rise to power. Malan's NP was gunning for the Afrikaner vote, which made sense, as the 1936 census showed that for every 100 English-speakers, there were 115 Afrikaners over the age of twenty-one and 185 between the ages of seven and twenty-one.[56] This cross-class mobilisation was done in close cooperation with the Broederbond and other emerging Afrikaner nationalist organisations in civil society.

Malan had the backing of nascent Afrikaner capital in the form of Sanlam and Nasionale Pers (owner of *Die Burger*), as well as large wine, fruit and wool farmers in the Cape. The Afrikaner nationalist elite had a cross-cutting presence in various structures. NP secretary WA Hofmeyr became the first managing director of Naspers. Among those who served on the company's advisory committees were JBM Hertzog and EG Jansen, who became minister of native affairs in Malan's first cabinet. Malan personified the intersecting roles which a group of Afrikaner nationalists played in an increasing number of public spheres. He was *Die Burger*'s first editor, a position he held even after becoming *hoofleier* of the Cape NP in 1915. As Piet Cillié of Nasionale Pers observed, he made no distinction between Malan the editor and Malan the party leader.[57] Malan rose through the ranks as a *dominee* and a leader of the Tweede Taal-beweging (Second Language Movement). This movement was initiated by *petit bourgeois* members whose livelihood depended on the entrenchment of Afrikaans as official language.

In the Transvaal, where the NP had only future prime minister JG Strijdom left at parliamentary level, Afrikaner nationalist mobilisation was extra-parliamentary and extra-party. It was led by the Broederbond, which was swelling its ranks with discontented members of the intelligentsia, such as DRC clergymen, attorneys, and academics at the universities of Pretoria and Potchefstroom, as well as *petit bourgeois* teachers, civil servants and small traders. The Broederbond's economic movement of the 1930s and 1940s was an organised attempt by these groups to build themselves into an industrial and commercial elite by mobilising support from Afrikaans-speakers through ideological and organisational means. This exposes Afrikaner nationalism as 'a shifting class alliance'.

For these groups, Hertzog's fusion with Smuts was 'a fatal collusion with the forces of capitalism and imperialism'.[58] *Die Burger* quoted Transvaal NP leader JG Strijdom as saying in December 1934 that the NP should 'combat capitalism. The strength of capitalism lies in the mines, and the means by which to oppose it lies in the gradual but inexorable nationalisation of the mines. The power of the great banks must be curtailed and at the same time capitalism in agriculture must be fought.'[59]

Malan proposed a motion in parliament in 1942 stating that the NP's envisaged republic should 'be effectively protected against the capitalist and parasitical exploitation of its population, as well as against the undermining influences of hostile and un-national elements'.[60] NP Free State leader Nic Diederichs claimed his party was the only reliable opponent of 'autocratic government and domination by large capital'.[61] This anti-capitalist posturing was misleading. What the NP was in fact after was to open the upper echelons of capitalism to Afrikaners. An essay on business in the 1953 NP publication *Die Triomf van Nasionalisme in Suid-Afrika* (The Triumph of Nationalism in South Africa) stated that the following connections had been made at the *volkskongres*: 'The Afrikaans *volk* became completely aware of the fact that no *volk* can maintain and build its own culture without putting its economic existence on a firm and healthy basis. The feeding source for the *volk*'s spiritual deployment is and should be a healthy and balanced economic life.'[62] Future cabinet minister Theo Dönges clarified at the *volkskongres* that the anti-capitalist struggle was not against capital as such, but against the concentration of capital in a few (English) hands. It was an obvious bone of contention around which to mobilise support. In 1938/9 the Afrikaner presence in the different economic sectors comprised single-digit percentages: a measly 5 per cent of financial; 1 per cent of mining; 8 per cent of commercial; and 5 per cent of manufacturing undertakings were owned by Afrikaners.[63] They still predominated in agriculture, producing 87 per cent of output. The *petit bourgeoisie* provided the services, credit, distribution and processing of farmers' products – hence the fortunes of the two were tied.

Similarly, says O'Meara, the process of urbanisation was 'exporting' the 'clientele' of the *dominees*, lawyers, traders and teachers from the *platteland* to the predominantly English-speaking cities and towns. By 1936, 58 per cent of Afrikaners were urbanised; by 1951, the figure was 69 per cent. Given the monopolistic, English-dominated structure of the economy, entry into the urban economy was difficult. Many Afrikaners joined the ranks of the poor whites, some 30 per cent of which could not feed or house their children in 1932. Living in racially mixed, dilapidated urban dwellings and slums, these were the 'Afrikaners' identified by the NP and the Broederbond as most at risk of being 'lost' to miscegenation – translating literally into a shrinking (potential) support base for the NP. These obstacles and pressures were attributed to discrimination against Afrikaners by capitalist monopolies and 'imperialism'.

Under the Pact government, enforced bilingualism enabled Afrikaner entry and advance in the civil service and therefore a secure base with potential for the lower middle class, including its intellectuals. For the lower middle classes to protect this base and the opportunities it contained, the NP had to regain control of the state.

To address these challenges, the *volkskongres* was called, leading to the formation of the Reddingsdaadbond (Rescue Action League). The fund was aimed at alleviating the poor-white problem, but, more importantly, the *petit bourgeoisie* and aspiring capitalists advocated the reorganisation of Afrikaner capital, buying and labour power. 'Wherever possible, the Afrikaner buys from the Afrikaner, procures his services via the Afrikaner cause and entrusts his savings to capital-controlling Afrikaner financial institutions.'[64]

In preparing for the 1948 election, the Broederbond's strategy was to alienate Afrikaner workers from unions that were regarded as too leftist or were not racially segregated. The Afrikaner worker was a prized target for which both the NP and the UP fought relentlessly. But Smuts still bore the burden of his heavy-handed intervention in the 1914 rebellion and 1922 mine strike.[65]

Pivotal to the Broederbond strategy, according to O'Meara, was not only to capture the working class to enable the NP to come to power, but also to harness their savings for the growth of Afrikaner financial companies. Diederichs exulted the reliability of Afrikaner workers and how they should be drawn into 'the nation' – 'there must be no division between class and class'.[66]

Together with the Broederbond, Afrikaner big business institutions such as Sanlam and Volkskas were directly involved in setting up committees and organisations aimed at luring Afrikaner workers away from English-dominated 'communist' trade unions. The Herenigde Nasionale of Volksparty (as the NP was known at the time) formed the Blanke Werkersbeskermingsbond (BWBB) (White Workers' Protection League) in 1944, with Jan de Klerk (FW's father) as its secretary and a representative from Sanlam on its board. The BWBB took on the task of saving 'white civilisation' by weaning Afrikaner workers off communism, uniting them with 'the nation' and 'preserving' them for the Christian National 'struggle'.

The Broederbond was behind the formation of the Reddingsdaadbond (RDB) via the Economic Institute (EI) attached to the FAK. For the RDB, *volkseenheid* was possible only by preventing Afrikaner workers from forming a class separate from any other. In summary, O'Meara explained the ideology into which Afrikaner nationalists sought to induct workers, thus: within the divinely ordained unity of the nation, the 'innate' inequality of individual members creates a hierarchy within which each individual has a place. The division of labour is in accordance with the will of God. Those who occupy the higher strata (no classes) arrived there through natural ability and accordingly have duties which match their privileges. Entrepreneurs should therefore provide a service in return for making profits, which are 'the just reward for the execution of Christian duty'.[67]

By accepting race rather than class as the basic social division, white workers could benefit without extra cost to capitalists. After all, black workers also had their 'place' in the God-given hierarchy – as 'hewers of wood and drawers of water'. It was the Christian duty of white workers to observe the 'correct' relationship between master and servant.[68] Dr EG Jansen explained that Afrikaners regarded black people as their responsibility and as people who would deliver the labour expected from them in the divinely ordained system.

In the end, the nationalists succeeded in taking over only the Mine Workers' Union – but more because of corruption among its leadership and their collusion with employers than due to political conviction. The campaign against 'communist' unions was successful insofar as it had created turmoil in the white working class by the end of the 1940s and confusion about the position of this class, thereby engineering an even wider chasm between white and black workers. Through the NP's ideology of racism and mythology of black, Anglo and communist threats, class and gender identities were rendered dormant, subordinated by an ethnic and racial identity consciousness. White workers were disciplined into adopting an ideology that neatly justified their exploitation and replaced class consciousness with race anxieties.

The NP's emphasis on 'saving' the Afrikaner worker from communism was reflected in the 1952 editions of one if its publications, *Skietgoed* (Ammunition), which dealt with the worker and communism, as well as pamphlets on the communist threat to South Africa. By the 1950s, Afrikaner workers had been incorporated into the nationalist alliance. In the end, the NP in government finished what the Broederbond and its front organisations could not manage: it smashed the unions through the 1950 Suppression of Communism Act, in particular the Garment Workers' Union. Much to the irritation of Malan, Verwoerd and Albert Hertzog, the 'Boeredogters' working in the clothing and textile sector firmly supported the GWU, despite several attacks on its secretary Solly Sachs, branded as a 'communist/Jew'. Sachs left the country in 1952 when he was banned.

Much time was spent convincing Afrikaners that the capitalists involved in the Eerste Ekonomiese Volkskongres were engaged in *volkskapitalisme* for the benefit of all Afrikaners, and not only capitalists. Pursuing economic interests was presented as 'positive', since Afrikaners, like English-speaking, Jewish and Greek South Africans, had to 'support' each other.[69] But small business cooperatives accused the larger members of the Afrikaanse Handelsinstituut of pursuing profit alone rather than acting for the benefit of the *volk*, as had repeatedly been claimed in the economic journals *Inspan* and *Volkshandel*.[70] This was confirmed by the allocation of only 10 per cent of the Reddingsdaadfonds to address the poor-white problem.[71] The bulk of the money went to Federale Volksbeleggings to channel capital to Afrikaans enterprises. The injection of capital benefited Broederbond members who had become directors of new businesses.[72]

The tension between big Afrikaner capitalist interests and the lower middle and working classes, which haunted the NP throughout its existence, was already visible in these accusations. *Volkshandel*, the official mouthpiece of business, cautioned capitalists to employ their profits in service of the *volk* and create jobs with benefits if they wanted to ward off allegations of not being truly anti-capitalist. The EI, RDB and AHI convinced farmers – the only sector with ample capital – to invest their funds only in Afrikaner-owned financial institutions. The *volksekonomie* would be one in which the state fostered private capital's great entrepreneurial spirit, declared *Volkshandel* in 1941. The NP stepped up to the plate. Its economic plan of 1944 supported a 'controlled economy' with private enterprise and private property. It favoured the abolition of trade preferences and a system of 'free trade' internationally. Trading licences would limit 'non-whites' to their 'own' areas (aimed at Indian traders). Banks would have headquarters in South Africa with local directors, while labour regulations would protect the 'position and civilisation of the white race'.[73]

The second Ekonomiese Volkskongres in 1950 decided that small undertakings should no longer receive capital support, and that all capital should be channelled to large companies. The greatest success of the Reddingsdaad movement was to redirect Afrikaner savings to Afrikaner institutions, thus allowing the growth of Afrikaner-owned financial companies such as Sanlam, Santam, Volkskas and Saambou. Afrikaner economic success produced a small group of financial capitalists grouped around Sanlam and a larger group of lower-middle-class traders in the north.[74] The Afrikaner share of business grew from 5 per cent in 1938/9 to 11 per cent in 1948/9 – mostly on the back of a leap in Afrikaner commerce from 8 to 25 per cent. Finance capital in Afrikaner hands doubled.[75] The north–south division would lead to further tensions in the following decades.

When the NP came to power, its labour and pricing policies ensured an improvement in capital accumulation for both Afrikaans- and English-speaking whites. But it was the Afrikaner-owned companies that benefited handsomely from NP rule. The Reddingsdaad initiative was so successful in channelling capital to Sanlam that, by 1950, the company was independent of agricultural capital. Then it received an even bigger boost. The NP in government redirected state tenders to Afrikaner companies, providing them with a massive new source of capital. By 1963, Sanlam was the second largest conglomerate in South Africa after Anglo American. The Truth and Reconciliation Commission would hear years later, in the 1990s, about the 'special' relationship Sanlam enjoyed with the NP government.[76]

The 1950 Ekonomiese Volkskongres was also the last. Such concerted actions had become unnecessary with the NP in power. The NP's anti-capitalist rhetoric disappeared as the Afrikaner capitalist class developed and it became glaringly obvious that the NP's anti-capitalist sentiments applied only to English- and Jewish-owned capital. Once in government, the NP pursued capitalist industrial development, while looking after its primary support bases: the white farmer and the white worker. Wages of white workers rose by 10 per cent in the first five years of NP rule, while those of black workers dropped by 5 per cent. State-owned enterprises such as Iscor, Sasol, Escom, Armscor, Soekor and Nufkor expanded throughout the NP's reign, with management almost exclusively in the hands of white Afrikaner men. The civil service was also Afrikanerised.[77]

The result was that Afrikaner nationalism modernised 'the Afrikaner', as academic André du Toit argues.[78] It was therefore a break with the past rather than a continuation.[79] Finally, while nationalists used colonial rhetoric to mobilise Afrikaners across different classes and to justify apartheid, the explicit aim was to gain political power in order to improve their socio-economic status. This goal had an elite bias, but in order for the elites to benefit, the working-class vote was needed to secure state power. Economic advancement resulted in the NP becoming a party of the middle classes by the 1970s. By 1980, the NP could afford to relinquish the much diminished working-class element of its support base.

Against capitalism and for national socialism

The NP's version of Afrikaner nationalism was never the only one, and its hegemony was always contested to a greater or lesser extent.

By the late 1930s, Hertzog, a veteran of Afrikaner politics, was a spent force. Ideologically, the newest contender for Afrikaner support turned out to be national socialism, as manifested in the proto-fascist Ossewa-Brandwag (Ox Wagon Sentinel) and the OB offshoot, Nuwe Orde (New Order).

The OB was born of the 1938 Great Trek centenary celebrations. Among other elements of national socialism, it borrowed the practice of seeking symbolism from the past to glorify and romanticise support for a radical ideology.[80] Its leader, former Afrikaanse Nasionale Studentebond head Hans van Rensburg, rejected 'capitalist democracy' while supporting Christian nationalism. During the Second World War, the ethnic-based extra-parliamentary OB found significant support among the population of just more than a million Afrikaners, numbering about 300 000 members in 1940. Its core principle was support for national socialism against capitalism and communism. The OB was opposed to the *geldmag* (money power); anti-democratic; racist and anti-Semitic; anti-British and English-speaking interests; and pro-Germany. Elements of the OB strongly supported violence as a tactic, leading to sabotage attacks on government targets and as many as 723 members being interned at one point. Among the detainees were BJ Vorster, who became prime minister a couple of decades later, and Hendrik van den Bergh, head of the Bureau of State Security (BOSS) during Vorster's reign.

The Nuwe Orde, headed by Oswald Pirow, was just as anti-democratic as the OB itself, regarding liberal-democratic elections as defective and outdated.[81]

In the run-up to the 1943 election, the Broederbond made concerted efforts to bring the OB and the NP together. For a short while, it seemed these efforts might bear fruit. At the NP's Cape congress in 1940, agreement was reached that the party would control all political matters pertaining to Afrikaners, while the OB would be responsible for their mobilisation in the 'non-political' economic, moral and religious spheres.[82] The OB agreed to respect the NP 'on party-political terrain as the only organ of the Afrikaner volk'.[83] Cooperation between the two organisations was so close that the OB drafted the NP's 1942 constitution, which demanded a state based on the Boer republics of the nineteenth century, rejected British liberal democracy, and agitated against 'the capitalist and parasitical exploitation' of Afrikaners.[84] Malan reiterated these principles in a parliamentary motion during the same year.[85]

The OB did not stick to its agreed mandate, and its propaganda for a 'partyless state' translated into a rejection of the parliament-based NP. Van Rensburg declared at a rally of 7 000 members in 1942 that the OB should rule the country. Then 'the most important man in a district would be the OB general and the most important in a ward would be the OB field-cornet. If someone seeks support from the state, only his relationship with the OB will be taken into account. In ten years South Africa will look very different than today. There will be no democracy. You will also no longer need the masses.'[86]

At the time, Malan was seeking a break with the OB. He found a reason when the OB published a pamphlet with overtly political content which, in terms of the two organisations' agreement, trespassed on NP territory.[87] Malan issued an ultimatum to the OB to withdraw the statements made. He declared that he could no longer force dual membership of the OB and his party on NP members. The NP also disowned the draft constitution.

The NP's break with the OB was partly based on ideology and partly calculated to neutralise it. At the 'crisis congress' in June 1941, where the NP had reiterated its position *vis-à-vis* the national socialist position of Van Rensburg and Pirow, the party confirmed that, like the Nuwe Orde, it was seeking the 'fall of the capitalist system'.

Malan argued that national socialism was the antithesis of Afrikaner history, given their quest for freedom and republicanism. The NP was also uncomfortable with national socialism's anti-Christian undertones, and the party could not deliver South Africa to German imperialism as Pirow's Nuwe Orde proposed. Instead, while the party was absolutely opposed to universal franchise, it did support a form of democracy, albeit one that catered for whites only. At the congress, the NP emphasised that it did not accept the British parliamentary version of democracy, since this did not offer adequate protection for the *volk*. Malan's version of democracy was based on the 'Voortrekker principles' of a Christian national republic, a *volksdemokrasie* in which the will of the people would prevail, as had been emphasised by Paul Kruger. The Boer republics represented the accepted model: representative of the *volk* and with the necessary guarantees against manipulation by the organised *geldmag* and the press. For Malan, a *volksdemokrasie* brought the *volk* into being, while a one-party system meant 'there would be no Afrikaner *volk* today'.[88] However, Malan never mentioned that Kruger exercised a personalised authority in which the political system revolved around one 'strong man', or that heredity still played a role in election to public office. Moreover, in Kruger's democracy, relatives and support-ers were rewarded with positions. Kruger intervened in the *Volksraad*'s decisions, was intolerant of dissent, and his populist rhetoric did not translate into real participatory decision-making.[89] This concept of democracy becomes especially significant when considering how the NP leadership exerted power after entering government. This could be seen in its approaches to internal structures, such as the parliamentary caucus, as well as towards supporters and branch members.

The 1943 election was the penultimate nail in the coffins of the Nuwe Orde and OB, as the NP remained the only Afrikaner nationalist party in parliament, and thus the sole bastion of demonstrable support among Afrikaners. The out-come of the Second World War – the defeat of national socialism and fascism – almost totally depleted the support for the two organisations. Ultimately, most OB members were absorbed into the NP, signifying acceptance by the Afrikaner radical right[90] of the parliamentary path to power rather than the use of violence. But the NP's flirtation with national socialism was more than skin-deep. For example, Malan declared as late as 1943 that he would still prefer a German victory to a communist triumph, which would be the case if the USSR should win the war for the Allied forces.[91] This comment illustrates the depth of anti-communist sentiment within the NP and sheds more light on the party's 'anti-capitalist' stance.

While the OB's presence on the South African political landscape was com-paratively short-lived, its level of support among Afrikaners made it a significant player at a crucial juncture. Had it not been neutralised, South African politics could have developed stronger authoritarian features than were subsequently seen under NP rule. The NP's liberal strand won the day over authoritarian impulses, as the party could ultimately not reconcile itself with the idea of gaining power through 'undemocratic' means and not allowing whites to elect their political representatives. Nevertheless, Furlong[92] argues that despite the OB's eventual demise, its ascendance did have consequences for South African politics, since it amplified radical right tendencies within the NP.

The successful elimination of the OB and winning over of its supporters reinforced rhetorical flourishes in the NP that were similar to those of the OB, such as invoking history and promoting Boer-republic-type democracy with its empty populism. While Malan was not immediately willing to accept OB members into the NP, they entered through the ranks of the Afrikaner Party, which was absorbed by the NP after the 1948 election.

In power on a minority vote
Racism, land grabbing, inhumane labour exploitation, movement control and the denial of black people's human rights were all hallmarks of colonialism,

especially the Spanish and British varieties. In the southern United States, black people bore the brunt of segregation at home, work and in mobility. Native Americans were relegated to shrinking reserves, as were Australian aborigines.

The apartheid plan, hatched in piecemeal fashion depending very much on personalities, was different from these contemporary events in one major respect. It was a retrogressive step in a world where the cruelties of the Second World War had spurred a drive towards acknowledging the human rights of all. This international change was due in no small measure to the horror evoked by the extreme demonstration of white supremacism in the systematic murder of Jews and other marginalised minorities such as gypsies, homosexuals and the mentally disabled. Yet no sooner was Hitler dead than South African whites voted into power a party with pro-Nazi leanings and overtly racist rhetoric and programmes. The irony of the NP being elected in the same year that the rest of the world adopted the UN Universal Declaration of Human Rights underlines the retrogressiveness of the step.

Liberal politician Dr Margaret Ballinger, who represented black people in parliament until 1960, was still recovering from this event in 1969 when she wrote that she had regarded an NP victory as a 'temporary aberration'. She could not imagine it being more than a momentary delay of 'the already belated adjustment of South African thinking and practice to the demands of twentieth-century developments'.[93] The confluence of historical realities, actors and interests nevertheless meant that she and others would remain confounded as NP power grew until the late 1970s. Indeed, through a combination of clever policy manoeuvres and state repression of dissent the party would remain firmly in the driving seat until 1990.

The NP did not have a strong start in government. Astonishingly, the party ruled for almost two decades before capturing the support of the majority of voters. In collaboration with Klaas Havenga's Afrikaner Party, the NP came to power in 1948 with a slim majority of five seats. In an election that attracted the participation of only about 42 per cent of those allowed to vote, the NP won despite drawing a lower percentage of ballots than the UP. The result was 38 per cent for the NP, as opposed to 48 per cent for the UP[94] – the NP had about 100 000 votes less than the combined opposition in parliament.

This undemocratic outcome reflected an institutional flaw created by the elite compromise of 1909. The constitution made provision for the regular revision of the country's electoral divisions to ensure that each contained the same number of voters. The number could be varied by 15 per cent either way, taking into account factors such as 'sparsity or density of population'. Liberal historian Leonard Thompson observed that the judicial commissions assigned to carry out the task in practice attached great weight to this principle, in the process advantaging parties with more rural supporters – like the NP.[95] Moreover, as Afrikaner reformist historian FA van Jaarsveld[96] points out, apartheid was not the issue that drew most support for the NP in 1948. The Afrikaner vote was *against* Smuts more than it was *for* Malan. Smuts had participated on Britain's side in the Second World War and had failed to address the labour needs of farmers, the heightened competition between black and white workers, or the pressures placed on towns and cities through urbanisation.

In the NP's election messages, apartheid was one among a number of issues. The obsession with communism remained a strong rallying point. Along with the NP's slim majority and the low voter turnout, this raises the question of how much actual support apartheid as a policy enjoyed among the enfranchised section of the population – the whites – at that stage. Given that a minority of voters had cast their ballots, it may be assumed that an even smaller minority in fact specifically supported apartheid. But apartheid soon became the centrepiece of NP policy, as white people benefited directly from the intensified racial discrimination. It was the ticket to consolidating Afrikaner nationalist and white power.

The NP's practice of appointing Afrikaner businessmen (always men) to state positions began when it came to power. Possibilities for Afrikaner business were also created through parastatals, such as the Industrial Development Corporation. The NP busied itself with the economy to promote Afrikaners in the private and public sector, the latter sometimes serving as a training ground for the former, with a view to reducing the threat of a widening wealth gap between Afrikaner classes.[97] Laws were passed in 1956 and 1959 to reserve an even wider range of jobs for whites in both sectors. Blacks could not hold positions of authority over whites and were blocked from skilled positions.[98] By 1970, 60 per cent of Afrikaners were in white-collar jobs, as opposed to less than 30 per cent in 1936.[99]

The party's hold on state power remained fragile during the 1950s. As that decade drew to a close, between a quarter and a third of Afrikaners were still voting for the UP. This insecurity not only spurred the party to tighten the screws on opponents and critics, but also to change the electoral system to ensure its dominance. The NP government disproportionately boosted the electoral representation of the 18 000 voters in the pro-NP South West African constituencies. According to the resistance group the Springbok Legion, each South West African vote had triple the value of a South African vote.[100] Lastly, coloured representation in parliament was removed through a drawn-out process that exhibited an extreme disregard for the rule of law and the basic principle of the separation of power. The reasons offered by NP politicians for the removal were quite blatant and underlined their attitude of white superiority. According to them, coloureds were being 'manipulated' into voting for the UP.

It was not until 1966, when Verwoerd was premier, that the NP finally managed to win a clear majority: 57.8 per cent, as opposed to 46.2 per cent in 1961.[101] That this was not achieved in the 1961 election is notable, given that Verwoerd had led the country to republican status the year before. The NP's continuous assurances to English-speaking voters about their social and economic status finally paid off in 1966, when it bagged 40.6 per cent of the vote in English-dominated Natal, as opposed to 16.7 per cent in 1961. Thus, by the mid-1960s the NP had established a nationalist hegemony among Afrikaners and had made major inroads into the English-speaking white electorate.

What is all the hubbub about?

In 1948, Jan Smuts, who had underestimated the NP to such an extent that he lost his own constituency of Standerton in the election, wanted to know from parliament: 'What is apartheid' – this thing that had 'raised such a hubbub?' At that point, the NP did not yet have a coherent apartheid policy. Verwoerd, who succeeded the meek Dr EG Jansen as minister of native affairs in 1950, was the first and last NP leader to hold a firm conviction that he knew what apartheid was.

As *verligte* journalist Piet Cillié remarked, rather than being a blueprint, apartheid was a set of policies that were continuously adapted to serve the NP's ultimate goal: staying in power. It was about power that was maintained by establishing Afrikaner self-determination and preventing another party – the UP – from winning an election.[102] This naked fact is obscured by the emphasis that some (Afrikaner nationalist) authors place on the idealistic aspect of apartheid. It is frequently claimed that Afrikaner nationalists had a 'grand dream' – they never meant to discriminate against anyone. If anything, the 'inconvenience' to black people was regarded as only temporary before the nirvana of ethnic nations, each in their own territory, was established. This was reinforced by NP propaganda.

After the NP's unexpected victory, Malan set about placating fears about apartheid, which, ran the argument, had been turned into 'a caricature'. Paternalistically, he assured black people that the NP sought 'the cooperation of the various races. There will be no discrimination against any section. We have a policy in regard to the non-Europeans but this involves no oppression or the removal of any of their rights. We shall protect them against oppression and bring about good relationships between them and the European population.' Apartheid would translate into 'a large measure of independence with the growth of their self-reliance, self-respect and at the same time the creation of opportunities for free development in conformity with their own character and capacity'.[103] And therein lay the rub. Who would decide what black people's 'character and capacity' were? Why, the whites, of course.

The NP developed a whole language to justify apartheid. It was presented as a 'form of democracy' that made 'good neighbourliness' and 'peaceful coexistence' possible. As minister of the interior Eben Dönges put it in 1951: interracial relations could only be improved by excising 'points of friction ... It is one of the fundamental principles of apartheid that points of contact should be removed as far as possible because the points of contact become the points of friction.'[104] Without apartheid, combustible racial tensions would be the order of the day. So seductive was the idea that apartheid made good neighbours of South Africans that *Die Burger*'s political columnist Dawie (usually the then editor, Piet Cillié) wrote in 1971 that South Africans 'live in separate, fenced yards to stay out of each other's hair, not to live in total isolation next to each other. We talk over the fence, we visit each other and [things] go calmly and are relaxed ... take [the fences] away and the good neighbourliness changes into hostility ...'[105]

Apart from the fact that few whites ever had contact with black people on an equal footing, Dawie seemed to have been under the impression that black people had some choice in the matter.

Another myth to justify apartheid was that other ethnic groups constituted 'nations' that would eventually develop the same nationalist aspirations as Afrikaners. This idea of the foreignness of especially black people had its ultimate manifestation in the Bantustans. Minister of Bantu administration and development MC Botha articulated this as follows in 1967: 'As [the Bantu] nations develop and become more attached to their own authorities and exercise greater powers, White-Bantu administration can be based increasingly on international agreements ... [meaning that] many matters which are now arranged by ... laws [on] urban areas, reference books [and] labour ... can then operate on agreements between the Black nation and the White nation'.[106] By the 1980s, this ridiculous notion manifested in the fact that the government's relations with the Bantustans indeed fell under the department of foreign affairs. The emphasis on black South Africans having their own 'nations' made possible the denial of discrimination, as 'the limitations on the Bantu in the White areas would not be discrimination ... but differentiation of the local White people on the one side and members of the remote Bantu nation on the other'.[107]

By the 1960s, the dominant discourse in the NP was along the following lines: people were 'different' to each other (read: black people were different), and admitting this fact did not make one a racist. To try to force the ('simple' and 'backward') 'black man' to become like the 'white man' is to perpetrate an injustice. Rather, the 'black man' should be allowed to develop at his own pace and according to his own customs. Apartheid provides this opportunity through the creation of an environment in which black people can develop. Apartheid is thus both 'ethical and Christian'. However, these justifications were never convincing to anyone outside the Afrikaner nationalist sphere, rendering Afrikaners more and more defensive as the years passed and the inequities of apartheid became starker.

Soon, the word apartheid itself was blamed as the source of the trouble. *Die Burger* declared in May 1960 that white South Africa could no longer 'afford' the word because of its negative connotations in foreign minds. The newspaper made a number of appeals to the government to accelerate the 'positive' aspects of apartheid and bemoaned the fact that 'the one hand is destroying what the other hand is building'.[108]

The first decade under Malan and his successor JG Strijdom was marked by what Afrikaner nationalists called 'negative apartheid'. This entailed the NP government entrenching white and particularly Afrikaner privilege through a piecemeal but still Orwellian system of control over every aspect of the lives of black people. Strijdom's crude *baasskap* rhetoric made way for Verwoerd's 'separate development', a euphemism that breathed new life into apartheid by soothing some Afrikaner consciences about the realities of the policy. *Die Burger* and other newspapers immediately took to the phrase, alongside other creations such as 'separate freedoms'.

Some historians, like Van Jaarsveld, credit Verwoerd with the 'internal decolonisation' of South Africa[109] through his idea of putting in place a common-wealth of 'multinational' South African states. However, Verwoerd's basic notions about black people and their rights differed little from those of Malan. In fact, while Malan might not have had as clear a vision of what apartheid would entail, he had already emphasised in 1944 that it was about developing blacks and coloureds under white leadership 'according to their character and ability'. In 1948 he said apartheid 'could mean equality but each on its own terrain'.[110] Equality therefore had a proviso: separation.

Many Afrikaner and later English-speaking white voters chose to believe the rhetoric despite the constant criticism, research and hard facts that showed the policy was ultimately impracticable. In a prescient address, Smuts pointed out in 1948 that reserves without industrial development could not work and that black urbanisation had become an inevitable process: 'The Native ... is part and parcel of industrial South Africa ... nothing can alter it.'[111] Liberal historian CW de Kiewiet put it more picturesquely in 1941: segregation had been 'denied by the sight of hundreds of thousands of natives dwelling permanently in the towns and on European farms ... To unwind the woven cord of native and European life is simply to require history to retrace its steps.'[112]

While the UP remained white supremacist, there were occasional liberal mutterings from Smuts's deputy Jan Hofmeyr, who served as a reminder that not all Afrikaners were nationalists. In 1947, when he was still a minister in Smuts's cabinet, he said that a time would come when black and Indian South Africans would have to be allowed into parliament.[113] The UP government appointed a commission under Judge HA Fagan in the mid-1940s to investigate the race question. Apart from proposing a national non-racial health system – radical for the era – the commission reiterated the growing feeling that black urbanisation had to be accepted and managed, not least through appropriate urban planning.[114] By the 1940s the reserves had a much reduced capacity for subsistence. The 'betterment' policies aimed at improving the situation through such measures as reducing livestock and moving people to villages led to a wave of rural protest. There was just not enough land in the reserves.

This was also the finding of the NP government's own Tomlinson Commission in 1956. The homeland system would only be able to remove 60 per cent of black people from 'white South Africa' – 40 per cent would still be living in white areas by 1980. The commission proposed that at least 45 per cent of the union's total territory be set aside for consolidated homelands. This was sure to be resisted, as any increase in land allocation to the reserves had been rejected by white landowners since a commission had investigated the issue some five years after union. The Tomlinson Commission thus proposed total territorial segregation. In the early years, the possibility of 'absolute apartheid' was mooted, but the NP leadership accepted it as impractical, given the economy's dependence on black labour. But that did not prevent Verwoerd from disingenuously suggesting at a cabinet meeting in 1956 that it should still be propagated as a means of whipping up more popular support.[115]

Admonitions about the unfeasibility of apartheid did not find fertile ground in NP structures. Branch proposals forwarded from the annual congress to the party leadership in March 1950[116] show that the leaders were reflecting what the party's members wanted. The proposals included the following:

- The 'high' minimum wages for natives were unacceptable and all further increments should be scrapped.
- Communist propaganda was rife in 'native areas' and on the *platteland* (rural areas) and agitators should be prosecuted.
- The government should appoint only 'sympathetic civil servants in key posts' and investigate monolingual civil servants who were appointed during the previous administration; residences should be built for young civil servants.
- A 'family allowance' should be introduced to encourage larger white families,

thus addressing concerns about demographics that surfaced frequently at NP congresses.

Branch proposals from the August 1950 congress[117] contained more specific pleas for protection against black competition, as well as more transparent examples of prejudice:

- Skilled positions in the construction industry should be reserved for whites.
- Municipalities should not be allowed to use only black people in construction projects.
- All natives and 'non-whites' working as drivers of government vehicles should be removed from their posts.
- Poor whites should be employed as drivers instead of blacks.
- Non-whites should not be addressed as Mr and Mrs in [state] departmental letters.
- Indecent assault by natives against white women should be punished with the death penalty, while other forms of assault should be dealt with through corporal punishment.
- Natives should be subjected to stricter penalties.
- Police should be given the right in unrest situations to shoot to kill and not only to frighten.
- As in the case of sheep skins and cattle, natives should have a letter from their '*baas*' when selling poultry and grain.
- Domestic workers should carry doctors' certificates to show they did not have tuberculosis.
- It should be a criminal offence for whites to appoint black people without passes.
- The taxes on natives should be increased 'so that they also pay a small amount towards their free education and medical services'.
- Taxes for urban blacks should be increased.
- The trust law in accordance with which 'kaffirs' were helped should be reviewed with a view to changing the unfair system that gave natives land, cattle and agricultural support from the government.
- Native children should be compelled to leave school at the age of sixteen, except when they could pay for their secondary school education.

The link between communist agitation and black discontent was made at that early stage. The congress requested that government 'send' the Russian consul out of South Africa 'because that is the source of all the agitation and unrest in the country'. Bechuanaland, Basutoland and Swaziland should also be incorporated into South Africa as soon as possible, as they were safe havens for communists.

A minority of proposals asked for 'lower living standards or higher beef prices'; improved salaries for civil servants; a review of the price of milk; more assistance for white farmers; a state-funded pension system; and limitations on immigration.

A bad omen

The NP was not long in the saddle before embarking on a campaign to disenfranchise coloured voters. While this may have seemed a logical step, given the party's policies, it is worth noting that, historically, relations between Afrikaners and coloureds were not always antagonistic. Up to the very end of the NP's existence, a strong ebb and flow of currents between these two population groups characterised party debates and policies. At the time of its demise in the 2000s, the NP had a substantial coloured support base.

After the 1948 election, groups such as the UP in parliament, the 'Circle of 13' academics and the Springbok Legion saw the makings of fascism or dictatorship in efforts to disenfranchise the coloureds. The NP's drawn-out campaign was a demonstration of how far the party would go to change laws and institutions to retain its hold on power. This was one of several tactics employed to build unassailability at the ballot box, and showed no regard for basic democratic principles.

According to an NP background document[118] from the mid-1960s, the party regarded black franchise and the 'danger of being ploughed under by the Bantu' as the predominant problem until 1929. Up to that point, coloureds were seen as a partner against blacks, and therefore 'deserving' of the vote. This changed when the 1932 NP Cape congress adopted a proposal for separate white and coloured voters' rolls. Hertzog changed his mind about the coloured vote when he joined Smuts to form the UP in 1933, accusing Malan of a breach of faith in white–coloured relations because of the NP decision to support racially separate voters' rolls.

In its 1938 election manifesto, Malan's NP advocated the scrapping of the Cape black franchise and the removal of coloureds from the common voters' roll. This was confirmed in both the NP's Sauer report, which advocated apartheid, and the party's 1948 election manifesto. Despite opposition outside and inside parliament, as well as within the NP itself, the party obsessively pursued the downgrading of the coloured vote for several years.[119] Towards the end, the campaign was driven by the hardliner Transvaal corps whose leader, JG Strijdom, saw even white representation of black people as a ludicrous concession that undermined the will of 'the people' – the whites. In 1949, Strijdom warned that 'Native representatives must not have the power to frustrate a White government or to overthrow it ... Can we tolerate a continuance of this state of affairs where the representatives of Non-Europeans are able to say which laws can be enacted in South Africa and which laws cannot be enacted?'[120]

In retrospect, given the obstacles that the NP faced in this regard, its determination to devalue the coloured vote seemed fanatical. However, throughout its tenure in government, the NP would 'adapt' the law to suit narrow party interests. There was, in fact, scant evidence of the benign picture painted by later authors, such as Broederbond chairperson Gerrit Viljoen, of the Afrikaner 'tradition of law and order'.[121]

The campaign against the coloured franchise proved that the NP would stop at nothing in its quest to entrench white supremacy. Neither the constitution, nor the courts, nor parliament were safe. The campaign was also about entrenching the party's position in government. It was a reminder that white supremacism served the NP because, by ring-fencing democracy and imposing a colour bar on participation in the political and economic life of the country, the party strengthened its hold on power. The coloured vote affected the NP's political fortunes at the time because the nine parliamentary seats for coloured areas usually went to the UP. Even the Communist Party had succeeded in sending a representative to parliament on the basis of the coloured vote. NP cabinet minister Eben Dönges accused political parties of using the coloured vote as a football.

At the beginning of 1951, the NP government tabled the Separate Representation of Voters Bill, which would remove coloureds from the existing voters' roll and place them on a different roll in the Cape and Natal. They would have four white representatives in the house of assembly, while the governor general would appoint a white person to represent coloured voters in the senate 'on the grounds of his special knowledge of the reasonable wants of the coloured people'.[122]

Direct representation of coloured people was limited to a proposed council that would have advisory powers only. It would be constituted according to coloured votes as well as nominations, and have eight coloured and three nominated representatives. The chairperson would be a civil servant appointed to the position.

The NP firmly believed that the law would be passed, even though the coloured vote had been entrenched in the South Africa Act of 1909. The opposition UP argued that the law would disqualify coloured voters from registration on the common roll, and therefore violated sections 35 and 152 of the South Africa Act. The NP contended that parliament, as the supreme law-making body, could determine its own procedures, that a two-thirds majority was not needed, and that the courts had no 'right' to decide on a law duly passed by the 'democratically' elected parliament.

Four coloured voters opposed the decision in the Supreme Court, which referred the case to the appellate division. An application was duly lodged, and the Appeal Court found that the amendment had to be passed with a two-thirds majority. Adopting the bill with slim majorities in the two houses of parliament did not pass constitutional muster, as this constituted a derogation of coloured voters' rights.

Malan was under pressure from the northern hawks in the party, as Strijdom would not accept the court's ruling. He immediately announced the NP's rejection of the judgment on the grounds that 'the legislative sovereignty of the lawfully and democratically elected representatives of the people is denied, and where an appointed judicial authority assumes the testing right, namely the right to pass judgment on the exercise of ... legislative powers by the elected representatives of the people ... The situation which has now arisen creates uncertainty and chaos where certainty and order should exist ... It is imperative that the legislative authority of Parliament should be placed beyond any doubt, in order to ensure order and certainty.'[123] Ironically, a similar argument would be heard fifty years later from ANC politicians when the Constitutional Court instructed the government to provide prophylaxis to prevent HIV transmission from mother to child.

Malan's address was followed by a statement from the four provincial leaders of the NP in which the issue was couched as part of the struggle against British imperialism. The leaders sent out a 'war cry ... to all Nationalists: Stand together in this new phase of the struggle for freedom. That struggle will proceed to its conclusion ... It is a clarion call to battle for the most sacred rights of a nation as it exercises them through Parliament. The action will be forceful and uncompromising.'[124]

For Margaret Ballinger, who later became leader of the Liberal Party, Malan's statement 'could not but revive and heighten every anxiety as to the nature and direction of the forces that were now in political control of the country'.[125] The NP's subsequent steps precipitated a constitutional crisis that lasted for most of the 1950s. It was 'a record of the lengths to which the forces now in control were prepared to go to put their own stamp on the country ... They were lengths which remained technically within the law. Were not Dr Malan, under whom the process began, and his successor, Mr Strydom [sic], under whom it reached its climax, repeatedly to underline that, however forceful and uncompromising, they were strictly legal in their actions? But the ingenuity that was put in commission to bend the law to their will could not fail to have its effect on the character and position of Parliament itself,' Ballinger later wrote.[126]

The NP came up with an extraordinary scheme to turn parliament into a 'court of appeal' with the power to deliberate and overturn those decisions of the courts that pertained to constitutional matters. This new 'court' would have the power to review all Appeal Court decisions with which the government disagreed. One of the justifications was alleviating pressure on the 'six old men of Bloemfontein' – as Malan's sidekick Paul Sauer called the Appeal Court judges – to make 'political' decisions. NP cabinet minister Tom Naudé declared in parliament that 'the people' did not want to be governed by paid officials, whether they were judges or not.

On 27 August 1952, the 'high court of parliament' duly overturned the Appeal Court's decision. The UP boycotted the session. *Die Burger* declared the bill a 'necessary evil', and said the 'high court of parliament' should be dissolved once it had completed its task, namely the removal of coloured people from the common voters' roll. Shortly thereafter the Supreme Court declared the parliamentary reversal of the decision null and void, and the Appeal Court dismissed the government's objection to this decision. The Supreme Court found that all persons were entitled to non-infringement of their entrenched constitutional rights, that it was the duty of the courts to uphold these rights and, that in doing so, they were not infringing the legislature's powers.

In the 1953 election, the NP again emphasised the virtues of apartheid and beat the drum of communist and British imperialist threats. As Transvaal NP leader, Strijdom pushed the republican ideal and *baasskap* – the 'white man's right' to govern 'the black man'. The NP managed to increase its majority by gaining another twenty-nine seats to hold ninety-four against the UP's fifty-seven, the Labour Party's four and the three seats for the white representatives of the Cape 'natives'. But this still did not give the party the two-thirds majority that Malan sought, and the governing party was still not supported by the majority of the electorate. Some 646 000 people had voted for the NP, but 722 000 had cast their ballots for opposition parties.[127]

In the 1954 provincial elections, the NP gained control of the Cape, Transvaal and Free State. The UP's poor performance at the polls, along with divisions over the coloured vote, was splitting the party. Its right wing was partial to derogation of the coloured vote, but the NP's willingness to shatter the democratic principle of the separation of powers by usurping the role of the courts was a bone of contention. The UP proffered an argument that would resurface as one of the NP's reasons for the creation of a tricameral parliament in the 1980s, namely that white cooperation with coloured people was necessary to avoid the formation of an anti-white 'Non-European bloc'. Negotiations with members of the UP did not deliver results and Malan introduced another bill, this time to enlarge the Appeal Court. The issue heightened divisions within the UP to the point where six members broke away to form another party, which supported the NP's bid.

Even with these new supporters and after months of manoeuvres, the NP was still short of nine votes. Meanwhile, the geriatric Malan retired, to be replaced by Strijdom, the outspoken advocate of *baasskap*. The hard-line reactionary contingent of the NP had gained control. Strijdom was close to Verwoerd and paved the latter's way to the top.

In 1955, the NP government pushed through the law that enlarged the Appeal Court from six to eleven judges and changed the requirements for a quorum to eleven in constitutional cases. Minister of justice CR Swart stated openly that the bill was designed to address the coloured vote issue. In another unexpected move, a bill was introduced to enlarge the senate and do away with proportional representation. In effect, the senate became a reflection of the national assembly and ensured the ruling party's dominance. In the process, the senate's intent was undermined, namely to ensure minority representation in the upper house as well as 'the federal element behind our unitary constitution'.[128]

Years later, of course, political expedience dictated that the NP change tack on the issue of majority rule, minorities and federalism.

But even with a simple majority determining the senate's composition, the NP still did not have the required two-thirds to change the constitution. So it increased the number of nominated senators from eight to sixteen. Four of the new nominees would be selected on the basis of their 'knowledge of the reasonable wants and wishes of the non-White races'. The senate was thus enlarged from forty-eight to eighty-nine seats, ensuring that in a joint sitting of the two houses of parliament, the NP had 171 votes to the opposition's 77. In this way, the NP fabricated for itself the majority it could not achieve through the ballot box.

NP politicians fought each other for the new positions, the first 'quali-fication' being a £50 contribution to the party's coffers.[129] In February 1956, parliament passed 'A Bill relating to the Separate Representation of Voters and the Competence of the Law Courts to pass Judgment on the Validity of Acts passed by Parliament', effecting with an undemocratically inflated 174 votes to 68 what the courts had blocked in 1951. The 45 000 coloured voters were removed from the common roll and placed on a separate one. The Coloured Representative Council was restructured – henceforth the majority of members would be nominated rather than elected. Lastly, coloured voters lost the right to elect coloured representatives to the Cape provincial council.

Attempts failed in the courts to overturn the two bills on the coloured vote and the senate. Shortly thereafter, branches passed a motion at the Transvaal NP congress thanking Strijdom for placing coloured people on a separate voters' roll.

The sorry tale did not end there. Coloured South Africans remained a thorn in the NP's side, and the Cape NP and *Die Burger* started to prevaricate on the issue of their rights. Verwoerd raised the possibility of coloured 'self-rule' at local level, suggesting in 1961 that the Coloured Representative Council be developed into a separate parliament, and even mooting the creation of a 'coloured cabinet'.

The debate reached a crescendo with deputy minister of justice PW Botha reprimanding those who wished to take 'the leadership out of the hands of those who have been called to govern'.[130] He reiterated Dönges's paternalistic point that coloured voters were used as a 'football' by the UP. According to Botha, political integration did not bring development to coloured people, who 'only succeeded on two terrains: they became teachers or preachers'. In other areas their position had deteriorated or they had struggled to survive, according to Botha. He pointed out that since the removal of coloured voters from the common roll, the attitude of whites towards coloured people had improved. The NP would thus continue to strive for 'the ideal of good neigh-bourliness' through the Group Areas Act and 'greater autonomy in own sphere' [*groter selfstandigheid in eie kring*]. The latter was supposed to compensate for the political 'ceiling' Verwoerd admitted the NP had imposed on coloured people.[131]

By 1968, coloured representation by white parliamentarians was replaced by a Coloured Persons' Representative Council for which coloured people could vote, and which would control local administration and service delivery. The NP's federal council contended at a 17 May 1968 meeting[132] that legislative power had to remain in white hands, because 'political integration will mean the death of the white man in South Africa'. Minister of labour and coloured affairs Marais Viljoen reported at the meeting that coloured people showed no resistance to the policy, and that they only wanted their own homes, not a homeland. However, Prime Minister John Vorster was still considering a coloured homeland as an option. He said at the meeting that while this would not be 'practical politics for now', members were 'free' to explore the idea. Contention in NP ranks over the issue led to the government stating in December 1970 that a separate homeland for coloured people was unworkable, because their dispersal throughout the country meant that one could be created only with 'great disruption and injustice'. This was in line with the NP's Cape media partner. In 1971, *Die Burger* advocated joint decision-making between coloureds and whites on coloured issues.[133] But the Nats in the north had other ideas.

Even after December 1970, the coloured homeland kept cropping up as a 'solution'. At the Free State NP's 1971 congress, a number of branches proposed such a homeland as a 'natural' manifestation of the policy of separate development. In the same year, the NP information service prepared a confidential document for the leadership on a congress of the NP-aligned student organisation, the

Afrikaanse Studentebond (ASB). Academic Gerrit Viljoen, who would in 1990 become the chief NP negotiator at Codesa, had raised the idea of 'separate freedom for coloured people in a geographical area or areas'. ASB president Roelf Meyer, who would replace Viljoen at the negotiating table in the run-up to the 1994 election, reiterated the need for 'consolidation' of coloured areas, but denied that he supported a coloured homeland.[134]

The coloured-only Labour Party participated in the CPRC, but, after gaining control of the council in 1975, halted its operations and demanded an end to racial discrimination against coloureds. The council was disbanded in 1980, and the NP extended a greater say to coloured people through PW Botha's tricameral parliament in 1983 – but still on white terms.

The divinely ordained right to protect racial purity

Of all Afrikaner nationalism's civil society extensions, the Dutch Reformed Church and its two sister churches, the Hervormde and the Gereformeerde Kerk, were the most crucial. Of the three, the DRC predominated by far. After the South African War, many Boers from the two former republics felt humiliated, under immense socio-economic pressure and alienated, due to Milner's policy of anglicisation. The church became a safe haven in those troubled times.[135] *Dominees* had a distinct interest in keeping Afrikaners white and Afrikaans, as these were the people who constituted their congregations. Theologians were thus seeking new ways to justify racial segregation. According to the philosopher GJ Rossouw, the idea of segregation rather than protection for Afrikaners had become an end in itself by the close of the 1930s. The poor-white problem was mostly resolved through economic growth during the Second World War, and Afrikaners' economic and political status had improved.

Dutch theologian and politician Abraham Kuyper influenced the DRC with his argument that the nation was a 'creational ordinance' from God. Therefore, 'nationalism became an expression of one's obedience to the will of God'. As the nation was defined along racist lines, 'Afrikaners had a divinely ordained right to protect their racial purity'.[136] Therefore, apartheid 'became the credo of the church, and obedience to this credo was equated with obedience to God'.[137]

The DRC enjoyed an intimate relationship with the NP, to the extent that clergyman GBA Gerdener was one of the members of the Sauer Commission, appointed by Malan in the late 1940s to flesh out the idea of apartheid. The Sauer report, which contained a section by Gerdener dealing with missionary policy, was incorporated into the NP's 1948 election manifesto. The NP was 'probably unique in the world' in that its party programme included a section on missionary work,[138] which serves as a vivid illustration of how central such work was in relation to apartheid. It was also an essential component of nineteenth-century colonialism, highlighting the similarities between apartheid and colonialism. Gerdener's own attitude was encompassed in his expedient admonition to 'Bantu' Christians: 'Let the missionary be your adviser, the Church your mother, and the Gospel your guide.'[139]

After 1948, the overlapping membership of party and church ensured that DRC members filled government and public service posts, and apartheid had become 'church policy'.[140] Power intoxicates. As 'general election after general election reveal[ed] increasing support for the National Party and its policy, the sense of power increased among Afrikaners, which was also evident among those who occupied church pews and Synod halls. The [DRC as] *landskerk* would move closer and closer to the government, until in the seventies she saw herself as guardian over *landsbeleid* [national policy].'[141]

The DRC had already declared in 1949 that it was not the place of the church to tell the government what policies it should adopt. It nevertheless agitated for certain policies – such as the Mixed Marriages Act of 1949 – and was obliged when they were adopted. In 1949, the church declared itself in support of a righteous application of apartheid policies, as this 'did not aim at or envisage any inferiority, much less suppression'. In this way, the church continued to convince itself and its members that apartheid was a just and moral system.

In perpetuation of this falsity, the DRC even allowed the NP government to erode the most basic pillar of its existence: its evangelical mission. In 1957, the church accepted Verwoerd's prohibition in a parliamentary amendment against black people attending church services in white areas. The church's calling to preach the gospel 'always, everywhere and to all people' was revised. After a meeting with Verwoerd, it accepted that apartheid had rendered 'everywhere' impossible.[142]

The church fed off the psychosis bred by NP rhetoric and practice, which led to black resistance, which in turn led to whites feeling more insecure. Afrikaner nationalist religion became Afrikaners' bulwark against the 'onslaught' from black people, liberals, communists and, in the end, the revered 'West' itself. Whites could cling to the idea of the justness of apartheid because of the physical separation that it effected. They chose to believe that 'apartheid was just another political strategy ... [rather than] brute racism which dehumanised their fellow South Africans'.[143]

Shortly after accepting that blacks could not be converted 'everywhere', the DRC synods buckled under pressure from Verwoerd, aided by the Broederbond, and renounced their own representatives who had adopted the World Council of Churches' Cottesloe Declaration in 1960. In the wake of the shooting of civilians by police at Sharpeville, the declaration rejected racial discrimination, including migrant labour, the colour bar in the labour market and the prohibition of racially mixed marriages.[144] Verwoerd doubtless noted the position taken by nine members of the DRC's synodal commission, who expressed their sympathy with the Sharpeville victims, though he would not have had too much cause for concern. These members remained firmly under the influence of NP propaganda, as was evident from their accompanying appeal to 'law-abiding non-whites' not to be intimidated by a 'small minority' of agitators.

They also condemned the 'devilish' accusations made in the international community against 'our land, people and church'. They confirmed the church's position: '… the church could condone and approve the policy of independent, autogenous development provided that it was applied in a just and honourable manner, without impairing and offending the dignity of people. The church also accepted that application of the policy, particularly in its initial stages, would result in a measure of upheaval and personal discomfort and hardship as, for instance, when slum areas are cleared.'[145] Apart from the self-delusion, the church's attitude remained typical of the paternalism of colonial missionaries.

In 1960, AP Treurnicht, who would later form the far-right Conservative Party, became editor of the DRC's mouthpiece, *Die Kerkbode*, which he used as a platform to advance Verwoerdian apartheid. Future prime minister BJ Vorster's brother Koot, who headed the Cape synod of the DRC, labelled the Cottesloe Declaration 'an impermissible application of the scripture', as it propounded church and social integration.

In 1966, Treurnicht and Koot Vorster conspired to finally eject Beyers Naudé from the church by having the general synod declare his Christian Institute 'errant' and a disturbance of 'the good order'.[146] During that time a friend of Naudé's, AS Geyser, was charged with heresy after he criticised another of the three Afrikaner sister churches, the Hervormde Kerk, for its racial exclusion. The Afrikaner nationalist clampdown on dissent was continuing apace.

In conclusion, the idea of racial segregation was far from new. Rather, it was a peculiar characteristic of British colonialism, of which the legacy could still in the twenty-first century be discerned in the reservations for Native Americans in the US and for aborigines in Australia. With Verwoerdian apartheid the Afrikaner nationalists developed their own variation on indirect rule, as found in Britain's colonies. But apartheid was a retrogressive step in a world where direct colonialism was being abandoned for subtler relations of domination and exploitation.

The majority of white voters did not support apartheid until the mid-1960s. They were increasingly seduced by the single-minded fervour with which the NP propagated its vague idea in contrast to the UP's befuddlement. The NP capitalised on the strong current of racism and underlying fear that predominated in white South Africa, as elsewhere in the world. Underlying white domination was a wilful denial of reality, made easier by racist concepts. JBM Hertzog spoke of the 'lower civilisation' of black people at a time when an emerging black elite, including the likes of Sol Plaatje, JT Gumede, Pixley Seme, Charlotte Maxeke, John Dube and Abdullah Abdurahman, already existed. While there is evidence that both Malan and Verwoerd reconsidered the apartheid policy at some point, with Malan not seeing it as permanent and Verwoerd starting to rethink the policy,[147] neither would upset the apartheid apple cart. It was the way to political power.

Apartheid, colonialism and racism

In order to understand how racism underpinned both colonialism and apartheid, it is necessary to trace its evolution from the 1600s to contemporary South Africa.

Reaction against the destructive socio-economic effects of British imperialism fortified elite attempts to band Afrikaners together by a single nationalist thread. Embedded therein was the notion of white superiority. As noted by George Fredrickson in his comparison of white supremacy in South Africa and the United States, there is no 'primordial and predetermined aptitude for "racism" common to American and South African whites [one may add Australians and New Zealanders] but rather the emergence of long-term, historically conditioned tendencies leading to more self-conscious and rigorously enforced forms of racial domination'.[148] Apartheid in its earliest manifestation was moulded out of the racist and paternalistic ideas that had characterised colonialism from the late eighteenth century onwards. The racism in apartheid and Afrikaner nationalism served a function similar to the racism inherent to colonialism. To justify repression on the basis of race, black people had to be presented as 'uncivilised', 'child-like', 'heathen' and 'innately inferior'.

The Afrikaner nationalist historian DW Krüger offers an ostensibly academic description that captures most of the fundamental ingredients of Afrikaner nationalism:

> The Afrikaner attitude towards black and coloured people was partly based on custom and experience of Bantu races with a low standard of civilisation, but in the republics especially it was justified by the people's interpretation of the Bible. They saw a parallel between the history of their own Trek from the Cape Colony through the wilderness of the interior and the history of the children of Israel, who as God's chosen people in ancient days had been led from Egypt through the desert to the promised land, miraculously preserving their separate identity among a host of heathens. As Calvinists they acknowledged the sovereign power of the Lord God of Hosts, hearing His mighty voice in the thunder of the heavens and in the howling of the storm. Like Israel of old, they have been guided to a new country and with

God's help they have withstood the onslaughts of mighty barbarian hosts. Like Israel they did not mix their blood with that of the children of Ham, but kept their race pure. In this last respect the future of the people's separate existence was in the safekeeping of a high-minded womanhood who taught their children the history of their people and instructed them in a fair knowledge of the Word of God.[149]

In fact, no hard evidence exists of a coherent ideology among the trekkers of a Calvinist calling or of being a chosen people.[150] Afrikaner nationalist historians such as Krüger were themselves espousing the powerful myth-making that characterised Afrikaner nationalism. As with all nationalisms, the Afrikaner brand entailed not only a discovery of common ties, interests, grievances and adversaries, but also a common past, reinvented through the projection of current concerns on that history.[151] Krüger's description, which is more of an ode, contains the primary elements used to justify colonialism: civilisation versus barbarism; Christian versus heathen; the need for racial purity in order to achieve or maintain nationhood.

In an international television interview around 1960,[152] Paul Sauer, DF Malan's confidant and one of the authors of the report on which the NP's 1948 manifesto was based, explained the 'responsibility' the NP government felt. Seemingly oblivious to the irony of his words, Sauer said that the government not only had a responsibility to the white people who had elected them, but also towards the 'barbarous and semi-barbarous' black people, even though the latter had not voted for them. Therefore, 'the responsibility that the white man feels ... should not be underrated ... The responsibility of his duty towards these underdeveloped people not capable of governing themselves and who would fall to pieces if we did not look after them.' He was speaking at a time when a highly articulate Nelson Mandela and other activists were being prosecuted for organising opposition to apartheid – but the mythical construction of the 'savage, underdeveloped black person' had to be maintained to justify apartheid.

By the 1960s, the NP's programme of principles declared that 'natives and coloureds' were regarded as 'permanent sections' of the country's population, but under the 'Christian trusteeship of the European races'. The basic principle of NP policy in regard to 'natives and coloureds' was strong opposition to any act that might lead to the mingling of 'European and non-European blood'. Accordingly, the NP wished to give non-European races the 'opportunity to develop themselves ... according to their natural gifts and abilities', while assuring them of just treatment under the law. The NP also declared itself in favour of the territorial and political segregation of the 'native', the separation of Europeans and non-Europeans in general and in residential areas, and, as far as practicable, in the industrial sphere. (The emphasis on coloured and black people as 'permanent' stemmed from the NP vision of repatriating the Indian population. The party pledged to protect all sectors of society against Asiatic immigration and competition by preventing further encroachment on European livelihoods and through an effective programme of segregation and repatriation.)

As late as 1990, the NP still employed rhetoric on 'civilisation' to mobilise support. Three examples will suffice: first, 'If the ANC therefore wants to fall in step with Western and civilised thinking and democratic developments, it needs to realise that MK has to be disbanded,' said defence minister Magnus Malan in 1990; second, black people interested in participating in the political system would have to pursue 'Christian values and civilised norms' as one of the guidelines, explained Chris Heunis, minister of constitutional development, in 1986. From the NP's point of view, the white population represented 'civilisation'. Third, former Broederbond head Gerrit Viljoen said in 1979 that Afrikaners' 'mission would be to remain here and accomplish our task as a civilised and Christian cultural group'.[153] In verbal displays of *kragdadigheid*, NP leaders from the era of DF Malan to that of FW de Klerk vowed to protect 'civilisation' on behalf of whites.

This argument can be traced back to the eighteenth century, when 'civilisation' was based on European notions of savagery, Christianity and biology.[154] Europe's age of enlightenment was replete with contradictions, such as rationalisations for prejudice and justifications for European expansion and exploitation. Thus, white 'civilisation' was placed in contrast with black 'savagery'. Those who did not live on the European continent were perceived as 'savage'. Up to the end of the eighteenth century, European attitudes to inhabitants of other continents were mostly characterised by curiosity, and even admiration. This changed to superiority and condescension. By associating African societies with unbridled 'nature' and denying African history, colonialism could be justified. The French writer Gobineau wrote in the 1850s that racial 'purity' was a prerequisite for civilisation, as 'mixed blood' produced decay and therefore the downfall of civilisation. By the 1930s, the notions of 'nation', 'race' and 'people' were still fused in European thinking. Similarly, DF Malan's South African 'nation' was white.[155] Racial 'purity' therefore had to be protected at all costs, and to this end Afrikaner nationalists created the *volksmoeder*. This prototype of the 'ideal' Afrikaner woman was dutiful, Christian, hard-working, selfless and docile, while policing the parameters of her own sexuality to keep the *volk* white. For example, due to their middle-class status, the Afrikaner women of the NP-aligned Suid-Afrikaanse Vrouefederasie (South African Women's Federation) had graduated to fully fledged *volksmoeders*. They promoted *volksmoeder* ideals among working-class and poor Afrikaner women who were regarded as dangerously close to the 'non-white', and hence to miscegenation and the decimation of the *volk*. The SAVF publication *Vrou en Moeder* said in 1943: 'The failed poor white on his unhappily low standard of living can so easily become *the companion and room-mate of the non-white* [author's italics]. Here, as well as at the communist meetings, the non-white learns to resist the idea of white guardianship and to regard himself as at least equal to the white.'[156] These ideas prevailed, as shown by a statement from PW Botha while he was deputy minister of justice in the 1960s. He explained in the NP publication *Die Kruithoring*[157] that coloureds were different because of history, biology and the 'fact' that the majority were 'backward'. Unless checked, coloured people with low living standards would become the bridge between 'the weaker part of the white population and the Bantu. This will pull the White down and would not only be the end of the whiteman [*sic*] but also the end of the Coloured.'

Hand in hand with 'civilisation' went Christianity, another dividing line used to validate racial distinctions. Using the Bible, it was argued that while all humans were descended from Adam, the master–servant hierarchy between Europe and Africa was justified by the curse of servitude placed on Ham. In late eighteenth-century South Africa, colonists claimed their rights to political and economic domination by contrasting their status as Christians with those of black people as heathens.[158] Paul Kruger declared black people to be the descendants of Ham, and therefore destined to remain hewers of wood and drawers of water. This justification was continuously proffered by the NP, notoriously by HF Verwoerd, to explain why blacks were 'suited' to inferior education. It was also reflected in DW Krüger's philosophy.

Another stream of European thinking was the justification of racial inferiority based on biological traits. In particular, British attitudes shifted from regarding blacks as inferior – based on culture and the Christian association of blackness with evil – to the development of a theory of racial inferiority. By the 1870s, most Europeans involved in imperial theory or administration regarded race as an external indication of inner abilities.[159] Black people were likened to animals in pseudo-scientific expositions from the late eighteenth century onwards. This kind of imagery persisted into the twentieth century, for example in a racist South African postcard produced in the 1920s with the face of an adult black man and a caption reading 'Luke – The Baboon Boy'.[160] Social Darwinism, popular in the UK and US by the end of the nineteenth century, posited a racial hierarchy. A pseudo-science of race developed, which culminated in eugenics and gave the world Nazism.

At the heart of Afrikaner nationalism sat the fear of *gelykstelling* (equalisation). DF Malan continuously identified the choice between *gelykstelling* ('the removal of all colour discrimination') and apartheid as the NP's primary concern.[161] This is a theme that recurs in different contexts over several decades, starting with justifications for the Great Trek, the centrepiece of Afrikaner nationalist mythology. Trek leader Piet Retief's niece Anna Steenkamp is quoted as saying that it 'is not so much their [slaves'] freedom that drove us to such lengths as their being placed on an equal footing with Christians [whites], contrary to the laws of God and the natural distinction of race and religion, so it was intolerable for any decent Christian to bow down beneath such a yoke; wherefore we rather withdrew in order thus to preserve our doctrines in purity'.[162] Karel Trichardt stated that the primary reason for the Great Trek was to avoid the 'equalisation of coloured people with the whites'.[163] It is not within the scope of this book to explore the myriad reasons for the trek. What is relevant here is the issue of equality.

The two Boer republics were 'the visible symbols of Afrikaner political dreams and aspirations, [while] at the same time the legal embodiment of inequality',[164] as the indigenous 'others' – black people – were excluded from basic citizenship rights. At the beginning of the twentieth century, General Christiaan de Wet emphasised that the impossibility of equality should be impressed upon black people. In April 1947, the Afrikaner nationalist publication *Inspan* cautioned black people who were 'organising themselves to improve their position' through strikes that equality was unthinkable.[165] In a private letter to DF Malan in 1946, JG Strijdom wrote that by allowing urbanisation and education of black people, they would 'necessarily' become 'civilised', which would make the colour bar impossible to impose and lead to equality.[166] He was frank enough to admit shortly after becoming prime minister in 1954 that 'the white man would not be able to maintain his superiority by merit alone and owed his dominant position to the fact that he had the vote. It was part of the essence of apartheid, therefore, that the Bantu should never have the vote in white areas, but greater rights in their own reserves under white supervision.'[167] Therefore, Strijdom seemingly did not believe that black people were inherently inferior to white people, and he acknowledged that systems of discrimination were required to maintain inequality between black and white. By the 1960s, this obsession had been taken to the ridiculous level of instructing government officials not to shake hands with black people, lest they encouraged 'tendencies towards social equality'.[168]

In his excellent study of white people's depictions of black people, Jan Nederveen Pieterse points out that racism is underpinned by the notion of inequality. Race serves to justify differences in status and class. In the nineteenth century, race was used as an indicator of both.[169] Race is invoked to reinforce hierarchy, the power of the few over the many. In times of change, those with power and privilege become even more insecure about maintaining their status,[170] hence racism flares up during such periods. Examples are the American South and

South Africa when slaves were emancipated in the nineteenth century, as well as the entrenchment of racist laws and practices during negotiations to establish the Union of South Africa in the early twentieth century.

Another example was the NP's rise to power in the mid-twentieth century when the UP's resolve to maintain segregation was faltering as competition from Indian traders became stiffer, and white farmers were having difficulty acquiring and retaining black labour forces. An added factor, which distinguished South Africa from other settler colonies, was the issue of numbers. Indeed, the formalisation of racial inequality through laws and institutions in South Africa, as opposed to more informal racial repression in the US, has to be seen against the background fear of *oorstroming* (being overrun), which was never a factor in the US.

British imperialism is another important element in understanding colonialism in relation to apartheid. White English-speakers' identity, linked to a global Anglo ethnicity, had historically dominated Afrikaners' identity with its ethnic/nationalistic discourses.[171] British imperialists projected themselves as a nation/race-based aristocracy.[172] This was articulated by Cecil John Rhodes, who regarded the British as 'the finest race in the world … the more of the world we inhabit the better for the human race'. Hence, 'the object to which I intend to devote my life is the defence and the extension of the British Empire'.[173] Foremost Victorian scholar Lord Acton found the British to be one of the few races to be the 'makers of history' and 'the authors of advancement'. For him, other races constituted 'a negative element in the world; sometimes the barrier, sometimes the instrument, sometimes the material of those races to whom it is given to originate and to advance'.[174] Moreover, the notion of trusteeship furnished Britons with a reason (expressed as a 'duty') to rule over 'child-like natives' 'not unlike the obligation that decent Englishmen owed to women, children and animals'. Jan Smuts had adopted many of these notions. He said in 1929 at Oxford that the Negro and the Bantu were 'a child type, with a child psychology and outlook'. As Pieterse observes,[175] the colonial paternalism of 'they are just like children' prevailed in South Africa for at least the rest of the twentieth century. 'Children' required trusteeship – another colonial building block Afrikaner nationalists utilised to justify their programme of apartheid.

Ultimately, Britons regarded black people as idle, immoral, devious, dirty, impulsive, excitable and unable to govern themselves – not unlike the Irish, their first colonial subjects, who were depicted as unstable, childish and womanlike, or violent and lazy.[176] In a 1903 British school textbook, 'the Negro' was described as having such an easy life 'that he has never developed the qualities of industry'. In 1911, Rudyard Kipling and CRL Fletcher wrote that Negroes worked only 'under compulsion. In such a climate a few bananas will sustain the life of the Negro quite sufficiently; why should he work to get more than this?'[177]

Some fifty years later, the NP secretary of information Winsloo du Plessis told an international television team that 'the black man in his traditional environment, fifty, sixty years ago, was not a worker. He was a soldier, a warrior. We had to teach him that work is something a man can do and still be a pride upon his woman. We had to teach him to work satisfactorily and we have now reached the stage where he likes work.'[178]

Ironically, while Afrikaner nationalists swallowed colonial and racist discourses on black people wholesale, they themselves had at one time been viewed in the same bigoted terms. European travellers described the trekboers of the late eighteenth century as 'miserable and lazy', differing from the Khoikhoi only in respect of 'physiognomy and colour', as their mode of land use and living was the same.[179] Lord Kitchener called the Boers 'uncivilised Afrikaner savages with a thin white veneer'.[180] Lord Randolph Churchill used every derogatory perception in circulation at the time: 'It may be asserted ... that [the Boer] never plants a tree, never digs a well, never makes a road, never grows a blade of corn ... He passes his days doing absolutely nothing beyond smoking and drinking coffee ... His simple ignorance is unfathomable.'[181] Similarly, in English novels of the era, Boers were depicted as 'slow-witted', 'fatalistic', 'childlike' and a 'simple race'. The British description of the burghers of the ZAR was not much different: dishonest, ignorant, backward and lazy. Positive stereotyping dubbed them hospitable, self-sufficient, peaceful, courageous and able to persevere.[182] Paul Kruger was dismissed as 'ignorant' and 'dirty' by British colonial secretary Joseph Chamberlain.[183]

Some of these characterisations persisted as late as the 1970s, when studies showed that English-speaking whites still regarded Afrikaners in terms of various clichés – both positive and negative – including simple, warm, uncultured, superstitious and lacking in efficiency.[184] English-speakers persisted in the use of pejoratives such as 'hairyback', 'rock spider' and 'plank' (denoting stupidity) when referring to Afrikaners. Afrikaner nationalism provided a language of *volkstrots* (people's pride), noble suffering and a Calvinist decency to contradict the inferiority complex that *verligte* Willem de Klerk continued to identify, as late as the 1980s, as a persistent problem fanning the fires of Afrikaner racism. In 1990, the Afrikaans newspaper *Beeld* objected to the *Financial Mail*'s refusal to use the word Spoornet, because the word 'spoor' (Afrikaans for rail) was not 'good enough' for them.[185]

This constructed inferiority of Dutch-speaking settlers and later Afrikaners fuelled racial anxieties as far back as the eighteenth century. The lack of apparent European-style progress among the Dutch/Afrikaners placed a question mark over whether the European advance into the African continent would indeed promote 'civilisation', or rather lead to white degeneration into barbarism.[186] More than a century later, in 1975, the stereotyping of Afrikaners as 'fanatic', 'intolerant', 'patriotic' and 'conservative' led analyst Nancy Charton to share the concerns of English-speaking whites that these 'Afrikaner characteristics' were a threat to the maintenance of white supremacy.[187]

These attitudes are particularly relevant given the use of racism to establish hierarchy. In South Africa, one class of settlers (the Dutch) was displaced by another (the British) in terms of access to resources and power. Thus 'the Afrikaner' was created as an intermediate class of people mired between their aspirations to the power and affluence of the British/English-speakers, while threatened by competition from black people and population depletion through miscegenation. This could be one explanation for the particularly reactionary application of an intensified colonial-style variant of segregation after 1948. The descendants of the original settler class (predominantly Dutch) were still holding onto the ideological tools of yesteryear when they unexpectedly came to power.

The Afrikaner nationalist obsession with racial hierarchy explains Afrikaners' uneasy relationship with coloured people. This had not always been the case, as Afrikaner nationalist practice was a far cry from that of their Dutch ancestors. The relationship started with the virtual annihilation of the Khoi people through coerced trade, cattle raids and territorial expansion. By the eighteenth century, many Khoi had either become voluntarily employed or inducted into serfdom through the system called *inboekelingskap*. Up to that point, white seizure of Khoi land and cattle was justified on the basis of the distinction between heathen and Christian. What is remarkable is that through most of the first three centuries of white settlement, a 'permissive' pattern of racial mixture was followed in the Cape, according to George Fredrickson.[188] The Dutch authorities tolerated and even encouraged intermarriage between colonists and slave or indigenous women. The initial model in the Cape colony was to incorporate the acknowledged children of white males and Khoi and slave females into settler society.

While this happened to a limited degree and was due to both practical and political considerations (the lack of white settler women and the urge to establish a white hegemony over indigenes), it would not have been possible were the Dutch committed to 'racial purity'. Racial preference was exhibited in that wives were usually drawn from the imported Malay, Indian, Ceylonese or Indonesian slaves, or women of mixed descent rather than the Khoi or slaves from Madagascar and Mozambique. Compared with North America and West Indian slave societies, legal intermarriage in the Cape Colony was surprisingly prevalent and socially acceptable. In all, 24 per cent of founding families included one spouse of mixed ancestry between 1688 and 1807.

Fredrickson concluded that 'the social acceptance by the European population of at least some of the offspring of legal interracial unions that were a matter of public knowledge represented a sanctioned form of "whitening" for which there is virtually no parallel in American history'.[189] This tendency seemed to reverse only at the end of the eighteenth century, when incidents of racial discrimination increased. By the 1820s, 'obvious intermarriage' had become limited to lower-class whites. Until the mid-nineteenth century, when whites started to complain, whites and coloureds still attended Dutch Reformed Church services together. The British equalisation of the Khoi before the law has been cited as one of the reasons for the Great Trek. When the ZAR was founded, its constitution specifically forbade intermarriage between coloured and white people.

The only instance in which the Dutch authorities took a different position was the intermingling of white and Khoi in far-flung areas of the colonial frontier. Offspring from these unions were not socially sanctioned, as indicated by them being called '*Bastaards*'. The Dutch authorities raised the spectre of the 'degeneration' of colonists into a 'savage horde' – a notion widely held in North America at the time, namely that the co-mingling of races could spell cultural suicide for European settlers.

This idea persisted under NP rule, and was employed in conjunction with notions of 'the degeneracy of the poor', resulting in their susceptibility to racial mixing. It influenced Afrikaner nationalist interventions to solve the poor-white problem, which sparked fears of downward mobility. It was the ideology of racism, as manifested in Afrikaner nationalism and applied under apartheid, which enabled the displaced, 'second-class' settler group to use their whiteness to improve their socio-economic standing *vis-à-vis* people who were black.

CHAPTER 2

The party:
Between accumulation and crisis

The church accepted that application of the [apartheid] policy, particu-
larly in its initial stages, would result in a measure of upheaval and
personal discomfort and hardship as, for instance, when slum areas are
cleared up. — **Members of the Synodal Commission**
of the Dutch Reformed Church, 1960[1]

Dr Verwoerd did the thinking for each one of us.
— **BJ Vorster, addressing his first cabinet**
meeting as prime minister in 1966[2]

All that is worthwhile in civilisation is being destroyed in South Africa.
What are you trying to preserve?
— **ANC pamphlet addressed to white people, early 1960s**[3]

FOLLOWING FORMATION OF THE UNION OF SOUTH AFRICA IN 1910, successive governments sought to protect white South Africans from economic competition by black people, while reinforcing white power. This was done through the routine and systematic denial and limitation of black people's political and socio-economic rights.

By the time the NP entered government, urban blacks were segregated and rural blacks were languishing in the labour reservoirs of the reserves, from whence they replenished the urban workforce through the migrant labour system. To segregate urban coloureds from whites was more complex and led not only to the razing of Cape Town's historic District Six, but also to the uprooting of entire communities, who would bear the scars and social consequences for decades to come.

As nationalists are wont to do, the NP borrowed and stole from the past, both for the development of apartheid policies and the justification thereof. Apartheid involved a more meticulous discriminatory circumscribing of black people's access to resources. State control over black people's lives was intensified, and there was an increasingly vicious clampdown on resistance.

A primary difference between colonial segregation prior to 1948 and apartheid was that state policy focused particularly on benefiting Afrikaners, as opposed to the white minority as a whole. This was most clearly evident from the marked advance of Afrikaners in the civil service and parastatals. English-speaking whites benefited from the system by virtue of their skin colour, but until the 1970s, the post-1948 government concentrated on raising Afrikaner living standards across class barriers.

The NP abused state power to neutralise resistance and used racially discrim-inatory patronage to win over the electorate. It entrenched itself in government by consolidating the support of Afrikaners, while reaching out to the English-speaking voter. Efforts to gain the English vote paid off from the mid-1960s, when the NP first attained an electoral majority.

What might have happened if the United Party (UP) had remained in power? Its Fagan report had accepted the irreversibility of black urbanisation. While it had put further limitations on Indian settlement, it had also extended some level of franchise to Indians, who could for the first time elect white people to represent them at parliamentary and provincial level. Smuts himself was opposed to tampering with the coloured franchise as it stood at that point. His deputy, Jan Hofmeyr, was publicly indicating that black parliamentary participation was inevitable. While the UP was still committed to segregation and white supremacy, hints of pragmatism and moral doubt were starting to shine through. In contrast, Afrikaner nationalist ideologues in the NP, the three Afrikaans sister churches, the Broederbond and civil society organisations were resolutely denying the im-practicality and moral reprehensibility of segregation and apartheid. Along with them, more and more white people exchanged reality for a warped insularity.

A cursory glance at the period before a revamped NP's second rise to power in 1948 reveals multi-level conflict within Afrikaner ranks. Author André Brink explained it thus: 'The widespread notion of "traditional Afrikaner unity" is based on a false reading of history: strife and inner division within Afrikanerdom has been much more in evidence than unity during the first three centuries of White South African history.'[4] While Brink also hovered close to accepting that an entity such as 'Afrikanerdom' had existed 'for centuries' – which would be incorrect – he did put his finger on the basic workings of nationalism: to construct a community where there is none.

Diversity among white Afrikaans-speakers was characteristic of the 1950s. After the NP managed to wrest control from the UP, it did not only have to face black people and many English-speaking South Africans' rejection of its brand of racist nationalism; it also had to contend with dissent from Afrikaners in the UP, Liberal Party, Congress of Democrats, Springbok Legion, Torch Commando, Communist Party, Garment Workers' Union and others. Some South Africans oversimplify the NP's core constituency, the Afrikaners, as a monolithic grouping with a singular set of characteristics, ideological viewpoints and aspirations. But such reductionism was typical of the Afrikaner nationalist depiction of 'the Afrikaner', and did not reflect reality. Opposition to the NP came not only from outside, but also from within the party, as well as its surrogates in media, religious and cultural organisations. The opposition from within was not limited to competing nationalisms (such as Hertzogite nationalism or the Ossewa-Brandwag's national socialism) and racist ideologies, but included questions about racist policies. That said, with the assistance of its extensions in the *volksbeweging* (people's movement), the party's achievement was to gather the disparate strands of nationalism and the various suggested approaches to the national question of race, and bind together increasing numbers of Afrikaans- and English-speaking whites long enough to implement its ethnic class project.

Despite the NP having achieved political dominance, the following fault lines could be discerned during its first couple of decades in government: whether to reach out to English-speaking whites; how to balance the interests of the working and lower middle class against those of the capitalist class; and whether strict Verwoerdian apartheid or a more pragmatic approach to white domination should be applied. These quandaries had a historical and provincial dimension. JBM Hertzog's position on English-speakers had alienated JG Strijdom, HF Verwoerd and CR Swart, while some Cape Nats were more accommodating. Strijdom and Verwoerd were also anti-Semitic, while some moderates in the Cape NP were not. Nic Diederichs was ideologically close to Albert Hertzog, who was anti-capitalist and wanted to 'save' the Afrikaner worker from communism.[5]

An early feature of the NP was *kragdadigheid* – which translated into the use of force to quell opposition with little hesitation. The ANC had informed DF Malan of its intention to stage the 1952 Defiance Campaign, only to be warned that the full might of the law would be applied against participants. Verwoerd declared in 1965: 'I believe in the supremacy of the white man over his people in his own territory and I am prepared to maintain it by force.'[6] BJ Vorster was the instigator of the NP government's move to draconian laws that enabled security force abuses.

Political parties exist to gain power. The NP built its position in state power with a policy that would afford the white electorate direct privilege in every aspect of their lives. By 1966, they had been won over, the white alliance with the NP cemented.

The economic prosperity of the 1950s and 1960s helped to entrench the NP. Its economic policy was import-substitution – a system of increasing industrialisation by producing sophisticated consumer goods that had previously been imported. The basis of the system was the growth of gold and other mineral exports. The mining sector subsidised white agriculture and enabled the development of manufacturing through capital investment and expertise, foreign exchange earnings, taxes and footing the extra costs brought about by protective tariffs. Mining's success, however, was contingent upon suppressing black wages to minimum subsistence levels.[7] South Africa was able to sustain annual economic growth rates at a high average of 4.9 per cent between 1945 and 1974, with a 'golden age' of 6 to 8 per cent annual growth between 1964 and 1972.

First apartheid, then capitalism

The ascent of the fuzzy concept 'apartheid' to government policy was met with concern and panic outside Afrikaner nationalist circles. The reason was the party's anti-capitalist rhetoric. DF Malan stated in 1941 in yet another of his speeches with the family as reference point – 'The party is the mother' – that the NP had 'always' been the country's 'anti-capital and anti-exploiter' party.[8] In a 1942 parliamentary motion, he indicated that one of the objectives of the NP's 'policy for the future' was protection of the (white) South African population from 'capitalist and parasitic exploitation'.[9] He noted that the 'anti-capitalism' of national socialism should not be regarded as inimical to Afrikanerdom.

In fact, for Malan, an anti-capitalist stance was one of a few hallmarks that distinguished true Afrikaners from 'un-Afrikaans' elements.[10] It was thus to be expected that the primarily English-speaking owners of capital would be fretful about what awaited them after the NP's surprise victory in 1948. Indeed, the radical right in the party, as personified by NP founder Barry Hertzog's son Albert, pushed for nationalisation[11] after the party came to power. However, English capital's fears did not materialise as, once in government, the NP quickly changed tack and instituted further policies that benefited capital accumulation, especially through more detailed control of black labour.[12] In the end, the NP's intention was not to disrupt English-speaking capital accumulation, but to open it to Afrikaner capitalists. The anti-capitalist rhetoric was geared towards reinforcing the Afrikaner nationalist class alliance and held little substance, except for a handful of leaders who were ejected in 1969.

The racist policies prohibiting sexual intercourse between blacks and whites, or restricting black people to certain entrances or public toilets (so-called petty apartheid) were not the central aspects of apartheid. Indeed, this was why the pro-capital *verligte* wing was quite happy to do away with such policies in the 1980s.

The heart of apartheid was not just about political exclusion and inclusion, but also about determining the terms on which ethnically defined sections of the population could participate in the economy. Hein Marais[13] points out that around the 'cultural, historical and political mythos' of Afrikaner nationalism, 'the Afrikaners' were being differentiated and organised into a political and economic force. This was built through state patronage, as racial policies explicitly advanced the cumulative ambitions of white people. An example is the displacement of Indian traders to the benefit of their Afrikaner counterparts.

The 1950 Group Areas Act blocked Indians from operating businesses in white areas. This followed a long campaign waged by the Broederbond and was in step with recurrent proposals at NP congresses that Indians' trade licences be revoked; that Indians be repatriated; or that Indians not be allowed to trade within a certain distance from white businesses. This intervention ironically disproved racist constructions of the inferiority of other races in practice and demonstrated the use of racism in neutralising economic competition. Similarly, while there was not a 'precise fit' between capital interests and apartheid interests, apartheid was functional to the needs of the capitalist classes. If it were not, 'the state would have been plunged into a genuine crisis'.[14]

The English-dominated mining sector benefited handsomely after 1948, as the NP continued to ensure that black wages were kept at the same appallingly low level. From 1911 until the early 1970s, the real wages of black mineworkers, including food, remained the same.[15] Cheap, expendable labour was what made the mining of deep-level, low-grade gold ore profitable, and thus worth the effort. Similarly, predominantly Afrikaner farmers benefited from strict controls over black labour, which ensured that farm workers' wages showed little change between 1866 and 1966.[16] This is not to say that all capitalists supported apartheid. Harry Oppenheimer of Anglo American and De Beers, Anton Rupert of Rembrandt and several others did not. The Association of Chambers of Commerce (Assocom) opposed apartheid, and issued a statement in 1960 requesting the gradual relaxation of black property ownership outside the Bantustans, trade union activity among black workers and abolition of job reservation. But the Oppenheimers and the Ruperts were careful not to upset the rulers too much – conditions were still mightily favourable for making money.

Verwoerd became very annoyed when pressure groups voiced their views on policy or the government in the media instead of behind closed doors. Assocom's indiscreet public declaration irritated him so much that he withdrew his acceptance of an invitation to open their 1960 congress. He responded to the statement by saying, 'those who have made such proposals often do not have the full facts at their disposal … and it therefore remains the task of government after consideration of all the facts and after consultation with its experts to make the necessary decisions'.[17] *Die Burger* backed Verwoerd's position, rejecting Assocom's stance in an editorial, because the business community 'has to consider the political consequences of their economic proposals'.[18]

Verwoerd was pro-capitalist, but the implementation of apartheid enjoyed priority in his mind. This was encapsulated in an address he made to Assocom and the Federated Chambers of Industry (which merged in 1990 to become the South African Chamber of Business) in 1951: the 'implementation of apartheid policies had to take account of economic possibilities ... [but] the desire for economic gain could not be allowed to take precedence over more urgent considerations ... [namely] the interests of preserving white civilisation'.[19] Similarly, Nic Diederichs, the former head of the Reddingsdaadbond who became Verwoerd's minister of finance, propounded that the economy would be 'bent' until it made apartheid work.[20] This was where the NP under Verwoerd parted ways with capital.

While Verwoerd was minister of native affairs, he took his belief so far as to propose at a cabinet meeting the total prohibition of black people entering the Witwatersrand, and especially Johannesburg. Colleague Ben Schoeman took him on with the support of other ministers, and he backed down. Verwoerd also rejected the Tomlinson Commission's proposal that, for reasons of viability, white business should be allowed into the reserves, because he wanted to 'keep the Jews out' and because blacks were not 'psychologically adapted to develop industries'.[21] He disingenuously claimed that allowing white business in the Bantustans would amount to 'neo-colonialism'. The issue led to clashes between him and Rembrandt's Anton Rupert. His decision was only overturned when Vorster became premier.

Rupert and Verwoerd had a number of confrontations, including 'a violent break' in the late 1950s, something that the Cape hierarchy had sought but was unable to rectify.[22] Rupert wanted Verwoerd's approval to set up a factory in Paarl in partnership with black residents. When Verwoerd heard that black directors would be overseeing white personnel, he indicated that the factory would be shut down. He then publicly attacked Rupert for wanting to 'exploit' black people.[23] In order to justify his own neo-colonial inventions, Verwoerd was regurgitating the anti-colonial discourses of *uhuru* that were sweeping across Africa at the time. Conveniently, he regarded only compliant chiefs and headmen, many of whom were not representatives of 'their people', as legitimate leaders. They were ostensibly living in accordance with their 'customs', unpolluted by Western influence. Urbanised black people he dismissed as 'imitation Englishmen'.

The NP's attitude towards business changed under BJ Vorster. While he was still a deputy minister in Verwoerd's cabinet, he told an AHI meeting that businessmen should attend to business and leave government to govern. But his position underwent a sea change after Verwoerd's death, when he and his cabinet were on the receiving end of perks from business. In 1964, when Anglo American all but handed a mining company to Sanlam, Verwoerd became concerned about the increasing independence of Afrikaner business and its closeness to

English capital.[24] Perhaps he was surmising – correctly – that economic consider-ations would ultimately override even the deeply entrenched racism in white society.

In the 1950s and 1960s, the NP was able to harmonise the increasingly com-peting interests of different capitalist groupings. In particular, mining interests sought the restoration of the reserve system to ensure a continuous flow of cheap migrant labour and replacement of redundant workers. Farmers wanted to stem the flood of workers to the urban areas, and therefore sought more stringent measures to restrict the movement of black people.

As the economy diversified and the manufacturing sector grew, factory owners who insisted on a stable, semi-skilled, urban-based corps of workers became more of a force.[25] Up to the 1970s, the NP could stave off their demands, but economic realities moved the party to introduce necessary reforms in this regard under Vorster and PW Botha. During the 1970s, with the country in the grip of high inflation and a stagnating economy, these NP strongmen were able to both ensure the security of the white population and project their ability to do so, gaining more and more votes in return, including many from English-speaking whites. This was the NP government's most significant contribution to the development of capitalism in South Africa: it managed to secure the conditions for capital accumulation in a society prone to destabilisation due to its high level of inequality.

NP personalities

The subjective aspects of NP politics – including leaders' contrasting person-alities – were a powerful influence throughout the party's reign.[26] As 'apartheid' was far from a formulated policy, different NP leaders had different conceptions about and approaches to it. Minister of native affairs Dr EG Jansen announced shortly after his appointment in the first apartheid cabinet that black urban-isation and population growth in the reserves would be stemmed, without providing any details.[27] In all probability, race-obsessed Verwoerd, the third NP premier after 1948, had the clearest sense of what apartheid would entail.

DF Malan, the inaugural NP prime minister, had epitomised the Cape faction of the NP through his overlapping leadership positions in the party and the private sector. He was the original editor of *Die Burger*, the first newspaper created to serve the Afrikaner nationalist cause, founded by Nasionale Pers. Later, Malan became chairperson of insurance giant Sanlam. These intimate connections with nascent Afrikaner capital in the Cape province were character-istic of a growing section of the party, which became known as the *verligtes* in the 1970s. The *verligte/verkrampte* distinction was at its root a separation of class. The *verligte* camp had closer relations with Afrikaner capital and was capitalist in orientation. It was founded on the professional classes, was strongly linked to the Cape province, and its race politics were regarded as 'liberal' by the *verkramptes*. The latter were rooted in the working and lower middle class. They placed retention of racial privilege above economic considerations and were predominantly based in the northern provinces. Among the early leaders, Strijdom and Verwoerd were *verkrampte* front-runners.

Documentary film footage reveals Verwoerd as a person who spoke with the fervour of one who believed in final solutions, which could explain why, of all the NP leaders, he was most frequently associated with Nazi Germany's social engineers. His tone of voice was patronising, as a father to a child, an impression reinforced by his slow, measured speech and confirmed by those outside his cabinet who had dealings with him. Joyce Waring, whose husband Frank was a minister in Verwoerd's cabinet, said of the assassinated premier:

'Verwoerd always assumed that you would not differ with him about what he said. He always implied "this is what will happen. I have explained everything to you, child, but you have to understand this is the law speaking."'[28]

His intractable belief in his own insights caused him to reject the Tomlinson Commission's findings, mainly because the commission was appointed by his predecessor, Jansen. During compilation of the report, Verwoerd had constant clashes with Tomlinson. Afterwards, he ensured that Tomlinson's career in the civil service reached a dead end.

Verwoerd was quite willing to bend the truth to manipulate supporters. He suggested at a cabinet meeting that, even though the NP thought absolute apartheid impractical, given the country's dependence on black labour, the opposite message should be relayed to build support. He was also known as the NP *hoofleier* who liked to manipulate white opinion by evoking the myth of the Afrikaners as God's chosen people, with a holy mission in 'darkest Africa'. Verwoerd was a shrewd operator who neutralised the Cape wing of the NP through cabinet posts and managed the Broederbond by giving it the task of formulating apartheid policy.

Entrenching apartheid

For the NP, the 1951 population statistics raised the spectre of 'the white minority … stand[ing] less and less chance [of] maintaining its superior position' due to 'the ever-increasing mixing of white and non-white people owing to industrial development'.[29] The forecast was that, by the year 2000, whites would constitute only 23.5 per cent of the population, while blacks would account for 62.4 per cent. By that time, it would be 'too late to apply apartheid'.[30]

The NP government wasted no time introducing legislation that would deepen existing discrimination wrought by segregation. The first laws were to prohibit marriage between people of different races (1949) and to extend the 1927 prohibition of sexual intercourse between black and white South Africans (an activity regarded as 'immoral', hence the name, Immorality Act) to include coloureds and Indians (1950). The Population Registration Act (1950) categorised all South Africans according to race, except for Indians, whom the NP, in keeping with previous governments, intended repatriating to India.

The absurdity of this idea seemingly dawned on them in 1959, when another category was created under the act: Asian. White parliamentary representation of the Indian population, instituted by the UP in 1946, had been promptly abolished when the NP came to power. The Group Areas Act (1950) elaborated on the Natives Land Act of 1913 (which gave black people 13 per cent of the country's land) and its 1936 amendments (which tightened control over blacks living on 'white' land). The Act gave government the power to determine all human settlement in the country on the basis of race.

The Bantu Authorities Act of 1951 put in place the basis of what would become Verwoerd's grand apartheid plan of separate black nations in separate countries. 'The Bantu' were subdivided into eight ethnic groups: South Sotho, Pedi, Swazi, Tsonga, Venda, Xhosa, Zulu and Ndebele. In 1953 the Separate Amenities Act prescribed the racial segregation of public amenities, with the proviso that such facilities need not be of equal standard. Signs went up throughout the country denoting that everything from park benches and lifts to post office queues and hospital entrances were for use by 'Europeans Only'/'Non-Europeans Only', and later 'Whites Only'/'Non-Whites Only'.

'Natives' were renamed 'Bantus' in laws such as the 1953 Bantu Education Act. This legislation was aimed at providing education to black people 'in conformity with their own traditions and needs', ending education as provided by missionaries and churches where 'frustrated potential agitators were bred who found no popular outlet for their limited talents', as Afrikaner nationalist historian DW Krüger put it in 1969.[31] He was echoing Verwoerd, the then minister of native affairs, who infamously declared in 1954 that there was no place for a black person 'in the European community above certain forms of labour. Within his own community, however, all doors are open. For that reason it is of no avail for him to receive a training which has as its aim absorption in the European community where he cannot be absorbed.'[32]

In the same speech, Verwoerd spoke of 'the creation of unhealthy white collar ideals' among black people, who could not occupy such positions because of the government's apartheid policy. In effect, Verwoerd was acknowledging that apartheid, and not inferiority, was the barrier between black people and high-level occupations. Yet again, this confirms the utility of apartheid in protecting whites against competition with blacks. This economic benefit was mostly hidden in the racism that coated apartheid and Afrikaner nationalist rhetoric.

In 1954, the Bantu Resettlement Act was passed to 'clean up' what were offensively called 'black spots' – including Sophiatown, a vibrant hub of the arts, and Newclare in Johannesburg. The misnamed Industrial Conciliation Act built on its 1924 version by giving the executive the power to segregate occupations (thus restricting black people to lower-paid and menial jobs) and prohibiting black, Indian and coloured workers from joining trade unions.

After decades of successful resistance, black women in urban areas were finally incorporated into the pass system through the amended Bantu Urban Areas Act as part of the NP's plan to control the flow of black labour to towns and cities. Poet Wally Serote captured the way in which the pass system demarcated black people's existence in a poem on Johannesburg:

> In this way I salute you:
> My hand pulses to my back trousers pocket
> Or into my inner jacket pocket
> For my pass, my life,
> Jo'burg City ...[33]

Standing up against the jackboot

The 1950s were a time of intense activity involving women and men of all races and different ideological persuasions, as democrats set about organising against the apartheid regime. As Stephen Clingman, Bram Fischer's biographer, put it: 'If the intent of the apartheid government [in the 1950s] was to prove some misguided point about God-given hierarchies and distinctions, then the anti-apartheid movement would show through its most intimate gestures as much as its wider institutional structures that not only were racial cooperation and harmony possible, but that the only kind of superiority there could be was moral.'[34]

Several gatherings and marches took place, aimed at formulating and mustering support for an alternative vision to apartheid. Activists met on the basis of principle and not race, and included luminaries such as Albert Luthuli, Nelson Mandela, Bram Fischer, Walter Sisulu, Ahmed Kathrada, Helen Joseph, Joe Slovo and Ruth First. The increased activity was the result of the consolidation of African nationalism.

The ANC, which had become largely dormant by the 1930s, had been revived by resistance against Hertzog's final disenfranchisement of black men in the Cape in 1936. However, under the leadership of Dr AB Xuma, the ANC still remained sceptical of mass-based action. This changed in the wake of the massive 1946 strike and squatter resistance, as new leaders such as Anton Lembede, Nelson Mandela and Oliver Tambo rose in the ANC Youth League. They were very much in touch with the wave of nationalism sweeping across the continent and the broader international swing towards democracy and human rights.[35] By 1948, black political aspirations had shifted: no longer were blacks seeking participation based on suspect notions of 'civilisation'. Instead, African nationalists were demanding an end to segregation, trusteeship and racial discrimination, to be replaced with full political rights and a common citizenship.[36]

The attempt to engage DF Malan had run aground. In the mostly peaceful Defiance Campaign of 1952, black people left their passes at home and disobeyed the petty rules of petty apartheid by entering public places through the 'Europeans Only' entrances. Those arrested refused to pay fines and were locked up. In the end, about 8 000 people were arrested. Mandela, Sisulu, Yusuf Dadoo, Ahmed Kathrada and Yusuf Cachalia were all charged and found guilty of 'statutory communism'. As Mandela pointed out, the Suppression of Communism Act was drafted in such a way that 'virtually anyone' who opposed the NP government was guilty of communism.[37]

The Defiance Campaign launched the ANC as a mass organisation and changed incarceration from a threat to an honour. Mandela writes about the psychological effect of the campaign: 'The campaign freed me from any lingering sense of doubt or inferiority that I might still have felt; it liberated me from the feeling of being overwhelmed by the power and the seeming invincibility of the white man and his institutions.... I could walk upright ... with the dignity that comes from not having succumbed to oppression and fear.'[38] However, it also brought home the message that the NP government was not interested in petitions and protests, regarding such actions as criminal rather than a civil right, as would be the case in a democracy. The intransigence of the NP government also made the ANC realise that there was no constitutional route to democracy.[39] It marked the moment when Mandela felt himself coming of age as 'a freedom fighter'.[40] But more than the ANC's actions, it was the spontaneous mobilisation of resistance by rural peasants (Pondoland, Zoutpansberg, Sekhukhuneland, Witzieshoek, Marico and Natal) and the women's anti-pass campaign that most effectively frustrated state control.[41]

In 1955, the Congress of the People brought together blacks, Indians, coloureds and whites to adopt the Freedom Charter. This document was too vague in its formulations to provide more than a normative framework for policies, but it offered a powerful vision of the different country that was possible.

In the 1950s, women conducted protests that temporarily upset the state's efforts at imposing passes on black women. In 1956, the ideologically and racially inclusive Federation of South African Women mobilised 26 000 women from across South Africa to march to the Union Buildings in Pretoria in protest. Lilian Ngoyi and Helen Joseph were among those who led the march. The government's response was to arrest 156 people and charge them with treason. The irony was that, not long afterwards, the same government forcibly revoked black people's citizenship, ostensibly so that they would become 'citizens' of the Transkei and other Bantustans. Liberals, communists and African nationalists came together in these campaigns – but the Afrikaner nationalists had the force of state power behind them, which they did not hesitate to employ. The NP was not about to relinquish power and no opposition would be brooked, even if this came from within white ranks.

The Springbok Legion was a predominantly white grouping that challenged the NP to ban it as part of its fervent opposition to NP rule. The organisation, led by AG Malan, consisted of ex-servicemen and women who had fought in the Second World War. They rallied round the issue of the removal of coloureds from the voters' roll, and by 1952 had 125 000 members.[42] In the run-up to the 1948 election, the leadership issued a pamphlet in Afrikaans and English to coloured members, urging them to vote: 'We ask you to recognise that the present [UP] Government has defended your right to vote and that the Nationalists cannot wait to abolish it. We warn you, beware of Nationalist propaganda. The Nationalists come to you and advise you not to vote at all … We are not the government's little brothers. But we ask you to support the United Party and the Labour Party because these parties offer you a chance.'[43] After the NP came to power, the Springbok Legion voiced its increasing concern about the clampdown on democratic space. 'The Nationalist Government does not believe in the right of others to criticise it … [T]he attempts to muzzle the press, the withholding of passports, the restriction of the rights of some Members of Parliament – these are proofs. Their cry is that criticism is sabotage, that opposition is treason. The right to criticise is fundamental to Parliament and to democracy. A Government which attempts to stifle criticism has something to hide.' These words appeared in a pamphlet released for general distribution and aptly titled 'Will we be banned for this?'[44] The government had threatened to ban the legion, and dismissed members as 'communists stirring up trouble'.[45]

The legion raised its concerns about the NP's willingness to change the constitution to downgrade the coloured vote; the boosting of government support by giving new constituencies too much electoral weight; the pass system; curtailing travel by government critics by revoking or refusing passports; the appointment of pro-Nazi Otto du Plessis as state information officer; and attacks on non-NP trade unions. By 1950, the Springbok Legion had joined forces with the War Veterans' Association to hold a torchlight procession against the NP's

plan to remove coloureds from the common voters' roll. This led to the formation of the Torch Commando, which had the support of the UP and some of the
English press in its opposition to the watering down of the coloured franchise.
The legion remained critical of opposition parties in parliament, where the UP
was being pulled to the right in a bid to win back support from the NP: 'You
have been divided and enfeebled by your own inner anti-native, anti-Indian and
anti-coloured prejudices – which our enemies have played upon and encouraged.
You have tried to show the country that your race and colour prejudices run just
as strongly as those of [DF] Malan's [sic]. And in that attempt you have succeeded only … in spreading dismay and confusion among your own forces.'[46]

As far as the Springbok Legion was concerned, the NP's fascist tendencies
placed it on a 'headlong rush to dictatorship'. All democrats had to stand up
against the 'jackboot'. In response to the Defiance Campaign and the Torch
Commando's call 'to bring the country to a standstill', the NP passed Public
Safety Act No. 3 of 1953, allowing the executive to declare martial law in case
of 'public danger' and to detain people without trial. In a classic example of
the UP's internal conflict, it supported both this bill and an amendment to
the Criminal Law Act, which outlawed mobilisation ('incitement') in support
of civil disobedience campaigns.[47] The Torch Commando was weakened when
members broke away to form the short-lived Union Federal Party, which
supported the proposed secession of Natal from the union and disappeared
after the 1953 election.

In 1953, the Congress of Democrats (COD) was formed. This was an
organisation of white anti-apartheid activists that allied itself in the Congress
Alliance to the ANC, the Coloured People's Organisation and the South African
Indian Congress in pursuit of the broad objectives of the 1952 Defiance Cam-
paign. The COD flowed from the Springbok Legion, the Transvaal Congress of
Democrats and the Democratic League of Cape Town. Its first president was
Piet Beyleveld, who conferred the military title of *Isitwalandwe* on Father Trevor
Huddlestone, Chief Albert Luthuli and Communist Party of South Africa leader
Yusuf Dadoo at the Congress of the People.[48]

While some members, such as Helen Joseph, were not communists, many
others were, leading to suspicion by the Liberal Party that the COD was a front
for a takeover of the Congress Alliance. Bram Fischer, Molly Fischer, Ben Turok
and Beyleveld were all communists, and joined the South African Communist
Party (SACP), reconstituted in 1953 after the banning of its predecessor, the
Communist Party of South Africa, three years before.

Founded in 1953 and led by Margaret Ballinger, who had been a 'native
representative' in parliament, the Liberal Party attracted both black and white
members through its support of a universal franchise. Prominent members

included Leo Marquard, an Afrikaans-speaking former member of Smuts's UP, and author Alan Paton, who later became president of the party. The party attended the Congress of the People at Kliptown as an observer, due to its concern that the Freedom Charter was socialist in nature. It finally rejected the Freedom Charter when the SACP adopted it. The Liberal Party never won a seat in parliament, and was eventually forced to disband in terms of the Political Interference Act of 1968, which prohibited racially mixed political parties.

Also liberal-oriented was the Progressive Party, formed in 1959 by a break-away group under Jan Steytler, which had come into conflict with the UP's right wing. The party had the support of Harry Oppenheimer, who had previously backed the UP. In 1961, the PP lost all its seats but one: that of the indomitable Helen Suzman. With the banning of non-racial parties in the late 1960s, the PP faced a crisis, but eventually decided to fight on in the arena of white politics. Until 1974, when Suzman was joined by more ex-UP members, she was the only PP member of parliament.

The PP supported a qualified non-racial franchise, which had become anathema for whites by the 1960s. Despite being a lone voice, Suzman battled the government's abuse of the rule of law from inside parliament, making herself highly unpopular with the all-male corps of NP parliamentarians, but at the same time ensuring that such abuse did not pass unnoticed or unchallenged.

In the early 1960s, the security forces exposed the activities of the small National Committee for Liberation (later renamed African Resistance Movement), which included some former Liberal Party and National Union of South African Students (NUSAS) members. Among those arrested were Hugh Lewin, Lynette van der Riet, Eddie Daniels and Baruch Hirson. After the ARM had been disbanded, a member on the fringe of the group, John Harris, planted a bomb at Johannesburg's Park Station, which killed a woman.

In a statement from the dock, Lewin, aged twenty-four, described the reasons for his 'terrifying' decision to join the ARM. He wanted to protest against the system in such as a way as to focus attention on the 'living conditions of the blacks. My previous attempt to do this had been completely ineffective. I thought that sabotage would shock the whites into an awareness of the conditions under which the blacks were living and, in due time, change the system.'[49]

During the Rivonia Trial in the same period, the ANC had distributed a pamphlet containing a plea directed at the 'white man'. It captured some of the burning issues of the time before pointing out the contradiction in the ruling party's rhetoric on civilisation:

Over 3 000 men and women, mostly Africans, but including all races, are in jails for resisting apartheid. More will be tried. They come from all over

South Africa. They are not criminals. Most of them are people of the highest integrity, intelligence and courage, gentle and compassionate, vitally concerned with problems of justice and freedom. In any normal society these people would be the rulers. Our land is not normal. Violence is used every day against our people. They are violently uprooted by the tens of thousands and turned out of their homes. Families are violently divided, people are deprived of the right to decent wages, proper education, normal homes. Our organisations are violently suppressed, our leaders forcibly removed from us. We have been deprived of every legal, every legitimate means of protest. When the Government wants to do something that conflicts with the rule of law, they pass a law to make it 'legal'. Then basest injustice becomes the law, and all those who oppose it become saboteurs. The Government prepares for open war against the people, training and arming every White man and woman, teaching schoolgirls to shoot, and schoolboys to fight the Black man, creating an atmosphere of fear and war ... ALL THIS IN THE NAME OF 'PRESERVING WHITE CIVILISATION'. All that is worthwhile in civilisation is being destroyed in South Africa. What are you trying to preserve?[50]

In 1960, the Pan Africanist Congress's Mangaliso Robert Sobukwe released a pamphlet[51] launching the PAC's 'positive decisive campaign' to demand the abolition of the pass laws, payment of a decent wage, and that workers and PAC leaders not be victimised as a result of the campaign. Black male workers were instructed to leave their passes at home on 21 March and surrender themselves at their local police stations. 'All men will go to jail under the slogan "No Bail, No Defence, No Fine"', Sobukwe declared. The idea was for workers to stay away from work for as long as possible. The iron fist of the state put paid to this idea and sixty-nine people died – many from bullet wounds in the back – when police opened fire on them at Sharpeville.

Die Burger's response on 23 March 1960 revealed a profound ignorance, apart from being an obvious attempt to entrench stereotypes about 'violent blacks' and to justify the killing of civilians. It was headlined 'Die veglus van die Bantoe' (The Bantu's lust for fighting), with subheadings 'Met geeste gepraat' (Spoke with spirits); 'Groot slagting' (Huge massacre); 'Honderd dooies' (One hundred dead); 'Vegters (Fighters)'; and 'Altyd hoender' (Always chicken). The article began by saying, 'The Bantu are easily agitated. This has become clear, yet again, following the unrest in Vereeniging and Langa.... Inciting hysteria and even violence among them is apparently an easy matter. They appear not to think as individuals, but as groups ...'

The writer then raked up the Xhosa cattle-killing of 1857, invoking images of superstition and credulity; the 1921 incident at Bulhoek involving members of the Israelite sect, dispassionately mentioning that the police had mowed down '163 people' (it was actually closer to 200); and the Zulu attacks on Indians in 1949 when 142 people were killed, omitting to mention that the NP's anti-Indian statements had contributed to the attacks.[52] These examples, according to *Die Burger*, offered proof that '[i]mpetuosity among the Bantu … is therefore nothing unusual and is known to have given rise to greater carnage than in this case. They are also wont to fight among themselves; without the police, there would be far more faction fights.'[53] Legitimate resistance against the iniquity of apartheid was dismissed time and again with neo-colonial rhetoric about how white people had to prevent black people from murdering each other. If anything, the Sharpeville attack had exhibited 'die veglus van die Afrikaner'.

The report in *Die Burger* included a reference to the 'black man' being a soldier and a fighter rather than a worker – startlingly similar to the comment made around the same time to an international television crew by the NP's Winsloo du Plessis, about the 'black man' being 'a warrior'.[54] NP rhetoric was diligently recycled in the Afrikaner nationalist press.

But Sharpeville shook the suburban complacency of Afrikanerdom. Poet Ingrid Jonker, who was disowned by her father, an NP senator, wrote her powerful 'The child who was shot dead by soldiers at Nyanga' with its prescient lines:

The child is not dead
not at Langa not at Nyanga
Not at Orlando not at Sharpeville
not at the police station in Philippi
where he lies with a bullet through his brain.
The child is the shadow of the soldiers
on guard with rifles Saracens and batons
the child is present at all gatherings and law-giving
the child who just wanted to play in the sun at Nyanga is everywhere.
The child grown to a man treks all over Africa
the child grown to a giant travels through the whole world
without a pass.[55]

Jonker would finally receive recognition for her courage to speak out amid deafening silence when President Nelson Mandela read this poem at the opening of the first democratic parliament in 1994.

The literary movement, the Sestigers, was also critical of the authoritarianism, insulation and self-satisfied materialism that had come to epitomise Afrikanerdom during the 1960s. In 1963, censorship laws were introduced to 'protect' white minds from liberal and communist influences. Etienne Leroux's 1964 novel *Sewe Dae by die Silbersteins* incensed the cultural commissars. Poet Breyten Breytenbach became radicalised when the government blocked his Vietnamese wife, Yolande, from entering South Africa in the mid-1960s on the basis that she was 'non-white'. While liaising with the ANC, he founded a 'white militant' organisation called Okhela, which aimed to end the capitalist apartheid order. He was arrested and incarcerated for seven years, a dehumanising experience he captured in his book, *The True Confessions of an Albino Terrorist*.

Like Bram Fischer, Breytenbach was the victim of a vindictive Afrikaans prison warder intent on avenging his betrayal of the *volk*. Breytenbach described him thus: 'A thin fellow, bristling little moustache, sharp, very pale green eyes, wild look, tight jaws, ears sticking away from his head. A complete marionette, fierce and violent. He opened my door with a brusque gesture, pointed to my bed which was a bunk built into the wall, and said, "Ek is die baas van die plaas [I am the boss of this place]. I will make you crawl here; you will get to know me yet." Yes, I did get to know him.'[56] Like all totalitarian ideologies, Afrikaner nationalism dug dark holes where inhumanity could be perpetrated with impunity.

Despite the vocal and visible stance taken by many black people and a few whites, there was no end to the criminalisation of the black population. By the early 1960s, 600 labour bureaus had been created, and the state had issued passbooks to 4 million men and 3.6 million women. The number of people convicted for breaking influx control laws rose from 164 324 in 1952 to 384 497 in 1962 – translating into 3 million convictions over a decade.[57] However, influx control was always only a temporary measure, as black urbanisation increased more rapidly than under previous governments that had exerted *less* control. In 1946, 23 per cent of black South Africans were living in towns and cities; by 1960, this had grown to 32 per cent.[58]

Socio-economic need compelled black people to challenge the barrage of laws and an increasingly arrogant police force in order to carve a livelihood for themselves. The criminalisation of black people was captured by Steve Biko: 'While those amongst the blacks who do bother to open their mouths in feeble protest against what is going on are periodically intimidated with security visits and occasional banning orders and house arrests, the rest of the black community live in absolute fear of the police. No average black man can at any moment be absolutely sure that he is not breaking a law. There are so many laws governing the lives and behaviour of black people that sometimes one feels that the police only need to page at random through their statute book to be able to get a law under which to charge a victim.'[59]

But the charade of apartheid as self-determination for all South Africa's 'peoples' continued. The Transkei was given control of its 'internal affairs' in 1963, with Pretoria still in charge of security, foreign affairs, immigration, customs and banking. In 1971, internal control was also extended to Ciskei, Venda and Lebowa.

Bram Fischer, *volksverraaier*

Bram Fischer, a foremost human rights lawyer and leader of the SACP, was banned in the 1950s. To Afrikaner nationalists, Fischer was nothing less than a *volksverraaier* (a traitor to the volk). His grandfather Abraham had been the leader of the Orangia Unie, allied to Botha and Smuts's *Het Volk* at the start of the 1900s. After the British had granted self-government to their former foes, Fischer's Orangia Unie won the 1907 election and he became prime minister of the Orange River Colony, as the territory was known by then. He served as a minister in the first union cabinet of Louis Botha, and was sympathetic to Hertzog's position.

Less than half a century later, Fischer's grandson was jailed for life for opposing what his grandfather had believed in. Bram Fischer was a communist and thus a proponent of that which was anathema to Afrikaner nationalists: *gelykstelling* (equalisation).

Fischer was the second most senior member of the legal team that defended Luthuli, Mandela, Sisulu, Helen Joseph, Lilian Ngoyi, Joe Slovo, Moses Kotane and eighty-five others in the Treason Trial of the 1950s. This case and the subsequent Rivonia Trial, in which the defence team also included Arthur Chaskalson and George Bizos, alerted the ANC to the possibilities of non-racialism. Luthuli remarked: 'If there is one thing which helped push our movement along non-racial lines, it is the Treason Trial which showed the depth of sincerity and devotion to a noble cause on the white side of the colour line.'[60] The trial ended in the acquittal of all ninety-two accused when the state failed to prove that the ANC wanted to overthrow the government violently, or to impose communist rule on South Africa.

Molly Fischer – married to Bram – was arrested in the nationwide clamp-down under the state of emergency that followed the Sharpeville and Langa shootings. Those arrested with her reflected the motley variety of the real South Africa: Mandela, Luthuli, Govan Mbeki, Kathrada, ZK Matthews, Sisulu, Slovo, Bettie du Toit, Rusty and Hilda Bernstein, Harry Bloom, Sonia and Brian Bunting, Hymie Rasner, Issy and Anne Heymann, Eli and Violet Weinberg, Harold Wolpe and Jack Simons. When the women went on a hunger strike, the Fischer daughters Ruth and Ilse arranged demonstrations by the children of some of those incarcerated. This prompted a column by Piet Cillié, editor of *Die Burger*, under his pseudonym Dawie, in which he lamented how far the apple (Bram) had fallen from the tree (Abraham). Ruth Fischer commented in a letter to her mother in prison that the article was without malice, but tinged with regret.

Bram Fischer's biographer notes: 'It was evident now that divisions that could once be contained within the larger Afrikaner family were becoming more definite ... The more vehement of Afrikaner nationalists increasingly began to regard Bram as apostate and irredeemable, a traitor to his people whose predilections were bluntly unintelligible, and whose lost promise could at best be regarded with nostalgia and dismay. The universe his children inhabited was the one they feared most of all because it looked like the end of their world.'[61]

Fischer was arrested under the ninety-day law in 1964, released, and rearrested along with ten others under the Suppression of Communism Act. He was scheduled to represent a client in a copyright court case in London. Senator Jan de Klerk (father of FW) first denied him a passport, then changed his mind. Fischer could have broken his bail conditions and stayed in the UK, but he came back to stand trial with other members of the SACP. Piet Beyleveld, a member of the SACP's central committee, was also arrested, but in the end it was his testimony, along with that of a police informant, that sank Fischer. Beyleveld had been a member of the party since 1956, was active at the Congress of the People and was a leader of the COD. His appearance as a state witness came as a severe shock to his comrades.

Halfway through the trial, Fischer absconded and went underground. His reasons, as read out to the court, were the following:

There are already more than 2500 political prisoners in our prisons. These men and women are not criminals but the staunchest opponents of apartheid.

Cruel, discriminatory laws multiply each year, bitterness and hatred of the Government and its laws are growing daily. No outlet for this hatred is permitted because political rights have been removed, national organisations have been outlawed and leaders, not in gaol, have been banned from speaking and meeting. People are hounded by Pass Laws and by Group Areas controls. Torture by solitary confinement, and worse, has been legalised by an elected Parliament – surely a unique event in history.

It is no answer to say to this that Bantustans will be created nor that the country is prosperous. The vast majority of the people are prevented from sharing in the country's wealth by the Colour Bar in industry and mining and by the prohibition against owning land save in relatively small and grossly overcrowded parts of the country where, in any case, there exist no mines or industries. The idea that Bantustans will provide any solution would deceive no one but a White South African.

What is needed is for White South Africans to shake themselves out of their complacency, a complacency intensified by the present economic boom built upon racial discrimination.

Unless this whole intolerable system is changed radically and rapidly, disaster must follow … To try and avoid this becomes a supreme duty, particularly for an Afrikaner, because it is largely the representatives of

my fellow Afrikaners who have been responsible for the worst of these discriminatory laws … If by my fight I can encourage even some people to
think about, to understand and to abandon the policies they now so blindly
follow, I shall not regret any punishment I may incur.[62]

Bitter words these turned out to be, as racist attitudes hardened even further
and the NP went from strength to strength. Fischer's words fell on deaf ears.
More and more Afrikaners were determined to remain blind and complacent.
The NP government did what it could to ensure their obliviousness. BJ Vorster,
minister of justice at the time, was determined to put Fischer behind bars.
His brainchild, detention without trial, made that possible when information
was extracted that led to Fischer's arrest while he was living under the alias
of Douglas Black. Sentenced to life imprisonment, he was subjected to daily
humiliation in the Pretoria Local Prison by a warder determined to punish this
former Queen's Counsel 'who consorted with kaffirs and Jews and communists'.[63]
Fischer was given the most ill-fitting clothes and a greasy, oversized hat, and
forced to scrub pipes with a toothbrush and clean toilets and urinals with rags.

On 27 January 1971, his twenty-three-year-old son Paul died after a lifelong
battle with cystic fibrosis. Bram's brother Gus was allowed to tell him this sad
news, but only through a perspex barrier. As Hugh Lewin put it: 'They wouldn't
let brother meet brother … That would threaten the security of the State.'[64]
Afterwards, Fischer was locked up as usual, alone in his cell for fourteen hours.
He was not allowed to go to his son's funeral, and his daughters and brother
Paul were denied a visit – to 'maintain the security of the State'.[65]

Fischer's health deteriorated, and in 1974 he fell and broke his femur. He was
not given medical attention until almost two weeks later and was then released
from hospital prematurely, even though he was unable to walk unaided. His body
was riddled with cancer, but requests to Vorster's government for the dying
man to spend his last days in the care of his family were blocked until three
months before his death. When he was finally released on 'compassionate grounds',
it was with the strict instruction that the semi-paraplegic, dazed man of sixty-
seven be confined to his brother's house in Bloemfontein, lest Johannesburg's
'commies' come crawling out to succour him. Bram Fischer died on Ascension
Day, 8 May 1975.

The NP government's treatment of Fischer can be explained by referring to
André Brink's general observations about dissidence: 'Apartheid, which has
defined Afrikaner unity since 1948, needs an image of historicity, preferably of
eternity, for its success; dissidence exposes it for what it is. And the reaction becomes even more vicious [if] dissidence … implies a revolt against the Afrikaner
power base itself'. Moreover, said Brink, 'if the Afrikaner dissident … encounters

such a vicious reaction from the Establishment, it is because he is regarded as a traitor to everything Afrikanerdom stands for (since apartheid has usurped for itself that definition)'.[66] But sometimes there was no reaction, as NP members spun a world of make-believe normality around themselves. One of many illustrations was the following, put forward by a branch at the Free State NP congress in 1971: We 'request that meat prices, as have been the case in the past, be broadcast after 6 pm over the Afrikaans transmitter.'

The hopes of the ANC, or of a Fischer or a Lewin, that their actions would awaken their slumbering white compatriots, were dashed. Throughout the 1960s, rank-and-file NP members continued to call for the intensification of apartheid policies. In 1966 the party leadership was considering the usual array of discriminatory proposals from branches: apartheid should be extended to retail outlets; Indian hawkers should not be allowed near white businesses; sport on Sundays should be banned (this was a perennial appeal). From Vanderbijlpark came a suggestion that the words 'of the Afrikaner' in the declaration on the back of NP membership cards be replaced with '*of white South Africa*', to read: 'To the best of my ability and with undivided loyalty, I will maintain the stated principles of the National Party as the political national front of white South Africa.'

In the same batch of proposals could be found one of the reasons for the inability of the party faithful to observe critically what was happening around them: slavish support of the leadership and a willingness to employ anti-democratic measures to protect the leaders. Stilfontein asked the government to pass laws that would force the press to show the necessary respect to the prime minister and his office. A proposal from Parys in the Free State reflected the sense of ownership of 'our' blacks: 'Given that non-whites are allowed to use alcohol, congress requests that drinking places be limited to Bantu areas.'

Dissent from within

The party's relationship with its supporters was based on the 'fundamental conviction among the Nats that the only true South Africans were those who professed allegiance to the volk as defined by the party and, in turn, that the only true members of the volk were those who supported the party, who adhered to official party policy and accepted an apartheid future'.[67]

Hardliner JG Strijdom, who succeeded Malan, unflinchingly demanded what he called '*eendersdenkenheid*' (uniform thinking). In 1948, he declared that opposition to apartheid was as treasonable as refusing to defend one's country if it was at war.[68] This attitude soon permeated Afrikanerdom. In the 1950s, the Afrikaans press acted as the party mouthpiece and was wholly intolerant of '*andersdenkendes*' (alternative thinkers), even within NP ranks, according to historian FA van Jaarsveld. In his *Die Evolusie van Apartheid* (The Evolution of Apartheid), Van Jaarsveld drew attention to a number of *andersdenkendes* among Afrikaner nationalists, including the Circle of 13 academics, who were subjected to a 'campaign' by NP supporters to discredit them.[69]

In May 1955, the Circle of 13, led by Professor PV Pistorius from the University of Pretoria, protested against the NP's attempts to remove coloured people from the voters' roll. They called themselves avowed 'nationalists' and 'supporters of the National Party', and argued that their position enjoyed the support of 'Afrikaans-speaking people and Nationalist circles'.[70] According to a statement from these academics, their position provoked 'hysterical reactions in certain [Afrikaans] Press circles ... The manifestation of this spirit proves to us how far we have already advanced in South Africa towards a State wherein it is dangerous for the individual citizen to have or to express an independent opinion'. They were particularly concerned about the implications of the NP's manoeuvres for South Africa as a constitutional state: 'The proposed legislation is being defended by the affirmation that we as a White group have no alternative at this stage ... This is another instance of the point of view that the "end justifies the means"'. The Afrikaans press reported on the Circle of 13 and its concerns, but they were concerns that NP supporters did not share.

About twenty years later, *Die Burger* finally also became concerned and warned that apartheid had become an end in itself, rather than a means to an end. The newspaper also admitted that far from dismantling colour prejudice, as had (absurdly) been hoped, apartheid had rather achieved the opposite. It had become a 'fossilised, unimaginative separation-for-separation's sake'.[71] Prominent figures who differed from the government became the targets of discreditation campaigns, especially in the Afrikaans press. In *Suid-Afrika Waarheen?* (Whither South Africa?), written in 1956, Stellenbosch-based DRC theologian Professor Bennie Keet assessed apartheid from a Christian viewpoint and asked whether it was not mere 'wishful thinking'. Apartheid was the 'easy' way out, as it was 'impossible' and therefore something to dream about, instead of grappling with reality.

In a front-page article, *Die Burger* denounced the book as a 'frontal attack on apartheid'. Piet Cillié dismissed it as a 'little piece of work' that avoided the question of power, which lay at the base of race relations. It was an 'empirical fact' that certain human relations had to be 'looser' in order for peace to prevail. This 'loosening' should not be an end in itself but, according to Cillié, apartheid was a means to peace and improved understanding between races.[72] In this statement, he employed one of the centrepieces of pro-apartheid arguments.

In later years, Keet's book was criticised for not dealing with white party politics and the pressure the electorate was exerting on parties[73] to adopt racist policies. But while Keet was appealing to Christian consciences, he did point out realities that were being popularly ignored. He emphasised that while it was whites who wanted apartheid, it was blacks who suffered under the policy; apartheid violated the dignity of black people and the migrant labour system was destroying black families.

Another Dutch Reformed theologian, Professor Ben Marais, also came under attack when he contradicted the dominant line in the church by saying apartheid could not be justified biblically. He predicted – correctly – that whites would not be able to implement total territorial and economic separation and would therefore have to accept black franchise.[74] Broederbonder Judge Henry Fagan's report for the UP, in which he described apartheid as the 'impracticable mandate', was publicly rejected by a group of seventy lecturers who insisted that apartheid was the only way to safeguard 'white civilisation'.[75]

The clampdown during the 1950s was so effective that voices of dissent against apartheid inside the party disappeared. The party structures were also run in a top-down manner that discouraged questioning. Malan gave his ministers some latitude, but instructed the caucus to confine itself to strengthening the party in parliament, as policy matters were the realm of the NP leadership in the executive. Nevertheless, the caucus did exert some influence. Pressure on Malan by the native affairs group in the caucus led to EG Jansen's removal and the appointment of Verwoerd as minister of native affairs.

Under Verwoerd, intolerance escalated. He already dominated the cabinet under Strijdom, since even the Lion of the North, as Strijdom was called, seemingly did not have the courage to stand up to him. The pedantic Verwoerd did not take kindly to any independent thinking. When he wasn't hatching his grand apartheid plan, he spent his time as prime minister sniffing out diversions and crushing dissent among South Africans, including Afrikaners. The Sharpeville massacre prompted a rethink among some of his ministers: Eben Dönges, Paul Sauer and Ben Schoeman even proposed the scrapping of one of apartheid's building blocks, the pass system. Verwoerd dismissed their suggestion with characteristic irritation.

During the 1960 state of emergency, Verwoerd was shot in the first assassination attempt against him. His temporary removal from the scene gave the Malanite Paul Sauer the courage for some rare soul-searching about the position of black people in South Africa. In a public address to his constituency of Humansdorp, he tested certain ideas: changing the pass system; raising black wages; boosting Bantustan development; and improving contact between whites and 'peace-loving' urban blacks. He was summarily repudiated by Verwoerd.[76]

The growing intolerance among Afrikaner nationalists led to some in their ranks advocating *lojale verset* ('loyal resistance'), *à la* NP Van Wyk Louw, who had written about this concept in the 1930s. It entailed the tempering of nationalist dogma with notions of Christian morality, justice and liberty.[77] Van Wyk Louw pleaded for a 'just existence' (*voortbestaan in geregtigheid*), but by the 1950s was still trapped in an Afrikaner nationalist world view, in that he saw South Africans as irreconcilably different on the basis of ethnicity. From the 1960s onwards, some *verligtes* increasingly latched onto *lojale verset*.

A means to an end

In the 1990s, *Beeld* journalist Tim du Plessis observed that the grand apartheid plan had been stored in Verwoerd's brain. When parliamentary messenger Dimitri Tsafendas stabbed him to death on 6 September 1966, that plan went with him to the grave. One could add that with the disappearance of the plan went the single-minded zeal to promote the apartheid model. Verwoerd's successor, BJ Vorster, confirmed this when he said that 'the cardinal principle of the NP is the retention, maintenance and immortalisation of Afrikaner identity within a white sovereign state. Apartheid and separate development is [*sic*] merely a method of bringing this about and making it permanent. If there are other better methods of achieving this end, then we must find those methods and get on with it.'[78]

Far from merely shuffling the ideological cards, this statement placed in sharp relief the reality that NP rule was, first and foremost, about white minority domination. Only the way in which this was achieved was flexible. Vorster continued to implement Verwoerdian apartheid, as he had promised when he was elected *hoofleier*, but began to tweak the policies here and there in reaction to new crises. His successor, PW Botha, built on this by pursuing revised strategies and constitutional forms of white domination more aggressively. Vorster and Botha both systematically applied repressive state power to stave off opponents. These two ideas – apartheid as a means to an end and the systematisation of state repression – converged in the utilisation of state repression as *the* method of entrenching white power.

Balthazar Johannes Vorster was a compromise candidate who became *hoofleier* of the NP despite being a relatively junior cabinet minister and having no solid support base. It was significant, however, that his appointment as a deputy minister was welcomed by *Die Burger* on 23 October 1958. His ascendance to *hoofleierskap* was similarly supported by both the Cape NP and *Die Burger*, and when Vorster became prime minister, it wasn't long before he took the first steps away from Verwoerdianism.

The first bone of contention was the NP's relationship with English-speaking whites. Ironically, this was one of the issues that had led to JBM Hertzog's isolation from Malan's NP: he had advocated a white nationalism across the divides of language and culture. In the 1960s, the Broederbond's Piet Meyer pushed for the Afrikanerisation of English-speakers. He used the vacuum after Verwoerd's death to jostle for more power for the Bond, saying the NP should confine itself to the political realm, while the Bond would look after the educational, cultural and economic needs of the volk. By contrast, Vorster made strong appeals to English-speaking whites, a trend his successor would continue.

As Dan O'Meara noted rather quaintly: 'The removal of "The Rock" Verwoerd brought into sharp relief the various creatures whose titanic battles had been hidden under his shadow. The simmering nationalist conflicts on the cultural terrain, in press wars and for control over the peripheral organisations of Afrikaner nationalism, now slowly boiled over in overt battle for control of the NP itself.'[79]

The stand-off was between what became known as the *verligtes* and the *verkramptes*. The foremost *verligte* in Afrikaner ranks, Willem de Klerk, coined the terms *verligte* and *verkrampte* in 1972, when he was still an academic at the Potchefstroom University for Christian Higher Education. *Verkrampte* he described as an attitude and school of thought hostile to anything new and determined to perpetuate the patterns of the past. Regarding race relations, *verkramptheid* was a traditionalism that sought to entrench the master/slave relationship. For De Klerk, the true Nationalist was between *verkramp* and *verlig*. In his original conception, *verlig* was not a positive term, but rather an open-mindedness that erred on the side of being unprincipled and tending towards compromise and pragmatism.[80] In later years, *verlig* came to be popularly understood as the more human face of the NP, but De Klerk's original definition revealed more about the true face of the *verligte*. Lack of principle, compromise and pragmatism became the face of NP rule.

With the achievement of the republican ideal and Verwoerd's vision for a white South Africa buried with him, the battle for the soul of the NP erupted. Vorster spent the first four years of his tenure fighting against the *verkramptes*. At one point, he felt so besieged that he threatened to resign. Albert Hertzog was an outspoken opponent of the relaxation of apartheid in the case of visiting black sports teams and individuals. He also made a statement to the effect that English-speakers could not be trusted with the maintenance of 'white civilisation' in South Africa. Vorster responded with a concerted effort to rid the party of Hertzog and his ilk. He dropped Hertzog from his cabinet in a reshuffle and went so far as to release a press statement that falsely indicated Hertzog had apologised to the caucus and withdrawn his statement on English-speakers.

A plan was contrived to force the Hertzogites to show their colours at the Transvaal NP congress, when a vote was called on four issues on which they had criticised government policy: immigration; relations with the rest of Africa;

English-speakers; and sport. The dissidents supported the first three policies, but seven abstained from the vote on sport. Their names were noted, and Hertzog and Jaap Marais were kicked out of the party within weeks. They formed the Herstigte Nasionale Party (HNP) in 1969.

The HNP was founded on the premise that it would protect the interests of the Afrikaner lower classes. Vorster called an election to convey the message that the NP was as strong as ever, and he was proved right, with the HNP managing to garner only 3.59 per cent of the vote. However, in order to neutralise the HNP and reaffirm itself as the true custodian of Afrikaner nationalism, the NP had run a campaign of speeches that were 'more right-wing than usual'.[81] In the process, some of the English-speaking vote was alienated, as nine seats were lost to the UP.

This pandering to the far right wing would be evident in the NP's message at all subsequent elections, and came to absorb most of the political energy in Afrikanerdom, at the cost of the primary challenge, namely democratic rights for black South Africans. This nigh obsession with the HNP and later with Andries Treurnicht's Conservative Party shows how the class struggle within Afrikanerdom occupied centre stage while the state applied increasingly repressive methods to block black demands.

The distance increases between leader and led

The discontent with the leadership that became noticeable during Vorster's tenure as *hoofleier* continued until the party's demise. It was characterised by feelings that the leaders were unaccountable, that followers were being misled and that leaders were benefiting from schemes that had not been mandated by their supporters. A memorandum and reports from the time reflected the growing distance between the leadership in government and the party as an organisation. This was partly the result of Vorster ceding his provincial power base as Transvaal NP leader to Ben Schoeman as a sop when the latter opposed Vorster in the race for the top position.

In lieu of a party power base, Vorster utilised the state apparatus to wield power and extend privilege and patronage. In a break with Verwoerd's dictatorial style, he allowed ministers full control over their portfolios, resulting in bureaucratic power bases becoming more important to NP leaders than the positions they held within the party. One example is the rise to prominence of Pik Botha, who held the portfolio of foreign affairs for almost two decades and contested the *hoofleierskap* twice, but only became Transvaal NP leader in the 1990s.

This shifting of power to non-elected bureaucratic bases moved the party further away from its support base and reduced accountability, while the government increasingly resorted to state violence to defend apartheid. The latter was not a problem for NP branches, but the increasing distance between leaders and supporters was. In the early 1970s,[82] NP branches in the then eastern Transvaal town of Nelspruit detailed their grievances in a memorandum submitted to the NP's federal council for consideration. The memo sheds light on the internal processes of the party and provides leads as to the sense of alienation between supporter and leader. On the one hand it points to the professionalisation of NP politicians who became less accountable in the process; on the other hand it points to the typical difficulty of translating party policies into government policies. Delegates were frustrated at the NP's much vaunted congresses, because not enough time was made available for debates on discussion points that branches put on the table. The ministers chaired the sessions 'autocratically', voting seldom took place and discussion points were seldom given effect. The result was that NP members no longer 'look[ed] up to congress as a democratic policy formulating institution', which led to members being unwilling to represent branches at congresses.

The memorandum identified a shift of power from the branches to the parliamentary caucus. By leaving the *hoofleier*'s election to the caucus, selection of a leader became the prerogative of 'a small group of people who are open to all manner of influences'. The caucus determined policy 'while it does not have that right'. Provincial leaders were made ministers, and then became 'virtually untouchable and they can apparently do as they please without being called to order'. In the process, provincial NP congresses had become the 'biggest farce'.

Ministers did not chair sessions at the congresses impartially, especially not when a colleague of theirs was being criticised. It was also a problem that ministers received the discussion points beforehand, giving them time to prepare, while branches did not have the same luxury, since ministerial responses were revealed at the congress. This meant that there was no place in NP structures 'where a member can confront a minister or a member of [the party] executive with an independent chairman presiding. This leads to superciliousness and autocratic behaviour.' As an alternative, the Nelspruit memorandum suggested that the provincial system be replaced with a national congress that would elect the *hoofleier* and a national chairperson, and determine policy.

Disgruntlement was not limited to Nelspruit. In the same period, the NP's secretariat held discussions with groups of members in two of the party's strongest constituencies, Christiana and Wolmaransstad. In the late 1950s, Wolmaransstad was one of the top party fund-raisers.

In the secretariat's 'Report on problems, complaints and grievances',[83] dated March 1972, the leadership came in for a bashing. Yet again, the strands of alienation that would stretch into the 1990s and beyond were visible. 'The government is overly sensitive and intolerant of criticism. People who ask questions or criticise are threatened with prosecution, ridiculed or silenced by being denounced as *Sappe* or *Hertzogites*.' Sappe referred to Smuts's old South African Party or SAP, and the Hertzogites were JBM Hertzog's followers. These were the two brands of nationalism that the NP had managed to trump and which were still strongly resisted in NP-supporting circles at the time.

Ideological 'confusion' due to the split in class interests within the NP was a theme that recurred frequently from the 1970s onwards. In the case of Christiana and Wolmaransstad, the Nationalists asked how it was possible that the NP leadership had rejected JBM Hertzog's son Albert, while actively recruiting historical foes – English-speaking white voters and big business. Another question was: 'What power does [Anglo American owner] Oppenheimer hold over the government?' They were suspicious about how ministers used their positions for personal gain and confused by the NP leadership's deviation from Verwoerdian apartheid, as on the question of how to deal with visiting black sport participants. This issue, which exposed the depth of racism in white society, was highly contentious at the time and led directly to the expulsion of Hertzog and others in 1969.

The NP secretariat noted that Nationalists were concerned that such concessions caused 'social mixing and raped our apartheid policy'. They pointed out that 'ministers are contradicting each other in public and confusing the voter', which confirmed the *verligte/verkrampte* division within the leadership. Division among followers was evident from the way the Christiana and Wolmaransstad branches bemoaned the 'irritating instruction' in the civil service to address black men as 'mister'. This clashed with the 'Afrikaner's view of things', they felt. They shared many of Nelspruit's points of discontent about the NP congresses and confirmed that branches were losing interest in the gatherings, with 'some openly calling this a waste of time'. Again it was felt that ministers 'dominated' proceedings and 'belittled' delegates.

'The feeling between MPs and the voter is becoming less close, especially before and after parliamentary sittings' – which showed that some MPs were not as involved in their communities, because when parliament was not in session, they should have been working in their constituencies. The sense of a lack of accountability is reflected in a comment that 'civil servants are running the country. They enjoy far too much power over the making of decisions ... and make decisions on matters without consulting ministers'.

This was an almost preternatural observation: barely seventeen years later, the zeal of a civil servant – Niel Barnard – would ensure the surreptitious pursuit of rapprochement with the ANC without even President FW de Klerk's knowledge.

The report ended with 'the deeply held view that the youth and the worker, who have always been the strength of the party, can orchestrate our downfall if their interests are not actively looked after'. This veiled threat, along with concern over big business and the racist views, were clear signs of the growing alienation of the Afrikaner lower classes, who were most threatened by black competition, from the NP leadership.

On 23 August 1972, Marais Viljoen, a cabinet minister and confidant of Vorster, shared with him frank 'thoughts for consideration by the honourable prime minister'.[84] It seems that Viljoen, who would later succeed Vorster as the last ceremonial state president (1979 to 1984), was acting on the above-mentioned reports about grievances and dissatisfaction. His 'thoughts' confirmed disquiet, not only about the party leadership moving away from Verwoerdian apartheid, but also about arrogant attitudes and leaders becoming distant from their support base. Significantly, one of the 'thoughts' was a remarkably candid reproach directed at Vorster himself: 'Party leaders should still appear dignified to the outside world, for example, answers to questions at public events should be friendly and not a rebuff.'

Vorster's biographer describes him as 'cold and formal, even rude', 'unsmiling, inflexible, fearsome and intolerant' towards opponents and critics.[85] Viljoen's discussion points suggest that the leader's attitude permeated the party – especially when read with the Nelspruit memorandum and the Christiana and Wolmaransstad report. The issue of inflated executive ego features yet again: Viljoen requested from Vorster that 'the impression should be avoided that ministers are superior to the *volk* and enjoy excessive comfort, luxury and privileges'. According to Viljoen, these privileges were pointed out as low house rental, owning second cars and arriving in 'long black ones' – luxury cars – at Newlands sport stadium in Cape Town. And again there was concern that classic apartheid was being jettisoned: 'the social mixing aspects of multi-ethnic sports events creates the impression that the government is moving too fast for the Afrikaner's public opinion; adjustments should be made to accommodate our *volk*'s conservative approach'.

Viljoen's notes reveal that not only was there a disconnection between leaders and branches, but also between MPs and the executive. While executive ascendancy over the legislature, judiciary and constitution was not limited to South Africa at the time, it was 'the dominant and inexorable feature of the system',[86] kept in place to a large extent by the power and personalities of the prime ministers and the constrictions of the caucus and party systems. This caused the role of parliament to change from 'policy formulation to policy legitimisation'.[87]

The note offers the view from the inside. In a forthright admission, he said parliamentarians felt like 'rubber stamps'. Important decisions that affected constituencies were made without consulting or even informing the relevant MP, resulting in embarrassment in front of voters: 'MPs are not always informed by ministers and their conclusion is that they are not trusted.' Ironically, the proposed solution was for ministers to assign tasks to MPs in order for their 'services to be better utilised' and their 'talents to be used optimally'.

Viljoen's note shows that the MPs clearly did not understand the notion of separation of powers, or they would have considered being of 'service' to South Africans by using their 'talents' to legislate or to hold the executive accountable. In that sense, they were firmly inducted into the party's culture as enunciated by Vorster. When he was an MP, he regarded the government's role as fulfilling the party's policy and defending leaders against attacks. 'I never saw it as my task and function to suggest or make policy within or outside parliament.'[88] This attitude prevailed to the end, and even when announcements had implications for their continued tenure in parliament, MPs were rarely consulted.

The racial aspects of the NP documents discussed here confirm that sections of the party's support base remained firmly committed to Verwoerdian apartheid. Vorster's moves away from Verwoerdianism elicited resistance from supporters, which suggests that as much as apartheid was being fed from above by elitists intent on staying in power, racist attitudes continued to ensure support for racist policies from below. Whites remained convinced that they were living in a country that was theirs alone – a white country – in which only they were fully entitled to citizenship. The disgruntlement reflected in the documents sprang from 'their' government not serving their vision of white/Afrikaner domination.

Afrikaner economic advance

The most obvious reason for the HNP's inability to make major inroads into Afrikaner support is that while many Afrikaners might have felt the government was moving 'too fast' for them, they continued to benefit handsomely from the NP's social engineering.

Dan O'Meara[89] detailed the economic advance of Afrikaners during apartheid. There was a discernible progression from the 1950s onwards – the direct result of explicit policies aimed at boosting Afrikaner empowerment. Looking at the occupational structure of the country, one can easily trace the improvement in the position of white Afrikaner males. Their presence in the lowest-paying economic category of agriculture, forestry and fishing fell by 30 per cent between 1946 and 1960. Afrikaner men doing manual labour dropped by almost 47 per cent in the same period, while unemployment among Afrikaner men fell by almost 12 per cent.

Over the same time span, Afrikaner men in professional and technical categories increased by more than 93 per cent; those in administrative, managerial and executive positions grew by about 70 per cent; and those in clerical positions by 136 per cent.

Comparatively speaking, English-speaking white men swelled the ranks of professional and technical occupations by more than 67 per cent; those of administrative, managerial and executive positions by more than 39 per cent; and of clerical positions by about 33 per cent.[90] Note the discrepancy in clerical uptakes, which reflected the different class structures of English- and Afrikaans-speaking whites, with the latter moving from a lower base. The lower percentages for English-speaking white males also reflected the Afrikaans bias of NP policies, as well as the fact that Afrikaners had historically been underrepresented in such posts.

Afrikaners in agriculture shrank from about 30 per cent in 1930 to 16 per cent in 1960, and to about 8 per cent in 1977. Overall, the Afrikaners' share of national personal income rose from 27.9 per cent in 1946 to 32.4 per cent in 1960, while that of English-speakers declined. After 1960, the share of both groups declined.[91] By the late 1970s, the per capita income of Afrikaners was 80 per cent of that of English-speakers, up from about half in 1946.[92] While this was a substantial increase, it revealed the gap within the white bloc.

Figures on Afrikaner ownership in the private sector showed that, despite apartheid-style affirmative action, Afrikaners still lagged behind English-speaking whites in 1975. Afrikaner advancement in the private sphere was nevertheless significant, as they increased their ownership from 9.6 per cent in 1948/9 to 20.8 per cent in 1975. In other words, Afrikaner private ownership doubled in the first three decades of apartheid. For the most part, NP policy maintained the existing levels of inequality among Afrikaners, even during the years of high apartheid. From 1946 to 1960, the Gini equality index for Afrikaners dropped slightly from 0.46 to 0.44, with 1 being highly unequal and 0 being equal.

O'Meara pointed out that the benefits were not spread evenly throughout the Afrikaner capitalist class. Some were more equal than others – in particular those in finance, mining, liquor and catering, manufacturing and construction. Afrikaner presence in finance and mining made the biggest leaps: respectively from 5 per cent in 1938/9 to 25 per cent in 1975, and from 1 per cent in 1938/9 to 18 per cent in 1975.

Insurance giant Sanlam formed the core of Afrikaner capital, from whence sprouted various initiatives into other economic sectors. Sanlam was formed by the 'very men who established the Cape National Party and its official press, and who sat with key Cape politicians on the board of Nasionale Pers'.[93] The founder of Santam, a subsidiary of Sanlam, was Willie Hofmeyr, who became managing director of Naspers after resigning as organising secretary of the NP.

Yet again, this demonstrates how the political and economic elite of Afrikaner capital in the Cape were one and the same. A history of shared directorships between Sanlam and Nasionale Pers culminated in Ton Vosloo being chairperson of both boards in the 2000s. NP politicians sat on the Nasionale Pers board of directors until the 1970s.

Another early Afrikaner economic investment was Sanlam's mining subsidiary Federale Mynbou, which was boosted by Anglo American's gift of General Mining in 1964, aimed at cementing links between English and Afrikaans capital.[94] This move was a harbinger of things to come: black economic empowerment deals would cement white and black elite relations in the 2000s. Federale Mynbou acquired control of Union Corporation in 1975 to become the second largest mining house in South Africa. By the 1980s it was known as Gencor, and in the 2000s became BHP Billiton – the largest mining company in the world. From Gencor emerged Derek Keys, who played a crucial role as economic policy strategist and advisor to Trevor Manuel and others in the ANC in the early 1990s. Keys resigned as the first post-1994 finance minister to become head of BHP Billiton after approving Gencor's access to foreign capital to purchase the company.[95] He was simply continuing what had become a tradition in the NP government.

Sanlam moved into manufacturing during the course of the 1950s, capitalising on the withdrawal of international firms in the wake of the Sharpeville and Langa massacres by buying up vehicle, technology and electronics companies.[96] Anton Rupert's Rembrandt Group had found a foothold in the brandy and wine markets during the Second World War and used that as a springboard to become internationally predominant in the tobacco industry, later spreading its wings to banking, finance, mining and engineering.

In his biography of Rupert, former *Die Burger* editor Ebbe Dommisse points out that Rembrandt never supported the NP with funds and that a lawsuit was brought against persons who implied that Rembrandt's directors were Nationalist-controlled. However, elsewhere in the book there is mention of Rembrandt donations to the FAK in the 1950s, along with various English-speaking white organisations. Connections between the Afrikaner business elite and the NP elite are also illustrated by the fact that Rembrandt's first chairperson, Dr AJ Stals, was a minister in Malan's first cabinet.

Volkskas and Old Mutual also extended their interests into manufacturing. By the 1960s, the dependence of Afrikaner financial institutions on the savings of the *volk* had waned. O'Meara cites the example of Sanlam, which increased its investment earnings from less than 20 per cent in 1946 to nearly a third in 1961, the year in which investments accounted for double the income from premiums on policies.[97]

As dependence on capital from farmers and workers diminished, so did the shared interests. Afrikaner big business increasingly floated free from Afrikaner nationalist appeals and closer to the English-speaking capitalist club.[98]

Under Vorster, there was little sign of the ambivalence about capitalism that had marked the Verwoerd era, and politicians and business people embraced each other more enthusiastically. In a sense, the *verligte* (capitalist) pressure from outside the party, which Verwoerd was able to ward off, finally broke through to the top of the party. NP politicians began to benefit directly from business deals. For example, fishing concessions were allocated to a subsidiary of Sanlam, which then issued shares to government officials and politicians. Cabinet members owned holdings in companies supplying products of which the prices were fixed by the government. Vorster personally benefited from the establishment of the petroleum company, Trek, in 1969 when he was awarded shares, along with nine ministers and deputy ministers. Shortly thereafter, the government approved Trek's involvement in a new petrol refinery.[99]

The NP's bias towards large capital concerns rather than smaller enterprises also had an effect on its traditional farming support base. NP policy boosted larger farms, leading to a simultaneous drop in numbers of white farms (118 097 in 1951 to 75 562 in 1976) and an increase in the size of farms (from 736.5 hectares in 1951 to 1134 hectares in 1976).[100] Farms became mechanised agri-businesses, with output doubling during the first fifteen years of NP rule. Farmers' average real income grew by more than 7 per cent each year between 1960 and 1975.

State subsidies remained crucial, representing 20 per cent of the average farmer's income. In 1967, agricultural subsidies totalled twice the amount spent on black education. But the relationship between the NP government and farmers became more strained. By the mid-1960s, farmers began to see labour controls as undermining agricultural growth. Afrikaner farmers did not enjoy the relative security of the private and public sectors. Maize farmers in particular found that the government's anti-inflation policies were bruising them by keeping the maize price down.

Blaming British imperialism or the legacy of the pro-imperialist Smuts government for continuing economic difficulties was becoming less convincing. Anti-imperialism was losing its value as 'the single symbolic target against which all classes of Afrikaners could be mobilised'.[101]

During the 1960s and 1970s, the rapid change in Afrikaner socio-economic classes was also reflected in Broederbond membership. In the 1950s, the Broederbond was dominated by teachers, academics, lawyers, farmers and clergymen. In 1950, not a single member defined himself (always a 'him') as a businessman. About a quarter of the members were teachers and farmers. In the late 1970s, businessmen and bankers formed the third highest category.

Vorster strengthened his own position by ensuring the recruitment of large numbers of police officers to the Broederbond in the 1960s. By the 1970s, the new Afrikaner capitalists had gained control of the organisation, their interests clashing increasingly with those of the farmers, the traditional support base. This fragmented the old network of Afrikaner nationalists.

By the 1960s, aided by Anglo American's transfer of General Mining to Federale Mynbou, Afrikaner and English-speaking capital were becoming increasingly intertwined.[102] A convergence of race and class interests was reflected in the fact that Vorster and Botha both succeeded in winning the votes of between a quarter and a third of English-speaking whites. What Vorster had in mind was a nationalism based on race rather than culture. Hegemony had been achieved within the white community by the 1960s, but it would be short-lived, as Afrikaner capitalists began to balk against the constraints of nationalist ideology.

Communist, liberal – what's the difference?

Film footage that can be viewed at Johannesburg's Apartheid Museum captures a different BJ Vorster than the one revealed in Afrikaner nationalist hagiographies. The footage was shot while, as minister of justice under Verwoerd, Vorster was trying to persuade a foreign news team that passes for black people were not at all sinister, since white South Africans also had to carry identity documents on their person. While making a big show of taking his ID from his jacket pocket, a malicious little smile appears on Vorster's face. His expression says: 'You know and I know that what I'm saying is hogwash, but you can't do anything about it.'

Vorster's malevolence was expressed more forcefully in repressive security measures that escalated in severity under his stewardship. It was he who set up the first institutional tool of repression, the Bureau of State Security – known by its defiant acronym, BOSS. He appointed his old Ossewa-Brandwag buddy Lang Hendrik van den Bergh as the boss of BOSS. Together, they elevated the police to the status of untouchables and systematically set about destroying not only what room for democracy remained, but also the opposition that emanated from any quarter at the beginning of the 1960s.

Both as minister of justice and then as prime minister, Vorster was the one who initiated the barrage of laws that created the environment for security force abuses. Police could shoot with impunity. Rule of law meant nothing. The constitution and parliament counted for little. *Kragdadigheid* was the order of the day, sustained by an air of self-righteousness. What happened under Vorster was not unlike events in Zimbabwe in the 2000s: the quashing of opposition was 'legalised' through the adoption of anti-democratic laws. In 1961, one of these laws enabled Vorster to deny then ANC leader Albert Luthuli the right to collect his Nobel Peace Prize in Norway. The decision was later reversed.

In 1962, Vorster banned the Congress of Democrats and the leftist publication *New Age*; prohibited protest meetings on the steps of the Johannesburg City Hall; declared 437 people communists; prohibited another 103 from speaking publicly or being quoted; placed eighteen under house arrest; and threatened action against the 'liberal' *Rand Daily Mail*. This was also the year in which Vorster revealed that he regarded liberalism as 'the predecessor of communism. The evidence of this is that whenever you take on the communists, every liberal cries for fourteen days. It is also typical of communism to use liberalism as a bulwark behind which it hides and which it uses to destroy democracy ... In South Africa it is a fact that communism believes in everything that liberalism believes in. Nevertheless, every liberal is not necessarily a communist. It is so that the difference between them becomes smaller and smaller and later you need a magnifying glass to see it.'[103]

The reason why Vorster was unable to see the difference between the two ideologies was because he was perturbed by their acknowledgement of the humanity of black people, something which the *Rand Daily Mail* spotted at the time: 'Mr Vorster, you are actually saying to the non-whites that those who respect their human dignity and who are truly worried about their grievances act like communists.'[104]

Unconventional methods

With the channels of democratic expression blocked in all directions, opponents of apartheid turned to violence. But these organisations – from the ANC to the SACP and ARM – decided to attack only hard targets, such as installations associated with the state, and to avoid hitting civilians. Most shared the vain hope that the mass of white South Africans would 'awaken'.

Vorster was intent on avoiding any such stirrings of conscience or justice. He instituted one of the most infamous siege measures of apartheid: detention without trial, in terms of which some 80 000 people were incarcerated between 1960 and 1990. Vorster heralded the era of detainees falling down staircases or from windows, or slipping on soap ... Questions were rebutted with the absurd insistence that the communists had been instructed by their commanders to commit suicide in detention. One after another inquest into deaths in detention found that 'no one was to blame' as the security police, the judiciary and district surgeons conspired to keep torture and murder under wraps.[105] Vorster and Van den Bergh devised the Sabotage Act of 1962, equating sabotage with treason and therefore punishable by death; putting the onus on the accused to prove that he or she was not guilty as charged; and enabling extended detention without trial.

The General Law Amendment Act of 1963 empowered any police officer to detain without a warrant anyone suspected of political activities, and to hold them in solitary confinement for ninety days without charge or access to a lawyer. It also provided for interrogation by police officers, leading to a spate of arrests based on evidence extracted through torture. Combinations of physical assault, electric shocks, solitary confinement, extended periods of standing in one place without moving and sleep deprivation were used against enemies of apartheid.

Between 1 May 1963 and 10 January 1965, 1 095 people were detained, of whom 575 were charged and 272 convicted.[106] On 11 July 1963, Walter Sisulu, Ahmed Kathrada, Lionel Bernstein, Arthur Goldreich, H Festenstein, Denis Goldberg, Bob Hepple and Govan Mbeki were arrested at Goldreich's house in Rivonia. Vorster felt vindicated after criticism from various quarters against what was called the 'most stringent peace-time security legislation in the history of South Africa'. His justification of such legislation was a prelude to the justifications of the Botha era, when state repression became more acute: 'People have to realise that the communists take incredible risks. These are not people who play according to the rules. To fight them with conventional methods is a waste of time.'[107] This statement, which Vorster made in 1963, became a refrain during the 1970s and 1980s. It marked the beginning of a time when the NP government shifted from ad hoc quashing of pro-democratic resistance to increasingly systematised subjugation.

In parliament in 1964, Vorster admitted that complaints of torture had been received, but said that of forty-nine complaints, thirty-two had been found false on investigation. The General Law Amendment Act was replaced by the Criminal Procedure Amendment Act in 1965, which provided for 180-day detention – with suspects invariably being rearrested upon release – as well as solitary confinement. The Terrorism Act of 1967 allowed indefinite detention without trial on the authority of a police officer with the rank of lieutenant colonel or higher.

Here we see the NP's tendency to learn from exploits elsewhere in the region: the Terrorism Act was first used in the former South West Africa to detain SWAPO members before it was implemented against the ANC and other liberation forces.[108]

In 1976, police powers were further bolstered when the Internal Security Act was amended to allow for 'preventive detention'. (Thirty years later, similar methods used by US president George W Bush's administration would provoke the ire of international human rights activists.) Prominent people killed during Vorster's tenure as prime minister include Dr Rick Turner, gunned down at his Durban home on 8 January 1978. A BOSS agent and the bureau's so-called

Z-squad were later implicated in his death, but this was never proved. BOSS was also linked to the intimidation of the Rev. Theo Kotze, Cape director of Beyers Naudé's Christian Institute, when a bullet was fired through the door of his home. The institute, which was subjected to constant police harassment, had initiated a project in which Turner participated.

The repressive actions of Vorster's government received broad support from rank-and-file NP members, as expressed at the Free State congress in September 1971. In a proposed resolution the government was asked to act 'drastically' against NUSAS and other student organisations that were 'hostile towards the Afrikaner's Christian National outlook on life'. It was further proposed that the government withdraw state subsidies or reduce them in cases where students were guilty of 'undermining authority'. Moreover, appreciation was expressed for steps taken by the government against students involved in 'activities with evil intent' and 'the promotion of communism'.

Were these positions the product of misinformation? William Beinart[109] points out that the 'political and cultural brokers of Afrikanerdom wished to deliver wealth to their people as well as to insulate them'. The effect was that Afrikaners insisted that they knew what black people – 'their' Africans – wanted. And, as many an NP leader would indicate, black people did not want the franchise. Arrogance and ignorance cocooned white society.

Beinart captures something of the apartheid mindset when he writes that '[m]ost whites were unable to see black South Africans during this critical period [1960–1970s] … Homelands, passes, group areas, social amnesia and powerful ideologies put them out of sight, literally and metaphorically.' The question remains: Was the leadership, which had much more access to information, as ignorant?

Relaxing black labour strictures

The unprecedented 1973 strikes – some 200 000 black workers mostly in Durban, but also in East London and the Witwatersrand, had had enough of low wages and bad working conditions – caught Vorster and the rest of the NP leadership off guard. Vorster appointed the Wiehahn and Riekert commissions to recommend changes to the labour regime, leading to the recognition of black trade unions and the scrapping of job reservation for whites. This more measured response to black resistance was partly due to the fact that big capital had been pushing for modifications in those instances where apartheid strictures had begun to undermine business.

While it was PW Botha who implemented the recommendations, they confirm that the change of attitude towards capital had started with Vorster. The party's rank and file reflected concern about the economic rather than political implications of the strikes; at the 1973 federal NP congress, a proposal was made that the 'exorbitant wage demands' be carefully considered in the light of inflation and that wage increases be allowed only in cases of improved productivity. What strikes one as strange is the claim that the demands were 'exorbitant'. Not only did the black share of total personal income decline from 22.2 per cent in 1946/7 to 19.3 per cent in 1970, but the ratio of per capita income of white and black South Africans grew from an already staggeringly unequal 10.6:1 in 1946/7 to 15:1 in 1970.[110]

The 'homelands':
Overpopulated and under-resourced

During Vorster's tenure, Verwoerd's 'homeland' scheme gathered momentum, with all blacks receiving 'citizenship' in 1970. Transkei became the first 'independent' state in 1976, followed by Bophuthatswana in 1977. Self-government was handed to Ciskei, Gazankulu, Lebowa, QwaQwa, Venda and KwaZulu by 1978.

Any plans that the Bantustan leaders might have harboured about integrating black people into white South Africa as citizens were dashed. After a summit held in 1973, they declared their rejection of the pass laws, proposed a federal state with the homelands as provinces and requested more land to improve the viability of the homelands.

To Vorster, a federation meant abandoning white sovereignty 'to other people or nations'. He thus reverted once more to the ideological fantasy of the 'foreignness' of black South Africans. Cabinet minister MC Botha was even more contemptuous: as the land would be a 'gift' from the whites to the blacks, 'we as the givers must determine what land should be given and it is not for those who receive to point out what land they should have'.[111] Botha's ignorance can only be explained by assuming that he had limited himself to reading the Christian National version of colonial appropriation of land.

A parliamentary committee confirmed that no more land would be added to the designated homelands, but recommended consolidating Bophuthatswana from nineteen separate patches to six, and KwaZulu from 108 fragments to ten.[112] The absurdity of the homelands is yet again apparent. A primary reason for the problem was that white landowners refused to give up their land. This had been anticipated by Jan Smuts as leader of the opposition as early as 1948, when he pointed out that 'whether you go to the Transvaal or Natal or anywhere else, you find the farmers say: "Are we going to part with our heritage? Are we going to sell the land of our fathers? We shall not."'[113] Whatever 'good intentions' the NP government purportedly had with the homelands – that black people could develop and form autonomous nations – they were not shared by their constituency. The issue was only taken up again during PW Botha's reign.

At the same time, the hardships caused to black people were tremendous. The homelands were areas to which the socio-economic contradictions of apartheid were displaced. Between 1960 and 1983, 3.5 million people were forcibly removed from their homes. While they were not moved to homelands, about 600 000 of those affected were coloured and Indian. Given their comparatively smaller numbers, this represented a large proportion of these groups. During the 1960s alone, the population in the Bantustans rose by 70 per cent, partly due to the black population explosion.[114]

By 1982, 600 000 people had been removed from 'black spots', which were mostly unproductive farms owned by black people outside the homelands and housing large settlements. The percentage of the black population inside the homelands grew from 39 (4.2 million people) in 1960 to 52.7 (11 million people) in 1980. However, there was not enough land available and the removals were tantamount to dumping, which meant that by 1980 about half of all black rural families had been rendered landless in what were basically rural slums without services, facilities or employment.[115]

Impoverishment could also be measured according to cattle owned. By the late 1970s, only about half of all families in Transkei owned cattle.[116] Poverty was transferred to the homelands, where child mortality and malnutrition were much worse than in towns and cities. The average black urban income was twice that of the rural areas. Population density in the homelands almost doubled between 1955 and 1969.[117]

NP members were egging on their government. At the 1969 Free State NP congress, the Rouxville branch bluntly requested the government to accelerate separate development and move 'Bantus' faster to 'their' areas, 'especially those who are redundant'. The Frankfort branch proposed the redirection of all housing funds away from black townships to the homelands. This had indeed been effected by the mid-1960s. At the Transvaal NP's provincial congress in 1969, branches put forward similar proposals:

- Reduce the number of 'Bantus' in white areas.
- Stricter control of black people in white areas and the accelerated 'tidying-up' of 'black spots'.
- 'Operationalise all that is needed to limit the settling of the Bantu, especially families, in the white areas and to amend existing legislation which gives "rights" to among others the Bantu who were born in a white area to limit such settlement.'
- The movements of 'Bantu' in white areas should be limited between 10 a.m. and 4 p.m.
- 'Bantu' should not be allowed to sleep on white premises.
- The policy of separate development should be taken to its 'logical consequences as quickly as possible'.

To tighten control over urban blacks, the controversial Bantu Affairs Administration Boards (BAABs) were established in 1971. They removed administration of black areas from municipalities and centralised it at national government level in the Department of Bantu Administration and Development. The BAABs intensified control over the daily lives of urban blacks, stepping up influx control and whittling away their rights. But Vorster's pragmatism also resulted in a policy reversal as the NP started to accept the permanence of black urban dwellers. Black people's right to own freehold property in the urban townships had been revoked in 1968, but in 1976 thirty-year leasehold on properties was reintroduced in black townships, and extended to ninety-nine-year leasehold in 1978.

While the percentage of the black population on white farms shrank from thirty-five in 1950 to twelve in 1985, the numbers grew slightly, showing that the 'surplus' generated by demographic growth was being removed.[118] Urbanisation was arrested at between 25 and 29 per cent of the black population between 1950 and 1980,[119] but steep population growth still ensured an increase of some 2.4 million people in the urban areas. A massive housing crisis ensued. By 1977, a backlog of 141 000 units existed, which mushroomed to 540 000 by 1982.[120]

William Beinart[121] points to the irony in the demographics, which were a cause of great concern to the NP and its supporters, as reflected in branch requests for state support to encourage larger white families. 'A central element in apartheid planning was to stabilise the African population in the countryside, and this had the effect of intensifying rural poverty. Many African families who might otherwise have migrated to the cities tried to hold on to some rural productive base. Simultaneously, it seems that they perceived a need for more potential workers and income-earners, as resources declined.'

While similar population-growth figures were seen in other African countries, the black population increased most rapidly at the height of apartheid in the 1950s and 1970s, suggesting that planners were inadvertently watering the thorn of black population growth embedded in white apartheid flesh. Up to 1951, the black and white populations each grew at about 2 per cent. Whites still constituted 20.9 per cent of the overall population. By 1970, this had fallen to 17.3 per cent, and by 1996 to 10.9 per cent.[122]

Black Consciousness

Just as the 1973 strikes caught Vorster unawares, so did the 1976/7 student uprisings. The arrogance of the ruling establishment was such that Manie Mulder, chairperson of the West Rand Administration Board, assured the media in May 1976 that 'the broad masses of Soweto are perfectly content, perfectly happy. Black–white relationships at present are as healthy as can be. There is no danger whatsoever of a blow-up in Soweto.'[123] His words were barely cold when, on 16 June, 15 000 schoolchildren marched in Soweto.

Cabinet member Andries Treurnicht's insistence that black pupils be taught subjects such as mathematics in Afrikaans was the last straw for a generation bearing the brunt of an economic recession and faced with a bleak future. One cannot escape the irony of the government illegitimately withholding citizenship from black people, yet simultaneously demanding that they be taught in one of the two official languages. Protestors carried placards rejecting Afrikaans as language of instruction – including one that turned the NP obsession with racial purity on its head: 'The black nation is not a place for impurities. Afrikaans stinks.'[124]

By the end of 1977, the uprising had spread from Soweto to Alexandra and Mamelodi, to the Eastern Cape and Cape Town. Workers became involved through stayaways, sometimes voluntarily, sometimes not. As the year drew to a close, some 575 people had been killed and another 2 389 injured. The Cillié Commission detailed the casualties, including those perpetrated by the police. The record showed that the security forces had used disproportionate force again and again. For example, thirteen-year-old Noel John Adriaanse was shot dead when he ran away after looting a shop in Hanover Park near Cape Town; nineteen-year-old Gary Sandy Bernardo was killed by a gunshot wound in his back after throwing stones at the police. The commission found what the NP government wanted to hear: the uprising had been orchestrated by outside agitators and had nothing to do with the drudgery and hardship of township life.

The ANC was caught as much by surprise as the Vorster regime. Black Consciousness (BC) was a much more significant influence on those who led the 1976 uprising.[125]

Security force action and incarceration of the ANC and PAC leaders in 1960 had forced the organisations underground and into exile abroad. Amid the economic boom of the decade, all seemed well to the NP – but not for long. By the end of the 1960s, BC had emerged as a powerful philosophy that wholly embraced the concept of black people as 'more than appendages to white society'.[126]

The leading voice in South Africa was that of Steve Biko, a young medical student who founded the South African Students' Organisation in 1969 after breaking away from the white-dominated NUSAS. The clampdown on the BC movement ended with Biko's torture and murder in 1977 and the banning of all BC organisations. An inquest[127] was held, which exhibited the arrogance and derision of the security forces at the time. The police justified transporting Biko naked in the back of a bakkie from Port Elizabeth to Pretoria by saying they feared he would commit suicide. One of Biko's interrogators, Major Harold

Snyman, testified mockingly that it was 'possible' to commit suicide with a pair of underpants.

Snyman referred pointedly to Biko's 'insolent attitude'. He also attempted to elicit an image of Biko reminiscent of nineteenth-century racist depictions of black people: Biko had attacked his interrogators out of the blue and with a 'wild look in his eyes'; it took 'five men' to restrain him; even when his hands and feet were manacled he had not 'calmed down at all'. It was admitted that Biko 'fell on a number of occasions'. The tone of the evidence was one of defiance, derision and wilful non-cooperation. It fitted right in with police minister Jimmy Kruger's callous comment that news of Biko's death had left him untouched ('cold').

Cold War justifications

During Vorster's tenure, South Africa stepped up interference in the internal affairs of its neighbours. Counter-insurgency theories gained popularity in South African security circles during the 1960s. Army chief Pop Fraser's book, *Lessons Drawn from Past Revolutionary Wars*, later became a blueprint for the NP government's counter-revolutionary strategy.[128] Instruction in counter-insurgency was introduced in the SAP and SADF in 1967 and 1968 respectively. The SADF's growing Cold War mindset was further reinforced.

A hallmark of those years was the departure from conventional use of the SAP as a force to protect civilians inside the country by deploying policemen beyond South Africa's borders. In March 1965, as part of a pre-emptive strategy, an SAP base disguised as an engineering company was established in the Caprivi Strip of then South West Africa. South Africa's war in the region started some fifteen months later with the SAP's first attack on SWAPO.

SAP members were sent into the former Rhodesia in 1967 to combat MK and ZIPRA (ZAPU) alongside the forces of Ian Smith's government. Vorster announced this at a ceremony where the town council awarded him honorary citizenship of Brakpan. He received 'loud approval' from those present, 'and within a few hours the first telegrams with congratulations streamed into Vorster's Pretoria office'.[129] The NP government received unequivocal approval for actions that disdained the basic democratic principle of the rule of law, despite all protestations. The British government's objection went unheeded, and in the end the SAP's 2 000 officers were withdrawn only when Vorster decided it was time, which was in 1975.[130] The NP's intransigent attitude towards external criticism had a precedent long before PW Botha perfected it.

The year 1975 was also when South Africa sent troops into Angola with the backing of the United States. Perhaps more than any other single act, this marked the debut of the securocrats, as neither the public nor the cabinet knew about what became known as Operation Savannah. The invasion was a contravention of the Defence Act of 1957, which did not allow for the deployment of conscripted forces outside the country. Yet again, parliament proved its status as a rubber stamp by hastily amending the law in January 1976. As troops had already entered Angola in October 1975, the amendment was made retroactive.

This action illustrates the increasing tendency by government to a lack of transparency and accountability, justified by 'the national interest', and a reckless contempt for the rule of law. General Magnus Malan, head of the army at the time, said in his autobiography that 'the government decided ... to get involved in the Angolan crisis'.[131] However, the invasion was raised at cabinet level only after news of the invasion had reached South Africa from abroad.

South Africa's clandestine military action was precipitated by Portugal's withdrawal from its African colonies of Angola and Mozambique in 1974. The defence force believed that Soviet policy was to extend its influence to Angola, Mozambique, Botswana, Tanzania and Zambia and to support the ANC, according to former SADF chief General Constand Viljoen.[132] These countries were regarded as buffer states in South Africa's resistance to the Soviet onslaught, but the coup that ended fascist rule in Portugal brought 'the RSA's defence line to its borders'.[133]

Like Botha, Vorster believed that the USSR's intention was to create a string of Marxist states along South Africa's borders and, ultimately, add South Africa itself to this string. Given his policy of détente with southern African states at the time, Vorster was not overly enthusiastic about invading Angola, but as minister of defence, PW Botha convinced him that it was the right thing to do. The withdrawal of US support led to an embittered South African government pulling its troops out in 1976. Instead of South Africa forging an alliance with anti-communist African states, as had been hoped,[134] the Organisation of African Unity (OAU) deadlocked on the issue before eventually accepting the MPLA government in Luanda as a member. That put an end to Vorster's détente and his vision of a commonwealth of southern African states.

Along with Zambia's Kenneth Kaunda, Vorster then tried to use Rhodesia's dependence on South Africa to bring Ian Smith to the negotiating table. The initiative failed, but just one month later Vorster brought leaders in South West Africa together – again with the hope of change on white terms, as SWAPO's Sam Nujoma was not invited.

In 1977, Vorster led the NP to the largest electoral victory for any party up to that point, winning 134 of the 164 contested parliamentary seats. But by September 1978 he faced an ignominious end: the Information Scandal – or Muldergate – had exploded. Some have suggested that Vorster's lenient running of the cabinet had led to his downfall.[135] Unlike Verwoerd, he expected his ministers to be on top of their portfolios and afforded them autonomy in their decision-making. The power that he had concentrated in BOSS as his institutional base came back to haunt him. BOSS was involved in the misappropriation of funds used in the NP government's quest to counteract negative messages from the international anti-apartheid lobby. The homespun propaganda campaign cost taxpayers R85 million.[136]

The scandal broke at a convenient time. Connie Mulder was the information minister, and it was from his department that funds had been secretly routed, for instance, to buy an influential US newspaper, the *Washington Star*, and to set up *The Citizen* in South Africa with the backing of business mogul, rugby supremo and later politician Louis Luyt. Mulder was also the NP's Transvaal leader and the crown prince of the *verkrampte* faction. In 1978, this made him PW Botha's chief opponent as *hoofleier*.

Despite all indications that he was the most popular candidate, Mulder could not escape the Info Scandal, and in the first round of voting for a new leader, he polled seventy-two ballots to PW's seventy-eight and Pik Botha's twenty-two. In the second round, PW came out on top, with ninety-eight votes to Mulder's seventy-four.

The Info Scandal cost not only Mulder and Hendrik van den Bergh their jobs, but also put an end to Vorster's political career. Already forced out of the executive into a grace-and-favour post as ceremonial state president, he was forced to quit public life and retired to a seaside resort – much as his successor would do eleven years later.

Botha took some of the *verligte* steps Vorster had initiated to conclusion, but his tenure was predominantly characterised by a rise in state violence. He shifted the institutional power point that he had inherited from the police to the military, his bureaucratic support base. The day of the securocrat had dawned.

In conclusion, the NP achieved political hegemony among whites by the 1960s. Afrikaner nationalism proved especially indispensable in entrenching an ethnic self-consciousness among Afrikaans-speaking whites, fortified by notions of race-based supremacy, historic and contemporary embattlement, and values such as loyalty, uniformity and conformity. Moreover, Afrikaners remained caught up in the romanticism and emotional appeal of being 'God's chosen people', placed on the African continent to bear the torches of 'white civilisation' and Christianity.

From the perspective of the rising international human rights tide against colonialism, the NP was the wrong party at the wrong time. International conditions were more conducive to social justice, but the NP was emphatically *not* the party to move South Africa towards greater equity. With its neo-colonial concept of race relations, it managed to capitalise on the fears of whites. Whatever doubts bubbled up in the collective white conscience were stilled by the powerful sweetener of rapid economic advance, especially of the Afrikaner.

What made apartheid particularly abominable was the foolhardy denial of black people's humanity. This was the fruit of an ideology of racism, which spawned more and more severe forms of violent repression. DF Malan's sidekick Paul Sauer called black people 'barbarous and the semi-barbarous' at a time when the ANC's Albert Luthuli was awarded the Nobel Peace Prize. It was not that there was no one to talk to. It was that the white leadership and their supporters did not want to talk. In post-apartheid South Africa, it is said that they were blind and deaf – they did not hear the appeals of black people. Strange, then, how quick whites were to silence the appeals they ostensibly could not hear. They supported the intensification of state repression to silence these 'inaudible' appeals. When some within their ranks resisted, such as the Circle of 13, they, too, were promptly silenced. Others, such as Bram Fischer, paid dearly for daring to contradict the ideology. His hope that fellow whites would be roused from their slumber came to naught in his lifetime. Opposition was quashed. Through a combination of patronage and *kragdadige* repression of democratic and egalitarian views and ideologies, the NP made its policies the only game in town. NP supporters would not hear anything else. Years later they would claim: 'We did not know.'

As apartheid exacerbated the socio-economic crisis of black existence while unsustainably bottling all political aspirations, white fears grew and entrenched the NP further in the warm pillows of power, as was illustrated by the NP's massive electoral victory in 1977. After Vorster came Botha – and with him, even more abuse in order *not* to hear and *not* to know.

CHAPTER 3

Building a black bulwark against resistance

The onslaught is aimed at the prevailing state structure that is the present South African democratic way of life as represented and symbolised by parliament.   **– General Magnus Malan, addressing parliament as minister of defence, 1981[1]**

September is the prettiest,
prettiest month.
Violets in the drawing room
and riots everywhere, across the land.
– Singer and author Koos Kombuis[2]

THE NATIONAL PARTY COULD NOT ACCOMMODATE THE DEMOCRATIC groundswell of 1976. It was in direct contradiction to its ideological objectives, precipitating a new era in South African politics and hastening the demise of the apartheid state.

The ferocity and extent of the protests caught the government off guard. Though the security forces were eventually able to restore a semblance of order, the unrest awakened some Afrikaners to rising black animosity towards Afrikaner rule, symbolised by the Afrikaans language.

The uprising took even the liberation movements by surprise.[3] This was spontaneous combustion from grassroots level, which would be much harder to control than resistance orchestrated from above. The youthfulness of the rioters was especially notable. Their parents' protests had been arrested by the mid-1960s in a security clampdown, but inferior education, poor living conditions and a lack of job prospects left the youth with no choice but to rise up against their oppressors. This mood was captured in the words of a song by a father about his sons in the 1970s, quoted in a short story written by Charles Rukuni:

Kill if you want to
I am not the one who started the war
After all what have I got to lose
My sons are now beasts of the jungle with no home
So what have I got to lose ...[4]

The social roots of the uprising required a response that went beyond security action. PW Botha's 'total strategy' was ostensibly devised to counter the external communist onslaught from the Soviet Union in cahoots with its 'surrogate', the ANC. But the socio-political dimension of total strategy shows that it was specially designed to annihilate the enemy within.

John Vorster was hamstrung by his conviction that a mere tweaking of the apartheid system would sustain it. He was the leader who had initiated reform through his appointment of two labour commissions in the 1970s and of a cabinet committee, headed by PW Botha, to find constitutional alternatives to the bankrupt idea of apartheid. When Botha replaced Vorster in 1978, Vorster's piecemeal approach made way for a sudden flurry of activity. A hint of what was to come was Botha's famous 'adapt or die' speech on 28 July 1979 in Upington, when he exhorted white South Africans to show racial tolerance and adaptability. He followed this with a visit to Soweto, becoming the first prime minister to venture into a black township.

Botha was pugnacious and opinionated, as well as unusually blunt and frank, about the limitations of grand apartheid. He emphasised the 'instrumentality' of apartheid, sweeping aside hallowed aspects of NP racial policy and introducing technocratic grit to the South African state. As a *verligte* who was close to Afrikaner monopoly capital in the Cape, he aimed to remove those elements of white domination that constrained capitalist growth. Botha's two primary policy directions were borrowed from the ideological currents in the West at the time: Cold War anti-communism and the rising ideology of neo-liberal capitalism. He managed to breathe new life into the NP by reforming apartheid with the help of the Cold War theory of 'total onslaught' necessitating a 'total strategy'. This he had appropriated while minister of defence, when he developed a close working relationship with military officers, a hallmark of his reign.

Botha also latched onto the rise of the technocratic response, which corresponded with the economism that came with the international advent of neo-liberal capitalism. He took South Africa into the age of technocratic government, which propounded economistic and managerial rather than 'ideological' solutions – an idea that remained in vogue into the twenty-first century. Botha's version entailed managerial bureaucratic responses imposed from above, notwithstanding democratic pressures or demands. As pointed out by political scientist Pierre du Toit,[5] this required centralising decision-making in the hands of unelected technocratic specialists who were unaccountable, while the decision-making powers of parliament and even cabinet were reduced. Integral to the technocratic vision was that economic growth through private enterprise was seen as the paramount objective of state policy, backed by stability imposed by the state. Growth was to be achieved at the cost of equity, and stability at the cost of democratic participation. This was done in combination with the Botha *verligtes'* willingness to discard age-old NP policies in favour of pragmatism.

Of course, the managerialism was applied in the service of white domination, and that, indeed, was what constituted NP *verligtheid* in the 1970s and 1980s. As former deputy minister of justice Sheila Camerer puts it: the *verligtes* believed that a 'ring of steel' was necessary to push through reforms to prevent economic collapse.[6] According to Leon Wessels, a deputy minister in Botha's cabinet, it would be 'fair' to say that the difference between the *verligtes* and the *verkramptes* was that the latter regarded economic development as subject to apartheid, while it was the other way around for the *verligtes*. An illustration would be the response to Biko's murder. In January 1978, a 'general discussion [and] meeting took place between members of the NP caucus and influential business leaders to orientate each other and influence each other's thinking ... The business people explained the effect of Steve Biko's death on international trade and commerce. Those who were sympathetic to this position were all National Party *verligtes*. Those who were averse argued that you could not allow the economy to dictate. Politics had to dictate the economy and you could not allow this bunch of business people to tell you how to formulate your policy. Your policy had to be formulated by the people who support and vote for you.'[7]

The *verligtes* opted for flexibility and compromise[8] – underpinned by a commitment to white supremacy and capitalism unfettered by apartheid's 'ideological' constraints. In this sense, *verligtheid* fitted in with the economism associated with neo-liberal capitalism. Economism suggests that 'economic issues are somehow apolitical'.[9]

Technocratic revisions were thus applied to revive capital accumulation by broadening the elite base beyond the white section of the population. In practice, this required the excision of working-class representatives among NP leaders, which happened in 1982 in an unceremonious shattering of the cross-class Afrikaner nationalist alliance that had been painstakingly stitched together by the Afrikaner elite four decades earlier.

These revisions were not meant to dismantle white domination. Under Botha, the NP's primary strategy was to shift its tactics from white cross-class mobilisation to multiracial elite mobilisation. The ruling elite attempted to forge new alliances to perpetuate historical patterns of domination, but in a revised form: as multiracial domination by the few of the many. In the process, the party sought to reinvent itself as the vehicle for this new elite alliance – a strategy that, despite Botha's accompanying convoluted policy permutations, failed miserably in the end. As the technocratic solutions failed, Botha's determination to preserve white control pushed him against a wall, and the militaristic option became increasingly predominant.

Characteristic of Botha's rule was an increased closeness with English-speaking capital and direct efforts by the government to address capital's concerns. This had started under Vorster. For example, the Wiehahn and Riekert inquiries followed a call in 1974 from Anglo American's Harry Oppenheimer for employers to acknowledge black labour unions and for a commission into black labour rights. While capital had flourished in the first two decades of apartheid, with a boom during the 1960s, the policy's effects came to seriously constrain economic growth. The over-regulated movement of black labour, coupled with the apartheid-induced skills shortage, started hampering economic growth in the 1970s. This was against the background of an international crisis in the capitalist order as growth stagnated and inflation rocketed. Until then, South Africa had followed a Fordist model in which racist power relations shaped economic development, with whites as the beneficiaries. In a context of suppressed black wages, government policies boosted white-owned manufacturing and agriculture relative to mining.

Industrialisation was intensified by the substitution of luxury imports with locally manufactured goods for the white population.[10] Parastatals accounted for a substantial share of local investment. But the system of import substitution was reaching its limits, and exacerbated a lack of competition. The consumer market remained artificially limited by apartheid, which inhibited the growth of the manufacturing sector. South African industry also remained overly dependent on imports for capital goods. The monopoly structure of the economy militated against new investment and growth. Capital was seeking solutions to these constraints, and PW Botha appeared to be the leader who could deliver them.

Shifting bases

By 1978, when Botha came to power, the NP had long abandoned its anti-capitalist ranting and was promoting especially big-business interests. Given its pro-capitalist policies, it was obvious that such 'anti-capitalism' was a reaction to Afrikaners being mostly excluded from the loftier heights of capital accumulation. During its first three decades in power, the NP used the state to promote Afrikaner capitalists, whether in big business, or as entrepreneurs or through state-owned companies, which sometimes served as a training ground for the private sector.[11] The party was a prime vehicle for the aspirations of the Afrikaner business and professional classes. However, for these aspirations to be fulfilled, these classes required the electoral muscle of Afrikaner workers. While building Afrikaner big business during the 1950s and 1960s, the NP had held on to the worker's vote through job reservation, which protected unskilled and semi-skilled whites from competition in the form of black workers.[12]

The NP's core class interests illuminate why the party did not act counter to big-capital interests when it came to power in 1948, and in the late 1970s responded favourably to big business's complaints about apartheid policies hampering access to skilled labour. The granting of labour rights to black workers at the end of the 1970s, in contradiction of apartheid philosophy and die-hard NP opposition to black citizenship rights, makes sense only when judged against the necessities of boosting capital accumulation by expanding the ethnic base of the consumer classes.

By the 1970s, Afrikaner capital was firmly entrenched in South African industry's monopolistic structures. Afrikaner agriculture had become relatively more mechanised, run by 'chequebook farmers' with business interests, as opposed to the struggling producers of yesteryear competing with urban capital for labour.[13] There were fewer but larger farms and therefore fewer farmers. The percentage of Afrikaners active in agriculture had shrunk from about 30 per cent in 1930 to 16 per cent in 1960, and to about 8 per cent in 1977.[14] The Afrikaner contribution to manufacturing turnover rose to 15 per cent, in finance to 25 per cent and in mining to 30 per cent by the mid-1970s.[15] Afrikaner control of companies on the Johannesburg Stock Exchange grew from less than 10 per cent in the late 1970s to 20 per cent by 1990.[16] Therefore, as apartheid succeeded in establishing Afrikaner capital, the NP's power base shifted from farmers and workers to capital, the professional and middle classes.

From the 1970s, the NP consistently moved closer to English capital, an ideal already espoused by Malan when the party came to power. This happened through corporate mergers and acquisitions, directorships and the state's utilisation of English-speaking whites with expertise and international connections.[17] By the end of the decade, the NP needed capital even more, as multinational corporations provided 'lifelines to outside loans, markets and know-how'[18] at a time of growing economic insulation. This increased the state's dependence on capital and forged closer links between state and capital.

Apart from the NP's shifting class bases, internal and external pressures had built up by the end of the 1970s, precipitating a crisis. The following factors were tipping the scales against NP policies:

- The mobilisation of black workers through illegal trade unions to stage disruptive strikes, starting in Durban in 1973.
- The ferocity of black urban discontent that exploded in the 1976 uprising – despite increases in government funding for education – and which was only contained *after* it had spread from Soweto to townships across the country.
- Demographic shifts in the wake of booming black population growth between 1950 and 1970, and rapidly growing urbanisation. Durban doubled

in size within two decades; townships outside Cape Town grew from having almost no black residents to 750 000; shacks in Katlehong on the East Rand mushroomed from 3 000 in 1979 to 44 000 in 1983.[19]

- The escalating recession after 1972 as the racial Fordist model became mired in its own contradictions of inhibiting growth of the domestic market; its inability to absorb surplus labour; and dependence of the manufacturing sector on imported capital goods.
- Spiralling costs of administering and enforcing the plethora of intricate laws controlling especially black people's lives.
- The mortifyingly poor performance of grand apartheid's flagship projects, the 'homelands', as they reeled under inefficiency, corruption and abuse of power.
- The deepening moral crisis among Afrikaners, with the Information Scandal being the final prick that burst the bubble of morally superior leadership, as the age of Verwoerdian smugness made way for greater introspection.
- The white electorate's move to the right as insecurity grew hand in hand with the crisis in apartheid.
- Mounting hostility towards South Africa as the last colonial power – Portugal – withdrew from Africa, Ian Smith's regime in Rhodesia collapsed and regional rulers rejected Pretoria's offers of cooperation.
- Heightened international pressure as the United Nations declared apartheid a crime against humanity and the 1976 uprising caused constraints in investment flow.

This was the context in which PW Botha shifted the gears of the NP government from paralysis to activity, drawing public and private players together and remotivating the white electorate with the borrowed ideological innovation of 'total onslaught'.

Capitalism, the panacea

The NP government was not alone in needing fresh ideas and new allies. Capital also needed the state more. Internationally, the 1970s marked the rise of economic stagnation and high inflation (so-called stagflation), and corporations were seeking ways to improve their dipping fortunes. This crisis, sparked by capital over-accumulation, was exacerbated in South Africa by apartheid policies. Milton Friedman, guru of neo-liberal capitalism, who was assisting Chilean dictator Augusto Pinochet at the time, visited South Africa in the mid-1970s to advise the government that 'free market capitalist politics are the only way to a free and reasonably peaceful South Africa'.[20] In fact, as the Soweto uprising showed, a free and reasonably peaceful South Africa was the only way to maintain capitalism.

The countrywide unrest of 1976 and 1977 made it clear that apartheid policies were wholly unacceptable to urban blacks. In addition, capital required readily available, urbanised and at least semi-skilled black labour rather than the unskilled labour that the migrant system provided. Historically, large volumes of transient black workers with no rights had formed the foundation of capital growth. By the 1970s, the increasing use of technology required at least semi-skilled labour. Insufficient numbers of skilled white workers were available, and apartheid was blocking black workers' upward mobility and skills development.

The relationship between the NP government and the English-dominated capital sector had previously been symbiotic, with capital adhering to an apolitical stance while benefiting from apartheid's over-regulation and coercion of black labour. The relationship had to move to a new level in order to deal with the conundrum of urban blacks and the demand for skilled labour. Faced with the inertia of the Vorster government in its last years, capital decided to mobilise 'business power' to force changes that would reactivate the economy and restore profitability.[21] The NP itself, as the party controlling the levers of state, became the terrain of political contest.[22]

This process was bolstered by the convergence of interests between English-speaking and Afrikaner capital, the latter with its 'privileged personal access'[23] to government. In the late 1970s, an English-speaker, Owen Horwood, was appointed minister of finance, and in 1977 the Urban Foundation was established at the behest of Anglo American's Oppenheimer and Rembrandt's Anton Rupert, in an illustration of the coming together of Afrikaner and English-speaking capital.

The Urban Foundation identified the lack of a black middle class as the primary obstacle to the survival of capitalism in South Africa. This became even more prominent as socialist slogans gave content to resistance against apartheid. A reversal of apartheid's artificial suppression of class formation in the black population was needed because it was resulting in a class gap, something that had concerned capitalists such as Oppenheimer since the 1950s.[24] As the political scientist Heribert Adam put it: '[I]nterest in potential lucrative profits ties in neatly with the traditional liberal political strategy of an alliance with an emerging African bourgeoisie that is also now [in 1979] advocated by sections of Afrikanerdom as suitable for the defence of capitalism.'[25] Afrikaner capital thus also moved to the position that a black middle class with 'Western-type materialistic needs and ambitions'[26] was sorely needed. By the late 1970s, the Afrikaans press had joined the chorus, calling the promotion of a black bour-geoisie 'a bastion against the attack on our free capitalist way of life'.[27]

The foundation became a 'testing ground'[28] for policies suggested to the government and which adopted the premise that the presence of blacks in urban areas should be accepted as permanent, and that their quality of life should be improved through housing and the general upgrading of townships.[29] Between 1977 and 1983, the foundation spent some R17 million on 250 projects designed to improve black education, partly to communicate to disaffected black urbanites that 'capitalism' could deliver 'benefits'.[30] The foundation also targeted black workers with a view to incorporating them into institutional collective bargaining and thereby containing upheavals in the labour market.[31]

As with capital, the growing crisis in apartheid was forcing the realisation on the ruling elite that racial concessions were unavoidable. And, as was the case with capital, the NP was seeking a model that would allow it to cling to white minority domination. Since 1971, NP politicians had been in contact with US political scientist Arend Lijphart,[32] who advocated 'consociationalism' – power-sharing arrangements in heterogeneous societies where minorities felt threatened by majority rule.

The possibility of sharing power spurred the NP's search for acquiescent and conservative black partners, a search that dovetailed neatly with the corporate elite's obsession of finding a black bulwark against the black masses. Rising star PW Botha was ahead of the pack in this regard, as shown by the complete deracialisation of the armed forces by the end of the 1970s.

The labour reforms of the late 1970s were the NP's first substantial shift away from the ideology that had put it in power. Vorster's appointment of the Wiehahn and Riekert commissions demonstrated the shared concerns of party and capital. Through Oppenheimer, big business had long advocated the scrapping of those apartheid regulations that 'get in the way of the free enterprise system'.[33] Proposals by the Urban Foundation impacted strongly on the findings of the two commissions,[34] which flew in the face of accepted Verwoerdian doctrine.

The Wiehahn Commission recommended that black workers be allowed the right to organise themselves through trade unions, but within parameters set by the government, and that discriminatory regulations such as job reservation be scrapped in order to address the skills shortage. The Riekert Commission proposed that the government allow urban black people property rights and higher wages, and improve their housing and education. It also recommended the relaxation of influx control – a cornerstone of apartheid. At the same time, the commission suggested the tightening of control over black people without residential rights in 'white' South Africa through punishment with a substantial fine. The commission's primary proposals boiled down to dividing the black population into urban insiders and rural outsiders, with the latter to be contained in their 'homelands' through stricter measures.[35]

Laws were passed in 1979 to effect most of the recommendations made by the two commissions. These policies resonated with the Urban Foundation's plans, including the eventual abolition of influx control, a bugbear for business because of its constraining effects on labour flow.

The split of 1982

The commissions' proposals were regarded as revolutionary by the conservative flank of the NP. Nic Wiehahn even received death threats, and the reforms brought divisions within NP ranks into sharper relief.[36] Business expected Botha to push on with the reforms promised at the Carlton conference between business and the government. Representatives of ten major companies, led by Barlow Rand, presented a five-point reform plan to Botha. They warned him that 'if his compact with business was to be meaningful', the follow-up Good Hope conference between government and business held in 1981 had to go beyond regional development. They prodded the then premier towards reform, even in the face of resistance from the Treurnicht faction in the NP.[37] Treurnicht's ousting, which catapulted FW de Klerk into the powerful position of Transvaal NP leader, constituted the final unshackling of Afrikaner elite interests from those of the worker. The prelude to this was the party's support for the crushing of the 1978 strike by Afrikaner miners opposed to the lifting of job reservation.

At an NP caucus meeting in February 1982, Treurnicht delivered a prepared speech in which he rejected Botha's idea of power sharing as 'Prog policy' (referring to the opposition Progressive Federal Party).[38] He was supported by speakers who threatened to resign should the policy be adopted. Treurnicht's subsequent attempt to rally the powerful Transvaal NP behind him amounted to a battle for the soul of the party. The immediate issue that forced the clash between Treurnicht and Botha was the inclusion of coloured and Indian people in the cabinet. But the larger question was whether the NP would revert back to pure Verwoerd-style apartheid, regardless of the consequences for capital accumulation, or pursue the interests of the latter and adapt – or even discard – apartheid where it hindered capitalism. The majority of members in the mostly conservative Transvaal had come round to the latter position. Surgery was necessary to excise that element in the NP leadership that would place the narrow, ethnically defined interests of Afrikaners, including those in the vulnerable classes, above the interests of capital. Treurnicht's attempt to swing the Transvaal NP leadership against Botha failed, and he resigned from the cabinet in March 1982. Sixteen MPs followed him to what became the Conservative Party.

The outcome of this stand-off heralded the end of the cross-class alliance in Afrikanerdom that had been bound by racist laws. Henceforth, Afrikaner workers' interests would not trump economic interests. As Dan O'Meara describes it: 'The large, self-confident class of Afrikaner capitalists brought into being through NP policies was not likely to abandon either its economic power or its now affluent, materialistic lifestyle for mystic appeals to the unity of the *volk*. Like their English-speaking compatriots, Afrikaner businessmen and managers were now exclusively concerned with the bottom line ...'[39]

When De Klerk replaced Treurnicht as Transvaal leader, it marked the moment when the NP's 'conservative' and 'liberal' factions came together across the provincial divide that had always demarcated class interests. De Klerk was known as an unquestioning adherent to NP policy, a true-blue Nationalist. He was the last in a long line of politicians from a family that included the highly conservative JG Strijdom.

The fact that De Klerk, a Transvaal conservative, linked up with the liberal Cape faction of the party and became instrumental in the removal of Treurnicht and his supporters symbolised the final split between the NP elite and blue-collar Afrikaners. It was official: Afrikaner capital interests in the Transvaal had caught up with their capitalist brethren in the Cape and had cottoned on to what was at stake.

Quoting a 1986 survey, political scientist and historian Hermann Giliomee emphasises that the NP's support across classes was not that different from the CP's support base. However, the figures showed a significant difference. The NP's 20 per cent support among people in the upper-middle category of household income was double that of the CP and Jaap Marais' Herstigte Nasionale Party (10 per cent). The latter two parties enjoyed 6 per cent more support among the lower middle and lower classes (41 per cent as opposed to the NP's 35 per cent). Among the middle-income group, CP/HNP and NP support levels were the closest: 49 per cent as opposed to 45 per cent.[40] While the CP's appeal was not limited to the workers and *petit bourgeoisie* and drew votes from the middle class, its appeal at the apex of white society – particularly among the big-business elite – was noticeably less. In the 1983 referendum, the liberal and far-right parties appealed to only 30 per cent of the electorate. The bulk of the middle class was still voting in accordance with the NP's position, while the poorer white urban and rural classes voted predominantly in support of the CP's position.[41]

The expulsion of the Treurnichites was a historical watershed: the end of the Afrikaner nationalist alliance that had brought the NP to power. It marked the ascendance of the big-business elite and the property-owning class over the lower classes. The *verligtes* retained control of the party and the state – and, therefore, over the mechanisms through which patronage was dispensed. Afrikaner nationalism as a cross-class project ended in 1982, but since the ideology could still mobilise some Afrikaners and like-minded English-speaking people, it survived, albeit with reduced class representivity.

The Afrikaner nationalist split removed the final obstacles encumbering unity between the Afrikaner political and economic elites and the English-speaking economic elite. Gavin Relly, then chairperson of Anglo American, confirmed in 1985 that the government and big business had reached agreement on the 'motif of South African society: free enterprise'.[42] The rearrangement of the Afrikaner nationalist class base was required to firm up the new intra-white class alliances, which then paved the way for the co-option strategies of the 1980s and the eventual interracial elite pact of the early 1990s.

Bringing together the state, capital and the military

Capital's increasing pressure on the policy-makers had prompted even Botha's predecessor to admonish his brothers in Afrikaner capital to 'keep out of politics'.[43] Botha as prime minister openly invited warmer relations between government and business at the highest level. According to Barend du Plessis, finance minister between 1984 and 1992, Botha 'encouraged those of us [ministers] who were able to have sensible interactions with business leaders to actively pursue them'.[44]

Apart from the Broederbond, the Afrikaanse Handelsinstituut 'could move in on the National Party leadership and really plant some body blows', as then MP Leon Wessels puts it.[45] According to him, the influence of thinkers such as Huntington and Lijphart was channelled through the AHI and the Bond. Moreover, 'it is not far-fetched to say that the *verligte* movement had the support of major Afrikaner business people and capital. The late [NP fundraiser] Otto Krause ran a campaign and, together with a group of his friends, collected funds to support the election campaigns of *verligte* MPs who were under pressure.'[46]

Botha's rise to the top of the party hierarchy cemented a 'compact of power'[47] between the government, the security forces and capital, across language lines. As a Cape Nationalist, Botha represented the 'liberal' capitalist bloc in Afrikanerdom, characterised by private wealth, professional qualifications and big capital such as Sanlam and Rembrandt.[48] He was a director of Nasionale Pers and had a strong bureaucratic support base, something that had become decisive in NP leaders' ability to entrench power as the distance between them and the party rank and file grew. Botha was backed by the defence force, which he had served as minister for twelve years.

In that position, he had expressed the desire 'to unite business leaders behind the South African Defence Force'.[49] When the British refused to sell South Africa weapons at the end of the 1960s, a military-industrial complex was created in the form of Armscor, with directors drawn from the private sector. Sanlam's Fred du Plessis was one of them. Numerous private companies became dependent on arms contracts: 5 600 businesses employed some 70 000 people by the end of the 1970s.[50] In the process, 'business leaders and senior commanders had grown accustomed to working together, and clear agreement was emerging on the need for "reform" of apartheid to make it militarily defensible.[51]

Botha brought business and the military together by utilising the paradigm of a multidimensional 'total onslaught' necessitating a 'total strategy'. This entailed coordinated action in all fields, including the 'military, psychological, economic, political, sociological, technological, diplomatic, ideological, cultural, etc.',[52] as enunciated in the 1977 White Paper on Defence. The official goal of total strategy was to ensure 'a guarantee for the system of free enterprise'[53] and, signalling convergence with the ambitions of business, included the explicit aim of involving a stratum of black people as stakeholders and beneficiaries.[54]

Apartheid thinking was the basis of total strategy, encoded in phrases such as protection of minorities, self-determination, civilised norms and Christian values.

Under Botha, the government actively sought engagement with the corporate elite (as opposed to business associations),[55] resulting in the Carlton, Good Hope and Bryntirion conferences of 1979, 1981 and 1986 respectively. At the Carlton conference, Botha emphasised how state and capital fitted together: 'The basic responsibility of government is to establish, maintain and protect the national and international order within which private enterprise can fulfil its functions of producing goods and services.'[56] At the first two gatherings, a politicisation of the corporate sector occurred with its institutionalisation as policy- and decision-maker.[57]

Between the Carlton and the Good Hope conferences, capital pressured the government to accelerate reform and presented policy proposals to this end. Extending his tradition of accessing advice from big business through his defence advisory council, Botha opened the executive arm to appointments from the corporate sector and the military, thus creating a triangle of military, corporate and governmental power at the highest level of the state. Members of the business community continued to serve on the defence advisory council when Magnus Malan replaced Botha as minister of defence.

The Botha reformists were able to put an end to the paralysis that had set in under Vorster because they were willing to be flexible about sacred apartheid principles. This was essential if new black allies were to be found. Broederbond chairperson Gerrit Viljoen, later tasked by FW de Klerk with finding constitutional alternatives, expressed it thus: '[P]ractical experience has taught us that many of our statutory bastions – particularly those that discriminate to our advantage at the expense of other population groups – actually create more perils and problems than they solve. Where excessive self-defence is to the detriment of others or violates their human dignity, it spawns a crop of bitterness and division that may create worse enemies for us at home than any that threaten us from abroad.'[58] The Botha government therefore removed those apartheid controls that were not essential for continued white domination and repealed the following laws and policies: statutory job reservation for whites (1981, phased out in the mining industry by 1987); the concept of urban blacks as temporary sojourners; influx control (1986); and the thirty-year-old preservation of the Cape province for coloured labour (1986). By 1986, the 'immorality' legislation that prohibited sex between people of different races, as well as race restrictions in immigration law, were also scrapped.

Botha's government also recognised the right of blacks to own immovable property, converted ninety-nine-year leaseholds to full ownership, and introduced uniform tax laws for black and white. In addition, Botha denounced the Separate Amenities Act of 1953 (the basis of petty apartheid), though it was only repealed in 1990. Towards the end of his tenure, he released political prisoners, including Govan Mbeki.

Moscow's 'stepping stone to world conquest'[59]

Botha's policies were based on theories expounded by French Cold War strategist General André Beaufre, Arend Lijphart and US conservative theorist Samuel Huntington.[60] The most influential of the three was Beaufre, whose counter-revolutionary conceptualisation of a 'total strategy' to meet a 'total onslaught' was the result of his experience in the French suppression of the anti-colonial struggle in Algeria. In true Cold War parlance, Beaufre posited that the Soviet Union and its surrogates were leading a total onslaught against Western Christian civilisation, a theory influential in US military circles and colleges where SADF chief Magnus Malan had studied.[61]

Botha also borrowed ideas from US Cold War theorists and picked up tactics from the Portuguese and Rhodesian forces operating in Mozambique, Angola and Rhodesia. South African military officer Jannie Geldenhuys (who later became chief of the army and then of the SADF) was appointed vice consul in Luanda to study the Angolan civil war, while others were seconded to Portugal's regional military headquarters in Africa.

Botha and his allies in government and the SADF went to great lengths to propagate the total onslaught version of what was happening in the world and in the country. During the 1970s, the SADF actively promoted total onslaught theories among all state functionaries, military and non-military, through lectures and courses.[62]

Botha's efforts to link the government's suppression of democracy with the ideological contest between the US and the Soviet Union began in the 1960s. In his world view, South Africa was part of the capitalist West under threat by communist expansion. South Africa had to prevent the disruption of its supply of minerals to Europe, which, in Botha's mind, the Soviets sought to do. The Cape sea route also had to be safeguarded. Even Britain disagreed with Botha's understanding, as shown by its refusal to sell maritime armaments to South Africa in 1967.[63]

Botha was sorely disappointed by what he regarded as 'a paralysis in the mind of the West to acknowledge the importance of South Africa'.[64] His sense of abandonment by the West was so profound that at one point he even hinted at forging an alliance with the communist bloc.[65] For Botha's NP, the South African state bore the light of Christian civilisation in darkest Africa, which was harbouring the terrorist and communist ANC enemy. Botha argued that 'there is an attempt, under Marxist leadership, to bring about revolution in southern Africa, more specifically in the Republic of South Africa. This can no longer be denied. The revolutionary elements are there, and nothing … can satisfy the hunger of those powers. They want nothing but the overthrow of the present order. They want nothing but the overthrow of civilisation in this country.'[66]

Embracing total onslaught theories made sense in more than one way, especially as a counter to the ANC strategy of the time. In 1978, senior ANC and MK members undertook a study tour to Vietnam, where they were briefed by a strategist who had devised victories over French colonial and US forces. This led to the production of *The Green Book* in 1979, which proposed combining an increase in armed attacks with mass organisation, interlinked by a fortified underground movement.

The ANC's focus remained on the military component of the strategy, and from 1978 onwards MK launched a number of attacks, including successful sabotage operations against Sasol in the early 1980s.[67] The most symbolic of attacks in the minds of white South Africans was the Church Street bomb on 20 May 1983 in front of the Air Force headquarters in Pretoria.[68] Civilians were counted among the nineteen fatalities.

Botha created the National Security Management System (NSMS) in response, and further strengthened the role of the State Security Council (SSC), a cabinet committee created in the early 1970s. But the total onslaught theory was created at least a decade before the ANC explicitly sought insight into anti-colonial revolutionary warfare. With such theories, a powerful, well-organised enemy with designs on world domination could be conjured up for supporters instead of the real ANC, under-capacitated and dogged by rivalries among people experiencing the multifarious tensions of life in exile.

What the Cold War theories did was provide the necessary ideological justification to defend apartheid. The total onslaught idea gave the conservative regimes of Thatcher in the UK, Reagan in the US and Kohl in Germany the rationale to support white rule in South Africa. It justified military deployment in the region to destabilise newly independent states that opposed apartheid, and it justified the stepping up of security action inside South Africa. These actions came at great human cost.

Ultimately, what was presented as a struggle against communism fitted neatly with repression of legitimate pressure for democratisation. By clothing repression in the language of a battle against the *rooi gevaar* (red peril), black resistance against apartheid iniquity was, as in the 1950s and 1960s, expediently reinterpreted as communism and terrorism. *Rooi gevaar* and *swart gevaar* (black peril) became the watchwords that obscured the legitimate demands of blacks for basic rights as citizens. Conveniently, they also allowed calls for sanctions and Mandela's release to be dubbed further examples of a total onslaught.

The NP's constituency eagerly imbibed these rationalisations of white domination, compounding white paranoia and the collective siege mentality. Afrikaner public discourses of the time displayed a pitiful lack of insight, bolstered by oscillating expressions of obstinacy, smugness and mass victimhood. The pretence at normality continued, as captured by Koos Kombuis in his song 'Swart September' (Black September), quoted at the opening of the chapter.

Executive lawlessness

Not least because of the atmosphere of fear and loathing created through total onslaught rhetoric, Botha was able to centralise power to an unprecedented degree. While NP politicians exulted South Africa's 'democracy' as the prize that the 'terrorists' were after, as Malan did in the quotation on page 109, the government was the very force eroding that truncated democracy even further. As law professor Laurence Boulle put it in 1994: NP rule had been marked by 'successive rampant executives cast[ing] aside rule of law imperatives as they ... made their powers more intrusive and more discretionary, and less responsible and less accountable'.[69] Botha took this to a new level of 'executive lawlessness'.[70]

He restructured the executive extensively, reducing the number of state departments from forty to twenty-two, while increasing the size of the cabinet to twenty members and setting up a full-time secretariat to serve the cabinet. The office of the prime minister was enlarged to ostensibly improve leadership, policy coordination and governance. Neo-liberal prescriptions of technocratic rather than 'ideological' solutions helped Botha to remove the few weak constitutional obstacles that still stood in the way of non-accountable white rule.

Starting with derogation of the coloured vote in the 1950s, the executive had steadily eroded parliamentary review. Even the NP caucus had little influence on executive decisions. This process of centralising power was pursued most forcefully under Botha. He dismantled the senate in 1980 and created in its place the president's council, a de facto 'extension of the prime ministerial office'[71] with advisory and legislative powers. The council was a typical Botha-esque variation on consociational elite pacting and included Indian and coloured members. It was assigned the task of making recommendations for a new constitutional dispensation, which led to the drafting of the 1983 constitution. It allowed Botha to draw in not only political representatives, but also businessmen and academics.

With his domineering personality and technocratic sensibility, Botha ensured that the new constitution revolved around him. The position of executive state president was created separate from parliament, and Botha resigned as an MP. As a result, the president was not accountable to any one of the houses of parliament. The president had the power to dissolve parliament, but, in the event of misconduct or inability to fulfil his duties, he could be removed from office only by the electoral college – which included white, Indian and coloured representatives – and not by parliament. In this way, an extra institutional hurdle was created between the president and the limited democratic system of the time – an additional obstacle to presidential accountability to even the handful of citizens who had the vote.

In what was, for South Africa, an unprecedented rendering of the head of government as the 'personification of the state',[72] the ceremonial and symbolic role of the state president under the 1961 constitution was incorporated into the executive functions. As political scientist Annette Seegers observes, the old post of prime minister 'acquired new powers of a symbolic and personalised nature' not drawn from the role of leader of the majority white party.[73]

While the racial composition of the national assembly ensured that the president would always be the leader of the dominant white party, he could broaden his political base by appointing people from other parties – and even from outside parliament – to cabinet. Thus the president had the prerogative to appoint people to cabinet without any demonstrable (white, coloured or Indian) support – another crack in the veneer of the whites-only 'democracy'. The president also appointed members of the race-based ministers' councils. Ministers appointed by presidential fiat had a twelve-month period in which to gain a seat, but why would one subject oneself to election if the head of state could also nominate people to become MPs, as became the case in terms of the changes Botha wrought?

The president also managed the levers of state control over the lives of black people through local authorities and regional services councils. His power to decide what comprised 'general' and 'own' affairs meant that parliamentary oversight could be bypassed in case of opposition to a particular law. The president could also refer controversial legislation to the president's council for approval. It didn't take Botha long to use this avenue: when approval of secret funds for the police was held up by the tricameral parliament, he sought and got it from the president's council.[74] In another example, the houses of delegates and representatives in 1988 obstructed the passing of laws on land, which included an amendment to the Group Areas Act. Botha reclassified the bills as 'own affairs' so as to have the white assembly adopt them, but when this, too, was unsuccessful, some of the bills were referred to the president's council, which duly passed them.[75]

Ultimately, the 1983 constitution was drafted to fulfil the political aims of the NP, despite the appearance of consultation and scholasticism.[76] In a 1986 interview, FW de Klerk encapsulated the government's attitude towards constitutional reform: 'The National Party, being the majority party at this point in time, is the "owner", in legal terms, of the house … [I]t says: "I want to build rooms onto this house. I want to accommodate you. Come and talk to us and tell us how we can do it."'[77] The illegitimacy of the NP's claim to ownership of the state would only dawn on the powers that be during the multiparty negotiations six years later.

One remedy against a recurrence of the Information Scandal, or Muldergate, was the ostensible institution of legally enforced audits of state spending. However, a plethora of laws during the 1980s placed secret departmental funds beyond the scrutiny of both the Auditor-General and parliament. Under Botha, 'the executive acquired [for the first time] the legal means of playing with public funds with impunity'.[78] Ministers were still able to block the auditing of some or all files. This continued up to at least the 1994 election, as the Auditor-General included an explicit proviso in his 1991/2 and subsequent reports to parliament that auditing pertained to financial authorisation, and not to 'the penal nature' or 'moral reprehensibility' of the actions.[79]

From 1996, evidence emerged before the Truth and Reconciliation Commission (TRC) of hundreds of secret projects involving billions of rand, even in the department of arts, culture, science and technology. The National Intelligence Agency alone reported 749 projects, with another 417 being disclosed by the foreign affairs department. In all, R2.75 billion in secret funds was spent by state departments between 1978 and 1994. This excludes R48.6 billion that passed through the SADF's special defence account, and a further R586.5 million spent on SADF 'sensitive line function projects' between 1974 and 1995.[80]

Indirect rule the Botha way

Democratisation was never the goal of the Botha regime's reforms in the 1980s. Rather, they represented another step in the evolution of indirect rule, the colonial system of co-optation and control perfected by the British and attempted by the Afrikaners in the Verwoerdian 'homeland' system.[81] Botha came up with a set of policies that constantly mutated as the reformers adapted them in their search for a neo-colonial version of indirect rule that still maintained white domination. This model involved the positioning of compliant black middle classes as a bulwark against the white nightmare of black people seeking rights. Botha's vision was of unelected regional and elected local structures. The quest was thus to find suitably pliable black leadership to attach to the white oligarchy, in the hope that this superficial compromise would breathe life into the status quo.

The ANC, with its nationalist cross-tribal character and demand for ordinary majority democracy, did not fit the bill. The NP was insisting on subdivision into tribes, as that would give whites, one of the largest 'tribes', more bargaining power numerically. This insistence was born of the desire to hold on to power. After all, polls conducted by the parastatal SA Communication Service from 1986 onwards indicated that the ANC would garner 60 per cent of the vote, as opposed to the NP's 19 to 23 per cent.[82] Despite this, in a typical NP refrain of the time, De Klerk stated in a 1986 interview that the banned organisations were a 'vociferous minority ... threatening and intimidating the silent majority and the leaders of the silent majority'.[83]

Botha had accepted Beaufre's thesis that counter-revolutionary strategy was 20 per cent military and 80 per cent political. On the one hand, black people had to be convinced of the desirability of Lijphartian power sharing while, on the other, the revolutionary onslaught would be met with violent force. Hence, Botha's total strategy had a dual dimension that was reflected throughout his eleven-year reign. He and Magnus Malan embraced Beaufre's theory of winning hearts and minds (WHAM) as part of the soft dimension of total strategy, entailing expanded welfare initiatives that corresponded to security objectives. In line with the Urban Foundation's proposals, the state launched concerted efforts to upgrade housing and infrastructure, especially in 'trouble spots'. Coordination between the SSC and state departments enabled such programmes, but they were overshadowed by the oppressive aspects of total strategy.

The Bantustans had provided the first example of NP-style indirect rule, as conceptualised by Verwoerd. In return for tribute, Bantustan leaders in cramped territories would contain those black people who were superfluous to 'white' South Africa's needs. This was presented as 'self-government' through which blacks would be able to express their citizenship and develop their 'nationhood', a fabrication much vaunted in NP rhetoric and readily believed by followers. As unease about apartheid grew among some Afrikaners in the 1970s, the homelands fallacy served to soothe consciences over the socio-economic ills under which black South Africans were so obviously toiling.

In the consociational line of thinking, the reformers planned to bring together multi-level, ethnic-based political structures with mechanisms to prevent majority domination. Botha was considering new race-based geographical entities, as he had become doubtful about the homelands. While Transkei, Bophuthatswana, Venda and Ciskei had all accepted independence by the end of 1981, the scheme had become an international embarrassment. No foreign power acknowledged these 'nation-states', their administrations were riddled with incompetence and corruption, and they continued to suckle on the central fiscus.

Botha revived Verwoerd's idea of creating a constellation of southern African states, including the homelands. But in Botha's case, this was an acknowledgement – at last – that the homelands could not survive on their own. The hope was that the constellation would improve the economic viability of the homelands by incorporating them into four cross-border economic development regions, which would be run by multiracial regional services councils. In 1986, provincial councils were scrapped and replaced by executive committees that would deal with 'general affairs', but not be elected democratically.[84]

The government intensified efforts to create an acceptable class of conservative black leaders. In the mid-1980s, the NP broadened the participatory possibilities for black leaders by inviting them onto the president's council and proposing a statutory council under the president's chairpersonship with representation from homeland leaders, 'other' black leaders and the cabinet.

This thinking also underpinned the centrepiece of Botha's version of indirect rule: the tricameral parliament. The status of coloured people had suddenly become of greater concern, especially to *verligtes*, in the 1970s. On the surface, this rethink was based on the commonalities between coloureds and Afrikaners, of which language and religion were the most prominent. But it also coincided with the rise of the Black Consciousness Movement, which re-conceptualised black identity and increasingly attracted the discontented coloured youth. Afrikaner intellectuals expressed alarm at the prospect of chasing coloured people into the arms of the black majority. Such an outcome would militate against the divide-and-rule idea of racial buffers, ethnic determinism and the prevention of racial alliances. New plans at local and national government level were required.

Along with the executive presidency, the tricameral parliament was created through the 1983 constitution. It was presented in NP information pamphlets as 'the solution that our country has so long been waiting for!'[85] Indians and coloureds received political representation in a system which ensured that whites still had the majority say, even though they were an ever-decreasing national minority. In this way, coloured and Indian elites would be co-opted into the system on the white rulers' terms.

Parliament consisted of three uniracial chambers, members being elected along racial lines. The cabinet was drawn from all three chambers, and was responsible for 'general' affairs such as defence, security, the economy, foreign policy and all matters related to blacks. Uniracial ministers' councils presided over 'own' affairs, such as education and local government. The executive state president, elected by a multiracial college, appointed the cabinet. In all these structures, whites outnumbered Indian and coloured members – justified as a reflection of demographic reality.

Botha selected one Indian and one coloured member to cabinet, but without assigning them portfolios,[86] demonstrating the bogus nature of these new structures. The new powers amounted to little more than political posturing. White vetoes were built into the institutional arrangements for regional, local or group autonomy, making a mockery thereof.[87] This not only translated into continuing white rule, but also into entrenchment of NP dominance.

Following further fragmentation of the UP in the mid-1970s, more members swelled the PP's ranks and, in 1977, it reorganised itself as the Progressive Federal Party, with twenty-four seats. Under a new leader, the young Afrikaner Frederik van Zyl Slabbert, the party increased its support to 19 per cent of the whites-only vote – translating into some 250 000 votes for a negotiated settlement between black and white, the PFP's stated policy at the time.[88]

The black urban 'sojourner'

Under Botha, the NP re-evaluated its stance on the eternal conundrum of black people inside 'white' South Africa. Government calculations in the 1980s found that some 50 per cent of the black population lived in the homelands; some 20 per cent in white rural areas; 20 per cent in townships dominated by a tribe with links to the homelands; and the remaining 10 per cent in tribally mixed townships such as Soweto. Botha made a notable leap by accepting what the NP had been in denial over since 1948, when the UP's Fagan Commission found that black people were a permanent feature of white urban areas – a fact that had to be managed. The NP had dismissed Fagan's findings, only to find apartheid planning haunted by black urbanisation.

The 1976 uprising and ensuing violence throughout 1977 had forced Botha to become the NP leader who would accept the reality that could not be wished away. His response was to accommodate black leadership at local government level, but with a view to using 'the local arena as a training ground for collaborative political leadership'.[89] This went hand in hand with the state's fiscal withdrawal at local level and its promotion of the privatisation of services, thereby shifting the burden of social reproduction onto the predominantly working class, as per neo-liberal dictates.

The next ten years saw a bewildering array of local institutions coming and going as the government tried and discarded various models aimed at containing black political aspirations. In 1977, community councils were created – a new tier of black municipal officials 'to absorb and defuse discontent'.[90] These elected councillors apparently had the power to make decisions about housing and services that would be executed by white officials at the controversial Bantu Affairs Administration Boards. In reality, everything from conditions of employment to operational matters was determined by the relevant minister, while the BAABs still made most decisions on housing and services. Significantly, the BAABs did not relinquish their power over the crucial policies of influx control and labour allocation.

The councils soon ran into financial crisis. The state's beer monopoly in the townships was a primary source of revenue, but was due to be forfeited because of privatisation. Long-standing restrictions on black business and trading rights had been lifted by the late 1970s, but not enough time had passed for the changes to contribute substantially to council tax bases. The councils attempted to phase out subsidies and recoup actual costs, which sparked widespread discontent. By 1980, the 224 community councils faced mass rejection. Elections had to be postponed twice, the polls were low and councillors were regarded as corrupt sell-outs.[91]

The 1982 Black Local Authorities Act was passed, with the official hope that 'these local authorities will serve to defuse pent-up frustrations and grievances against administration from Pretoria', as expressed by PJ Riekert of commission fame.[92] Power was devolved to allow greater urban autonomy through municipal elections and control over security and health services. Another law was passed to reinvent the BAABs as 'development boards', which were later incorporated into black local authorities.

Elections in November and December 1983 for the 'improved' councils delivered even lower turnouts: 21 per cent, compared to 30 per cent in 1978.[93] All the while, violence continued, as 'bomb attacks on councillors, death threats and court cases alleging fraud, murder, theft and assault punctuated the business of councils'.[94] To counter mounting resistance, the government created paramilitary forces in accordance with the Black Local Authorities Act.

By 1984, the government was again changing tack: the objective now was 'to depoliticise local government through the creation of a series of technical management bodies controlling the provision of essential local services'.[95] The Regional Services Councils Act of 1986 would create structures that provided services at local level, but separated decision-making according to the 'general/own affairs' distinction. Voting shares were based on the proportion of revenue that local authorities paid for services, ensuring the dominance of white areas.[96]

The Local Government Bodies Franchise Act of 1984 standardised voting criteria across the races, but entrenched separate voters' rolls. The voting powers of property owners were enhanced – black people regained the right to own freehold property in townships in 1985. By that time, a new model for 'cooperative coexistence' had been proposed, incorporating an assembly for urban black own affairs linked to the tricameral parliament and the Bantustans in a supra-parliamentary structure.

These reforms merely added fuel to the fire, and boycotts of rent and electricity fees converged with struggles around education, unemployment, price increases and a rejection of the tricameral dispensation. The 1986 repeal of another cornerstone of apartheid, influx control, to be replaced by 'orderly urbanisation' and the creation of 'grey' central business districts, failed to stem the nationwide unrest. Representative black local authorities held elections in 1988 in which a low 26 per cent of registered voters participated.

Botha's ally, constitutional affairs minister Chris Heunis, managed the new multiracial constitutional institutions. His department controlled a plethora of organisations, including the council for the coordination of local government affairs, which governed local authorities and regional services councils; regional development advisory committees set up to advise on economic development priorities in the economic development regions; and multilateral coordinating bodies, which liaised with the Bantustans.[97]

Under Botha, the NP finally moved away from the compartmentalisation of 'black affairs' in one state department, as had been the case since 1948. Instead, labour bureaus were moved to the department of manpower, while – ludicrously – 'relations' with the Bantustans became the purview of the department of foreign affairs. The substandard education of black children fell under a new department of education and training, in line with the 'own affairs' approach.

To prevent black solidarity, different arrangements were made for coloureds and Indians at local government level. A mere decade after coloureds were finally robbed of their last remaining voting rights at municipal level (in 1971 in the Cape), the NP government was backtracking. Existing local committees enjoyed no legitimacy, partly because their powers were limited to an advisory function, and partly because all popular representation had been suppressed. Services had been neglected and the committees did not receive adequate financing.

These committees were attached to white local authorities that were disinterested in cooperation, further hindering attainment of the goal of autonomy that the NP government had supposedly set in a 1962 amendment to the Group Areas Act.[98] The 1976 uprising caused the NP to revisit its plans and, after a series of commissions and a president's council report, it was proposed that overarching metropolitan structures be created to enable universal franchise for whites, coloureds and Indians at local level, with a bias towards property owners. The broader fiscal base of such structures was aimed at addressing the socio-economic crises in coloured and Indian areas.[99]

The growing international outcry nudged the NP towards finding a moral basis for its racial policies. This had started with the attempt under Verwoerd to move away from the universally repugnant term, apartheid, and replace it with 'separate development'. The NP was at pains to present the homeland scheme as the only humane policy towards the real fulfilment of 'Bantu rule by the Bantu for the Bantu according to the ways of the Bantu'.

These moral protestations were belied by the overriding theme of under-commitment. Not enough land was made available to ensure the viability of the homelands, nor were enough funds allocated to make black, coloured or Indian local councils feasible. And although the lack of capacity in black, coloured and Indian local government was known, it remained unattended.

The white 'parent' authorities were unwilling to provide the necessary support to make the new schemes work. Part of the reason was continuing racist attitudes, but it all came down to the underlying problem: even such limited reforms remained half-hearted, because the real intent was to sustain white domination. And black people knew that, as the insurrection showed.

Resistance ignited

The NP's efforts at addressing the bane of Verwoerdian planning – the urban black inhabitant – by extending labour rights to black trade unions and local government representation to community leaders were thwarted. Similarly, attempts to position a coloured and Indian buffer of co-opted leaders had floundered. Instead of submission, the reforms precipitated a groundswell of resistance – as Huntington had predicted they would.

Protest was first enunciated through peaceful means. Black, Indian and coloured voters stayed away from the polls. Franchise at local government level was correctly perceived as a consolation prize for black exclusion from the tricameral parliament. Support from those directly 'benefiting' from the new-fangled dispensation was not much better. While 61 per cent of coloured adults and 57 per cent of Indian adults registered to vote, only 30 per cent of the former and 20 per cent of the latter cast their ballots in the first election under the new constitution.[100]

The reforms went hand in hand with repressive legislative measures, such as the introduction of preventive detention in the aftermath of the 1976 uprising. In 1982, the Internal Security Act was amended to provide for indefinite detention. People could be held for indeterminate periods while being interrogated and held in solitary confinement. Detention orders could not be overturned by the courts, but magistrates could extend the fourteen-day 'preventive detention' of someone regarded as a threat to public safety, regardless of how low-ranking the arresting officer. Suspects held under Section 29 of the Act were subjected to torture.[101]

Boycotting elections was merely the beginning. August 1984 marked the start of mass-based and widespread civil resistance, one of the factors that eventually drove home to the white elite that Botha-esque apartheid was *also* unsustainable. The United Democratic Front (UDF) was formed, comprising 575 community, church, women's and youth organisations and trade unions, with the single aim of ending apartheid.

The UDF organised demonstrations against the tricameral parliament, which dovetailed with rent boycotts and protests against electricity price hikes. These attempts by financially strained black community councils to improve their primary source of income added insult to the injury of co-opted black councillors. Bus companies suffered boycotts against higher fares. Every town and homeland was affected as resistance spread across the country. Black fury had grown beyond the NP's imagination. In flare-ups in the Vaal Triangle, councillors who were regarded as sell-outs were killed. By the end of 1984, official figures put the death toll at 175, sabotage attacks against state departments at 58 and attacks on police at 26.[102] The following year saw unprecedented levels of civilian unrest, ranging from strikes to school boycotts and attacks on government collaborators. Workdays lost to strikes increased exponentially, from 680 000 in 1985 to about six million in 1987.[103]

A securocracy to die for

As the limited version of Lijphartian reforms and the WHAM dimension of total strategy failed, security grew to be the dominant aspect of the Botha era.

Beaufre's theories slotted in well with those of Huntington on how reformers could outmanoeuvre revolutionaries. In the early 1980s, Huntington had told a conference in South Africa that reforms would have to be timed in such a way that new constituencies were brought on board without alienating old ones.[104] This resonated with Lijphart's views. Huntington also predicted that reform would raise expectations and therefore unleash political activism and violence. The government would thus have to exert more control – even if this amounted to 'enlightened despotism' or authoritarianism.[105]

The moribund SSC, reactivated by Botha and Magnus Malan, was the structure that could fulfil this function. With parliamentary oversight already fatally compromised, even the cabinet was sidelined as the SSC became the pivot of Botha's securocracy, deciding vital issues such as the need to declare a national state of emergency in 1985. The experience gained over the following twelve months prompted the securocrats to refine the system to meet the heightened levels of resistance.

The SSC comprised a working committee and full-time secretariat and presided over eleven joint management centres (JMCs) at regional level, sixty sub-JMCs at district level, and some 448 subcommittees or mini-JMCs at local level. Reflecting Beaufre's dual approach, the state's security strategy was synchronised with other, 'softer' functions. This was done by connecting the NSMS to state departments through another two sets of committees divided according to departmental portfolios and issues (information; the security forces; political, economic and social; strategic communication). The results manifested in a national joint management system encompassing the entire state apparatus.

With the SSC chaired by the president at its pinnacle, the NSMS further entrenched the power vested in the office of the executive state president through the 1983 constitution. In theory, a line of command existed from the president down to community level. Annette Seegers commented that under the SSC, 'a de facto pattern of decision-making emerged which undercut the real influence of the cabinet ... Belief in an onslaught against South Africa encouraged militaristic measures about which the military personnel of the SSC had the best advice and plans. Even if this belief was not shared by top politicians, [Botha] was an ardent believer ... Under his leadership, deliberations of the SSC generated a decision-making momentum that was hard for the cabinet to stop ... The NSMS took powers of presidential executive discretion to previously unknown heights.'[106]

Leon Wessels,[107] who served as deputy minister of law and order from the mid-1980s until 1991, confirmed that it had been difficult for the cabinet to overturn decisions taken at SSC meetings. The ministers in charge of the security forces would indicate that they had information which necessitated certain action. They would frequently not reveal the nature of such information, according to Wessels, which rendered ministers in charge of non-security portfolios impotent to challenge decisions taken at SSC meetings that preceded those of the cabinet. Botha held so much sway over decisions that when he agreed with an SSC decision, it was impossible to amend.

Wessels cited the bombing of Khotso House and COSATU House as examples. Law and order minister Adriaan Vlok did not propose such a resolution to the SSC, but was requested by Botha himself to undertake the operation. Botha received information from his trusted military advisors, made decisions and gave orders. He was the proverbial spider at the centre of the web – the one who knew more than anyone what was happening, where and who was involved.

His trust in the military appears to have been absolute, as was his belief that pro-democratic resistance was in fact the work of a few instigators acting in the service of communist masters. This justification had been integral to NP propaganda since the 1940s and was still being plied by the 1980s, as seen in the following quotation from a Standard 7 textbook aimed at fifteen-year-olds and used in Christian National Education in 1984: 'Even before the start of the Malan administration, communist agitators had begun inciting dissatisfaction among the Non-Whites.... A legal ban on communism did not mean that the danger disappeared, however. It was merely driven underground and continued to undermine, particularly by making use of the "African National Congress" (ANC).'[108] By 1989, Botha noted with apparent surprise that his '[military] campaign' had not resolved the security crisis. He relied on the security forces to provide solutions and allowed the military to influence him. It seems he became increasingly convinced that the militarist option would deliver the security needed to perpetuate white domination, departing from the dictum of a 20 per cent military and 80 per cent political solution. The influence of the securocrats came to an end only after FW de Klerk became president.

With parliament having long since been turned into a rubber stamp, the SSC's emasculation of the cabinet was the latest step in the NP's dilution of oversight and accountability. Continuing the trend that had started under Vorster, bureaucratic power was strengthened even more. The 1985 adjustments to the NSMS put 'wide discretionary powers'[109] in the hands of public officials, unaccountable to the oligarchic electorate and their parliamentary representatives. In the process, the state became an interest group in its own right, creating its own alliances and suppressing or mobilising other interest groups, thereby ceasing to be a neutral arbiter.[110]

The TRC later heard from one Major General Griebenauw of the security police how the securocracy worked in practice.

> During my term in office in Cape Town, extreme pressure was placed by the Joint Security Management System on the security branch, in particular to stem the tide of murder and violence. And obviously I gave members under my command instructions to do everything in their power to apprehend people who were guilty of these things and to extract as much information as possible from the detainees ... I was ... very much aware that the members' success could be ascribed to the use of unconventional questioning or interrogation methods. It would have been naïve for me to believe that they would extract information in any other way from a well-trained terrorist and to do so quite quickly ...[111]

Other former security force members told the TRC that Botha and the two other pivotal members of the SSC, Malan and Vlok, had visited the Eastern Cape in 1985 to instruct them that 'the area had to be stabilised at all costs and that they had to do whatever was required to achieve this – no holds barred'.[112] According to Port Elizabeth security branch member Harold Snyman, 'pressure was exercised from the government's side to act in a drastic way to neutralise activists and to help the security situation to normalise'.[113] Shortly afterwards the so-called Pebco Three – Sipho Hashe, Champion Galela and Qaqawuli Godolozi of the UDF affiliate, Port Elizabeth Black Civic Organisation – were murdered on 11 May 1985. Several Port Elizabeth security branch members, including Gideon Nieuwoudt, applied for amnesty for these killings. The operation was carried out with assistance from askaris – activists who had been 'turned' – from the police hit squad at Vlakplaas near Pretoria.

Within six weeks, the so-called Cradock Four – UDF activists Matthew Goniwe, Sparrow Mkhonto, Fort Calata and Sicelo Mhlawuli – were abducted and murdered on 27 June. At the time, in terms of a covert plan devised by the SSC's strategic communications branch,[114] it was publicly declared that their deaths were the result of conflict between the Azanian People's Organisation (AZAPO) and the UDF.

On 15 October, the highly publicised Trojan Horse killings took place in Athlone, Cape Town. Police officers hiding behind crates on an unmarked truck shot three children dead exactly one day after an SSC meeting with local security forces called by Vlok.

In 1993 the inquest into the deaths of the Cradock Four was reopened, following the emergence of a message from the SADF's Eastern Cape command to the SSC secretariat, recommending Goniwe's 'permanent removal from society'. The judge found prima facie evidence that members of the security forces had killed the Cradock Four. Yet again, there was a link to Vlakplaas, confirmed when the unit's former commander, Eugene de Kock, sought amnesty for his knowledge of the killings.

The murders of Florence and Fabian Ribeiro in Mamelodi were another example of the SADF working in tandem with the police. It was alleged at the TRC that General Jannie Geldenhuys, chief of the defence force, had instructed Major General Joep Joubert, the officer commanding the SADF special forces, to identify 'hot spots' that demanded such collaboration. Geldenhuys admitted to the TRC that he had been informed about the Ribeiro killings, but took no steps towards prosecuting those responsible.[115]

The economy at the Rubicon
South Africa's political prospects became bleaker than ever after Botha's in-famous Rubicon speech on 15 August 1985 at the Natal NP congress. Foreign

affairs minister Pik Botha had drafted a paragraph for the speech, announcing Nelson Mandela's release, and alerted the international community to a momentous statement. All eyes and ears were on South Africa, but at the crucial moment PW's inner white supremacist got the better of him. He excised the reference to Mandela's release and, harking back to the laager, regurgitated the rhetoric of white fear. While he made a noteworthy admission that black people in urban 'white South Africa' would have to be accommodated, this was overshadowed by apocalyptic visions and promises that he would not lead his people 'to abdication and suicide'.[116] He denied that a relationship of domination existed between whites and blacks, and emphasised the hoary old NP myth that South Africa was a country of minorities, where political rights had to be exercised as groups rather than individuals. Indeed, Botha exhibited the hardy NP trait of purporting to know best when it came to black aspirations. He assured his audience that black leaders and 'most reasonable South Africans' were opposed to a system of 'one man-one vote in a unitary system'.

According to Leon Wessels, PW Botha believed that he alone would define the Rubicon that white South Africans had to cross. For him, such crossing would be about winning the indulgence of the international community and the business sector through policy decisions, as well as taking on and defeating the ANC as the NP's primary opponent. But in reality, says Wessels, the NP had to confront the quandary of normalising a political situation in which a significant number of people who were accepted as 'role-players' by the majority of the population were banned, imprisoned or exiled.[117]

In the second half of the 1980s, Botha's decision-making became mercurial. In 1986, he instructed then finance minister Barend du Plessis to inform British prime minister Margaret Thatcher that he did indeed intend releasing Mandela, but he wanted this to be seen as a result of pressure applied by 'constructive South Africans' such as Mangosuthu Buthelezi rather than the international community. Would she and her cabinet ministers thus please desist from calling for Mandela to be freed? Thatcher agreed, but Sir Geoffrey Howe, British foreign secretary, commented that it was not a very practical request, given the pressure building in civil society in the West for Mandela's release.

The Rubicon speech exacerbated an existing economic crisis. In the wake of the Soweto uprising, the South African economy suffered a net outflow of capital, which turned briefly between 1981 and 1984 on the back of a surge in the gold price and international lenders seeking markets in the midst of debt crises in Mexico, Argentina and other developing countries. The higher gold price proved temporary, however, and after Botha's speech capital outflow continued with a vengeance.

According to Barend du Plessis, South Africa had 'a war economy, a siege economy. There was an international capital war against us.'[118] Capital flight persisted until 1994, peaking at 3.4 per cent of gross domestic product between 1985 and 1988.[119] Du Plessis recalled being telephoned the morning after Botha's address with news that anti-apartheid lobbying had finally led the major US bank, Chase Manhattan, to withhold further loans and to demand payment of outstanding debt as it fell due.[120] Other international banks followed, forcing Pretoria into a debt standstill until March 1986 and an intricate renegotiation of repayment terms.

Available reserves, together with the expected foreign trade surplus for 1985, stood at less than $5 billion, while total net foreign debt amounted to $16.5 billion. The straw that threatened to break the camel's back was that 67 per cent of these debts were due for settlement within twelve months.[121] The rand lost a third of its value within a week after Botha's speech.

In 1985 and 1986, trade sanctions were imposed against South Africa by the US Congress, the European Community, the Commonwealth, the United Kingdom and other governments. In all, 120 US companies had pulled out of local subsidiaries and companies by June 1987. However, the most damaging impact was made by restrictions on capital and credit, as capital inflows virtually ceased.[122] The chronic balance of payment problems due to a lack of access to foreign exchange forced the government to limit expenditure on imports, thereby sacrificing growth, since essential intermediate goods such as plastics, copper and chemicals and capital goods could not be purchased. In the process, South Africa became a net exporter of capital.[123]

The world closed the door to South Africans, and the government worried about debt collectors seizing exports, or even aircraft, in lieu of payment.[124]

According to Barend du Plessis, the 'economic disaster' soured relations dramatically between the Botha government and big business. Further evidence is found in the 1980s that shows the substantial difference between *verligtes* and *verkramptes* as the willingness of the former to adapt apartheid to capitalist imperatives, while the latter saw it the other way round.[125] NP *verligtes* had a close relationship with especially Afrikaner capitalists, and had been wooed away from state interventionist to neo-liberal capitalism from the 1970s. By the mid-1980s, government economic policy had many of the hallmarks of neo-liberal policies: a focus on growth as opposed to development; an emphasis on monetary and fiscal discipline; the limitation of inflation and government spending; cutting taxes; supporting small business; and privatising state entities.[126] Barend du Plessis developed a friendship with the British ambassador to South Africa, Robin Renwick, who arranged for him to meet Margaret Thatcher. Du Plessis was keen to do so, as he unquestioningly believed that 'Thatcherism absolutely pulled Britain out of the ditch and restored it as an internationally important economic power'. Thatcher's ascent was synonymous with the global spread of neo-liberal capitalism, as was Reagan's rise in the US. Du Plessis also enjoyed a 'wonderful' working relationship with prominent figures in the business sector, such as Wim de Villiers (head of General Mining, who became minister of privatisation under FW de Klerk), Meyer Kahn (head of South African Breweries) and Kerneels Human (economist and head of Federale Volksbeleggings).

However, in the second half of the 1980s the economic crisis was such that big capital and the government were frequently at loggerheads about how best to get out of the quagmire. Protectionist impulses clashed with neo-liberal impulses, as the following examples illustrate.

According to Barend du Plessis, Botha's relationship with the head of Sanlam, Fred du Plessis, was extremely close.[127] Consequently, Fred du Plessis' access to Barend du Plessis as finance minister was such that he would arrive without an appointment and simply expect to be slotted into the minister's daily schedule.

Such meetings – of which there were 'several' – would start with Fred du Plessis announcing that he 'had just come from the president', who had endorsed certain economic policy proposals. He would then proceed to discuss the proposals with Barend du Plessis. These meetings took place frequently after the 1985 debt standstill, when South Africa experienced a shortage of foreign exchange, which was mostly being earned through commodity exports – some of which were being smuggled, according to the former minister. Fred du Plessis convinced Botha of economic policies such as asserting total state control over interest rates and exchange control, which, as Barend du Plessis puts it, 'happened nowhere else in the world except in the communist states' at that time. Another proposal was that the 1984 figures for imports be used as a basis to proportionally allocate foreign exchange to importers in 1986 and thereby determine the use of foreign exchange.

The minister opposed this, saying that it would create an 'import rand', a third currency alongside the commercial and the financial rand. The idea fell through.

When Barend du Plessis arranged through business contacts to meet with the Japanese government 'at the highest level and in secrecy' to discuss the advance sale of gold, he latched the visit onto his attendance of an International Monetary Fund meeting in Seoul, Korea. However, he and Gerhard de Kock, governor of the Reserve Bank, had barely arrived in Japan when he was called back for an emergency cabinet meeting. Botha had again accepted advice from Fred du Plessis, this time to institute 'total import control as in the old days'.

After consultation with Pik Botha and De Kock, Barend du Plessis confronted the president at a cabinet meeting with the fact that this would mean cancellation of the customs agreement with Botswana, Swaziland and Lesotho. That idea was also sunk.

Another example was a salary increase for civil servants, which pushed more money into an already overheated economy. As a countermeasure, Barend du Plessis proposed a 2 per cent interest rate hike, to which Botha agreed. At the next day's cabinet meeting, Botha challenged him out of the blue: 'Colleague, that 2 per cent plays right into the hands of the *geldmag* [capital power].' It transpired that Botha had met with Fred du Plessis, Kerneels Human and others the previous evening and they had convinced him that it would be 'unbearable' to raise interest rates. As a result, the interest rate increase was at a lower level than originally proposed. Later that day, Barend du Plessis confronted Botha about the suggestion that he was 'an instrument in the hands of capital power'. The minister had had enough of external interference in economic decisions. He asked Botha directly whether his 'conduct in cabinet was being regulated by people in powerful positions in the private sector instead of the best interest of the country'. Botha replied in the negative. Barend du Plessis' conclusion was that, despite appearances, PW Botha acted under the influence of 'whoever left his office last'.

These examples indicate conflict between more typically protectionist policy proposals and the ministry of finance's resistance to them. They also show just how open Botha's door was, especially to Afrikaans big business, and how entwined business and the NP government had become, resulting in business having a direct influence on the policy and practice of sanctions busting.

Conflict between the government and business escalated over handling of the economic crisis, leading business to seek other escape routes. Less than a month after the Rubicon disaster, a delegation of 'leading representatives of large-scale monopoly capital', fronted by Gavin Relly, travelled to Lusaka to meet with the ANC in exile. There they 'put forward their class programme to break the political impasse'.[128]

But even as Botha was tightening the screws, he continued to pursue softer options. Mandela's profile abroad had grown immensely, and his long incarceration had made him a powerful catch-all icon for apartheid injustice, a problem for the NP that could be rectified by his release. Mandela had previously refused NP offers aimed at co-opting and splitting him from the rest of the ANC leadership, but in 1985 he decided to take the initiative and – without the ANC leadership's knowledge – wrote to Kobie Coetsee, then minister of justice. There was no official response until Coetsee visited Mandela in hospital, a step that must have been approved by Botha. Cabinet ministers did not venture much without Botha's say-so. Coetsee and Niel Barnard, head of the National

Intelligence Service and a hand-picked Botha protégé, then formed a committee and met with Mandela several times in secret.

Neither Botha loyalist Chris Heunis nor FW de Klerk was informed of this development. Leaving De Klerk out of the loop was probably a consequence of the distance he kept from the securocrats, but Heunis was minister of constitutional development, after all. Moreover, Heunis had appointed a committee of forty senior civil servants from non-security departments in 1987 to investigate and report on ways to break out of the political stalemate. In a March 1987 report dubbed *Skrik vir Niks* (Nothing scares us), they recommended the opening of negotiations with representatives of all South Africans; universal franchise; the scrapping of discriminatory laws; the lifting of the state of emergency; the institution of human rights; and the rule of law.[129] Roelf Meyer, who was a deputy minister at the time, later said that the report in all likelihood went nowhere because 'it was ahead of its time', and because Coetsee's talks with Mandela were in progress.

The nature of the Coetsee–Mandela interaction suggested another possibility. The government mindset was still one of co-option, and the committee was trying to persuade Mandela to abandon key issues such as majority rule, links with the SACP and the armed struggle. The NP thus hoped to gain major concessions from its foe while it still held the upper hand. Moving Mandela from Robben Island in 1985 and again in 1988, to a house in the grounds of Victor Verster Prison, was probably part of the strategy to wear him down. But Mandela did not budge.

Meanwhile, all was not well in the Botha government. Heunis, a *verligte*, was opposed by the more conservative Coetsee and De Klerk. Meyer was reportedly already close to the latter and was still of conservative persuasion in the late 1980s. Both he and Barnard were implicated in the blocking of the *Skrik vir Niks* report, allegedly acting on behalf of Botha, who wanted to hear nothing of the recommendations.

The report showed that, by the beginning of 1987, senior state officials outside the security establishment had rejected the reformist, piecemeal adjustment of apartheid. They criticised the government's attempts to maintain white domination by denying the 'legitimate aspirations of black people'.

In the second half of the 1980s, the strategy of legitimate and transparent activities aimed at political change, backed by illegal activities to weaken opponents, gave way to state terrorism, which would become worse in the 1990s.

The church rethinks apartheid
With Verwoerd's ban on black attendance of 'white' church services, most religious denominations became divided along racial lines, whether in dogma or

in practice. Some churches allowed themselves to be used by the government to neutralise dissent. The Apostolic Faith Mission, for example, preached that opposition to apartheid was a communist plot aimed at destroying Christianity.[130]

After the Cottesloe Conference in 1960, the largest of the white churches, the Dutch Reformed Church, took fourteen years to formulate its position on race in *Ras, Volk, Nasie en Volkereverhoudinge in die Lig van die Skrif* (Race, *Volk*, Nation and Peoples' Relations in Light of the Bible). While criticising migrant labour as disrupting the family unit and intimating that coloured people needed special consideration, the church reaffirmed that the 'autogenous development of different population groups' was justifiable and that mixed marriages were 'undesired and unauthorised' – despite an absence of biblical proscription in this regard.

Criticism slowly emerged against *Ras, Volk en Nasie*. In 1979, the Cape Synod of the DRC suggested tentatively that racial discrimination contradicted biblical brotherly love. Then eight lecturers from the universities of Stellenbosch and Pretoria reprimanded the church for not eradicating 'unloving and racist attitudes'. The response from its official mouthpiece, *Die Kerkbode*, was that the church was addressing these issues. In a publication on ecumenical relations and reconciliation, concern was expressed that the church was being compromised because of its links with the *volk*, the Broederbond and the NP, and that it should declare that apartheid had negative consequences despite the 'good intentions'.

An open letter from 123 Dutch Reformed theologians and clergymen in 1982[131] insisted that the primary task of the church was to be a 'ministry of reconciliation'. They further argued that a system in which 'irreconcilability is elevated to a communal principle' and which promoted estrangement through laws on mixed marriages, race classification and group areas could not be rooted in scripture. The church establishment perceived the letter as an attack.

In 1982, the World Alliance of Reformed Churches declared that apartheid was a sin that demanded a *status confessionis*. Thus the synod of the segregated DRC Mission Church adopted the Belhar confession, which stated that the white DRC was guilty of heresy and idolatry because of its theological justification of apartheid. The DRC Synod's response to the WARC was that the church was being misrepresented and that the alliance had been influenced by liberation theology. The synod also condemned racism as a sin, but said the law prohibiting mixed marriages could be justified. The academic Willie Esterhuyse commented that the synod did not hear Belhar, because 'no one is as deaf as those who for ideological reasons do not want to hear'.[132] The church was criticised for following the government and not providing leadership.

In 1983, the DRC finally admitted that the ban on mixed marriages was not based on scripture, which also did not prescribe separate development, and that if the latter led to racial discrimination, it was a sin. In 1986 the church's new position was published as *Kerk en Samelewing* (Church and Society), and membership of the DRC was opened to all, along with an admission that 'apartheid as a political and social system that wronged people and wrongfully favoured one group above another could not be accepted on Christian-ethical grounds'.[133]

Affronted by the church's 'liberalism', some 20 000 members broke away from the DRC in 1986 and formed the Afrikaanse Protestante-Kerk. It seemed 'the distance between synod halls and church pews was vast'.[134] It took another twelve years, but the DRC Synod finally accepted in 1998 that apartheid was a sin, and that its biblical justification constituted a heresy that demanded a confession from the church.

CHAPTER 4

The emperor strikes back

I committed these acts in my capacity as general commander in the Special Forces. I saw it as part of my duty ... My actions were never motivated by racist considerations, personal enmity or personal gain. It [sic] was aimed at ensuring the survival of the government of the day. Individuals who were eliminated were identified as people who played a material part in the struggle or could play such a part and were thus a serious threat to the state ... I considered the country to be in a state of full-scale war. I never questioned the validity of the war and only served the country to the fullest of my ability and convictions.
– **Major General Joep Joubert, former head of SADF Special Forces**[1]

Hold me, corporal.
I'm a child, totally lost ...
Blinkers ensure a clean conscience
It's my duty, not my choice
Here I sit, I sit and waste away
It's not my fault but I shut my mouth
– **Song about conscription, Bernoldus Niemand, 1984**[2]

A S A GROUNDSWELL OF RESISTANCE SWEPT ACROSS THE COUNTRY, Pretoria was forced to reassess the internal security situation. From 1985, a marked change of tone crept into State Security Council documents, the phraseology shifting to include words such as 'eliminate' and 'destroy'.[3] At the same time, the ANC decided to exploit the popular revolt by stepping up a 'people's war'.

Two issues are significant here. First, the government ramped up its counter-revolutionary activities in direct response to the ANC's change of tack. Second, both the ANC and the NP were playing catch-up with the popular insurrection. Even the community-based UDF was trailing behind the surge of grassroots protest. ANC insurgency increased as militants entered the country and launched attacks – 45 in 1984, 230 in 1986 and a peak of 281 in 1988.[4] In a contradiction of basic democratic norms, the Botha government deployed troops in the densely populated black townships. According to the then defence minister, this deployment internally was 'inevitable', as 'unrest' had grown to unprecedented proportions.[5]

In yet another example of the NP paying lip service to legality, the Defence Act of 1957 had been duly amended to include among the SADF's responsibilities 'service in combating and repressing terrorism' and 'service in preventing or suppressing local unrest within the Republic'. In July 1985, security force powers were further bolstered with the declaration of a state of emergency. It was the first since the 1960 Sharpeville massacre. The emergency regulations indemnified the police from prosecution for misconduct or excesses, 'reinforc[ing] their understanding that they enjoyed impunity for the extensive abuses committed in the interest of state security'.[6]

In the first eight months under the state of emergency, 8 000 people were detained and 22 000 charged with protest-related offences.[7] During the course of 1985, the death toll climbed to 879, the number of attacks to 136 and the number of strikes to 390, involving 240 000 workers. Deaths linked to the police showed a staggering five-fold increase between 1984 and 1985, to about 500.

The state of emergency was lifted briefly due to international pressure, only to be reinstated from June 1986 to 1990. Extraordinary powers enabled the police to detain an additional 26 000 people in a single year. Unofficial estimates placed the total number of people in detention by the beginning of 1987 at 30 000.[8]

In amnesty applications before the Truth and Reconciliation Commission in the late 1990s, death due to torture was admitted in a number of cases. Some activists had died anonymously; others had been more prominent leaders, such as Stanza Bopape. There was a long list of names of people who had died under suspicious circumstances while being held under security laws, including Neil Aggett ('suicide'). Security policemen admitted to the torture of people who later came to hold government positions: Father Smangaliso Mkhatshwa, Raymond Suttner, Barbara Hogan, Tony Yengeni and Pravin Gordhan, among many others.

The uprising became multi-levelled. While youth organisations frequently initiated protest action, they found wide community support. Funerals became displays of political solidarity as people exalted their heroes who had died in the struggle. Voices rang out singing Enoch Sontonga's religious poem, which had become a freedom anthem: 'Nkosi Sikelel' iAfrika' (God bless Africa). The toyi-toyi trot moved large crowds down streets as they sang new and old resistance songs, accompanied by Black Power salutes and the slogan 'Amandla! Ngawethu!' (Power to the people!) The growth in support for the ANC and its ally, the South African Communist Party, was seen in the unfurling of their colours at funerals.

Official figures of 'unrest-related incidents' were: 14 000 in 1986, 4 000 in 1987, 5 000 in 1988 and 17 000 in 1990.[9] The insurrection also took on another dimension as black local government structures collapsed under the weight of boycotts, bloodshed and the resignation of councillors who feared retaliation for cooperating with the regime. Such fears were not unfounded, as the murder of councillors showed. Informal structures were set up, including 'people's courts'. Boycott breakers and those suspected of being collaborators or informers were punished, mostly by young comrades. Many died by the inhumane method of 'necklacing', where a tyre is placed around the victim's neck, doused with petrol and set alight. Such incidents peaked at 306 in 1986. William Beinart[10] interprets this practice as '[t]he cast-offs of industrial affluence ... being recycled to purify society – in the minds of the perpetrators – by fire and death'. The slogan of 'ungovernability' had taken on a grim tone.

While the state managed to quash the uprising in most places by 1987, a veritable civil war raged on in Natal, especially around Pietermaritzburg, as Inkatha and the UDF/ANC engaged in attacks and counter-attacks. This and other township violence was conveniently presented by the government and the media as 'black-on-black violence'. However, studies showed the disingenuity of this description. Apart from a battle for political control, factors such as competition for scarce resources; independent landowners resisting Inkatha influence; generational conflicts; and the weakening of traditional and patri-archal hierarchies fuelled the violence.[11] 'Black-on-black violence' also hid an essential strategy of the NP government, honed in neighbouring countries: its support of proxy forces against its enemies. These forces included Inkatha and local vigilante groupings.

The opposition extended beyond the urban areas and into the Bantustans. Even some of the homeland puppets thumbed their noses at their political masters' plans. Reacting to the 1983 constitution, Bantustan leaders issued a state-ment declaring the homeland policy unworkable and calling for negotiations on a constitution acceptable to all South Africans. Later, most rejected Pretoria's offer to join a 'great indaba' on a future South Africa. The UDF grew strongly in Lebowa, and was also able to engineer the rejection of 'independence' by KwaNdebele in 1986.

As the crisis deepened, the whites-only 'democracy' developed increasingly authoritarian overtones. Defence spending ballooned from 6 per cent of the total budget in 1960 to 15 per cent in 1980, and between 17 and 20 per cent for the rest of the 1980s.[12] White society became militarised through conscription for white men, paramilitary cadet training at white schools and compulsory 'subjects' at Afrikaans schools, such as *Jeugweerbaarheid* (youth defence) and *Geestesweerbaarheid* (spiritual defence).

In 1977, the period of conscription for white young men was extended to two years, and they could be recalled to camps or 'commando' duty. More than 400 000 servicemen could be mobilised.[13] But dissidence in white society grew.

The End Conscription Campaign (ECC), involving mainly English-speaking white men, was founded in 1983 and gained some support, especially when the state deployed white soldiers in the townships. While the ECC remained small, the NP government perceived it as a serious threat. Members were harassed and prosecuted, and the ECC was banned in 1988.

Apart from the singer Bernoldus Niemand, Afrikaans author Koos Prinsloo articulated the confusion and alienation of conscripts in his books *Jonkmanskas* (literally 'Young Man's Cupboard'), published in 1982, and *Die Hemel Help Ons* ('Heaven Help Us'), published in 1987. The latter earned him the wrath of *Groot Krokodil* PW Botha himself, as he blocked the award of a literary prize to Prinsloo by *Rapport*, the NP-aligned Sunday newspaper, in the late 1980s. The reason: in Prinsloo's documentary style of fiction-writing he illustrated white racism by having a character in the short story 'Grensverhaal' (Border Story) make a racist and crude reference to Botha as a *meidenaaier* – someone who fornicates with black women. But apart from a handful of such examples, the majority of white men responded to their enlistment without protest at the time. Not until a decade later, after the dawn of democracy, did some Afrikaner men publicly revisit the issue of military conscription from a critical vantage point, for example in journalist Chris Louw's 'Boetman is die Bliksem in' open letter to the media.

This is our 'hood – applying lessons learnt

The NP government's counter-revolutionary strategies in neighbouring states served as precursors for suppression of internal resistance during the 1980s. There was a dual dimension of constitutional and coercive efforts. As the constitutional option faltered in the face of reality, the coercive option became dominant. This involved both overt and covert actions, ranging from economic blackmail (retarding the passage of Zimbabwean goods through harbours, for example) to cross-border attacks and campaigns, supporting puppet leaders, and training and arming proxy forces. The resulting terrorisation and large-scale killing of civilians accounted for more than a million casualties and thousands of refugees in neighbouring countries – in addition to the further destabilisation of weak states still reeling from the effects of colonialism.

In the government's quest to establish a constellation of moderate states as a buffer against the Soviet onslaught on the subcontinent, Zimbabwe was crucial. After the loss of Portugal as colonial ally in Angola and Mozambique, the NP government supported a controlled dismantlement of white supremacy structures in Rhodesia and South West Africa, where the days of white rule were numbered. These processes would serve as valuable experience when South Africa embarked on its own negotiations. According to analyst Adrian Guelke, South Africa enlisted the help of Zambia and Britain in Rhodesia,[14] fearing that a violent transition would catapult the 'wrong' (in other words, Marxist) organisation to power. Therefore, it played an important role in getting Ian Smith and Bishop Abel Muzorewa to the table at Lancaster House and applying pressure on the front-line states to 'deliver' ZANU-PF's Robert Mugabe and ZAPU's Joshua Nkomo to the negotiations.[15]

The NP government firmly believed that its favoured candidate, Muzorewa, would win the 1980 elections in Zimbabwe. The first setback to the Botha government's plans was Mugabe's decisive victory. This was ameliorated by the constitutional safeguards cemented at Lancaster House, but the second setback was the formation of the Southern African Development Coordinating Conference (SADCC) in 1980, with the aim of reducing the dependence of southern African states on South Africa. Not only did the SADCC wipe Pretoria's proposed constellation off the table, but even the NP government's allies in the region, Malawi and Swaziland, joined the organisation,[16] leaving the idea dead in the water.

The final blow to Botha's dream was when South Africa's neighbours changed their previous orientation as front-line states against Rhodesia to make South Africa the new front line. It became clear that other African governments were not about to fall in with the apartheid regime's plans for the region. These setbacks precipitated an aggressive response. The SADF launched bloody attacks against Angola in 1980, and more followed: Matola (Mozambique) in 1981; Maseru (Lesotho) in 1982; Maputo (Mozambique) in 1983; Gaborone (Botswana) in 1985; Botswana, Zambia and Zimbabwe in 1986; Gaborone yet again in 1988.

The cross-border attacks on Botswana, Zimbabwe and Zambia on 19 May 1986 were an indication of the internal dynamics in the NP governing elite at the time. A Commonwealth Eminent Persons Group (EPG) paid a much-publicised visit to South Africa in 1986. As a result of consultations with role-players ranging from PW Botha to the still incarcerated Nelson Mandela, the EPG released a set of draft proposals for a negotiated settlement. It included a section compiled by then foreign affairs minister Pik Botha and approved by PW, which declared that the government was not 'in principle' opposed to releasing Mandela and other political prisoners, nor to unbanning organisations; was 'committed' to ending white domination and removing discrimination from the statute books and broader society; and would not prescribe who might represent black South Africans at the negotiating table for a new constitution.[17]

In a provocative move that bears testimony to PW Botha 'The Hardliner', he authorised cross-border attacks by the SADF against three neighbouring Commonwealth member states while the EPG was still in the country. Neither Pik Botha nor PW's ally, Chris Heunis, had prior knowledge of the raids. Former defence minister Magnus Malan later told the Truth and Reconciliation

Commission that it had been his decision to launch the attacks. He had approached PW Botha alone, which had not been the normal routine, and was given approval for his action but ordered that it be kept quiet because of the sensitivity involved. Malan indicated to the TRC that he had been well aware that such attacks would receive widespread international media attention, and said no other minister was informed because of 'leaks' in the past, possibly in the ministry of foreign affairs[18] – an apparent swipe at Pik Botha.

The message could not have been clearer, and the EPG departed swiftly. The securocrats in Botha's administration still held the upper hand. PW Botha confirmed this two months later, when he told the London *Times* that the international community would not be allowed to dictate a political solution to his government.[19]

Former finance minister Barend du Plessis' account of his mission to convince Thatcher to downplay foreign calls for change (in the previous chapter) suggests that PW Botha was particularly irked by inferences that his government was capitulating to outside pressure. Du Plessis maintains that all ministers – not only those involved in security matters – were convinced of the necessity for military operations against the communist onslaught, but that all such action remained subject to approval by the political decision-makers.[20]

Magnus Malan justified South African aggression in the region by saying in parliament on 4 February 1986 that 'this government will not permit murderous gangs to complete their planning, training and preparation in the security and protection of neighbouring states and from there act against South Africa. The security forces will hammer them wherever they find them. What I am saying is the policy of the government ... I therefore warn the states of this subcontinent that the security forces ... will act against our enemies across the borders.' Pik Botha had put it even more bluntly in 1983: 'Out – they must get out. There is no compromise on this one.'[21]

'They' seemed to include the governments of certain neighbouring states, especially as South Africa's precious colonial *cordon sanitaire* had disappeared with the long overdue withdrawal of the Portuguese and the removal of Ian Smith in Rhodesia. To get 'them' out, Pretoria went well beyond cross-border raids. South African security forces became actively involved in Rhodesia, Zambia, Angola and Mozambique. Activities included supporting and supplying reactionary proxy movements, namely the Mozambique National Resistance (RENAMO) and the National Union for the Total Independence of Angola (UNITA). In line with classic Cold War doctrine, Pretoria aimed to displace the Marxist threat in Angola and Mozambique with client regimes.

In Rhodesia, Ian Smith's regime was amply assisted with armaments, SAP personnel, funds and military support from the late 1960s. Once it became clear that Smith would not prevail, Pretoria pinned its hopes on Muzorewa, raising R12 million for his election campaign, of which half came from state coffers and the rest from the private sector in response to fund-raising efforts by Pik Botha.[22]

Similarly, Pretoria backed the Democratic Turnhalle Alliance (DTA) in the election in South West Africa in 1989, spending R185.5 million to weaken the South West Africa People's Organisation (SWAPO). This was done through misinformation campaigns, intimidation of supporters and the disruption of political rallies. The SADF was given 70 per cent of the money budgeted for these activities and set up an electoral media centre under the name of Africa Communications Project in Windhoek. Money was also spent on activating the white right. An organisation called Aksie Kontra 435 was created, referring to the United Nations resolution on independence for South West Africa. The TRC would receive an amnesty application for a grenade attack by members of this organisation on an office used by UNTAG, the UN monitoring force in South West Africa.[23]

South Africa's secret invasion of Angola in the mid-1970s did not prevent the MPLA from coming to power after the Portuguese withdrawal. When Jonas Savimbi's sorely depleted UNITA was identified as a partner to combat the MPLA and SWAPO from the mid-1970s onwards, the SADF turned UNITA's dwindling fortunes around with military supplies, logistical support and back-up on the ground to such an extent that, by 1983, the rebel movement had 40 000 well-trained fighters and controlled one-third of Angolan territory.[24] Several military campaigns followed, including a raid on the Cassinga military and refugee camp in May 1978 in which 600 people, including non-combatants and children, were killed. The SADF occupied Cunene province until 1989 to safeguard it as UNITA's operating base.[25]

More than 8 000 'terrorists' – SWAPO and Angolan army combatants – were killed in ten operations between 1981 and 1988, but no tally was kept of civilian deaths. However, civilian centres were targeted and whole towns destroyed, leading to the conclusion that thousands of civilians had died. In a 1981 operation, 160 000 Angolans were left homeless, and the United Nations Children's Fund (UNICEF) estimated that up to 100 000 Angolans had died from war-related famine between 1980 and 1985. The organisation also put at 333 000 the number of children who had died from unnatural causes in Angola between 1981 and 1988.[26]

An even closer relationship existed with RENAMO, whose leaders were living in South Africa and were on the SADF payroll. The Mozambican resistance movement comprised both white and black members of the Portuguese colonial army and secret service and later also included disaffected former members of the FRELIMO government's security agencies. The SADF took control of

RENAMO in 1980 and commenced training of its members at bases in the Northern Transvaal and the Caprivi. RENAMO was supported with arms, clothing, food and agricultural equipment, as well as intelligence and even delivery of insurgents by sea and air.[27] The support continued in contravention of the Nkomati Accord (signed in 1984 with the Mozambican government), and apparently without the knowledge of PW Botha and the SSC, but with the authorisation of then SADF chief General Constand Viljoen.[28]

The SADF attempted similar destabilisation by proxy in South West Africa. The failure of the project – the surrogate was unviable due to SWAPO's popularity in Ovamboland – led to the creation of the SAP unit Koevoet in 1979 to combat SWAPO through extra-legal means.

The model for Koevoet was the Portuguese *Flechas* and the Rhodesian Selous Scouts, and it started with 'turned' ex-SWAPO combatants. The practice of 'turning' activists was also the origin of the Vlakplaas askaris. Eventually, Koevoet had ten to fifteen black members for every white officer. The whites had been trained in counter-insurgency – many with the Selous Scouts – in order to meet the unit's aims, as stated by police minister Louis le Grange in 1984: to go beyond conventional warfare to 'wipe out terrorist gangs' in South West Africa.[29]

This was another classic example of NP doublespeak, given that it was Koevoet that was operating as a terrorist gang. Its members, realising that they were a law unto themselves as long as they did the NP regime's bidding, left a trail of horror and destruction in their wake. They raped women, brutalised civilians, including children and the elderly, drove through people's houses and crops in their Casspirs, and tortured people to extract information. Koevoet's 'cash-for-corpses' policy – members were paid a bounty for each person killed – ensured a 1:32 ratio of prisoners to fatalities.[30]

Analyst Stephen Chan suggests that the South African government used Botswana, Lesotho and Swaziland as 'laboratories'[31] to test policies before employing them elsewhere in the region. The same was true for the internal strategies of repression implemented in the 1980s and 1990s. Several factors confirm the emulation of regional operations as a model for domestic repression. First, regional operatives were redeployed on covert internal operations. Multiple murderer Eugene de Kock was one example, having moved from fighting on the side of Ian Smith's regime in Rhodesia to Koevoet before becoming commander of Vlakplaas in July 1985.

Second, the SADF's Directorate of Special Tasks was created in 1976 as a conduit for support to UNITA and, from the early 1980s, to RENAMO, but switched in the mid-1980s to supporting Inkatha (Operation Marion) and operations in the Transkei and Ciskei (Katzen). This formed part of a trend of 'indigenising' the conflict, as was done by recruiting South West Africans into a force under SADF control, and black men as *kitskonstabels* and municipal police in South Africa.

Third, similar methods were used, such as 'false flag' operations initiated by the Selous Scouts in the Rhodesian war and by askaris and Koevoet members in SWAPO uniforms in South West Africa. Fourth, vast sums of money were spent on attempts to install client regimes in the then South West Africa and Rhodesia. Similarly, vast amounts were spent on propping up Inkatha as an alternative to the UDF/ANC in South Africa.

The South African government had decided to take the war to the enemy in the late 1970s. Strictly speaking, the 'enemy' was the ANC, but this approach also indicated a mindset of alienation from the rest of the continent. The disproportionate onslaught against critically underdeveloped states embroiled in the difficulties of state building leaves one no choice but to concur with the TRC's finding that 'factors of race and racism should not be dismissed when attempting to explain South Africa's conduct in the region. From the evidence before the commission it appears that while some acts of regional destabilisation may have been a defence against communism the purpose of the war was also to preserve white minority rule in South Africa and it was, therefore, a race war.'[32]

Pretoria's approach towards black people both inside and outside South Africa exhibited degrees of racism, manifested as hostility in cases of resistance against its schemes, and condescension in instances of compromise. It was a neo-colonial mindset that persisted, horribly demonstrated in the adoption of the same extreme methods of violence utilised to defend other settler societies in Rhodesia and the Portuguese colonies. It was a mindset that obviated the imagining of different potentialities, thereby entrapping white South Africans in a destructive spiral of their own making. It also meant the continuing misjudgement of the level of black discontent with white supremacist rule – whether in Mozambique, Rhodesia, South West Africa or South Africa – as revealed by repeated patronising attempts to foist illegitimate leaders onto civilians weary of human rights violations and racism.

The similarity in misconceptions and methods employed by the white regime to those of other colonial regimes draws a question mark over Afrikaners' popular perception of themselves as 'not colonial'. It also negates the idea of South African exceptionalism: that neo-colonialism and institutionalised racism was somehow different in South Africa than in other settler societies.

A symbiotic relationship

The state's counter-insurgency methods inside the country included creating vigilante proxies such as the *Witdoeke* (known by their white headgear), who terrorised communities in the Cape Town area, killing at least sixty people and destroying 10 000 homes in the 1980s. Unemployed black men were recruited to become *kitskonstabels* (instant constables) on the state's payroll to destroy UDF structures. But it is the relationship between the NP government and Mangosuthu Buthelezi's Inkatha that warrants closer inspection, since Inkatha was the largest of these groupings and became particularly significant as a potential NP partner during the transition.

Inkatha was founded in the 1920s and lay dormant for decades, until Zulu royal Buthelezi revived it in 1969. KwaZulu came into being in 1972 with Buthelezi as chief minister. Inkatha played an ambivalent role from the 1970s onwards, on the one hand participating in the Bantustan system and organising along tribal lines, and on the other hand undermining grand apartheid by rejecting 'independence' for KwaZulu. Buthelezi presented Inkatha as more than an ethnic movement. While Inkatha opposed violence as a political means and supported free marketeerism, it was also projected as a liberation movement working towards universal franchise. Because of this, the ANC initially saw Buthelezi, an ex-ANC Youth League member, as an ally.

Inkatha's declared pro-democracy stance was contradicted by its domination of KwaZulu, which was total to the extent that the KwaZulu government and police, Inkatha and Buthelezi himself became so closely associated with each other as to be indistinguishable.[33] Soon ANC members were labelling Buthelezi a sell-out, and public verbal battles ensued between him and UDF leaders in the early 1980s. Inkatha's hopes of dominating black politics came to a halt with the rise of the UDF.

Still, Inkatha did not abide slavishly by Pretoria's plans. In the early 1980s, Buthelezi dismissed the enlarged president's council with coloured and Indian leaders as merely an extended 'laager'. Along with other Bantustan leaders, he rejected the 1983 constitution as an effort to entrench white supremacy, and in the late 1980s he made participation in Botha's proposed indaba contingent on Mandela's release. A Buthelezi-appointed commission investigating constitutional options emerged in 1982 with proposals for a consociational government based on ethnicity.[34] The government dismissed the report, but it did point to an ideological convergence with the NP beyond economic policies.

It was from 1980 onwards, having lost its hegemony to anti-apartheid forces in the Natal region, that Inkatha resorted to violence.[35] Paramilitary camps were set up to train Inkatha members to 'discipline' school-goers who were boycotting classes. Buthelezi announced the creation of Zulu impis to restore order.[36] Clashes erupted between anti-apartheid activists and Inkatha members, especially in cases where students were critical of Buthelezi or Inkatha, or where Inkatha-dominated local authorities were identified for incorporation into KwaZulu.

After the Ngoye incident in 1983, when Inkatha members attended a rally addressed by Buthelezi at the University of Zululand and four students died in violence, Buthelezi proclaimed in the KwaZulu legislature that 'our youth did no more than defend my honour and the honour of his majesty the king. I must warn South Africa that if this kind of provocation continues ... Inkatha youth will demonstrate their strength and prowess.'[37] Inkatha members challenged the UDF's policy of 'ungovernability', as it threatened Inkatha's claims of being representative of the region, and from 1984, violence escalated. Inkatha needed a united support base to project itself as a significant national political player.

The security dimension of the government's relationship with Inkatha was cemented when Buthelezi – after receiving assassination threats – made a request for training and weapons in the mid-1980s. He had requested firearm licences for Zulu chiefs in 1974 and again in 1985, when he sought permission to issue permits.[38] The SSC made a decision in 1985 that amounted to employing the same strategy of repression through surrogate forces inside the country as it was following in neighbouring countries with forces such as UNITA and RENAMO.[39] During the course of the 1980s, Inkatha became an internal proxy for the regime's security forces, supported by the SADF's Directorate for Special Tasks and Special Forces. According to FW de Klerk, 'considerable sums of money' were given to Inkatha to assist with the creation of a trade union, the United Workers Union of South Africa (UWUSA), to counter the newly formed Congress of South African Trade Unions (COSATU). Funds were also provided to assist Inkatha with 'political organisation', as well as for large rallies.[40]

The first evidence of state complicity with Inkatha is the so-called A-Team vigilante group operating in Chesterville, Durban. The convergence between Inkatha structures inside and outside KwaZulu with NP government structures could be seen in this case. The A-Team apparently consisted of Inkatha members and was aligned with Inkatha. It was established in the wake of a call by the KwaZulu minister of justice for vigilante groups to join the KwaZulu Police.

A Durban SAP riot unit member testified to the TRC that the A-Team was created by Military Intelligence and aided the SAP in 'curbing' anti-apartheid organisations. In return, it received resources and protection from the SAP. The A-Team conducted a terror campaign between 1985 and 1989, murdering at least ten people and committing numerous arson attacks.

Inkatha received an overt armed capacity from the apartheid state in the form of special constables, of whom 150 had been ostensibly trained to protect KwaZulu VIPs. However, this training had a distinct military flavour, since it was provided by the SADF in the Caprivi Strip in an operation code-named Marion. Operation Marion provided Inkatha with a covert capacity for violent suppression,[41] and seems to have been the first high-level secret project involving the SSC command and Buthelezi himself.

While De Klerk subsequently vaguely claimed that 'most' ministers did not know about 'most' such projects, he did acknowledge 'there was widespread respect [in government] for Inkatha's refusal to support the ANC's armed struggle or sanctions. At the very least, it was felt that Inkatha should be helped to resist the encroachments of the ANC and its internal front organisations.'[42] This presents a contradiction, as he denied support for repressive action while simultaneously acknowledging the need for it. One finds a similar contradiction in Buthelezi's original press statement in response to Inkathagate, as exposure of Operation Marion in 1991 was called.

Buthelezi denied that the IFP 'ever trained one single person for hit squad activity' or 'for any killing against anybody or against any organisation anywhere'.[43] However, he linked the 'VIP training' to the 'intensification of ANC revolutionary activity … no-holds-barred violence against South Africa'. The KwaZulu Police, with Buthelezi himself as their minister, had decided that 'effective action should be undertaken to protect KwaZulu VIPs from the kinds of attacks that revolutionaries were boasting they were going to make'.

'VIP protection' seems a nonsensically mild response to a problem as grave as 'no-holds-barred violence against South Africa'. Indeed, the actual violence perpetrated by Inkatha supporters offers evidence that the organisation waged full-scale war on the ANC, with the help of elements (at the very least) in the NP government. The Caprivi group was explicitly told by SADF instructors that they were being trained for hit squad activities.[44] They received salaries from Military Intelligence until their absorption into the KwaZulu Police in 1989. Several also served as instructors at Inkatha's self-protection training base at Mlaba. Their dispersal throughout Natal exacerbated their impact on the people of the area, with tragic consequences.

The TRC found that between fifteen and twenty Caprivi trainees had acted as a hit squad in the Pietermaritzburg and Mpumalanga areas in Natal until 1988. In 1996, General Magnus Malan was prosecuted for murder along with Buthelezi's personal assistant, MZ Khumalo, and others, for the KwaMakhutha massacre on 21 January 1987 in which thirteen people, including children, were killed. The accused were acquitted, but the court accepted that two SADF members had planned the massacre, which was perpetrated by Inkatha members trained in the Caprivi. One trainee, Gcina Mkhize, headed a hit squad based at Esikhawini near Richards Bay, which was set up at a meeting attended by Khumalo and KwaZulu ministers.[45]

Lastly, De Klerk admitted in his autobiography that the cabinet had discussed the training of KwaZulu Police to protect KwaZulu politicians. However, Buthelezi alleged in his August 1991 press statement that he was told a security company would provide the training. It is improbable that Buthelezi would not have been informed of the true source of the training. Neither De Klerk nor Buthelezi apparently found it suspect that this training was conducted clandestinely in the Caprivi Strip.

Affidavits collected during the second half of the 1980s by the Black Sash's Natal coastal branch testify to large-scale intimidation by Inkatha-aligned individuals, frequently assisted by the security forces or unknown white men. Examples included the following:

- In KwaMashu, the local Inkatha councillor was alleged to have set up a committee in 1986 with the instruction 'to attack all youth indiscriminately'[46] if they did not belong to the Inkatha Youth Brigade. The committee was supplied with home-made weapons for which the councillor supplied all ammunition. The use of home-made weapons is noteworthy, given that evidence exists that Vlakplaas members manufactured weapons for Inkatha after 1990 on the basis of an instruction from Major General Krappies Engelbrecht to Eugene de Kock.[47]
- A woman's house in Hammarsdale was stoned while white police officers looked on. She was later interrogated by a white police officer about her political affiliation. When she told him she had none, he responded by saying that 'people who are ... having [sic] affiliation do not stay at Hammarsdale ... only Inkatha people stay here'.[48] In fear of their lives, she and her family then fled Hammarsdale. Other affidavits alleged attacks on COSATU and UDF members by the KwaZulu Police, vigilante groups, and white and black police officers.

By 1988, the violence gripping Natal had three characteristics: it was publicly perpetrated, in most cases by local Inkatha leaders, earning them reputations as warlords; it exhibited 'extreme, even symbolic, brutality'; and it was indiscriminate, killing toddlers, the infirm, relatives and friends.[49] Police seldom intervened in the conflict between Inkatha and the UDF, and mostly did so only to arrest UDF members. In particular, SAP Riot Unit 8 was directly involved in facilitating Inkatha attacks, of which the Trust Feed massacre of eleven people in 1988 presents a devastating example. It was executed by special constables led by Captain Brian Mitchell of the SAP, and planned by local police officers and Inkatha leaders in the community.[50]

The utilisation of black surrogates enabled the projection of 'black-on-black' violence to the NP's white constituency and the international community, thereby obscuring the regime's involvement, while justifying security measures. 'Black-on-black violence' was an NP propaganda creation that served local and international racist conceptualisations and was eagerly embraced by the local and foreign media. In the mind of white South Africa, 'the blacks' were attacking each other as they were wont to do, confirming the correctness and necessity of apartheid. In the popular white mind, 'black-on-black violence' proved how essential apartheid was in keeping 'order' between contending black 'tribes'.

Who knew what?

As the strategies of co-option of the first half of the 1980s failed, the state increasingly turned to the military option. In line with total strategy, this meant counter-revolutionary warfare, involving cooperation between the SAP and the SADF.[51] The shift resulted in higher death tolls from 1985 onwards,[52] including extra-judicial killings, as well as an explosion in incidents of torture, random intimidation of communities and assistance to proxy forces. Probably the most vexing question about the last years of the apartheid era remains: Was this the result of decisions made by the country's political leaders, or by its military chiefs?

Chile's Pinochet, Paraguay's Stroessner, Uruguay's Bordaberry, Serbia's Milošević and Liberia's Taylor could all be directly linked to murder. This set the wheels of prosecution in motion, though this progressed significantly in only two of the cases, while two more were stymied by natural deaths. But in South Africa, the post-1994 offer of amnesty in exchange for disclosure did not produce conclusive answers as to who was ultimately responsible for state abuses. The issue came to the fore most forcibly during the TRC hearings in the late 1990s, when the last NP president, FW de Klerk, denied knowledge of any such decisions on behalf of the entire party leadership. These incidents were ascribed to 'rogue elements', but this was refuted by several of the foot soldiers in court and TRC testimony.

SSC documentation in the 1980s shows an 'increasing anxiety regarding the seeming inability of the security forces to bring an end to the internal unrest'.[53] The TRC found 'a growing acceptance'[54] in the government and among members of the security forces that legal methods were inadequate to combat what they regarded as a revolutionary onslaught in a war situation. Then minister of law and order Adriaan Vlok admitted as much: 'In an attempt to promote stability and relative peace, the further instrument of the emergency regulations was introduced by the declaration of states of emergency and that was also made available to the security fraternity. At best this could only be preventative in the short term but *it was clear from an early stage onwards that the revolutionary onslaught would not be stemmed by these means. These measures also did not enable the Security Police to, by means of legal conduct, stop or combat the violence and unrest in the country and to normalise the situation.* To put it in brief, if the revolution [could have been stopped] with arrests, detention, banning orders and court interdicts and the application of other measures ... then it was a different matter'[55] (author's emphasis).

The switch can be traced back to the early 1960s, when state forces brutally smothered black resistance. The then minister of justice BJ Vorster declared that conventional methods were insufficient to capture 'communists'. He thus hatched detention without trial, one of a barrage of repressive laws. The message that such steps must have sent to the security forces was that all methods were justifiable to defend the status quo.

Apart from changes to the legal environment, which created the climate for abuse, institutional arrangements were made. The police had its C1 unit based at Vlakplaas near Pretoria. Evidence of its extra-legal activities began emerging in the late 1980s through revelations made to the independent Afrikaans and English press, while testimony to the TRC brought more proof to bear.

Captain Dirk Coetzee was snubbed by the pro-NP Afrikaans newspapers of Nasionale Pers when he approached them in late 1989 with his first-hand experience as commander of Vlakplaas in 1980 and 1981. The Afrikaans alternative weekly newspaper *Vrye Weekblad* published the details. The police unit was originally devised to 'turn' and re-train[56] ANC and PAC militants for counterinsurgency operations. From at least the early 1980s, the unit was involved in the murder and torture of ANC supporters. Coetzee received amnesty for Natal lawyer Griffiths Mxenge's 1981 murder, while his successor at Vlakplaas, Eugene de Kock, was sentenced in the late 1990s to two life sentences plus another 212 years for his activities. He claimed consistently that he had acted only on orders from the highest level of government.

The TRC testimony of Major General Joep Joubert, Special Forces commander during the crucial period between 1985 and 1989, provided more insight into how extra-judicial killings by the security forces were decided upon and justified. Joubert applied for and received amnesty from the TRC in three cases involving the killing of thirteen people, including Florence and Fabian Ribeiro in Mamelodi in 1986.[57] The SADF's multiracial, multinational Special Forces had been involved since the 1970s in the government's destabilisation campaigns against neighbouring states, particularly through surrogate forces. The unit included reconnaissance experts and a small covert group called D40, which became known as Barnacle.

When the second state of emergency was declared in 1986, Barnacle's role was extended, civilian front organisations were set up and the name was changed to the Orwellian-sounding Civil Cooperation Bureau (CCB). This was done with the 'full knowledge of all people at the highest level but it operated according to its own set of financial rules and regulations which had been approved at [that] level', according to Joubert. The CCB's work was of such a nature that it bypassed the normal command structure by reporting directly to the chief of the SADF, with some operations being vetted by the minister of defence or the state president.[58]

Joubert described the security strategy at that time as follows: 'In the middle to late 1980s, one of the main aims ... was to halt the mobilisation of ... revolutionary forces, especially the ANC's. The acceptance of this aim contained far more than was immediately apparent. In the mid-1980s it was clear that the onslaught could not be countered in normal conventional ways, so the defence force or the security forces had to become unconventional themselves. Military reaction depends on violence, uses violence as a means of achieving peace. The success or value of violence lies in its intimidatory nature ... participants, sympathisers and helpers must be disrupted and destroyed.'[59] In his submission to the TRC he wrote that 'covert aspects entailed, among others, (a) ANC members and people who contributed to the struggle, had to be eliminated; (b) ANC facilities and supporting structure had to be destroyed and ANC activists, hangers-on and people who supported them, also had to be eliminated'. Thus, according to Joubert, civilians were regarded as legitimate targets. 'Elimination' included 'killing'. This fits the interpretation of Beaufre's total strategy: 'The enemy's military machine is attacked as well as its domestic support.'[60] Joubert also testified that the NP cabinet and the SSC had known about the operations, but did not intervene.

Joubert testified to the TRC that Magnus Malan and SADF generals Jannie Geldenhuys, Constand Viljoen and Kat Liebenberg were involved in a decision before the second state of emergency in 1986 that the ANC had to be stopped 'at any cost', including by means of unconventional methods.[61] Minutes were also produced from a 1987 meeting between Joubert and Geldenhuys, then chief of the SADF, where the latter indicated that he did not consider Special Forces' actions as murder, but as attacks on enemy targets.[62] Joubert testified that Geldenhuys instructed him to devise a strategy for assisting the police inside the country.[63]

Despite the coherence between Joubert's understanding and official statements of policy, Geldenhuys vehemently denied in his testimony that he had given Joubert permission to kill people. But Geldenhuys admitted to the TRC that he had been informed about the Ribeiro killings but took no steps towards prosecuting those responsible.[64] Neither Geldenhuys nor Joubert testified at the subsequent inquest, and the deaths were covered up. Joubert was under the impression that the police senior command had authorised the killings. Geldenhuys took steps to put in place procedures to ensure that no such future operations were conducted without approval.

On behalf of the TRC, advocate Glen Goosen pointed out to Geldenhuys that the fact that he (Geldenhuys) regarded Joubert's assumption of approval as bona fide and took no steps against him, indicated implicit approval for the elimination of identified individuals. Geldenhuys again denied this.

The CCB was responsible for murdering SWAPO secretary general Anton Lubowski and University of the Witwatersrand academic David Webster. In his 1997 submission to the TRC, Magnus Malan admitted that he had approved the forging of the CCB 'in principle' to infiltrate, gather information and 'disrupt the enemy'.[65] But he insisted that the organisation's operations in Region 6, as the whole of South Africa was called in CCB jargon, were activated without his knowledge. He only became aware of such operations in November 1989, he said. Nevertheless, he felt the CCB had provided the SADF 'with good covert capabilities'.

His statement became more contradictory. Malan said the instructions to SADF members 'were clear: destroy the terrorists, their bases and their capabilities. This was also government policy.' At the same time, '[t]he killing of political opponents of the government, such as the slaying of Dr Webster, never formed part of the brief of the South African Defence Force.' This is where he contradicts commanding officers such as Joubert and De Kock.

Malan stuck to the excuse trotted out by soldiers the world over: some of his instructions as a professional soldier and minister of defence resulted in civilian casualties due to 'cross-fire', which he 'sincerely regrets', but regarded as 'unfortunately ... part of the ugly reality of war'. Nevertheless, he insisted that he 'never issued an order or authorised an order for the assassination of anybody, nor was I ever approached for such authorisation by any member of the South African Defence Force'.[66] Malan's denials were echoed by other former heads of the SADF, such as Geldenhuys and Georg Meiring.

The only orders admitted to by the NP government were the bombing, of the headquarters of COSATU and the South African Council of Churches, which also housed Black Sash offices, in 1987 and 1988. Vlok applied for amnesty for the attacks, conceding that PW Botha had approved both. Neither attack caused fatalities, with Vlok alleging that they had been planned that way. Seemingly, he admitted to the bombings in an attempt to 'prove' that the government had not authorised operations in which someone would knowingly be killed, and therefore had never conspired to kill its opponents. However, despite his protestations and those of other NP leaders, one finds recommendations such as 'neutralise the ANC leadership' in *Strategie ter bekamping van die ANC* (Strategy to combat the ANC), adopted at an August 1986 meeting of the SSC, and 'intimidators must be neutralised by way of formal and informal policing' in *Konsep Nasionale Strategie teen die Rewolusionêre Oorlog teen die RSA* (Concept National Strategy against the Revolutionary War against the RSA), adopted by the SSC on 1 December of the same year.[67]

Another SSC document, dated 24 January 1987, directed the security forces to 'identify and eliminate the revolutionary leaders and especially those with charisma'.[68] Other phrases found in SSC documents are *fisiese vernietiging* (physical destruction), *uithaal* (take out) and *ander metodes as aanhouding* (methods other than detention).

Pik Botha and Vlok both admitted before the TRC that members of the security forces would have interpreted such phrases as orders to kill. Botha said that without instructions from senior command structures, operators would not have distinguished between killing 'terrorists' who threatened the lives of civilians and people who did not pose such a threat, but belonged to the same organisations as the 'terrorists'.[69]

According to Vlok, expressions such as 'eliminate', 'neutralise', 'take out' and 'destroy' were commonly used and were a reflection of the 'war psychosis' that existed at the time. He disingenuously suggested that NP leaders had erred by omitting to ensure that such terms were clarified. Vlok insisted that while the SSC took 'no decisions' for the security forces to act illegally, in hindsight 'it would have been unavoidable that people who did not experience the spirit and intent of [SSC] meetings could very easily come to other conclusions and apparently they have indeed done so, especially the divisional commanders and their troops on the ground who were constantly reliant or were responsible for controlling uncontrollable situations and to normalise abnormal situations, and on whom there was extreme pressure from amongst others, their commanding officers, politicians and society in general. [T]hese people would not easily have linked an innocent interpretation to these expressions.'

Absurdly, Vlok acknowledged that SAP Strategic Communication (Stratcom) instructions could have resulted in unlawful conduct, but said his participation in such decision-making was 'unconscious'.[70] There 'can be no doubt that I possibly used words and expressions which the people under me could have interpreted as something other than what I had intended it to be, namely as an instruction to act illegally. The same goes to a certain extent for the apparent ratification of illegal action by policemen during the struggle.'[71]

The investigation of other methods of combat included considering the creation of a 'third force'. De Klerk, Malan and Vlok all admitted to the TRC that the option arose in 1985 to establish a third force to deal 'exclusively with unrest and counter-revolutionary matters'.[72] The SSC assigned Vlok to head up a committee to look into the issue. A work group recommended the '*restructuring of the South African Police instead of the establishment of an independent force*' (author's emphasis).

On 24 March 1986, the Vlok committee resolved to recommend 'against the formation of a third force *in favour of* the further development and restructuring

The 1909 South African convention – the first elite transition. Notable among the delegates were the following people: Front row from left: JW Sauer, John X Merriman, MT Steyn and Abraham Fischer. Louis Botha is fourth from the end. Second row: General Christiaan de Wet is fourth from right, with LS Jameson of Jameson Raid infamy third from right. General Barry Hertzog is second last in the row. Third row: General JH de la Rey is first and General Jan Smuts is second last

The excluded. From left, Thomas Mapikela, Walter Rubusana, John Dube, Saul Msane and Sol Plaatje. They formed the 1914 delegation of the South African National Native Congress to London to lobby for black South Africans' rights

The founder. James Barry Munnik Hertzog at the time of the National Party's genesis. He served as prime minister from 1924 to 1939

Afrikaner national socialists. An Ossewa-Brandwag meeting in Johannesburg, *c.* 1943–44. From left: Emmie du Toit, JJ Smith, Adv. J de Vos, OB leader Dr JFJ (Hans) van Rensburg and Rev. SJ Stander

Nationalists in power. The first National Party cabinet of 1948. Back row from left: BJ Schoeman, FC Erasmus, TE Dönges, AJ Stals, EH Louw, SP le Roux. The last two persons are unknown. Front row from left: CR Swart, EG Jansen, Prime Minister DF Malan (1948–54), Major G Brand van Zyl, NC Havenga, JG Strijdom, PO Sauer

Fighting the disenfranchisement of coloured voters. A meeting of the Torch Commando in 1952 to protest against the National Party's attempts to change the constitution to remove coloured voters from the common voters' roll

20 000 women march. On 9 August 1956, Sophie Williams, Radima Moosa, Helen Joseph and Lilian Ngoyi (from left to right), along with women from across the country, delivered petitions to the prime minister's office at the Union Buildings, Pretoria, to protest against the extension of pass laws to black women

The lion of the north and his protégé. Prime Minister Johannes Gerhardus Strijdom (1954–58) delivering an address with minister of native affairs Hendrik Frensch Verwoerd by his side. Verwoerd succeeded him in 1958, ruling until 1966

Sharpeville 1960 – symbol of things to come. Sixty-nine black people lay dead after a police shooting during one of a number of demonstrations against the pass system

Poet Ingrid Jonker (1933–65).
'I am ... with those coloured, African who are robbed', she wrote in her poem 'I am with those'

'Cold and formal, even rude'.
Balthazar Johannes Vorster, prime minister from 1966 to 1978, with a rare hint of a smile

Soweto 1976. The children rose up against the imposition in education of the Afrikaans language, which had come to be one of the symbols of National Party oppression

The securocracy swings into action. From left to right: minister of defence General Magnus Malan and President Pieter Willem Botha (1978–89) pay homage to the cannon

The second elite transition commences. President Frederik Willem de Klerk (1989–94), with ANC deputy president Nelson Mandela next to him, speaks after the conclusion of the Groote Schuur Minute on 4 May 1990. First row from left: Pik Botha, unknown, Joe Slovo, Walter Sisulu, Alfred Nzo, Moses Mayekiso. Second row: Dawie de Villiers, Gerrit Viljoen, Mathews Phosa, Penuell Maduna. Third row: Ahmed Kathrada, Stoffel van der Merwe, Adriaan Vlok, Ruth Mompati, Joe Modise. Fourth row: Beyers Naudé, Cheryl Carolus (bending down), Thabo Mbeki, Lieutenant General Basie Smit, Jacob Zuma, Roelf Meyer, Barend du Plessis. Behind Du Plessis is NIS head Niel Barnard. Back row: General Chris Willemse, JP Roux

Death toll rising. South African Defence Force members in the streets of Alexandra township in Johannesburg in March 1992 as conflict escalated between ANC and IFP members

Boipatong anger. Residents display their views on the police, the Inkatha Freedom Party and FW de Klerk on 20 June 1992, the day De Klerk visited the township to offer his condolences after the massacre and had to flee from 3 000 ANC and PAC supporters

Who's emulating whom?
NP chief negotiator Roelf Meyer (left) and ANC chief negotiator Cyril Ramaphosa

Democracy dawns. Nelson Mandela and other ANC MPs cheer FW de Klerk on 10 May 1994, the first day of the democratically elected parliament

Exposed. Like other NP leaders, Adriaan Vlok found his actions as minister of law and order subjected to unprecedented media scrutiny at the Truth and Reconciliation Commission hearings in 1997

Elite convergence:
ANC finance minister
Trevor Manuel (right) received
an honorary doctorate from
the University of Stellenbosch
in 2001, along with his two
predecessors, NP member
and former Gencor head
Derek Keys (left) and
Chris Liebenberg, also a
former Gencor head before
becoming 'non-partisan'
finance minister in 1994

'Initiator of change'. Billionaire Anton Rupert with President Thabo Mbeki in 2004. Mbeki later hailed him for his role in 'transforming' business

Done deal. Marthinus van Schalkwyk, the last NP *hoofleier* (1997–2006), with new comrade Mosiuoa Lekota, ANC chairperson, in the background in 2004

of the capabilities of the South African Police' (author's emphasis). This proposal was presented to the SSC in a discussion document entitled *Establishment of a Special Anti-Revolutionary Ability (including a Third Force)*, dated 9 May 1986. It is thus clear that there was support for the SAP to be restructured to adopt 'third force' functions. At a meeting on 12 May in the same year, the SSC accepted the restructuring of the police, which led to the SAP enhancing its counter-insurgency capabilities.

Malan denied in his TRC testimony that Operation Marion had been aimed at creating a third force. He also denied that any 'sinister covert or unlawful aim was intended' with a third force. However, training Inkatha operatives who then became involved in extra-legal activities constitutes a function of a third force. It seems that the security forces were indeed fulfilling the function of a third force, as proven by extra-judicial killings, torture, and the supportive role of the police to Inkatha in KwaZulu and the East Rand violence. This conclusion is confirmed by Vlok's testimony to the TRC that the creation of a separate third force was rejected because its powers and functions would have overlapped with those of the SAP, apart from the extra expenditure that it would have entailed. Subdivisions of the SAP acting as a third force were also confirmed in Malan's TRC submission, for example the SSC's acceptance on 8 May 1989 that the municipal police and the extended riot control unit fulfilled the function of a third force.

In its submission to the TRC, the NP insisted that human rights violations by the security forces had been perpetrated by a handful of rogue elements who took the law into their own hands. However, the TRC found '[t]hat these were not just a few low-ranking Security Branch members who had misinterpreted their instructions is evident by the extent to which authorisation or knowledge of such killings frequently involved leadership echelons such as divisional heads of the Security Branch, staff at Security Branch headquarters as well as the commanding officers of the Security Branch, Special Forces, the chief of the SADF and, in at least two cases, the minister of law and order'.[73]

Leon Wessels conceded in his TRC testimony that 'it was foreseen ... that people would be detained, people would be tortured, everybody in the country knew people were tortured'.[74] Thus, despite NP leaders denying that they had ever approved human rights violations by the security forces, the government had year after year passed legislative measures that made them possible. One would have had to be extremely naive to believe that abusive methods were not used to extract information from detainees.

Furthermore, having legislated an environment for the use of 'unconventional' methods, the government took no steps to prevent abuse, despite official acknowledgement as early as 1964 of alleged police excesses. Torture is one step away from murder, which is the ultimate way to halt resistance against the system. Denials about the results of total strategy policies are unconvincing, given that total strategy was about either 'persuading' opponents to the NP government's position (the soft option) or eliminating them (the hard option).

White fright

In his amnesty application, Major General Sakkie Crafford described the purpose of extra-judicial killings as threefold: scaring and demoralising activists, sowing distrust among them and dissuading others from providing support; keeping information gleaned through interrogation from being disclosed; and giving 'white voters confidence that the security forces were in control and winning the fight against communism and terrorism'.[75]

That fight, however, was a war against those seeking democracy. Most abominable was the fact that the black population was terrorised and young people in particular were murdered to 'improve' the credibility of askaris posing as MK militants. Such operations amounted to additional attacks in which more civilians were killed, while conveniently boosting the claims of a total onslaught. One of the most infamous and tragic examples remains that of the Gugulethu Seven, among whom were teenage boys.

Mandla Mxinwa, Zanisile Mjobo, Zola Swelani, Godfrey Miya, Christopher Piet, Themba Mlifi and Zabonke Konile were offered military training that they would in all probability never have accessed otherwise. They were then led into an ambush and killed. Two askaris received R7 000 *kopgeld* each, R1 000 per 'head' delivered.[76]

Another case was brought to the TRC by former police commissioner General Johan van der Merwe. While head of the security branch, he sought approval for the killing of eight 'troublemakers', students who were members of COSATU. Notorious askari Joe Mamasela posed as an ANC activist and recruited the students, who were alleged to be planning attacks on black councillors and police officers in East Rand townships. They were trained in the use of hand grenades and limpet mines and assigned to blow up an electricity substation. However, they were supplied with hand grenades and limpet mines that had been booby-trapped by Vlakplaas operatives. Eight people died and seven were seriously injured. Van der Merwe admitted in his amnesty application that approval had came from Louis le Grange, minister of law and order at the time, and that police commissioner General Johan Coetzee had been involved in the planning. However, the former head of the Northern Transvaal security police and Vlakplaas, Brigadier Jac Cronjé, said in his amnesty application that Van der Merwe had confirmed to him that PW Botha personally authorised the operation.[77]

Booby-trapping was done by security force members to create the impression that MK operatives were inept, as well as to mislead the public about the true identity of the perpetrators behind the attacks. Weapons were planted in cases where unarmed people were killed, while others were necklaced to create the impression that they were victims of 'black-on-black' violence. This had the added spin-off of persuading the white electorate to 'once again vote for the National Party in light of the black onslaught', as police operative Sampina Bokaba told the TRC.[78]

A milder version of this strategy was Vlok's admission that bomb threats were 'created' following the release of the film *Cry Freedom*, which depicted Steve Biko's life and death. Security branch members pretending to be right-wingers telephoned threats to cinemas, and explosive devices were placed at cinemas in Durban and Roodepoort.

'I judged the risk that this film would have and it was so enciteful [*sic*] that this risk was too big,' Vlok told the TRC.[79] The bomb threats allowed the state to ban the film in terms of media regulations under the state of emergency. Similar operations included the bombing in 1988 of the 'Why Not' club in Hillbrow, Johannesburg, which injured patrons, and the bombing of the toilets at a 'whites only' beach at the Strand in the Cape in an effort to implicate the UDF, which had launched its 'Open the beaches' campaign.

The white community was flooded with propaganda about the communist onslaught that South Africa faced. The propaganda was spread through state schools, NP structures and extensions in civil society, such as church and cultural organisations, the public broadcaster and pro-NP media. The entrapment killings of black activists formed part of the propaganda campaign. Such incidents offered a pretext for further state intervention, which created a sense of trust in the security forces and the government among white people living in fear because of total strategy propaganda. This points to a cyclical reinforcement of white fear as one of the vital ingredients in keeping the NP in power.

White rule was being reproduced through not only the spread of misinformation about the level of danger to white South Africans, but also the 'creation' of attacks. Booby-trapped attacks increased the volume of incidents and justified further state action to shore up white rule, which was presented as being under threat. The state could justify undertaking whatever action it deemed necessary.

But not all white people or all Afrikaners were swallowing what the rulers were serving up. This was exemplified by the alternative weekly newspaper *Vrye Weekblad* and the Voëlvry alternative Afrikaans music movement in the late 1980s. Johannes Kerkorrel (aka journalist Ralph Rabie) with his group, the Gereformeerde Blues Band; Koos Kombuis (aka author André Letoit); and Bernoldus

Niemand (aka musician James Phillips) toured the country despite harassment by the security forces. Their music gave voice in Afrikaans to the mood of dissent among a growing section of Afrikaners. In the song 'Energie' (Energy), Kerkorrel criticised the prevailing uncritical mentality and compensatory patronage among Afrikaners that created the space for apartheid repression:

> Don't ask questions
> About the things that bother you
> You must learn to keep quiet
> You'll get a gold watch.[80]

Fascist impulses

Some commentators note that capital's enthusiasm for the Botha regime and its reforms was somewhat dampened by 1985. Economist Sampie Terreblanche ascribes this to the failure of early reforms in the 1980s to quell black opposition.[81] After all, some of these reforms were put forward by capital itself, and rejected resoundingly by the black majority as insufficient.

The crisis of political legitimacy that had exploded in 1976 gained force as the tricameral compromise and efforts to co-opt black workers were snubbed, and the space created by the reforms utilised to further undermine the system. Instead of becoming acquiescent, the newly recognised black trade unions became more demanding. Consequently, the corporatist solution envisaged by capital and the state as part of the black insider/outsider scheme floundered.

Corporatism aims at creating a rift between those who are granted resources to organise and have access to political power, and those excluded from such resources and access.[82] The black trade unions entered into a relationship with state and capital, but insisted on their own terms, thereby knocking another hole in the NP's strategy of 'reforms', while putting more pressure on its concomitant strategy of repression. By the mid-1980s, the NP was losing the initiative. In their paltriness, the reforms ignited more black political expression, which could not be effectively doused.

It is little wonder, then, that PW Botha was gearing up for a step witnessed elsewhere in the world with devastating effects. After having suffered what was possibly his second stroke, Botha announced his resignation as *hoofleier* – but not as state president – on 2 February 1989. He had decided to disengage himself from the majority party in parliament and 'rise above party politics', but did not indicate whether he would carry out NP policy in future, saying merely that he would 'take note' of decisions emanating from NP congresses.

Having unshackled himself from parliamentary oversight in his 1983 constitution, and now also from whatever little party caucus oversight existed, he planned to hold on to his position as executive state president, from whence he would exercise unfettered power. By cutting himself loose from the majority party, he would sever the last thread of parliamentary accountability for the presidency. According to Botha, he would act from the assumption that his power base rested among 'all good South Africans'.[83]

In his analysis of Italy before the Second World War, Robert Cox[84] argued that the failure of capitalist corporatism to contain social and economic crises produced fascism. Conditions in the South Africa of the 1980s reveal noteworthy similarities. An economic crisis had existed since 1981 – the country's deepest and longest-ever recession. Finance minister Barend du Plessis was pursuing policies of fiscal conservatism, as had his counterparts in Italy and Germany in the 1930s. Efforts by capital and state to manage black labour conflict through institutionalisation were failing. Accountability to parliament had been replaced by an executive presidency heading the elaborate National Security Management System, designed to repress resistance down to community level. Finally, the apartheid state shared the same origins as the fascist state, namely growth from a distortion of the interventionist welfare state.[85]

The potential for descent into fascist dictatorship, amid a worldwide swing to democracy, was ripe. But South Africa was not to repeat the Olympic-scale feat of swimming against global currents, as it had done in 1948. Too many factors militated against another such regression. Ironically, one of these factors was the party of apartheid itself.

By splitting the NP *hoofleierskap* from the state presidency, Botha had single-handedly robbed himself of his power base within the party. For De Klerk, Botha's surprise action illustrated to what extent he had lost touch with the NP leadership. In the ensuing battle for the *hoofleierskap*, Botha supported Barend du Plessis, indicating his desire for continuation of the alliance between the *verligtes*, as representatives of capitalism, and the military.

The fact that Botha did not select defence minister General Magnus Malan as his preferred candidate signalled that, while the military under Afrikaner leadership had become a significant force during the 1970s and 1980s, it was still trumped by the civilian element in the NP leadership. De Klerk's election as party leader confirmed that the civilian element had won out over the securocratic element.

The NP leadership would have none of Botha's plans and, increasingly concerned about his political judgement given the stroke he had suffered, moved to force his resignation. The party's federal council voted twenty-two to seven in favour of the posts of *hoofleier* and state president becoming one again. Those opposed were Botha crony Heunis and other members of the Cape NP. The parliamentary caucus supported the decision unanimously.[86] The cabinet was also unanimous in its support of De Klerk's proposal that Botha should go on sick leave and appoint an acting president.

Not only did Botha's preferred candidate not make the grade, but the members of cabinet and the parliamentary caucus were predominantly opposed to the idea of Botha as 'everybody's president'. His ambitions were snuffed inside the NP, illustrating that the multi-level external and internal crises had proved too much for the intra-class alliance that Botha had set up between capital, the reformed Afrikaner nationalists and the military. The libertarian flickers within the NP had won out over the autocratic inclinations. The significance of Botha's ousting is akin to DF Malan's NP triumphing over the national socialist Ossewa-Brandwag and Nuwe Orde. For a second time, fascist tendencies within Afrikaner ranks had been defeated.

Having said that, I do not wish to suggest that apartheid was a democratic system. Clearly it was not, and by the second half of the 1980s, it had shifted even more decisively towards authoritarianism. It had always involved an oligarchy, a system with limited democratic features for the few. But even this limited democracy was being whittled away towards the end of Botha's tenure, through military deployment inside the country, media and other restrictions. For white minority rule to be maintained, these repressive measures would have had to be intensified, and it was that option which the NP leadership rejected when they removed Botha.

Why did the NP not go the dictatorship route? In Italy, the fascists rose to power when the dominant capitalist classes lost faith in the ability of their political parties to maintain conditions for profit-making. They 'connived to create a power they themselves could not control'.[87] In South Africa, Botha was unable to lure the capitalist classes into such a deadly deal. Not only had the relationship between Botha and business cooled considerably to a state of tension by the late 1980s, but the militarist option as demonstrated by the declaration of a second state of emergency in 1986 also clashed with South African capital's libertarian leanings. Pronouncements in the 1980s and the Urban Foundation's programmes showed that capital sought the increased liberalisation of society, including politics.

The shifts in the class base underpinning the NP also served to block Botha, as since the 1970s Afrikaner capitalist classes had expressed their disdain for what Sanlam chairperson Andreas Wassenaar called the 'communist' tendencies[88] in the NP government. For 'communist', read 'state interventionist'. Afrikaner capitalists developed an aversion to the very state interventionist policies that had established Afrikaner capital and wanted the NP to discard those policies. This new class force in the NP would not support the option of an even heavier-handed government.

Remarkably, this remained the case even after Botha had used his extended powers as state president in 1986 to iron out bureaucratic obstacles in the way of business. The *verligtes* within the NP were also not prepared to follow Botha where he was heading. Comparing the rise of fascism in Zimbabwe and Italy, the analyst Timothy Scarnecchia finds that political survival gained precedence over economic planning in Mugabe's Zimbabwe.[89] This did not happen in South Africa. As will be seen, even after 1990 the militarists threw their lot in with the capitalists.

The final factor that steered NP leaders away from autocracy was that the world was quite a different place in the 1980s than the one that gave rise to a fascist Italy. By the 1930s, *laissez-faire* capitalism had produced too many contradictions; in the 1980s, *laissez-faire* capitalism was very much on the rise. Neo-liberal globalisation had gathered such impetus that countries were bound together much more tightly. It had become difficult for any state to ignore external pressure, especially as a middle-level power on the periphery of the world capitalist system. South African capital was looking towards reincorporation into the world economy as the panacea for its stunted growth. This became apparent when all the primary representatives of organised business, including Afrikaner and black capital, illustrated their affinities with liberal capitalist countries by handing US senator Edward Kennedy a 'wish list' when he visited South Africa in 1985. Among others, they called for black political participation.[90]

After the disastrous Rubicon address, business associations and the Urban Foundation released a statement calling for negotiations, not least with black leaders in detention. However, the statement also confirmed business's continued ideological synchronisation with white minority domination, since it called for 'genuine power-sharing', but not universal franchise.[91] In 1985, disappointment in the NP regime led business to Lusaka under Anglo American chairperson Gavin Relly to meet with the ANC's Oliver Tambo and others, one of the first trips of its kind.[92]

Following the visit, ninety-one business leaders, including Relly and Harry Oppenheimer, called for 'equal opportunity, respect for the individual, freedom of enterprise and freedom of movement'. Again, no mention was made of one person, one vote. Instead, a fuzzy constitutional arrangement was suggested that would accommodate South Africa's 'extremely heterogeneous society'.[93] Big business's libertarianism only allowed it to go that far.

The Washington connection

In addition to pressure from big business, the NP government faced the considerable influence of external players, such as the World Bank and the International Monetary Fund. These financial institutions, both based in Washington, DC, had been goading the South African government towards neo-liberalism since the 1970s. Firmly under the control of the West and especially the US, they had provided loans to the NP regime from 1951 onwards, assisting Eskom, railways and harbours, and later the Lesotho Highlands Water Project.[94]

The bulk of IMF loans to South Africa were supplied after 1970, when the world capitalist system entered a crisis of accumulation. The largest loans were provided at the time of the Soweto uprising in a typical display of imperviousness to anti-democratic conditions – an ideological position for which both the World Bank and the IMF came increasingly under fire from the 1990s.

In the 1980s, Pretoria went into security overdrive amid severe economic recession. As a result, its reliance on loans from the IMF and private banks increased. The NP government's application for another IMF loan in 1982 was concealed for a few months at the request of the US state department, because it was expected to be controversial. This proved correct, and the United Nations, human rights groups and others argued against it on political grounds. Some of the IMF's executive directors were also opposed, citing economic grounds. Ultimately, the loan was approved thanks to the support of the US and Britain.

The IMF's assistance proved critical at a time when the government had recurring balance of payment problems.[95] In the international financial realm, support from the IMF and the World Bank was and remains a stamp of approval for a country – it opens the door to loans from private banks. The implications of IMF backing for Pretoria therefore went beyond direct financial benefits and arguably served as a lifeline that delayed the necessity of substantial political change in the 1970s and early 1980s. The public relations fallout from the 1982 loan forced a change in the US, with a law pertaining to funding of the IMF being passed with an anti-apartheid amendment. No further loans were extended during the 1980s. Political economist Vishnu Padayachee puts this down to a realisation among Western states that their interests could not 'be served in the longer run under an old-style apartheid form of state', and that a peaceful settlement of the political conflict was necessary to prevent 'the danger of South Africa slipping out of the Western sphere of influence altogether'.[96] Therefore, withdrawal of IMF loans was part of a strategy to apply pressure on the South African government. This was done in order to pre-empt more radical change, ensuring that South Africa 'become[s] "respectable" again within the world capitalist system', thereby enabling the West to hold on to South Africa as a politically sympathetic country in the southern African region.[97]

At the end of September 1990, on the first visit of a South African head of state to the US since Jan Smuts, FW de Klerk specifically met with the IMF and the World Bank. He was relieved to be given a hearty welcome by US president

George Bush Sr, as this signalled the reception he could expect from the two financial institutions.[98]

While political conditions apparently did not form part of the 1982 approval, economic considerations did. The NP extended the neo-liberal policies that it had tentatively launched in the 1970s. Capital outflows increased as exchange controls for non-residents were lifted, while monetary control was tightened, interest rates increased and consumer subsidies frozen.[99]

IMF teams continued to advise the NP government throughout the 1980s, facilitating its shift to neo-liberalism. In the late 1980s the IMF-dictated policy of privatisation benefited the Afrikaner elite, who were able to buy up state assets, much as politicians in several African states parcelled off state assets courtesy of the World Bank's structural adjustment programmes during the same decade. The IMF also devised the government's adoption of value added tax in 1991.[100]

De Klerk appointed businessperson Wim de Villiers as minister of privatisation in his first cabinet. This portfolio was later taken over by De Klerk's confidant, Dawie de Villiers. Sasol was one of the parastatals sold off at that point, while Telkom was commercialised in preparation for privatisation.

In conclusion, the centralisation of power during the Botha era protected not only white rule, but specifically NP rule. Maintaining state power had everything to do with maintaining NP power. The state was the lifeblood of the party, and the NP leaders made no distinction between the two. This was evident in the use of state structures and funds to essentially extend the life of the party and its policies. The administration of apartheid demanded a huge bureaucratic base – which resisted attempts at its own dismantlement. This emerged even more strongly during the transition, as NP politicians clung to their positions and pensions while protecting the interests of one of their primary constituencies, white civil servants. Thus, while the NP was cutting back state spending, it promised civil servants that their jobs were safe.[101]

The 'militarisation of society' may be a euphemism for what was happening in reality. Under Botha, South Africa was moving towards centralised executive state power devoid of parliamentary sanction, to prohibition on political expression, media freedom and freedom of association, punctuated by overt and covert violent repression in cases where the prohibitions were violated. While the apartheid state had always exhibited authoritarian overtones, Botha's imperial reign saw tyranny's claws sink ever deeper.

By 1988, PW Botha realised that the writing was on the wall and asked Barend du Plessis to assess his remaining level of support in the caucus.[102] At that juncture, the feeling within the NP leadership was that resources and energies should be concentrated on finding a workable constitutional solution.

There remained little confidence that Botha was able to lead the country and the party out of the quandary, and the general feeling was that he should retire at the beginning of 1989. After Botha's first health setback in January 1989, a delegation of his colleagues visited him with the request that he should resign. Botha became furious and defiant. Like all NP leaders before him, he was unwilling to go voluntarily. But unlike other NP leaders, especially his successor, he turned the situation into a spectacle and it finally took a palace revolution to get rid of him.

The rise of the *verligtes* during the Botha era meant that by the time the NP sat down to negotiate with the ANC, the party had made the shift from Afrikaner nationalist to white capital, elite and middle-class interests, Afrikaans and English. It had selected the libertarian, capitalist option and rejected the reactionary path to autocracy as propounded by Botha. It was seeking ways to retain some political power.

Through a series of innovative policy and institutional models, the NP had exhausted the possibilities of maintaining white rule through the co-option of coloured, Indian and black middle classes as a bulwark against the majority. The obvious next step after crossing the language and cultural barriers between Afrikaner and English elites was to establish a class alliance across racial lines to secure the 'free capitalist way of life'.

CHAPTER 5

The negotiations and the violence

We have got to look for our salvation to that fascinating business of constitution making. — Harry Oppenheimer,
head of Anglo American, 1980[1]

Even the head of an illegitimate, discredited minority regime has certain moral standards to uphold. — Nelson Mandela,
ANC president, 1991

The state contributed to a general pattern of violence that was obviously repressive, and on the other hand there were individuals who acted on their own. — Roelf Meyer, former NP deputy minister
of law and order and chief negotiator, 2006[2]

THE MULTIPARTY NEGOTIATIONS BETWEEN 1990 AND 1994 PUSHED the NP into unfamiliar political terrain. Its grip on South Africa became shakier as talks with the ANC proceeded. Their verbal power tussle started officially on 20 December 1991 and passed through turbulent moments before its end on 18 November 1993. The culmination was an interim constitution and South Africa's first democratic election on 27 April 1994.

These were years scarred not only by duplicity, suspicion and games of brinkmanship among political leaders, but also by the highest number of political deaths ever recorded in a country drenched by intermittent bouts of bloodshed since the days of colonisation. Citizens were drawn into a low-level civil war that at times verged on full-scale conflagration. Activities aimed by both the state and political organisations at terrorising civilians were at their peak. The anonymity of assailants, dubbed a 'third force' by the ANC, heightened public fear, as it was no doubt intended to do. People were being thrown off trains, hacked to death in their flimsy homes, shot in the back at political demonstrations and butchered at night vigils for the dead. Children were counted among the casualties again and again. South Africa was peering into the abyss, as political scientist Willie Esterhuyse observed.

Political violence decreased after April 1994. The euphoria, the widely felt sense of something described with the nebulous concept 'miracle', was born of the sheer relief of having teetered on the edge, and surviving. A number of years would have to pass before South Africans could allow themselves to question their 'miracle' and acknowledge that the problems facing them were even more indomitable than imagined. Examination of the transition, sometimes tainted with cynicism, could take place only within the luxury of putting several years between themselves and widespread murder.

National disputes erupted over the nature and outcome of the negotiations. From the conservative, mostly white vantage point, the claim was made in media columns and letters to newspapers that the ANC had outmanoeuvred the NP, with the latter sacrificing white interests by agreeing to a simple one-person, one-vote democracy – what one could call the 'we wuz robbed' allegation.

From a critical-theory vantage point – which this book supports – the assertion was that the NP, in concert with the ANC, had successfully created an 'elite transition'.[3] South Africa was in the grip of the second elite pact of the twentieth century, the first of which was the alliance of maize and gold across language and cultural lines in 1909; the second was across racial lines in 1993/4. The result was the broadening of interests to give the upper echelons of the economy an increasingly multiracial character, without diminishing white interests. This was done by adopting a liberal-democratic constitution that safeguarded individual rights and, most significantly, property rights.

Seemingly unfamiliar with the critical-theory position, one-time NP supporters launched a campaign of complaint about the party leadership's betrayal of its support base on radio talk shows and in newspapers. As affirmative action policies and black economic empowerment initiatives kicked in, aspersions were cast on the quality of NP leadership at Codesa, leading De Klerk to exclaim to this author in a 1999 interview: 'It was not capitulation!'[4]

In scholarly articles, books and Nasionale Pers publications, historian and political scientist Hermann Giliomee analysed where the NP had 'failed'. He blamed De Klerk. A strong case could be made, said Giliomee, 'for the view that under President PW Botha ... or under several possible successors other than Frederik W de Klerk, the NP could have and would have dominated the country into the next century, including [through] new but quite unworkable policies designed to keep Afrikaner control'.[5] Giliomee acknowledged that white domination strategies would ultimately have been futile. Indeed, the alternative was to increase state repression to the extent of South Africa becoming a full-blown dictatorship.

But undertones of resentment were noticeable in Giliomee's arguments, as indicated by the title of one article, 'Surrender without defeat'. He maintained that De Klerk misled those whites who had voted 'yes' in the 1992 referendum, as the NP did not ensure power sharing as promised, but buckled under pressure for ordinary majority rule. He was also scathing of De Klerk's management of the transition process, particularly his selection of negotiators.[6] Giliomee bemoaned the rising generation of leadership in the early 1990s, including chief

NP negotiator Roelf Meyer, who personified what Giliomee called 'free-floating political entrepreneurs'.[7] By this he meant that the collapse of Afrikaner nationalism had freed them from the rigours of accounting to the *volk*. Other commentators called the NP's position a 'strategic surrender' and a 'disguised surrender'.[8]

In a column in *Rapport* in February 1997, Giliomee again castigated the NP for surrendering Afrikaner self-determination. This led to a raging debate in the Afrikaans press, which the conservative editor of *Rapport* at the time, Izak de Villiers, joined: 'The dam wall has broken. The great word has been spoken; the Afrikaner, nay, the non-black, has been routed at the negotiating table.'[9]

De Klerk responded in an article in *Rapport* that 'the new dispensation (with all its shortcomings) was neither a victory nor a defeat for anyone, but a product of mostly reasonable compromises by all the major role players.' In March 1999, Giliomee again argued that the outcome of the negotiations showed that De Klerk did not honour the mandate he was given by white voters.[10]

However, it was rather a case of De Klerk and the NP navigating the rough seas of the negotiated transition while remaining as close as possible to their goal of entrenching white power. While they ended with a political result that fell short of this goal, they managed to embed white economic power for the foreseeable future – with the aid of other players. Mainstream analysts tend to err by excluding economics from their assessments. Without regard to the economic concessions made by the ANC between 1990 and 1993, the significance of the outcome of the negotiations remains opaque.

The *Groot Krokodil*'s last sputter

A persistent point of contention is why De Klerk, whose reputation was that of NP conservative, made his monumental announcement on 2 February 1990. Surprise over his apparent change of tack is overplayed, in the process obscuring the options available to the NP government at the time.

As *hoofleier*, De Klerk applied party policy. Since the 1970s, the NP had sought ways to create elite alliances. This was evident in Botha's bid to find new allies among the black middle class, and it was the strategy touted by capitalists for many years, taken further by the Urban Foundation and the Wiehahn and Riekert commissions. Labour market reform ensured better remuneration and rights for black workers. Government was in full pursuit of black conservative leaders through its policy on representation at local level. Under Botha, the NP also attempted to accommodate Indians and coloureds politically, dispensing with the Afrikaner lower classes in the process. The NP had coalesced with the libertarian and capitalist position of the English-speaking economic elite, with class subsuming race as its fundamental obsession. The NP leadership realised that its efforts to make South Africa safe for white capital accumulation had to include blacks if such accumulation was to continue.

These initiatives included secret discussions between minister of justice Kobie Coetsee and National Intelligence Service head Niel Barnard with Mandela from the mid-1980s onwards. Mandela steadfastly refused to buckle on the armed struggle, majority rule and the ANC's alliance with the South African Communist Party.

Botha's piecemeal, watered-down versions of consociational compromise backfired. The various small carrots held out to the black leadership corps produced no takers, not even among the more malleable leaders. The reason was simple: it was clear that the NP wanted to hold on to white domination, and any concessions made were inadequate to achieve an elite transition. Botha's reformism peaked in 1984, overtaken by increasing authoritarianism to quell resistance.

By the end of the 1980s, South Africans had reached a political impasse. The economic crisis and the nature of civil upheaval meant the state could not suppress resistance absolutely. On the other hand, the state still possessed enough power to prevent the political forces associated with resistance from defeating it. Carrying on along the same path would have wrecked prospects of economic recovery. But how to get out of this cul-de-sac?

Botha's last years marked the re-emergence of the intellectual drought that had started under BJ Vorster, encapsulated in lyrics by the alternative Afrikaans rock group, the Gereformeerde Blues Band, at the time: 'Does anybody have another idea? / No more ideas, no more ideas'.[11] Botha's answer was increased militarisation, the refuge of the ideologically bankrupt. His 'total strategy' reactivated the possibilities for white domination, but turned South Africa into a siege society. But then the *raison d'être* of total strategy was negated as the overstated communist threat disappeared in the dust of a crumbling USSR. The NP leadership became impatient with Botha. In the face of unrelenting pressure, he resigned as president on 14 August 1989.

The leadership's rejection of the ailing Botha was an acknowledgement that the military option had ultimately become unsustainable. The election of De Klerk confirmed that this position was widely held, as he never shared his predecessor's militarist convictions. He had, in fact, become alienated from Botha towards the end of the latter's term in office.[12] However, the end of Botha did not mean the end of his strategies. Just as the NP persisted with Botha-esque consociational reformist approaches, so did belief in the militarist option – including legal and illegal actions – among some within the ruling bloc.

Just three weeks after the palace revolution against Botha, the NP leadership faced a general election on 6 September. It crafted a five-year action plan based on a June 1989 Broederbond document titled *Basic constitutional conditions for the survival of the Afrikaner*. In the plan, the NP indicated its intention to create a 'new South Africa', describing it as 'a democracy where no group should dominate or be dominated by another; the independence of the judiciary should be respected; civilised norms should apply; an economy based on free enterprise should flourish; everybody should live safely and orderly; [and which co-exists] in good neighbourliness with the international community'.[13] Thus the NP emphasised that it rejected *oorheersing* (domination), that it believed in democracy, and that this was possible without *oorheersing*.[14]

The agenda for the NP's federal (national) congress held in the first half of 1989 catered for discussion on 'A democracy: Participation by everybody' and 'No domination: Protection of groups'.[15] De Klerk told parliament in the run-up to the election that the NP was 'planning a constitutional system in which [no] group will ... be put in a position to dominate over another. Black majority government is as unacceptable as white minority government!'[16]

The NP thus rejected a common voters' roll and still believed at that point that parliamentary representation should be on the basis of racial categorisation, that a veto mechanism should be created in place of the president's council and that decision-making should remain split along the lines of 'own' and 'general/joint' affairs. It reiterated its support for 'a great indaba' – a position the Democratic Party and its predecessor the PFP had been advocating but which, until the mid-1980s, the NP contended would lead to capitulation.

At the same time, the NP stressed the import of dealing with 'unrest, violence and terrorism'.[17] NP rhetoric before the election relied heavily on the fear factor and open assertions that the ANC threat could not be handled legally: 'It is not difficult to imagine what the result of an election on the basis of one man, one vote on a common voters' roll would be if a violent organisation like the ANC is let loose in the non-White townships ... We know from experience what will happen. Intimidation will be rife and assaults – and even murder – will be the order of the day. The DP [Democratic Party] plans to deal with such atrocities through the normal legal channels, *which have been shown to be inadequate in the counter-revolutionary struggle*. It is therefore clear that the implementation of DP policies would result in uncontrollable violence, bloodshed and the eventual transfer of political power to the perpetrators of it all'[18] (author's emphasis).

The NP was therefore openly pitching its ability to yield state power outside of legal channels as part of its promise to safeguard white domination. The message kept the party in power, but 1989 marked its worst showing in thirty years: it took 93 of the 166 seats in parliament, losing 17 to the Conservative Party and 12 to the newly formed DP, headed by the troika of Zach de Beer and former NP leaders Denis Worrall and Wynand Malan. Significantly, the

NP drew more support from English-speaking voters than from Afrikaners – 50 per cent as opposed to 46 per cent. The party had all but shed its cultural character. The CP managed to push its support up from 26.4 per cent in 1987 to 31.2 per cent in 1989. The DP drew 20.4 per cent of the ballot, which was less than the 27 per cent of the liberal vote collected in 1981 by the New Republic Party (ex–United Party) and the Progressive Federal Party together. The shrinking of the liberal vote – after its improved showing in the 1970s – reflected the siege mentality that gripped the white community at large during the 1980s.

Academic Janis Grobbelaar ascribes the CP's success to the fact that it had positioned itself as the torch-bearer of Afrikaner nationalism. Led by a former Dutch Reformed Church *dominee* and Broederbond president, the CP promised 'a way back. It provided psychological security, a familiar group consciousness and the conviction that the dream of white Afrikaner self-determination was, notwithstanding, defensible and viable. It promised the return to a *gemeinschaft* ethos that had once been the hallmark of Afrikaner nationalism – away from growing alienation.'[19]

De Klerk leaps

Announcing Nelson Mandela's release from prison and the lifting of the ban on the ANC, SACP, PAC and other organisations on 2 February 1990 was the NP's loftiest moment. In orchestrating these decisions along with other players, De Klerk pressed on where Botha had faltered. He believed that Botha had been on the right track, but that policies had been executed in a 'counterproductive'[20] way. Instead of Botha's blustering onslaught on friend and foe alike, De Klerk adopted a cool-headed approach to the challenges presenting themselves globally, regionally, domestically and internally in the NP. He was imbued with the same 'sense of urgency' that had become almost palpable in NP top structures at the time. He told the federal congress in 1990 that the 'moment of truth' had arrived.[21] The NP-supporting press exhorted readers to hold their criticism against the NP and give its action plan a chance, because there was no more 'time for games'.[22]

De Klerk's swing from NP conservative to dismantler of apartheid generated reams of text. How and why did this happen? He argued that the label of conservative had been attached to him unfairly while he was the minister responsible for own affairs in the 1980s, since he was merely doing his job well. But from interviews it emerged that, as with the majority of NP leaders, De Klerk's *volte face* was not the result of a Damascus experience. There was no single moment when the realisation of apartheid's folly suddenly tipped him off his donkey. As an anonymous interviewee told me: 'FW did not believe in what he was doing.' He did not have a change of heart – he opted for pragmatism. He faced the frightening prospect of maintaining white minority government through ever-increasing state violence, amid economic meltdown.[23] There was a sense in cabinet that room to manoeuvre had dwindled.[24]

The first factor in De Klerk's decision was the initiative started by Botha to engage with the ANC. This process, of which De Klerk was unaware, had been in place for four years when he assumed the mantle of president. Botha reached out to Mandela and the ANC through the ministry of justice and the National Intelligence Service. He had met with Mandela at Tuynhuys on 5 July 1989, where the latter proposed contact with the ANC in exile. Two NIS officials, Mike Louw and Maritz Spaarwater, met with the ANC's Thabo Mbeki and Jacob Zuma in Lucerne, Switzerland, on 12 September 1989. Barnard and civil servant Fanie van der Merwe were present at subsequent meetings.

De Klerk was not informed about the first meeting despite being acting president at the time. Years later, the director of the FW de Klerk Foundation saw in this a 'possible indication of the extent to which the securocrats claimed powers for themselves which they were not constitutionally entitled to'.[25]

Furthermore, foremost Afrikaner liberal Frederik van Zyl Slabbert publicly accused academic and Mbeki ally Willie Esterhuyse of inflating the roles of both the intelligence services and Mbeki in the negotiations. In the book *Africa, Define Yourself*, which Esterhuyse edited with Essop Pahad, minister in Mbeki's presidency, it was claimed that agreements reached at these talks had made the negotiations possible. Esterhuyse, who was also a Broederbond member, was asked by the NIS to make the initial contact with Mbeki, which he did on 31 May 1989.[26]

In a public response to Slabbert, Esterhuyse awarded credit for the start of the transition in the following way: 'If I had to divide 1 000 drops of water among members of the white establishment who helped before 1990 to let the rain of negotiations fall over our parched political earth, my count would be: 500 to the Niel Barnards, Louws, Spaarwaters and the National Intelligence Service; 200 to PW Botha; 100 to Kobie Coetsee; 100 to FW de Klerk; 50 to [Anglo American's] Gavin Relly; and the rest to the Dakar participants and a few others.'[27] De Klerk piled into the argument using his spokesperson and the director of his foundation, Dave Steward. He concurred with Slabbert that the NIS and the ANC had not agreed on the framework for the negotiations, as the NIS 'did not have the mandate'. The February 1990 announcements had been devised by De Klerk and his cabinet, Steward insisted.[28]

Mbeki then joined the debate through his weekly 'Letter from the President' on the ANC website: 'Ultimately, the ANC and Government delegates who were meeting in Switzerland agreed on the conditions that needed to be created to enable negotiations to take place, including the release of Nelson Mandela, and negotiated all the issues that had to be addressed to enable the ANC delegation to travel from Lusaka to Cape Town in 1990, to begin the open negotiations that led to the 1994 elections. The meeting that negotiated the return of our leaders was held in Geneva on 20–21 February 1990.'[29] Thus, while Mbeki hinted that the discussions had contained substantive issues, he also admitted that the return of ANC exiles had only been agreed upon *after* De Klerk's monumental address.

De Klerk was convinced that Botha's policies had not produced the desired results because he had lost the initiative. Regaining that initiative *vis-à-vis* general resistance was essential for success after a decade of playing catch-up. It was also crucial given the historical confluence of events. Major ideological shifts were afoot globally – the second factor in De Klerk's leap.

By 1987, the USSR's Mikhail Gorbachev had signalled his willingness to resolve conflict in the developing world, along with the US. Moscow withdrew its influence from southern Africa, leaving normalisation of the region to the US. The eventual collapse of communism was good news for the NP, since it also meant that the ANC had lost its backers. However, the threat of communism had long been a primary justification for state violence and, with its fall, the NP also faced the loss of its international allies. The absence of the *rooi gevaar* posed the risk of rendering the South African government redundant to the West, its total onslaught policies an outmoded overstatement.

The third factor was that the ANC was faltering. It had become even less of a danger than the NP government wanted white South Africans or its international friends to believe. Internally, the government had re-established control by the end of 1987, halting large-scale insurrection. A few weeks before De Klerk's address, ANC office bearer Alfred Nzo read out a document by mistake at a press briefing. It contained a frank assessment of the ANC, including the fact that it did not have the capacity to step up the armed struggle 'in any meaningful way'.[30] Umkhonto we Sizwe commander Joe Modise admitted shortly afterwards that armed operations had been downscaled, and attempted to downplay the difficulties the organisation was experiencing. Reporters visiting the ANC offices in Lusaka were struck by the inefficiency and malaise in activities. According to ANC expert Tom Lodge, by 1990 'it was uncomfortably obvious that Umkhonto's war had failed to achieve its primary purpose, the generation of a popular insurrection ... [and] it was unlikely to progress any nearer to it in the foreseeable future'.[31]

The timing of De Klerk's announcement was in keeping with the decision of an October 1985 meeting of the government's coordinating intelligence committee that negotiations should start only when a position of strength had been reached.[32] This was reaffirmed in a 1989 full-page NP press advertisement that advocated confronting 'the revolutionary threat' with 'negotiation from a position of strength! We are stronger, suppler, fitter and more uniquely capacitated for dynamic new economic progress.'[33] De Klerk was on track.

The fourth factor instrumental in De Klerk's leap was the deepening economic crisis. De Klerk was worried that a point was looming where 'not one box of grapes, one crate of fruit or a single ton of coal could be exported'.[34] The NP was intent on gaining access to foreign investment and re-establishing full economic relations with the rest of the world. The first step towards recovery was the lifting of sanctions and access to international credit – and even investment. Given that both the US and British governments at the time were positively disposed towards the NP regime, chances were that moves towards democratisation would spark favourable results without too many questions asked. This proved correct when the US government under George Bush Sr lifted sanctions against South Africa in July 1991.

The fifth factor involved a way of broadening the search for cooperative black partners, given that those allied with the NP suffered from political illegitimacy. Several efforts had been made throughout the 1980s to engage black leaders. Towards the end of the decade, the NP caucus held a think tank under NP minister Stoffel van der Merwe's leadership to find a way of incorporating blacks politically and extending the vote.[35] De Klerk took the obvious next step. Opening up the field by unbanning the ANC and others created the potential of hooking leaders with clout. De Klerk hinted at this by commenting in his 2 February address that opening up political competition would see parties judged on their policies.

The hope was that this would crack the anti-apartheid front. It did not seem to occur to De Klerk and his colleagues that the NP itself could become a victim. They had apparently pinned their hope on what Lijphart had argued for close on two decades: that the NP's 'real choice was between sharing power and losing power',[36] meaning that negotiations did not necessarily translate into the transfer of power and that the NP could hold on to (some) political power.

The final factor that exerted noticeably more influence over De Klerk's cabinet than that of his predecessor was legitimacy. While the economic crisis was pressing, the most profound problem was that of legitimacy. The doubts expressed by individual Afrikaner academics, writers and poets since the 1960s had converged with a chorus of external rejection from developing states, civil society organisations and, eventually, Western governments. Apartheid had not seemed such an aberration in a world where separate amenities were still enforced in the American South of the 1950s, or where 'half-caste' children were forcibly moved into serfdom or sexual slavery in Australia (until the 1970s). But by the late 1980s, apartheid was *the* international moral issue, drawing together countries that differed widely on other issues. In a sense, it came to symbolise the collective global injustice of North against South, as manifested in colonial and neo-colonial relations. Pressure groups in developed countries brought their governments round to what African states had been saying since their independence: apartheid was a crime against humanity. Many Afrikaners could no longer avoid the basic moral reprehensibility of a system applied in their name.

Minister of constitutional development Chris Heunis, tasked with finding constitutional alternatives in the 1980s, admitted that the fundamental problem with apartheid was that it was discriminatory. His successor Gerrit Viljoen told the 1990 Transvaal NP congress that the time had come to adopt a constitution that was acceptable to all, demanded the participation of all and was 'practicable', as experience had taught that the old way could no longer be followed. The old ways would no longer do. As finance minister Barend du Plessis said to a regional NP congress in the Northern Transvaal in 1991: 'The CP wants an election to take over government. To do what?'

De Klerk and his colleagues in the NP leadership seemed far more aware of the consequences of illegitimacy than the technocratically minded Botha and his military cronies. One of the first things De Klerk did after 2 February 1990 was to instruct his cabinet members to conduct an audit of all remaining apartheid laws with a view to repealing them. The fundamental legislation – the Population Registration Act and the Group Areas Act – was swiftly scrapped. Throughout the transition, De Klerk and his coterie sought entry to the political heaven of legitimacy – but it evaded them until the eventual demise of the party.

Within the NP, shifts were also taking place. Some of the leaders were less insulated and therefore less susceptible to old racist notions. Race was becoming less of a factor, while class interests gained import. As in the past, the *verligte/verkrampte* split governed the competition of ideas within the party. Roelf Meyer put it as follows: 'The Afrikaner's ideal of liberty clashed with that of the black community. The ideal of the Afrikaner to keep himself free could no longer be sustained because of the political, social and economic pressures. It became more and more apparent to at least the *verligte* element that the situation could not be maintained much longer. The *verkrampte* element was holding onto separation, willing to struggle until death for the sake of the liberty of the Afrikaner. [Their] paradigm was that the white person is in the minority and should therefore stay in control of the country.'[37]

The *verligte* element had been boosted after the 1987 election when half of the forty-five new MPs were recruited by veteran *verligte* Pik Botha into a 'Club of 22'. They were mostly English-speaking and they were ready for change, according to Sheila Camerer. They were a new generation of NP politicians, some of whom – like Camerer – had been exposed to black activists in their working lives. Standard old-style *swart gevaar* rhetoric did not impress them.

For example, a senior police official's briefing on the 'wickedness' of COSATU provoked much mirth – especially for Camerer, who had previously been part of a legal team representing COSATU members. While De Klerk as *hoofleier* would not tolerate Botha's empire building – he admonished Botha and the Club of 22 was disbanded – these MPs still supported Du Plessis in the leadership contest two years later.

De Klerk read the outcome of the NP *hoofleier* election in February 1989 as a message to speed up reform *à la* Botha. He beat Botha's unofficial candidate, Barend du Plessis, by a hair's breadth (69 against 61 votes), and concluded that the latter's strong showing was indicative of an 'urgent desire' within the normally conservative NP caucus to accelerate change. The message from the 'Young Turks', as represented by Du Plessis, was that the party needed renewal and that they were willing to move away from the tradition of reverence to senior leaders. In De Klerk's acceptance speech, he stated that a 'quantum leap' was necessary to extricate the NP from the corner into which it 'had been painted – or had painted [itself]'.[38] Du Plessis' response was that if De Klerk made the jump, he would land where the *verligtes* in the caucus already were.[39]

After De Klerk's election as *hoofleier*, he announced in parliament that he intended change. In a speech to the 1987 intake of MPs, De Klerk started by saying, 'I know you didn't vote for me.' He thus also felt pressure to gain the initiative *within* the party, given the close election results. In his 2 February address, he jumped further than anyone had expected when he was elected *hoofleier*, says Barend du Plessis.[40]

But, either in a bid to keep the conservatives on board or to counterbalance the *verligtes*, De Klerk appointed to his first cabinet all the conservatives who would later strongly disagree with the direction the NP was taking in the negotiations. They included Hernus Kriel, George Bartlett and Danie Schutte. But he also moved Gerrit Viljoen, the *verligte* former Broederbond head, to the crucial portfolio of constitutional development, with Roelf Meyer as his deputy.

Securing minority whites

Indications are that De Klerk was concerned about taking the white electorate with him on 2 February 1990. He took care in his epic address to parliament and the world to emphasise the link between the 1989 election outcome and his announcement: 'The general election on 6 September 1989 placed our country irrevocably on the road of drastic change. Underlying this is the growing realisation by an increasing number of South Africans that only a negotiated understanding among the representative leaders of the entire population is able to ensure lasting peace.'[41]

He constantly emphasised negotiations as 'part of the process of reforms

[as] a logical step in the progression of NP [policy],' says former health minister Rina Venter.[42] But her campaigning among NP supporters on the ground showed that the February 1990 announcement had been a 'radical break' for them. Having had to repeatedly allay the fears of voters in 1989 when she visited homes in several constituencies, Venter was concerned that many people did not grasp the implications of the course the NP had embarked on. According to her, the party's message did change somewhat at that point, but, at the same time, white voters were being mollycoddled: 'We were still saying: Don't be worried, we are not going to hand over power. We will entrench minority rights.'

This was a primary bone of contention that contributed to the party's eventual demise. De Klerk, like other NP leaders, is adamant that, far from betraying its supporters, the party was given a 'clear mandate for the continuation of reform and the creation of a new dispensation'[43] in the 1989 election. However, while the NP was suggesting change, the rhetoric followed the old recipe, fanning the flames of white fear and racism. The 1989 campaign message was vintage NP. References to 'civilised norms', to which a whole session of the 1989 federal congress was devoted, confirm that a neo-colonial mindset still prevailed in the party at that late hour. The NP's public messages also continued to portray whites as the victims of an internationally orchestrated onslaught.

The disingenuous conjuring up of images of bloodshed and intimidation by 'the enemy' would come back to haunt the NP in subsequent revelations of security force atrocities. These messages by no means came from only the conservatives within the party. By the late 1980s, *verligte* Barend du Plessis was still reaffirming the false connection between 'revolution' and international pressure on the South African government to democratise. Pik Botha, the longest-standing NP *verligte*, regularly made speeches reminiscent of George Bush Jr's latter-day Christ-like admonition that 'if you're not with us, you're against us'. Botha said, for example, that 'regarding foreign affairs, [the NP government] enjoys country-wide support of all South Africans that put South Africa's interests first'. Was it not PW Botha who used to say that 'responsible South Africans' agreed with the NP?

Even as the NP was taking comparatively unusual steps towards normalising politics, it was communicating in terms that obscured what was really happening. The party line was that it was in control, safeguarding white ('civilised') interests. For example, at its conference for election candidates in June 1989, the NP suggested that it would decide which black leaders were representative by insisting that only those who were 'recognised' could participate in the creation of a new dispensation.

Rina Venter ascribes the rhetoric to the established NP strategy of playing to the conservative gallery to prevent the far right from siphoning off more of its support. The party was sending a double message – always keeping one foot in the past. The NP's policies had historically been about mobilising people by exploiting racial anxieties and promising rewards on the basis of whiteness. The party had built an inherent fear of black majority rule, which continued to play on the minds of supporters, she says.

The NP also continued to use Christian rhetoric – this time to sell democracy to its members. At the 1990 Transvaal congress, Viljoen declared that 'Christian values, rules and prescriptions in the Bible' demanded that the political system be changed to allow for 'the elementary demands of democracy which require that the whole population in all its parts be involved in decision-making'.

Apart from using rhetoric to mobilise support, there were other indications that NP leaders were not planning to 'surrender'. There was no hint that the NP would agree to a simple majority democracy, as the leaders firmly believed this could be avoided. Venter, selected by De Klerk to serve first in parliament and then in the last NP cabinet, is among those who say that giving up power was the last thing on his mind when he made the 2 February 1990 speech. De Klerk realised that 'South Africa would never be the same'[44] afterwards, and told his wife Marike so that morning. However, he was seemingly unaware that he was about to unleash forces that his own party, in the end, would prove unable to withstand.

De Klerk was at pains to muster his cabinet's support. Unlike PW Botha, he was a team player. In December 1989, the cabinet had unanimously agreed to lift the prohibitions on the ANC.[45] De Klerk drew together a group of people who devised the package of announcements he would make. Viljoen, as minister of constitutional development, and Kobie Coetsee as minister of justice were involved, as was Niel Barnard, head of the NIS. Coetsee had a close working relationship with NIS, and both he and Barnard had been in contact with ANC luminaries since the mid-1980s. Magnus Malan was informed and apparently on board, despite doubts among some about whether he and the other securocrats would go along with the plans.[46] Dawie de Villiers, De Klerk's confidant, was certainly in the loop.

At its penultimate meeting before the opening of parliament, the cabinet was given a broad policy overview of De Klerk's proposed announcements. Some final details still had to be thrashed out, and at its next (and last) meeting before 2 February, the cabinet went through the address point by point. De Klerk then asked each minister in turn for approval of the content.[47] Their agreement was unanimous. Every member of De Klerk's cabinet, hawks and doves alike, was on board.

But that was their last moment of solidarity. As the negotiations unfolded, halted and started again, enmity became the ruling sentiment among the NP's executive leadership.

As per party tradition, the caucus was not consulted prior to De Klerk's momentous address. Their exclusion was justified on the grounds of confidentiality and to avoid the consequences of possible dissent. While the caucus had shed some conservative members in the 1987 election, then deputy minister Leon Wessels is of the opinion that a vote would have delivered a resounding 'no' to De Klerk's proposed announcements.[48] 'What would we have done then?' asks erstwhile foreign minister Pik Botha.[49]

Wessels says De Klerk was following Huntington's counsel: the reformist president acting decisively to gain the initiative over the revolutionary force. Because of the secrecy, the country was indeed taken aback, and De Klerk's headlong leap towards political liberalisation did secure the initiative for the NP once again. He not only released Mandela, but also unbanned the ANC and thirty-one other organisations, committing the government to prioritising negotiations aimed at creating a constitutional dispensation with a bill of rights and an independent judiciary.

The speech emphasised points that were of concern to the white electorate. Therefore, while it marked a turning point in South Africa's history, the address stuck to the infamous NP mantra of group rights: 'The formal recognition of individual rights does not mean that the problems of a heterogeneous population will simply disappear. Any new constitution which disregards this reality will be inappropriate or even harmful. Naturally, the protection of collective, minority and national rights may not bring about an imbalance in respect to individual rights. It is neither the government's policy nor its intention that any group shall be favoured over or in relation to any of the others.'[50]

The NP continued to view South Africa's political economy through a prism tinged with anxiety about whites being in the minority. The solution to allaying such fears? The NP's version of Lijphartian consociationalism, which they called 'power sharing'. In June 1989, the Broederbond's exploration of the various permutations of 'power sharing' produced a set of constitutional guidelines.[51] These moved slightly beyond what the NP had put in place with the 1983 constitution. There was still a distinction between 'own' and 'general' affairs, but provision was made for a single national assembly where 'general affairs' were to be decided by consensus.

De Klerk chose Gerrit Viljoen to lead the negotiations. In addresses to parliament soon after 2 February, Viljoen explained the NP's vision of protecting minority rights. While the party supported 'full and equal franchise and other political rights within an undivided, multi-party, democratic South Africa',[52] it rejected a unitary system with a single common voters' roll. To allow majority domination would be to undermine democracy. The proposed model for power sharing with various checks and balances consisted of the following:

- A cabinet representative of parties with substantial support.
- A presidency rotating between the dominant parties.
- A parliament consisting of a house of representatives based on universal franchise and a senate with representation based on ethnic groups, in which each would have equal say, regardless of numbers.[53]
- Decision-making in both houses based on consensus, with the senate able to veto legislation.[54]
- Decentralisation of power to provincial and local governments.[55]
- A two-thirds approval of parliamentary and cabinet decisions.
- Prevention of arbitrary changes to the constitution through a 75 per cent provision.
- A bill of rights to protect ethnic groups and individuals.[56]
- Sovereignty vested in a constitution interpreted by an independent judiciary[57] to prevent abuse of the parliamentary system by a dominant party.

To avoid the constitution being created by parties reflective of actual democratic support, as would happen in a constituent assembly, the NP insisted that the constitution be drafted by the main negotiating partners *before* an election was held. But above all, power sharing had to include adequate protection of minority rights. This was the very least expected by De Klerk's conservative cabinet colleagues in return for making the 'quantum leap'.[58]

Almost from the outset, the NP had an uphill battle to sell power sharing to the ANC, its allies in civil society and the international community. It was a slippery concept perceived as an attempt to sneak in a white veto. In fact, the NP was explicit about seeking a veto: its 1990 national congress decided that the new constitution should ensure that minorities 'with regard to really vital and fundamental issues have a guaranteed influence in the decision-making, whether by provision of veto powers or by a specially loaded majority requirement'.[59]

Power would be shared through an 'elite pact', apparently *the* buzzword in NP circles in the early 1990s.[60] The party leadership envisaged the ANC and NP political elites coming together. This was a continuation of machinations set in motion in the mid-1970s, when state and capital embarked on their search for conservative black partners.

Under Viljoen, Broederbond strategists produced the president's council constitutional report in October 1990, which included veto rights.[61] A core NP assumption was that it could count on the West to support its proposals on power sharing. Instead, the US undersecretary of state for African affairs announced that majority rule had to be accepted, as complicated arrangements 'to guarantee a share of power to particular groups'[62] would eventually frustrate effective government. All the white minority group could hope for was safeguards – not vetoes.

This signalled that not even De Klerk's announcements had succeeded in lifting the NP's legitimacy crisis. The ANC, with charismatic Mandela at the helm, was winning the public relations game. It constantly reminded the NP from whence it had come. The most blistering example was Mandela's verbal attack at the end of Codesa I in December 1991: 'Even the head of an illegitimate, discredited, minority regime [such as De Klerk's] has certain moral standards to uphold. He has no excuse, because he is a representative of a discredited regime, not to uphold moral standards.'[63]

This was the line taken throughout the negotiations, with NP representatives being subjected to a 'brutal attack on their integrity'.[64] As minister of health, Rina Venter had an early taste of things to come when trade unionist Jay Naidoo walked into her office during the 1990 hospital strike and lambasted her. 'One could not defend oneself. How do you justify them [the problems created by apartheid]? Much of what he said was true.' Indeed, a new dynamic was setting in, one that the NP misjudged at the time. The more legitimate the ANC became in the eyes of the West, the less the NP was needed as a counterweight or alternative. This trend continued throughout the 1990s, gnawing at the NP's foundations.

De Klerk instructed his cabinet to produce plans for the dismantling of apartheid in state structures and service delivery by repealing laws. Some supporters protested. Venter says that her announcement of the rationalisation of seventeen health departments in existence at the time provoked bitter responses. She received a letter from a *tannie* in the Karoo who said that for her entire life, she had voted '*Nasenaal*' [Nationalist], but that she could no longer do so. How, she asked, would she explain this to her dead father when she arrived in heaven one day? Another correspondent was outraged at 'black bodies' in 'white beds'. Yet another letter, from a 'university professor', started with 'Dear Lord, what else?' instead of the customary 'Dear Minister'.

So far apart

Both the ANC and the NP were founded in the crucible of early twentieth-century South Africa, just two years apart. It was a time of escalating political rivalry against a backdrop of high levels of mineral wealth and rapacious capitalism. Black civil rights had been traded for Afrikaner compliance with British imperial demands, so while both black people and Afrikaners were feeling thwarted in their attempts to improve their lives, Afrikaners were in the ascendancy, while blacks had just suffered another setback in the shape of the whites-only agreement establishing the Union of South Africa.

Since then, both parties had gone through not only name changes, but also different ideological permutations. The ANC commenced its upward battle as a bourgeois party, but experience caused transmutations in its ideology and strategies. These experiences included decades of political exclusion despite numerous pleas, and later, democratic action and violence; the influence of Marxism-Leninism and the South African Communist Party; and the opportunities afforded by the Cold War in the form of training and support from the Soviet Union. The organisation had become radicalised and had shifted leftwards. When Mandela walked out of prison in 1990, he was ready to embark on a process of nationalisation to fulfil one of the clarion calls of the Freedom Charter: 'The people shall share in the country's wealth!' At the same time, however, protection of individual property rights had been included in the ANC's *Constitutional Guidelines for a Democracy* in 1988 and in its 1990 discussion document on economic policy drawn up in Harare, which supported 'redistribution through growth' – a neo-liberal model that found equal favour with the NP. The two schools of thought within the ANC would battle one another for decades, with Thabo Mbeki even stating in 2002 that the ANC was not and had never been a socialist party.

The NP also suffered from contradictions. Its bourgeois leadership was equally known for anti-capitalist sloganeering before it came to power in 1948. Both parties adapted their positions – the ANC in the short period between its unbanning and the country's first democratic election, due to the influence of business interests, international forces and the NP itself. The latter dropped the anti-capitalist rhetoric after using it in the 1930s and 1940s to weld the support of the Afrikaner working class onto its elite base.

Other factors complicated matters for De Klerk and the NP. The SACP's Joe Slovo said at the time that all he had ever prepared himself for was to sit at a round table and negotiate. In contrast, the NP had only the broad strokes of a plan, and a support base that still had to be convinced of the wisdom of releasing Mandela and unbanning the ANC. Moreover, the ANC leadership had taken the NP by surprise. When prohibitions on the organisation were lifted, the NP knew little about the ANC or the qualities of its leaders, according to Pik Botha.

De Klerk mentions in his autobiography that a number of the ANC delegates at the Groote Schuur meeting were unknown to him. The NP was surprised not only by the ANC's cunning at the negotiating table or the support it enjoyed on the streets – both big enough factors, given the NP's overestimation of its own abilities and support – but also because the NP had begun to believe its own propaganda. Over decades, the ANC had been reinvented as a bogeyman, which turned out to be far removed from the reality. Instead of terrorist thugs and communist Antichrists, the NP was confronted with normal people, a variety of personalities and convictions, many of them likeable human beings who exhibited a sophisticated level of political thought. Many in the NP leadership were unprepared for such an assault on their prejudices.

Petulant bedfellow

The NP hoped to reinvent itself by becoming 'non-racial'. By the end of 1990, the party's provincial congresses had all accepted changes to the NP constitution that opened membership to all South Africans. This was yet another departure from its founding principles.

Within the NP, two options were being considered in the early days of the transition. The first was to draw the ANC into an elite pact through power sharing. The NP saw the ANC as a potential alliance partner from the start, with the caveat that it had to shed the SACP. In November 1991, Viljoen opened the door a little wider, saying that if a party's adjustment of its policies made it acceptable to the NP, the NP would have to reassess cooperation.[65]

The second option was for the NP to shore itself up by pulling together a 'multiracial' right-wing alliance of parties. This was strongly mooted around October 1990, and would have included the white DP and the coloured Labour Party. Part of this strategy was to insist that the governments of the Bantustans be part of the negotiations, no matter how small their support base; and that the Bantustans existed as separate polities.[66] The NP was still asserting the latter as late as February 1992.

By then, the feeling within the leadership was that such a bloc would boost the NP to a level of support that would place it in an 'equal position' with the ANC, says Meyer. In the end, only the Labour Party was absorbed into the NP, despite some of its more progressive leaders vowing to fight 'until we are liberated on political, spiritual and social level and also freed from poverty and suffering. We will fight for our people.'[67]

The NP's perennial conundrum reared its white head yet again. All the potential black partners among the Bantustan leaders enjoyed even less support than the NP itself. The largest was Mangosuthu Buthelezi's Inkatha Freedom Party, for which the NP had always harboured an affinity, despite Inkatha being a Zulu nationalist juggernaut under volatile leadership.

It has since been argued that there was no evidence of cooperation between the political leadership of the NP and the IFP.[68] Former NP members of the executive refute this,[69] with Wessels typifying relations between the two at the end of the 1980s as 'warm', a 'relationship of sympathy'. In Afrikaner popular discourses the cantankerous Buthelezi was touted as the 'moderate' black alternative to the 'terrorist, communist' ANC, given his support for Christian values, his free-marketeerism, his federal inclinations, and his opposition to sanctions and to the armed struggle as a means to gain universal franchise. The ANC, says Wessels, was presented as 'diabolical' because of its disinvestment campaign and support for a violent overthrow of the government.

After the ANC and the NP decided in October 1991 to commence multiparty talks, the NP met with Inkatha. Several bilateral *bosberade* (literally, conferences in bush settings) were held to discuss the basic principles for a future constitution and Inkatha's vision for a future KwaZulu. The meetings were not all work. NP leaders such as Viljoen's negotiating partner Tertius Delport enjoyed socialising with IFP leaders over *braaivleis en pap* when the talks adjourned for the day.

The relationship was such that the NP was sensitive to IFP criticism of government actions. After Buthelezi complained to De Klerk about the centralisation of control over health facilities, Rina Venter flew to Ulundi – the IFP stronghold in KwaZulu – to discuss the issue with senior IFP leader Frank Mdlalose.[70]

On 19 July 1991, the sinister side to the cooperation between the government and Inkatha emerged as Inkathagate exploded into public view. The government had a strategy to assist the IFP in broadening its support base – hitherto limited to the rural areas of Natal – in order to beat back the ANC's advance in the urban areas of the Witwatersrand. It was called Operation Marion, and included the creation of a security management system in KwaZulu, similar to the national security management system, the training of the KwaZulu Police and the setting up of a paramilitary force.[71] At the time, the media exposed secret government funding to boost the IFP's organisational capabilities, and the provision of military training and weapons to the murderous KwaZulu Police.

Press revelations of this subterfuge dealt a crushing blow to the NP's dreams of partnership. The disclosures offered the first tangible proof of duplicity on the NP's side after repeated accusations by the ANC that the security forces were instigating the violent tide washing across the country at the time.

De Klerk admitted later that while 'most ministers' did not know of 'most such projects',[72] they probably would have approved them, if presented with the details. He distinguishes between funds and assistance on the one hand and the training of the KwaZulu Police on the other. For the most part, the cabinet did not know about the funding, but probably would have approved, according to him. The training was indeed discussed in cabinet *and* supported as provision of security for leaders of a legitimate structure, namely the KwaZulu government. It was never presented to or perceived by the cabinet as the training of an 'anti-ANC strike force', says De Klerk.[73] He also describes it specifically as the training of 'KwaZulu Police', while the TRC found that the trainees were Inkatha members – some of whom were appointed to the KwaZulu Police, while others became *kitskonstabels*. All received monthly salaries from the SADF until they were all eventually absorbed by the KwaZulu Police.[74]

De Klerk's position was that a decision to train KwaZulu Police to protect KwaZulu leaders was 'logical' because of the violent conditions prevailing.

However, if it were so logical, why all the steps to ensure that the project remained secret? Magnus Malan and two previous SADF chiefs were unsuccessfully prosecuted for the KwaMakhutha massacre on 21 January 1987, as the state was unable to prove a link between the decision to train the IFP members and the killing spree that ensued. De Klerk argued against the prosecution. He regarded the conflict as having been between the ANC, the IFP and 'faceless elements' within the security forces.[75]

Nevertheless, the TRC found that evidence indicated that Buthelezi had personally requested military training from government security forces, a request that had included the setting up of hit squads.[76] Malan admitted that Buthelezi had requested the formation of a paramilitary force. He, minister of police Louis le Grange and constitutional development minister Chris Heunis had met with Buthelezi in January 1986 to thrash out the security forces' 'assistance' plan, which was subsequently approved by the State Security Council and cabinet.[77]

Regarding the relationship between the NP and the IFP after 1990, it is worth noting that De Klerk went out of his way to keep the IFP in the negotiating process. For example, he engaged in 'extraordinary' shuttle diplomacy between Buthelezi and Mandela over the issue of allowing traditional weapons at rallies.[78] Another instance was the signing of a peace code in September 1991 when Buthelezi bussed in a 2 000-strong Zulu impi and petulantly refused to shake hands with De Klerk and Mandela. Afterwards, De Klerk made public excuses for Buthelezi's behaviour.

De Klerk ascribed his efforts to wanting to promote an understanding between Mandela and Buthelezi in order to end the violence. While this might be true, his actions also indicated his anxiousness to keep Buthelezi as a partner at the table. Given the overlapping concerns of the NP and the IFP, keeping the latter on board would have strengthened the NP's hand. A relatively significant black partner would have boosted the NP's position considerably, with implications for the eventual outcome of the negotiations. But two factors militated against De Klerk's efforts.

First, he was up against a joint ANC–COSATU campaign to discredit Buthelezi and the IFP in the eyes of the black populace. An open turf war between the IFP and the ANC erupted in mid-1990, shortly after COSATU and the ANC had launched the campaign to 'isolate Buthelezi', which included ignoring his repeated calls to meet with Mandela and to address rallies together.[79] Secondly, as the incident at the signing ceremony showed, De Klerk was ironically being undermined by Buthelezi himself. This had been a threat since the 1980s, when Meyer and Wessels had met Buthelezi in Durban to discuss ways of smoothing the friction between him and that other pugilist of the time, PW Botha. They agreed that Buthelezi would not make aggressive public pronouncements before Meyer and Wessels had spoken with Botha. Botha concurred and said he would like to 'even out the road' between himself and Buthelezi.

These attempts floundered when Buthelezi made a hostile public address at the beginning of 1989 while Botha was abroad. When confronted by NP representatives, his unconvincing excuse was that the speech had been prepared for him and that he did not have time to study it before delivery.[80] Wessels was particularly disappointed, as he had come a long way with Buthelezi, attending his annual prayer meetings with former NP member Wynand Malan.

Through political violence, the IFP forced a more prominent place for itself in the transitional process than the other Bantustan representatives. This afforded De Klerk the opportunity to try to establish a three-way engagement between the NP, ANC and IFP in early 1991, which the ANC promptly rejected. The ANC's blocking of Buthelezi drove the IFP to more extra-legal actions to improve its political foothold – a strategy that ultimately failed, as it did not derail the negotiating process. Moreover, the IFP was robbing itself of the opportunity to influence the negotiations. Buthelezi played into the ANC's hands by withdrawing from the talks, as he not only gave up whatever influence he might have had, but also caused a split between himself and the NP. The latter pursued a different strategy by staying the course in the negotiations.

While Inkathagate with its association of dirty tricks tainted the NP–IFP relationship, the NP continued its overtures to the IFP. This fits in with the theory that a double strategy was being pursued by the ruling establishment. In the aftermath of the scandal, the De Klerk leadership tried desperately to re-build the NP's image as a legitimate political actor and negotiating partner. This resulted in De Klerk's decision to appoint the Goldstone Commission to investigate the violence, and the Kahn Commission to probe secret government projects.

Inkathagate was the beginning of the parting of ways between the NP and the IFP. In the process, the NP lost its only possible black partner with significant support and thereby its chances of building a substantive conservative alliance. The other effect of Inkathagate was that the ANC and other parties proffered the scandal as final proof of why an interim multiparty government should preside over the negotiations instead of the NP. Inkathagate confirmed the ANC's suspicion that the NP was prone to abusing state resources to bolster its position. ANC pressure for an interim government, a proposal the NP had dismissed, grew immensely.

De Klerk moved to placate the ANC. First he demoted law and order minister Adriaan Vlok and defence minister Magnus Malan to lower-ranking cabinet portfolios. Then, about six months later, De Klerk delivered his second significant surprise in two years. On 20 December 1991, at the start of the

Convention for a Democratic South Africa (Codesa I), he yielded to the ANC's demand that a democratically elected government should draft the final constitution.

Was he pushed or did he jump?

The media described the NP's acceptance of an elected government drafting the final constitution as a 'breathtaking policy switch'.[81] It effectively amounted to the NP ceding its power to exercise control over the final negotiations as the party occupying the institution of state. This concession made a democracy based on majority rule unavoidable.[82] The drafting of the final constitution by an assembly based on an electoral outcome rendered the NP, as a minority party, unlikely to find enough other takers for its idea of a consociational arrangement.

Transitions are fluid and volatile processes, and much depends on how political actors read the state of play. In 1991, the NP was losing the initiative. A bold move was necessary, and De Klerk was willing to make it. The decision makes more sense measured against the following realities of the time:

- Inkathagate was a political embarrassment, a rude interruption of the NP's attempts to hold on to some veneer of respectability. For some in the NP leadership, Inkathagate was enough of a reason to abandon hopes of co-operation with Inkatha. Moreover, the upper hand in the leadership at that point was not held by hard-nosed oligarchic leaders like their predecessors. They did not regard violence as ultimately viable. They wanted to retain their respectability with a view to building the party's future in a democratic South Africa.

- As the NP's crisis of legitimacy persisted, it suffered isolation from both left and right. An alliance called the Patriotic Front emerged between the ANC, the SACP and the PAC, together with parties with which the NP had thought it could align itself, including some Bantustan governments and the DP. NP negotiators were upset, reading this as 'ganging up'.[83] Moreover, the ANC was successfully building its coherence as an organisation and as part of the internal anti-apartheid movement. While the ANC seemed to be finding partners, De Klerk was snubbed from the left by the liberation movements when he called a peace conference in May 1991, even though it did even-tually result in an accord supported by the significant players. From the right, his very life was under threat, as when he visited the AWB stronghold of Ventersdorp in August 1991. All the while, the CP refused to come to the table.

- As the ANC settled in, its leadership became more susceptible to influence from the rank and file, as when members castigated their leaders at the consultative conference in December 1990 in Soweto about the lack of consultation on the Groote Schuur and Pretoria Minutes. Members, picking up a whiff of an elite pact in the making, complained that Mandela was too autocratic, that his working relationship with De Klerk was too intimate and that the leadership had conceded too much when it suspended the armed struggle. Leaders' efforts at shifting policy towards relaxing sanctions faltered in the face of strong resistance from the floor. Pressure resulted in an ultimatum from Mandela to the NP with demands and threats to withdraw from the negotiations. The NP leadership was concerned that this would cause a delay during which the more radical viewpoints of the rank and file could sway the ANC leadership. The ANC's first national conference held internally in South Africa after its unbanning – in July 1991 – again contrasted the militancy of the rank and file with the more amenable attitudes of the leaders. Resolutions were adopted that the ANC should remain a liberation movement rather than become a political party, and that sanctions, mass action and the underground structures should be retained. The pressure was on the NP leadership to save the working relationship with their ANC counterparts before they drifted too far apart. The ANC did, after all, allow almost a year to pass before Codesa I finally got off the ground.

- The ANC declared 1991 a year of mass action, and it ended with millions of South Africans embarking on a two-day strike in protest against the institution of VAT in November 1991.

While it is true that the NP as the party with its hands on the levers of state was in a more powerful position than the ANC, state power became a paradoxical asset. The NP had far more to lose than the ANC. If the NP had hardened its stance and wielded the state apparatus to hold on to political power, it would have had to return to Botha-style militarisation. The levels of social insurrection would have increasingly demanded outright military force to push the country's crippled economy along.

The question confronting De Klerk and his colleagues was: What would be the best mode of survival – trying our hand at being a legitimate political player and a potential partner in a future government along internationally accepted lines, or not? The global context had changed to such an extent that South Africa's conservative allies in the US and UK had set their sights on more profitable playgrounds in the newly liberalising ex-Soviet bloc. As the international focus moved away from Africa, foreign support for states on the continent was diminishing. Given the worldwide post-communist drive towards democratisation, overt outside support for a military regime would have been scarce.

Selecting the civilian option, and thus deciding against the utilisation of coercive state power to entrench its position, required the adoption of a strategy to attain political legitimacy in order to survive in a democracy. This is one reason for the NP's insistence on constitutional continuity between apartheid and what came after, and that the transitional processes be supported by laws passed by the NP-dominated parliament. As the transition rolled on, clinging to political power became less and less of an option, while economic prospects weakened as violence bloodied the rural enclaves and the urban wastelands of the townships.

The pivotal year 1992: Codesa breaks down

At Codesa I, working groups were established which met during the first months of 1992 to work on a climate conducive to elections; constitutional principles; the terms of the transition; the status of the Bantustans; and a plan to implement decisions. At Codesa II, as the resumption of negotiations in 1992 was named, parties managed to agree on basic liberal-democratic principles to be contained in an interim constitution, on the basis of which an election would be held to constitute a parliament. This new parliament would serve as a constitutional assembly that could change the constitution to arrive at a final constitution. These changes could only be effected with a majority of votes.

Tertius Delport, who was Gerrit Viljoen's sidekick in Codesa II's Working Group 2, says the NP's agreement to an interim government and constitution opened the door to an interim constitution written *not* on the basis of a majority electoral outcome, but on consensus.[84] This was because of the principle of 'sufficient consensus' at Codesa, which meant that the NP and government delegations (they were separate) had to agree, giving the NP 'an effective veto over change'. The sway the NP held, combined with ANC intransigence, led ANC negotiator Kader Asmal to dismiss Codesa as a 'debating society'.[85] The NP's approach was that it would block progress if it did not 'get what it wanted'.[86] As Delport says, 'We did not have to allow anything in that constitution that was not acceptable to us.' This attitude was bolstered in the beginning by the NP's sense that it held state power.

For the NP to ensure that its preferred outcome would triumph, it needed the ANC to agree to high voting percentages in parliament for the adoption of the final constitution and the bill of rights. Therefore, the NP insisted on thrashing out these finer details in the interim constitution-making process. Having agreed to let a democratically constituted government determine the final constitution, the NP was obviously reluctant to leave too many details to such a government, as it would be dominated by the ANC.

The NP's proposals to Working Group 2 in March 1992 comprised a two-chamber interim parliament, including a senate with regional representation that would allow minorities to block decisions by the elected lower house, and a rotational presidency that operated by consensus.[87]

The ANC's Cyril Ramaphosa, on the other hand, emphasised time and again that parties should enunciate broad, rather than detailed, principles.[88] For the ANC, Codesa was not a democratic body and therefore lacked the legitimacy to decide over the details of a future dispensation. The ANC was worried that the NP's proposals for an interim arrangement held the seed of permanence. ANC legal advisors Firoz Cachalia and Fink Haysom alerted the ANC to the possibility that the NP was aiming to finalise the constitution at Codesa.[89] The NP was pushing for a parliamentary majority of 70 per cent before the constitution could be changed, and 75 per cent before the bill of rights could be changed. The NP's offer boiled down to minority parties being able to veto a new constitution if the majority party was unable to secure 75 per cent of the vote. The high percentages would mean that production of a final constitution could be indefinitely delayed, which could have paved the way for the interim constitution to become final.

The issue of percentages led to the collapse of Codesa II on 15 May 1992. Delport admits that the NP had had in mind a permanent arrangement. Like De Klerk, he contends that it had been the ANC and not the NP that had forced the breakdown of Codesa II. According to Delport, this was because the ANC had realised that the NP's plan was to cement the final constitution in the drafting of the interim document. He quotes from the ANC's *Negotiations Bulletin* of the time: 'Many people have been left with the impression that the deadlock was merely over percentages (i.e. should decisions be taken by special majorities of 66.7 per cent, 70 per cent or 75 per cent). The conflict over percentages is a symptom of a much deeper problem. So what was the real issue at stake? ... The ANC and other Patriotic Front organisations at Codesa agreed to the idea of an interim constitution provided it would be replaced as a whole by a new constitution drafted by [a democratically elected] national assembly. The regime ... set such stringent conditions that the national assembly would take many years to draft a new constitution. This would mean that the interim constitution would remain in force and even become the final constitution. This was the trap set by the National Party. We were therefore forced to deadlock rather than make such an unacceptable compromise.'[90]

The 'stringent conditions', in the view of the ANC, were the allocation of powers of the senate, entrenchment of the demarcation of the boundaries and powers of provincial government, and the NP's insistence on a majority of 70 per cent for changes to the constitution and 75 per cent for changes to the bill of rights. In its last offer to the NP, the ANC came close to the NP's demands on majorities. Added to that, however, the ANC noted that the national assembly might not be able to reach agreement with such high percentages, and therefore proposed a deadlock-breaking mechanism: if more than 50 per cent of national

assembly members supported the contested draft, its fate would be democratically tested through a referendum.

The NP rejected this proposal out of hand, because it meant that the final
constitution could be written on the basis of a simple majority (50 per cent + 1)
in which majority groups would be under no obligation to listen to smaller
parties, says Delport. He maintains that the ANC's dogged majoritarian approach
sank Codesa II, while De Klerk later argued that the left-wing element in the
ANC had got the better of it and forced the breakdown.

At this stage of the negotiations, the NP still held the power. It was standing
firm on the issue of power sharing. Superficially, the breakdown of Codesa II was
merely about a conflict over percentages.[91] In reality, it reflected the ideological
differences between the two main players. It was the NP's insistence on power-
sharing elements and the ANC's insistence on simple majority principles that
led to the collapse of the talks.

In its submissions to Working Group 2, the NP made it clear that it was
seeking 'meaningful participation of political minorities' as a general constitutional principle; it rejected a monopoly of power by any party; it wanted a
strong second chamber in parliament reflective of the country's ethnic groups
but not their relative sizes; and autonomous provincial governments, deriving
their powers from the constitution.

The IFP agreed with most of these proposals, as it was pushing for the right
to self-determination. However, the ANC position was that the protection of
rights allocated to individuals – not groups – in a multiparty democracy with a
free civil society would sufficiently protect minorities. In the view of Cachalia
and Haysom, constitutionalism obviated the need for power sharing because of
the safeguarding of basic rights and the principle of judicial review, both of
which already had the support of the NP.

Instead of protecting groups, power sharing would guarantee power for
losing political parties, Haysom and Cachalia contended. They opposed an
elected interim government in favour of one based on informal agreements
between parties. The ANC asserted that minority concerns could be accommodated through proportional representation (which guaranteed a parliamentary
presence for small parties), a two-thirds majority for adoption of the constitution and constitutional principles that would set the parameters for the final
constitution.[92] The ANC later dropped constitutional principles as minority
guarantee.

The role of both ANC and NP personalities, and the different political
agendas within the NP, were significant in the breakdown of Working Group 2's
deliberations. Valli Moosa stood in for Ramaphosa, who returned towards the
end, having missed most of the meetings.[93] He had a much more hard-nosed

attitude than Moosa. This happened at a time when Viljoen left as chief negotiator for the NP due to health problems. Delport was left to negotiate these essential transitional items with an increasingly aggressive ANC.

The ANC was suspicious of the closer cooperation between the NP and the IFP that emerged at that juncture, with more and more convergence between the demands of the two parties. The IFP opposed an elected constitution-making body and strongly supported federalism, which fitted well with the NP's idea of constitutionally autonomous provinces. It was also no coincidence that the IFP seemed closer to the NP after Delport took the reins from Viljoen. The NP hawks were far more partial to cooperation with the IFP,[94] and Delport, a hawk himself, drew the IFP closer.

The relationship between Delport and Ramaphosa was marked by open conflict, with Delport expressing his frustration because Ramaphosa negotiated 'like a trade unionist'[95] – which of course was true. He'd cut his teeth as National Union of Mineworkers general secretary in negotiations with Anglo American before becoming ANC secretary general. Ramaphosa, in turn, accused Delport of being unwilling to move towards an agreement, and therefore forcing a deadlock. Some say he outmanoeuvred Delport and that the latter overplayed his hand.

This is only relevant to the argument that the NP should have accepted the ANC's offer of a 70 per cent majority in parliament for adoption of the final constitution. However, that offer included a referendum in the event of a deadlock, which totally militated against what the NP was seeking. It is spurious to lay the blame for the breakdown on Delport. He did not have an open-ended mandate from his party to adapt positions as the negotiations proceeded. The proceedings of Working Group 2 were frequently interrupted by Delport having to telephonically clear decisions with De Klerk and other members of the NP leadership.[96] He was, after all, a relatively junior member of the executive, having only been elected to parliament in 1987.

Viljoen's withdrawal came at a particularly inopportune moment: one week before Working Group 2's final meeting. For De Klerk, his departure was a huge blow, as he had been crucial to the NP's plan. Delport was instructed to stick with the plan, and that was what he did. Roelf Meyer, who later became chief negotiator, sat in on the last meeting of Working Group 2 but did not intervene to assist Delport. The previous day, Meyer had issued a statement in which he defiantly reaffirmed the government's insistence on power sharing, its rejection of 'a monopoly of power' and its commitment to a dispensation that would prevent abuse of power by a majority.[97]

At the last meeting, Ramaphosa rejected his colleague Valli Moosa's proposal that the issue of a senate, as proposed by the NP, be resolved at a later stage. This would have brought Working Group 2 closer to a resolution, but Ramaphosa insisted on the issue being resolved there and then. Yet again, this confirms that what precipitated the Codesa II deadlock was the NP's commitment to power sharing and the ANC's insistence on majority rule in a democracy.

After Codesa II failed, the ANC embarked on a mass action campaign with the apparent intent of achieving the so-called Leipzig option, an idea derived by leaders such as Ronnie Kasrils from the last days of communism in East Germany, where mass action toppled the regime.

Delport reiterated the NP's position[98] that 'the composition of the senate should reflect regional and minority interests ... prevent[ing] a situation where a majority simply rides roughshod over minorities'. He rejected suggestions that this was tantamount to a 'white veto', a phrase picked up by the international media, much to the irritation of the NP leadership. In the immediate aftermath of Codesa II, the NP was resolutely sticking to its guns.

De Klerk had been pushing the more conservative members of the NP leadership to the fore, but when the talks broke down, Ramaphosa was adamant that he could not work with Delport, and De Klerk was forced to replace him. This cost De Klerk a measure of control over the negotiations. But from the hawks' point of view, his decision to appoint Meyer in Viljoen's stead as minister of constitutional development and, therefore, chief negotiator, indicated that he 'doubtless' preferred Meyer's approach.[99]

The NP's defiant stance during Codesa II could be ascribed in part to the decisive 69 per cent 'yes' vote in the referendum on 17 March 1992. De Klerk had called the referendum in a calculated move following the loss of NP stronghold Potchefstroom to the CP in a by-election. There was great concern that the NP was fast losing the support of the white electorate as a whole, given that it had held the seat for decades with large majorities. De Klerk decided that a referendum should be held. The matter was discussed at length in cabinet, and the conclusion was that there was no other option. For the NP leadership, the referendum was crucial for continuation of the negotiations.

The party had thrown down the gauntlet to white voters. The only alternative to negotiations was retaining power through force, says Venter. The large margin of victory emboldened the party, since it was seen as proof of its status as representative of white people in the country. Kobie Coetsee claimed at Codesa II that he had delivered a 'yes' vote in the Free State in spite of widespread doubt that he would be able to do so.[100] The far right managed to convince only some 30 per cent of the white electorate to vote 'no'.

The result was met with 'general jubilation' at Codesa II, showing that not only the NP, but all parties involved acknowledged the importance of having the white minority on board.[101]

The impasse and the ANC's withdrawal from Codesa II 'forced the NP back to the drawing board,' says Meyer. 'We had to ask ourselves: what is it that we want to see in a future constitution, as opposed to what we are trying to retain from the past? How best can we serve our own as well as the national interest?'

In the process of debating these issues, the NP adopted a new constitutional framework that formed the basis of its subsequent engagements with the ANC. This led to Meyer's rapprochement with Ramaphosa, and the drafting and adoption of the pivotal Record of Understanding (ROU) in September 1992. The ROU split the NP leadership in two along the historical *verligte/verkrampte* lines. But while the *verligtes* now became distinctively dove-like in their approach, the *verkramptes* refused to accept that the writing was on the wall for white minority rule. They still clung to some misplaced idea of 'Afrikaner self-determination', which they believed could justifiably be achieved through suppression.

A dual strategy?

In the period between 2 February 1990 and April 1994, more people were killed than during any other period in South Africa's history.[102] Half of the statements on killings submitted to the TRC related to incidents during this period: a total of 5695 from 1990 to 1994 – showing the prevalence of violence, as the TRC's mandate covered events from 1960 to 1994. Other sources indicated that 14000 people died in politically related incidents.[103] The number of deaths from political violence doubled in the year of De Klerk's groundbreaking announcements: 3699, compared to 1403 in 1989. The major escalations were in Natal – 1279 political fatalities in 1989 against 1811 in 1990 – and the Transvaal, where the increase was dramatic: from 54 to 1547.[104]

The steep rise in conflict after the ANC's unbanning came just months after Buthelezi had requested additional assistance from the security forces, including the creation of hit squads.[105] The types of weapons used correlates with the Inkathagate revelations of security force involvement. Even as the NP and the ANC reached agreement through the Groote Schuur Minute of 24 May 1990 on measures to curb violence and intimidation, the conflict was spreading.

When De Klerk finally lifted the last state of emergency regulations, he kept them in place in Natal in response to what was by then a low-level civil war. Mandela was constantly in contact with De Klerk about the issue. Towards the end of 1990, Mandela was openly accusing the state of complicity in the conflict, saying the NP government could end the violence if it so chose. By December, the ANC was fingering 'trained death squads' utilising 'systematically orchestrated'[106] violence to destabilise the organisation. This was vehemently denied by De Klerk, who insisted that he referred all cases brought to his attention to the police.

De Klerk was never one of PW Botha's securocrats. He reincorporated the State Security Council into the structures of the cabinet, reducing it to the level of an ordinary committee, as when it was created in the early 1970s. His different approach to the security forces was obvious from an early stage of his tenure. At a cabinet *bosberaad* in 1989, the securocrats, as usual, made presentations on the security situation in both the country and the region. Several scenarios were proffered as possibilities. At the end of the presentation, De Klerk took the wind out of their sails with the following question: What if peace prevails? It was the one scenario that the securocrats had not considered.

Given the rampant violence, the vexed question of political accountability again arises. Was the military subordinate to the civilian government?[107] As war theorist Clausewitz put it: Was war policy still being subordinated to political policy? Did the NP stick to an above-board strategy of negotiation and courting the African nationalist elite, or was the party engaged in a more sinister two-pronged strategy of talks backed up with covert violence?

The NP leadership, and De Klerk in particular, denied knowledge of all illegal activities, including extra-judicial killings and other human rights violations. Meyer argues that the truth was never ascertained about allegations of institutional violence or the conundrum of the increase in violence during the negotiation process. 'Even the TRC did not have answers [to] what the background of the violence was and where it was coming from. I don't have an answer to that. I can honestly not tell where the violence was coming from. There were at no stage any decisions by government in this regard that I am aware of. Or by ministers. There seems to have been institutional support for that kind of violence, but when that question was put to the police, they could provide no conclusive answers. There was never a purposeful double strategy that was decided on formally that I am aware of.'

The fact, though, is that in the dying days of the Botha regime, the ruling establishment was confronted with two options. The first was to participate in a negotiated transition to democracy. The second was the Botha model. The latter entailed the continuation of co-option strategies to establish a multiracial oligarchy, which would then have had to resort to increasingly authoritarian measures to stave off popular discontent. The resounding denial of Botha's autocratic ambitions sent out a clear message that his model was redundant, even in the eyes of the majority of the NP leadership.

Yet, state violence was inherent to the maintenance of the apartheid system from its earliest days, exemplified by the Sharpeville massacre, deaths in detention and forced removals. Botha's total strategy institutionalised state violence. The structures and policy regimes of Botha's securocracy were all still in place when De Klerk assumed power, along with myriad security players in the ruling establishment. Members of the security forces continued to defend what they believed was a legitimate state. Meyer describes the NP government's 'view from the state' in a way that is typical of any regime: to use and maintain state power to the 'benefit of the country and the welfare of everybody, as it was seen in those days'. It was this last proviso that set the apartheid government apart. While the NP insisted that it was acting in the best interest of all South Africans, it was serving white supremacy. This involved the ideological positioning of the apartheid state as legitimate and its opponents as illegitimate. This was the context in which policy decisions were taken and in which we find the self-perpetuating state bureaucracy.

The latter is found in most states, and the vast securocracy in South Africa was no different. Indeed, as was seen in the 1980s, the military takes on a life of its own when allowed to do so by political masters. Meyer cites the example of a security policeman named Chappies Klopper. When Leon Wessels confronted him about a bomb attack against the house of Ivor Jenkins, who did 'relatively innocent' work to establish reconciliation in the townships, Klopper's response was: 'We thought we were doing you a favour.' For Meyer, this personifies 'elements in the security forces who acted on their own under the false idea that they had the authorisation of the State Security Council to do what they did'.

Meyer admits that the state should take responsibility for these attacks, as they were the result of an interpretation of functions within a particular context of protecting the state. Then there were those who acted entirely of their own volition, with no reference to any state mandate, according to Meyer. The government could not have known what the latter were up to, he contends. Therefore, he suggests that the state 'contributed to a general pattern of violence that was obviously repressive, and on the other hand there were individuals who acted on their own'.

De Klerk denies any complicity on the side of the state, saying that '[a]lthough it is now indisputable that some elements of the security forces were involved in secretly instigating and perpetrating violence, their actions were in direct violation of explicit instructions and of everything that my government and I had been trying to achieve since my inauguration. In cabinet and in all my interactions with the responsible ministers and generals I continuously exerted pressure to ensure that the security forces would act within the law. In cases where there was sufficient evidence, we acted firmly against suspected transgressors, and where possible they were prosecuted. In the end, the actions of the security forces were directed as much against the government and its reform policies as they were against the ANC and its allies. The question that Mandela should have asked himself was why the government and I should instigate – or connive at – violence which seriously jeopardised the initiative into which we had sunk all our moral and political capital?'[108]

Coup Scenario I

Whether the security forces were indeed trying to undermine the government's reforms is debatable. Barend du Plessis points out that events were following a course that was acceptable to the defence force. In Meyer's view, both the SADF and the police acted in a professional manner and gave their support to the negotiation process. De Klerk also describes both Malan and Vlok as 'strong supporters of the reform process'.[109] Meyer points to the lack of a 'substantive rebellion or uprising' by the security forces as 'one of the success stories' of South Africa's transition. Asked whether a military insurrection ever was a real possibility, he says the 'fear existed very strongly in ANC ranks' – more so than among the NP leaders. The ANC's Joe Slovo pushed for a government of national unity as one way of avoiding a backlash from the security forces. The business sector had similar fears.

This information suggests that the securocrats continued to support the *verligte* agenda, as they had done during Botha's reign. Indeed, it is written[110] that the SADF high command consisted of well-educated technocrats working at a high level of sophistication and having a good grasp on the demands of political legitimacy. This was reflected in their dictum that any solution would be '20 per cent military; 80 per cent political'. Speculation during the 1980s was that if ever the military staged a coup, it would be to prevent extreme right-wingers from assuming power.[111] This was because the military was co-opted into government as policy-makers. Having been part of policy formulation, the SADF strongly identified with the values of the state and this, in turn, reinforced the military's loyalty to defending the state.

This is the most likely explanation for the fact that no security force revolt followed De Klerk's demotion of Malan and Vlok. It also helps one understand the docile reaction to De Klerk's dismissal of twenty-three SADF officers following an investigation by Lieutenant General Pierre Steyn in December 1992.

As the result of the special investigation into violence headed by Judge Richard Goldstone, De Klerk had instructed Steyn to probe the SADF's intelligence functions. Steyn found that 'a limited number of members, contract members and collaborators of the SA Defence Force ha[d] been involved, and in some cases [were] still involved, in illegal and/or unauthorised activities and malpractices'. In what was dubbed the 'Night of the Generals', De Klerk placed seven SADF officers on compulsory leave pending further investigations, while another sixteen, of whom the most senior was a lieutenant general, were forced to take early retirement. Still there was no retaliation, despite Malan later denouncing De Klerk's actions as 'a breach of trust between the government and the security forces' for what was seen as De Klerk's willingness to 'bend the knee' before the ANC, as when he had moved Malan and Vlok to other portfolios.[112]

According to Malan, the NP leadership had fallen for the ANC's continuous allegations against the security forces and 'gradually started to accept that the propaganda might be true'. He argues that the ANC, intent on splitting the ruling bloc, managed to create the perception that the SADF had its own agenda, which clashed with that of the government. If, as former Meyer ally Annelizé van Wyk[113] asks, the SADF was such a loose cannon, how was it possible for De Klerk to 'just fire' the top brass without major repercussions? The worst some of the sacked officers did was to take their cases to court. Not even their ejection sparked an armed uprising. This could only be explained as support for the course on which the government had embarked. According to Van Zyl Slabbert, the last SADF chief, Georg Meiring, had told him that the militarists were convinced that they could take over the country, but 'if we did, what do we do the next day?'[114]

The bureaucratic continuation of a military immersed in defending the state as they saw it aided a dual strategy. Botha's total strategy, to which the security forces had been exposed in one form or another since the 1960s, stemmed from the dualistic nature of Beaufrean counter-revolutionary approach and may serve to explain why Chappies Klopper had told Leon Wessels he thought they were assisting the negotiators.

While the security forces were supporting reform, they could simultaneously have used violence – directly or by proxy – to strategically weaken the government's opponents. Simply by turning a blind eye, the government could have benefited, though De Klerk denied this. It is also conceivable that the security forces were applying a counter-revolutionary or dual strategy as a form of insurance, exactly as the ANC had Operation Vula, a plot to seize power by force that was uncovered by the security forces in July 1990. Oliver Tambo had authorised the plan in the mid-1980s, and the ANC leadership sustained it as a fallback position in the event that negotiations failed. ANC operatives infiltrated the country, and Mac Maharaj was among those captured and charged at the time. De Klerk confirmed that Operation Vula had reawakened the suspicions of the securocrats about the ANC.[115]

The effect of the mutual distrust that prevailed at the time should not be underestimated. De Klerk knew full well that the security forces represented the government's final power base, and that they were also the ultimate guarantor of constitutional change.[116] He was thus attempting to strike a balance: on the one hand, he thought it was 'essential ... to maintain the integrity of the SADF and on the other to root out any possibility for the continuation of abuses'.[117] Maintaining integrity meant keeping the SADF's capabilities intact, even if they were scaled down. The De Klerk cabinet did not dismantle covert operations; it merely amended the rules.

While De Klerk replaced Botha's National Security Management System with the National Coordinating Mechanism (NCM), the structures and those involved remained mostly the same and seem to have performed the same functions as before, even though De Klerk insisted they would concentrate on welfare functions. For example, the police killed twenty-one-year-old activist Meshack Bekinkosi Kunene three months after a senior officer informed the Alexandra Advisory Committee that councillors had asked the police to 'wipe out troublemakers'. The AAC had formerly been a joint management committee, which was part of the NSMS and still had all the same members, including the police, defence force and local (co-opted) councillors.[118]

There was still ample room for abuse. Guidelines adopted by the cabinet on 29 June 1990 in respect of 'unavoidable secret operations' dictated that they should take place only in cases where departmental line functions were inadequate and where the political head accepted full responsibility. Ministerial approval of projects had to be in writing, no indemnity from prosecution would be granted and accounts would be scrutinised in terms of the Auditor-General Act of 1989. But the guidelines also allowed for plausible deniability, though this 'should wherever possible be avoided'. Moreover, the 'need-to-know' principle remained in force, with the minimum number of people being informed about any secret operations.

De Klerk restructured and downsized the NSMS, then continued to utilise it, with the line of authority reaching right to the pinnacle of government. According to the TRC, an SADF raid on a house in Umtata that killed three teenagers and two twelve-year-olds in October 1993 was authorised at an SSC meeting attended by De Klerk, Pik Botha and Kobie Coetsee. De Klerk was later at pains to say that he had acted on information supplied by the SADF and had issued instructions that minimum force should be used.[119] According to SADF intelligence, the house was a hideout and arms cache for APLA operatives. Only a few months had passed since APLA cadres attacked the congregation of the St James Church in Cape Town, killing twelve people and injuring another fifty-six. The threat was thus real. Afterwards, De Klerk expressed his regret about the loss of civilian life and, as a member of the government of national unity, endorsed a statement describing the attack as 'unjustified and inexcusable'.[120]

During this period, the extraordinary powers of the police remained in place. Even when the state of emergency was finally revoked, the police still had the legal right to use extreme measures. By declaring specific locations 'unrest areas', they could invoke similar powers to those they had under a state of emergency. These included the vaguely defined 'necessary force' to restore public order; arrests without warrants; detention for up to thirty days; the blocking of access to an area; prohibiting residents from being outside their houses or in vehicles; and a ban on gatherings. These regulations were applied in the townships and the security forces frequently used disproportionate force to halt demonstrations, indiscriminately shooting civilians in the process.

In March 1990, police action led to 281 people being injured in Sebokeng, 127 of them shot in the back.[121] In other cases, targeted killings of activists occurred.[122]

In 1990, too, De Klerk appointed Kat Liebenberg head of the SADF. Significantly, he had made his name as head of Special Forces, which was responsible for numerous covert structures including Barnacle, which became the Civil Cooperation Bureau. In 1992, Pierre Steyn recommended that De Klerk's purge of the military should start at the highest level, but De Klerk felt that dismissing Liebenberg would be too drastic a step, given the unproven nature of the evidence gathered and the delicacy of the transition. Liebenberg thus remained well situated to continue covert actions against the NP's enemies, should he have chosen to do so.

Conversely, De Klerk's decision to retain Liebenberg as well as Malan and Vlok suggested that he wanted to keep them close. He insisted that he was neither personally complicit in abuse, nor had he lost control of the security forces,[123] yet he admitted that he had had no knowledge of the CCB's existence until it was publicly exposed. At the very least, therefore, De Klerk was not in full control of the security forces with its Byzantine structures – especially those that were clandestine. While the dominant players in the securocracy were in support of De Klerk's reforms, cracks started to appear.

Coup Scenario II

While the *verligte*-aligned securocrats had not contemplated staging a coup, former SADF chief Constand Viljoen confirmed to the TRC that he had had plans to establish a *volkstaat* by force. This was the closest that security force elements came to openly organising themselves against the negotiations. Viljoen founded the committee of generals in May 1993. It consisted of retired generals such as former Military Intelligence mandarin Tienie Groenewald, former SADF chief of operations Koos Bischoff and former deputy police commissioner Lothar Neethling.

After a series of meetings with people across the country, the Eenheidskomitee 25 (Unity Committee 25) was founded. This was extended to the Volkseenheidskomitee (Volk Unity Committee), which became known by its acronym, Vekom, and formed the basis of the Afrikaner-Volksfront. The inaugural meeting in May 1993 brought together an array of white right-wing organisations including the CP, the Herstigte Nasionale Party, the Afrikaner-Volksunie, Afrikaner-Vryheidstigting, the Iron and Steel Workers' Union, the Mynwerkersunie (later renamed Solidarity) and the Ku Klux Klan–like Church of the Creator. Groenewald drew in more militant organisations, such as the AWB and the Boere-Weerstandsbeweging (Boer Resistance Movement), which had its own armed wing, the Boere-Republikeinse Leër (Boer Republican Army). Through the Boere-Vryheidsbeweging, a *volksleër* or people's army, consisting of 10 000 members, mostly farmers, was activated. Yet again one sees a connection with the counter-revolutionary strategies and regional destabilisation links of the 1980s, as the *volksleër* allegedly had links with RENAMO and included members of the CCB, 32 Battalion and Koevoet. The former commander of 32 Battalion, Colonel Jan Breytenbach, headed the *volksleër* for a while. (Fifteen years earlier, his brother Breyten had served time for opposing the state that the military man was defending, a tale which encapsulates the split among Afrikaners.)

Three theories exist to explain the creation of the Afrikaner-Volksfront: either it was a vehicle created by security force operatives to defuse the armed right-wing danger by drawing them into the ambit of the negotiations; or it was created as a 'right-wing threat' to strengthen the NP's bargaining position; or it was indeed an independent organisation forged with a view to taking control of the country.[124] Meyer says Constand Viljoen was regarded as someone who could have mobilised 'elements in the security forces' to halt the transition to democracy. Georg Meiring also confirmed that he knew Viljoen could mobilise 30 000 armed people.[125]

Mandela and Mbeki went out of their way to court Viljoen and convince him to join the constitutional process, leading to right-wing accusations later that Viljoen had sold out the cause, having became too enamoured of Mandela. It has been suggested that the AVF was an MI invention, and while this would fit the strategy of the time – MI was involved in setting up numerous front and bogus organisations – the white far-right clearly had its own agenda, and it was not the same as that of the NP. The NP was probably able to gain some political capital, as it could be seen as the reasonable face of Afrikanerdom in contrast to the AVF's reactionary and militant complexion. But this was probably an unintended side-effect.

To most of the white far-right, the NP negotiators were traitors. The militant faction made no distinction between NP offices, a DP councillor, a mosque, buses transporting black commuters, the National Union of Mineworkers, the progressive Afrikaans weekly newspaper *Vrye Weekblad* and the NP-supporting newspaper *Beeld*, all of which were attacked by right-wing organisations in the early 1990s. For the white right, all of these targets symbolised political change, which they were willing to oppose by force. In many cases, existing or former members of the security forces were implicated or prosecuted for these crimes.

The white far-right threat was real – demonstrated forcefully by its concerted efforts to derail the negotiations. The most dangerous of these was the assassination of SACP general secretary Chris Hani in April 1993, which involved members of the CP. The record shows a litany of incidents perpetrated with the explicit intention of undermining public order, overthrowing the government and disrupting the negotiations. The AWB and the BWB in particular propagated the overthrow of the government by force.

Despite access to trained soldiers, military equipment and arms, however, deep divisions and internal disagreement diluted the impact of far-right-wing politics. The fragmentation was such that, by 1994, close on 100 right-wing organisations existed in South Africa. Their influence was also diminished by the gung-ho machismo of some groups, as illustrated by the embarrassing attack on the World Trade Centre – home of Codesa – in June 1993. Some 3 000 khaki-clad AWB members invaded the building, drove a Casspir armoured vehicle through the glass entrance doors, shouted racial abuse, sang 'Die Stem' and prayed. Some urinated in the building. While negotiators were intimidated, the incident exposed the AWB's true core as a gang of racist buffoons.

War talk continued in white far-right circles, with CP leader Ferdi Hartzenberg (who succeeded Treurnicht when he died) threatening civil war if the multiparty transitional executive council took over from the NP government. The low level of preparedness was evident from right-wing magazine *Dexter*'s non-ironic warning to its readers that while 'guerrilla war' held the benefit of making black people flee the country, it would mean no salaries and the 'guerrilla fighters' would be unable to repay their mortgage bonds.[126]

The danger of AWB leader Eugene Terre'Blanche's mix of bombastic bluster and recklessness was confirmed with the organisation's next 'invasion' – of Bophuthatswana in March 1994. Gun-toting thugs drove around, spewing racist slurs and shooting at black people. The fiasco culminated in the cold-blooded killing by Bop security force members of three AWB members who were pleading for their lives, in full view of the media. It was a chilling demonstration of the nihilism of Terre'Blanche's brand of white supremacist hooliganism. Constand Viljoen, a disciplined militarist whose instructions to the AWB to stay out of Bophuthatswana had been flatly ignored, realised what he was letting himself in for. He pulled out of the AVF and entered the constitutional process as the leader of the newly formed Freedom Front. His decision was also based on the fact that the military lacked alternatives to the policy route that the NP government was pursuing.

Bophuthatswana was the reality check that sank most right-wing fantasies of violently seizing state power. Thanks to his stature, Viljoen was able to lead much of the white right into the elections. The course of these events dashed hopes that an extra-constitutional process would deliver the white right's demands for self-determination. It seems highly unlikely that such an outcome could have been contrived by the NP government or security elements. The Bophuthatswana incident made the constitutional route more viable, and both the NP and the ANC went out of their way to draw the white right into the process. This led to the last-minute inclusion of clauses on a *volkstaatraad* (literally a council for a people's state) and Afrikaner self-determination in the interim constitution. According to academic Janis Grobbelaar, 'the white right wing should be understood to embody and symbolise not only the historical guardianship of the Afrikaner nationalist dream but also its [post-1994] striving for self-determination'.[127]

The white right and Inkatha

Given De Klerk's statement that violence was also aimed against the constitutional reforms, it is conceivable that security force elements used their counter-revolutionary training to this end. Some activities were aimed at terrorising the civilian population. The period 1990 to 1993 saw 572 people killed in more than 600 incidents of train violence.[128]

At first, large groups of up to 300 men wearing red headbands and using weapons ranging from iron rods to machine guns would indiscriminately attack commuters, either from train platforms or inside coaches. This violence raised the spectre of South Africa's covert activities in neighbouring states during the 1970s and 1980s yet again, as statements made to the TRC and the media indicated that some of the attackers were foreigners who had been forcibly recruited. One such statement came from a Mozambican who was a member of the SADF's 5 Reconnaissance Regiment. Train attackers were accommodated at Vlakplaas, he alleged. He also alleged that a unit of former Selous Scouts and RENAMO members were involved, and that railway security included ex–Special Forces operatives. Amnesty applications were also received from members of the police and the IFP, which strengthened evidence of connivance between the two.

The attacks seemed random and without a clear target, and therefore aimed at generally terrorising civilians – similar to incidents documented by the Black Sash in the Eastern Cape in the late 1980s. Most significantly, though, there was a distinct pattern of spikes in the incidence of train attacks and milestones in the negotiations, for example in July 1993, when the date for the first democratic election was announced. For Meyer, the escalation in train violence was especially noticeable in August 1990, when the Pretoria Minute was signed. The ANC had suspended its armed struggle just days before signing the document, which included agreements on the release of political prisoners. 'Every time we made progress, it flared up,' says Meyer.

The use of proxy forces, in line with total strategy, can be seen in the continued relationship between the security forces and the IFP and other vigilante groups, presenting 'overwhelming evidence ... of police collaboration with Inkatha'.[129] Of course, most details remained hidden through elaborate attempts at subterfuge, but the TRC hearings divulged much about the form and content of the collaboration. The TRC found the IFP to have been the 'foremost perpetrator of gross human rights violations in KwaZulu homeland and Natal province in the 1990s'.[130] There was evidence of a meeting between Buthelezi and MI officials in October 1989 during which Buthelezi requested assistance in the form of hit squads.[131] The SAP supplied weapons to the IFP via Vlakplaas, and Eugene de Kock had the permission of Major General Krappies Engelbrecht in or around 1990 to supply the IFP with home-made weapons.[132] Weapons supplied by Vlakplaas to IFP leader Themba Khoza were linked to the 1990 Sebokeng massacre.[133]

However, Wessels insists that the NP government never had 'an agreed strategy to support Inkatha to destabilise [the ANC] ... That people could have interpreted it that Inkatha should be supported at all costs and then follow that route via certain line functions and secret funds is possible.' However, in his mind, security force operations at Swanieville were somehow connected with Inkatha. Some 1 000 IFP-supporting hostel dwellers from Kagiso on the West Rand descended on Swanieville informal settlement in an early morning attack on 12 May 1991, killing twelve people and injuring numerous others. Various suspicious factors pointed to police complicity in the attack, including the seizure of weapons in a raid on Swanieville the day before the attack, by police who made no effort to disarm the IFP. In addition, armoured police vehicles escorted the assailants to Swanieville; the police told residents to go to bed early and stay off the streets; and white men wearing balaclavas participated in the violence.[134] Wessels also received information to the effect that the security forces had supported the IFP in the attacks. 'But I have not been able to figure this out to my own satisfaction,' he says.

Opposition to an NP–ANC-managed transition brought the black right wing, the white right wing and elements of the security forces together. The most visible illustration of this was the creation of the Concerned South Africans Group (Cosag) after the ROU of September 1992. It was a multiracial right-wing alliance combining the CP with the IFP and the governments of Ciskei and Bophuthatswana.

Both the black and white right had tentacles that stretched into the state. Many of the new white right organisations had former or serving CCB, MI, Special Forces and SADF operatives as members. Some links were cooperative and dated from the 1980s, especially with the IFP. AWB and IFP members on the Natal North Coast and Johannesburg's West Rand helped each other with arms procurement and training. At Cradock in the Eastern Cape, a planned joint IFP/AWB attack on a police station was foiled.[135] There was also a convergence of ideas with right-wing elements *within* the state.

These unlikely bedfellows – white supremacists and black reactionaries – were not only opposed to the transition, but shared secessionist ambitions. They could meet on this point despite the white right consisting of innumerable permutations of 'self-determination', represented by a proliferation of radical groups. The white right's mix of ethnic chauvinism with territorial ambition was not far from Buthelezi's dream of a Zulu nation.

Here we see the connection with the conservative wing of the cabinet. Buthelezi's ideas were quite similar to those of Delport and the KwaZulu-Natal NP. Delport had a 'language map' that he proffered at one of the many *bosberade* of the time. His argument was that power could be more effectively distributed through a regional division on the basis of language. His chart showed that if a line were drawn from Port Elizabeth to Kimberley, the area to the west would be predominantly Afrikaans. Therefore, the post-1994 provinces of the Northern Cape and the Western Cape, with a sizeable chunk of the Eastern Cape, would have fitted into a predominantly Afrikaans province or state. KwaZulu and Natal would be Zulu and English; the Free State would be Sotho and Afrikaans, and so forth. He was advocating 'near independence' for regional entities based on the geographical boundaries of provinces. Delport's ideas synchronised with those of the NP's leaders in Natal – including Danie Schutte, Con Botha and Renier Schoeman. They supported autonomy for KwaZulu, from which flowed a mutually appreciative relationship with Buthelezi.

In terms of ambitions for self-determination, the right wing thus stretched outwards from the cabinet, intensifying in extremism and militancy as one moved further to the right. However, the right wing was not coherent, and thus, when the crush of a liberal-democratic agreement landed on Delport's shoulders, he had neither the stomach nor the security force connections to activate a violent reaction to block the negotiated interim constitution.

CHAPTER 6

Clinching the elite compromise

The democratic state will exercise fiscal discipline in order to avoid inflation.   – ANC, *Ready to Govern*, 1992

The National Party commits itself to continuing the fight against inflation ... Fiscal discipline, in the form of suitable and coherent monetary and fiscal measures, must be maintained.
       – NP manifesto, 1993

Ouma Hannie: After 1990, there were only two NP members left: your father and FW de Klerk. After 1994, only your father.
       – Author Antjie Krog[1]

HARD-LINE APPROACHES WERE TRIED AND, HAVING FAILED, discarded by both the ANC and the NP in 1992. The harsh reality of life outside the comfort of the negotiation halls jolted politicians into action, resulting in a Record of Understanding.

Attacks on homes in the Vaal Triangle township of Boipatong on the night of 17 June were a wake-up call. Among the forty-five people who died and the 108 injured were ten children, one of whom was paralysed. One of the victims, Rebecca Motaung, described what happened: 'I heard people crying and stones were thrown at our squatter shack. A group of black men came into the shack, one stabbed me with a knife then let me go. Someone asked in Afrikaans: "Did you kill the woman?" and someone said: *"Yebo, inkosiyana."*'[2]

The victims were apparently pro-ANC; the assailants (some 300 of them) were IFP supporters from nearby hostels, who allegedly acted with the connivance of the security forces. Despite numerous affidavits containing detailed descriptions of white men participating in the attack, the Truth and Reconciliation Commission found that the security forces had not been involved. In 2003, ten IFP members received amnesty for the attack.

Boipatong gave the ANC a reason to formally withdraw from the stalled Codesa II. What made a grave impression on the NP leadership was the attack on then president FW de Klerk's convoy when he visited the township to express his condolences to the survivors. De Klerk's life was physically threatened, and the NP had yet again to face the growing anger over atrocities against black people. It sent a stark message that not even De Klerk's stature, as the leader who had heralded the 'New South Africa', immunised him against aggression. The incident humiliated De Klerk in front of the world's media and was a reality check indicating how little black support the NP could rely on. Time was not on their side.

This was also true at economic level, as the longest recession in the country's history deepened from early 1989 to late 1993. Real economic growth turned negative; real fixed investment growth remained negative (even though it improved from −7.4 per cent in 1991 to −3.1 per cent in 1993); there was a net outflow of foreign capital equalling 2.8 per cent of GDP between 1985 and 1992; private investment stood at 10 per cent of GDP, as opposed to the average of 20 per cent in comparable economies; real per capita disposable income was still declining (by 11 per cent between 1980 and 1993); and unemployment increased as almost eight in every 100 positions became redundant.[3]

The ANC leadership was still smarting from the reprimand it had received from rank-and-file members at its December 1990 conference. ANC members had caught the odour of an elite pact in the making and indicated their displeasure in no uncertain terms by hauling the leadership over the coals. The leaders were under pressure to deliver tangible advances at Codesa, but ANC structures were not giving feedback on documents as instructed, and negotiators felt that they were losing touch with their constituency. The Boipatong massacre demanded a response.

The ANC launched a campaign of rolling mass action, which enabled the leadership to reconnect with supporters and demonstrate common cause. After a meeting between COSATU, the SACP and the ANC in May 1992, the tripartite alliance announced that mass mobilisation would continue, whether an agreement was reached at Codesa or not. 'If Codesa II deadlocks, only mass action will ensure that the democratisation process remains on course. If Codesa II produces a breakthrough, mass mobilisation will be critical to ensuring the effective and urgent implementation of the agreements.'[4]

In a sense, mass action was to the ANC what the March 1992 referendum was to the NP. The massive street protests were a nightmare come true for NP leaders. They were concerned about the popular pressure being put on ANC leaders, the implications thereof for an elite agreement and the consequences for international relations, especially in the economic sphere.

From the viewpoint of the NP *verligtes*, economic deterioration necessitated movement. The pressure on negotiators to deliver results was also felt as an effect of the referendum. Internationally and locally, expectations of progress became more pronounced, compounding the pressure that NP participants felt. This played a decisive role in the NP's keenness to get the negotiations back on track.[5]

The *verligtes* were sensitive to foreign opinion and influence. Willingness to concede to an interim government came after De Klerk's first trip abroad. British premier Margaret Thatcher in particular was a precious ally of the NP government. Commonwealth member states applied pressure on her that contributed to the decision to unban the ANC.

During the first half of 1992, De Klerk moved Roelf Meyer to the constitutional development portfolio, and added defence to the conservative Kobie Coetsee's justice portfolio. The cabinet *verkramptes* were dejected by Meyer's appointment as chief negotiator instead of Tertius Delport, who had been Gerrit Viljoen's sidekick at Codesa. At the time, the gossip was that De Klerk wanted someone who could be manipulated.

Rina Venter[6] dismisses this, saying Meyer was a more appropriate candidate because he was not belligerent. In this sense, Meyer and De Klerk had a similar approach to the negotiations, seeking compromise rather than conflict. For Venter, this also meant that Meyer's business-like but amiable demeanour could lead to him buckling when he should have stood strong. Leon Wessels had a different impression. He argues that in the 'open market of an exchange of ideas in the cabinet', Hernus Kriel, Coetsee and Delport could not keep up. They just did not possess the requisite abilities to be chief negotiator. 'There was no alternative [successor] for Gerrit Viljoen apart from Roelf Meyer.'[7]

De Klerk instructed Meyer to contact ANC chief negotiator Cyril Ramaphosa, and the rapport that developed between the two of them created an axis of continuous interaction between the ANC and the NP. Their relationship became the dynamo that drove the negotiations towards agreement. This roused the suspicion of other parties and led to complaints that the negotiations were too much of a bilateral affair. But it was precisely the bilateral engagement between the ANC and the NP that allowed the negotiations to proceed. Meyer and Ramaphosa debated for hours on end over a period of three months before finally agreeing on the contents of the ROU, the next milestone in the transitional process after Codesa II.

The process of arriving at the ROU highlighted the increasing contestation of ideas between the *verkramptes* and the *verligtes*, as well as the convergence of interests between the securocrats and the *verligtes*. Disagreement about general amnesty almost scuppered the September 1992 summit at which Nelson Mandela and De Klerk were to sign the ROU.[8] The NP attempted at first to make the release of political prisoners part of a general amnesty for all who had committed crimes with a political motive, including government forces. The ANC was dead set against this, arguing that a government cannot 'give itself amnesty'.[9]

At last-minute talks, the NP backed down and agreed that the issue be addressed by the elected government of national unity. Hardliner Coetsee joined the government delegation only after the NP had made this concession. When a draft ROU was presented on 18 September, he immediately proposed an amendment that would extend amnesty to the security forces. The NP delegation – comprising Meyer, deputy law and order minister Gert Myburgh, constitutional development director and former intelligence head Niel Barnard and constitutional development advisor Fanie van der Merwe – held a separate meeting. Meyer and Coetsee exchanged 'heated words', but the latter remained intransigent. The ANC delegation was informed that the NP negotiators were at loggerheads, and the meeting was called off.

Coetsee was not alone in his conviction. De Klerk was against granting amnesty for serious crimes,[10] arguing that the temporary immunity given to exiled ANC members, together with the Indemnity Act of 1990, which provided indemnity to prisoners and exiles who had committed political offences, was adequate. Moreover, the internationally accepted Norgard principles were followed, which excluded perpetrators of wanton murder of civilians and pre-meditated or especially violent crimes from consideration for amnesty. The ANC's Jacob Zuma had signed an agreement with Coetsee acknowledging that the NP had abided by its commitment to release political prisoners. Zuma's agreement was dismissed by his colleagues, who demanded the release of all those imprisoned for political crimes, including offences that failed the Norgard test.

Meetings between Mandela and De Klerk to resolve the issue ended on 24 September, with Mandela threatening to pull out of the summit. Internally, the *verligtes* felt that the ANC's demand was not too high a price to get the ne-gotiations back on track. Coetsee dropped his insistence on blanket amnesty and the ROU was adopted on 26 September 1992. He admitted later that the NP sacrificed blanket amnesty to get the ANC back to the negotiating table.[11] At the time he was upset, as he had planned to use the issue as a bargaining chip in subsequent talks. He threatened to resign, but De Klerk persuaded him to stay on. De Klerk also mused that, 'in retrospect, it is possible that others in the security establishment might have had their own reasons for favouring the widest possible definition of political crimes'.[12] Significantly, this suggests a point of convergence in the interests of the *verligtes* and the securocrats. It also serves as a reminder that the militarists were always in full support of the *verligte* agenda – a point that is illustrated by Pik Botha's emphasis on PW Botha (as *verligte*) being the true originator of change rather than the conservative De Klerk.[13]

De Klerk also confirmed that *über*-securocrat Magnus Malan was a loyal supporter of the reform process. The *verligtes* accepted that reform could take place only within a 'ring of steel'.[14] It is not unthinkable that they would also have wanted indemnity to be available to those who formed this security cordon. The Further Indemnity Act of 1992 was passed as a result of the ROU, applying to people on both sides of the spectrum who could make the case that they had committed an offence for political reasons. De Klerk denied that it was a mechanism to slip amnesty to security force members through the back door.[15]

The impression was that the NP had lost its grip on the transition as the result of concessions made to the ANC in the ROU. For the NP, failure to reach a settlement would have meant yet another dead end. Wessels insists that the only option that would have remained 'was to force conflict, as was done at Codesa. Then you would have again run into the cycle of violence and mass action.' The escalation of violence since Codesa II impelled the *verligtes* to seek a resolution. By that time, Wessels realised that 'the best opportunity in negotiations is where you find yourself at a given moment. Circumstances seldom get better. The circumstances from Codesa I to Codesa II deteriorated. Similarly, our circumstances from the middle eighties to the middle nineties got worse.'

Boipatong reminded the NP of the hard facts on the ground in 1992. The second tragedy of that year served as a similar reminder for the ANC. Hardliners in the organisation sought to disrupt governance in the Ciskei by arranging a demonstration and then attempting to storm buildings in the capital of Bisho on 7 September. Members of the Ciskei defence force opened fire on the demonstrators, who included leaders such as Ramaphosa, Ronnie Kasrils and Chris Hani, killing twenty-eight of the 70 000 protestors. Events at Bisho brought home to the ANC that mass action as a tool had its limitations. The Leipzig option was not to be.

Boipatong and Bisho precipitated a retreat by the hardliners in both parties. Meyer underwent a 'paradigm shift'; De Klerk made a pragmatic reappraisal and invested his support in a more dove-like Meyer. Mandela became convinced that there was no alternative to negotiations.[16] And Ramaphosa, having had a close shave at Bisho, began engaging with Meyer to get the negotiations back on track.

Newborn liberal democrats?

The Record of Understanding of 26 September 1992 demonstrated a fundamental shift in the NP's approach to the negotiations. For Ramaphosa and Mac Maharaj, this marked the moment when the NP lost the initiative, as Mandela gained a 'psychological ascendancy' over De Klerk.[17] Personalities did indeed play a role – those of Mandela and De Klerk, as well as others. Mandela acknowledged the interdependence between him and De Klerk when he told writer Patti Waldmeir that, despite the personal animosity between them, 'my worst nightmare is that I wake up one night and De Klerk isn't there. I need him.'[18]

De Klerk's leadership was invaluable to the success of the transition. It is doubtful that any other NP politician, whether *verlig* or *verkramp*, would have been able to pull off what he did. As a conservative, he had enough clout with the white electorate to carry the majority with him. The same applies to the right-wing element in the NP leadership. The *verkramptes*, who were generally more hawkish than the *verligtes*, were trying to claw back lost ground. De Klerk's non-confrontational temperament doubtless helped him to contain the hot-heads. Generally, he seemed to have carefully weighed the options, electing to go with the *verligtes* in cabinet at crucial moments. Given his political credentials, this appeared out of character, but De Klerk's conservatism was imbued with moderation, and his consultative and supremely pragmatic approach to the multifaceted crises at hand made his the perfect personality for the moment. His stormy relationship with Mandela could have lured him into unwise knee-jerk responses, but it did not. Instead, he mostly stuck with the new generation of NP leaders, all of whom were of the conciliatory variety: Roelf Meyer and Leon Wessels, along with De Klerk's confidant, Dawie de Villiers.

According to Meyer, De Klerk was fully aware, at the time of the 2 February 1990 announcements, that there could be no turning back – 'Mandela could not be put back in jail.' De Klerk had committed himself to a negotiated settlement and, as the process unfolded, says Wessels, 'logic and momentum' kept him on the side of the negotiators. Towards the end of 1992 the pace of negotiations picked up dramatically, and the options put forward by the conservatives in cabinet seemed less and less viable.

The ROU allowed the NP to be reborn as 'liberal democrats'. On the surface, the party seemed to have met every demand made by Mandela in a newspaper interview a short while before the ROU was adopted: the release of politi-cal prisoners; enforced prohibition on the carrying and display of dangerous weapons in public; the fencing of hostels to prevent attacks on townships. However, the ANC's original demands had been whittled down from fourteen to three, and two of those were never enforced. Shortly afterwards, Inkatha – furious at having been excluded from the ROU negotiations – demonstrated that the ban on public displays of dangerous weapons was unenforceable by staging a provocative march through central Johannesburg. Impis brandished knobkieries and assegais. De Klerk's excuse was that a few police officers could not disarm 'thousands of Zulus' without people being killed. The fencing of hostels never took place either.

More importantly, for both De Klerk and Meyer, the ROU bound the ANC to an agreement that it had managed to sidestep by leaving Codesa II. For Meyer, the ROU was 'the moment of settlement' on which future engagement was built.[19] It was the point at which the NP's chief negotiators finally broke with the 'old paradigm' of clinging to a minority veto and group rights, says Meyer. Until then, the NP had operated from the premise that, in order to survive, white people as a minority grouping had to hold a monopoly on political power.

For Meyer, 1992 was the year of the paradigm shift. 'This is not a superficial or academic observation. Two things needed to happen: an intellectual move based on pragmatism, and an emotional acceptance. My own experience was that I became driven to ensure that we reached the end of the new road that we had set out on – to see the process through to its final phase, with all the consequences.'

While the NP had made liberal-democratic noises before the ROU, the events of 1992 pushed the *verligtes* closer to these values. The NP moved from minority to individual rights; embraced a liberal-democratic constitution; supported a bill of rights; and accepted a Constitutional Court as the highest decision-making body in the country. In this process, the *verkramptes* trailed behind, looking for ways to hold on to white power.

For Meyer and Wessels, the moment also marked a milestone for the ANC. Most significantly for Wessels, the dominant sections of both parties accepted constitutionalism, which was not the point at which they had started. The Harare Declaration of 21 August 1989, spearheaded by the ANC, had confirmed continuation of the armed struggle to 'fight and eradicate' the apartheid system.[20] The first ANC consultative conference inside the country in December 1990 resolved to expand the 'people's army', Umkhonto we Sizwe, and the underground structures to act against 'enemy-orchestrated violence' by creating self-defence units and pursuing mass action to pressurise the government into ending the violence.[21]

The 1990 conference reiterated the Harare Declaration that an interim government would replace the NP to oversee the drafting of a new constitution and the transition to democracy, including the first election. Instead, the NP managed to remain in government and be a dominant force in the drafting of the interim constitution. For the NP, convincing the ANC to accept that a constitutional vacuum should not be allowed was a victory. In that way, the NP secured its place in the 'orderly' development of a future constitution. By the end of Codesa II, the concept of constitutional principles holding an elected parliament to liberal-democratic guarantees had quietly fallen off the ANC's list of commitments. The ROU forced the ANC to commit itself anew to binding constitutional principles that would frame the first democratic parliament's deliberations on the final constitution after April 1994.

But while Meyer and Wessels emphasise that the ANC had also to revise its thinking, it had historically espoused the principles of democracy and human rights. The Harare Declaration had reaffirmed the ANC's commitment to a constitutional order based on democracy, liberty, equality, a bill of rights, equality before the law and an independent judiciary. In its May 1992 *Ready to Govern* policy document – released two weeks after the breakdown of Codesa II – the ANC committed itself explicitly to constitutionalism, including a bill of rights upheld by a Constitutional Court.[22] For Meyer, the ANC's concurrence with the latter as the supreme authority – higher than parliament – was a watershed moment. But the NP had to make far more radical adjustments to its world view.

In order to engage in the contest of ideas that is a negotiated transition, the NP had to abandon apartheid principles. The idea of 'group rights' was contaminated by the moral stain of apartheid, hence the NP's inability to peddle the concept to either its primary negotiating contender, the ANC, or its traditional allies in the West. By 1993, it had finally accepted that group rights as such would not be protected, and opted for the more acceptable protection (in the liberal-democratic paradigm) of cultural, religious and language rights.

At last the international political mood was gripping the NP, as exemplified by the party's changing attitude towards a bill of rights. In the 1970s, the dominant feeling in Afrikaner Nationalist ranks was still that the UN Universal Declaration on Human Rights was '*vanuit die bose*' – evil – because it propagated a secular humanist approach that attempted to put together that which 'God' had not ordained should be together. In the collective Nationalist mind of the 1970s, the doctrine of apartheid gave expression to 'God's will' that birds of a feather should flock together. Beneath this veneer of religious justification lay the very real situation of a white minority parliament that could not allow its own position to be threatened by a justiciable bill of human rights.[23]

The NP's revulsion to the concept of universal human rights held sway until the mid-1980s. In 1984, Kobie Coetsee reaffirmed this stance in a statement, but a mere two years later the NP revisited its position. Coetsee asked the South African Law Commission to devise a bill of rights, but for individuals *and* groups. Later that year, the Transvaal NP congress put its stamp of approval on his decision. In 1989, the commission came up with a proposal that protected individual rights, but offered little in the way of group rights. This prompted the government's *Proposals on a Charter of Fundamental Rights* in February 1993, which confirmed its 'conversion to the idea that individual (human) rights are best entrenched in a justiciable bill of rights mindful of liberal democratic values', according to constitutional experts Lourens du Plessis and Hugh Corder.[24]

For Wessels, the Law Commission's proposals paved the way for the NP's final official affirmation in 1993 that it had abandoned the concept of group rights. As had become the habit, the party was still ruling by commission – and the commission's inability to conjure up ways to protect group rights was yet another sign that the NP had no choice but to move towards the increasingly global norm of liberal-democratic protections. But throughout these developments, the party remained aware of its conservative support base and the difficulty of retaining it while moving towards liberal democracy, says Wessels. A 1989 poll found that only 7 per cent of English-speaking whites and 5 per cent of Afrikaans-speaking whites supported a unitary state with one parliament and universal franchise. Even among DP supporters, a 1990 poll found that only 8 per cent thought the ANC was capable of running the country.[25]

Recalcitrant supporters, combined with die-hard white supremacists in *verkrampte* ranks, translated into the leadership moving only as far as they had to – which meant democracy with a strong libertarian tone. The negotiations on a bill of rights for post-apartheid South Africa during 1993 became marked by urgency on the NP's part to embed the 'libertarian' concept of human rights in the constitution.

Libertarianism is in perpetual conflict with egalitarianism, in that it holds individual liberty rather than equality as the paramount human right, and demands a hands-off attitude from the state in relation to individual autonomy.[26] Therefore, contrary to what the expectation might have been, the NP fought much harder to maximise the guarantees for rights. The multiparty negotiations were not representative of democratic support, which gave the NP – as government – disproportionate say over development of the constitution and its bill of rights.

This was why the ANC had resisted the entrenchment of guarantees and adopted a minimalist position on the level of detail to be included in the charter of rights. The NP's reasoning was, ironically, that such rights could safeguard the citizenry against the abuse of power by a politically dominant party in future. More cynically, ensuring these rights also meant the protection of vested white interests and was in step with the party's perennial fear of *gelykstelling* [equalisation] – so long-standing that, were the NP a living organism, it would have become part of its genetic programming.

The NP's adoption of libertarianism brought it firmly into the camp of the liberal capitalists. As was to be expected, the corporate sector supported the libertarian position on human rights, as illustrated in 1986 when the South African Federation of Chambers of Industry set out its preferences in the *Business Charter of Social, Economic and Political Rights*. The NP was thus in line with the political tradition most closely identified with English-speaking capital – that of parties such as the Progressive Party, the Progressive Federal

Party and the Democratic Party. The DP's May 1993 bill of rights, compiled by future Democratic Alliance leader Tony Leon, put forward a 'preponderantly libertarian' position, despite emphasising the harmonisation of equality with liberty.[27]

According to Du Plessis and Corder, the 'older liberals' – business and the DP – welcomed the NP as ally in their 'efforts aimed at preserving certain "structures of privilege" and "maintaining standards"'.[28] They met on the point of concern about preventing a disturbance to existing patterns of wealth distribution, which the NP's charter on human rights also promoted. The party had finally come to realise that it did not have to cling to race as a category of discrimination to ensure the perpetuation of white privilege.

The NP used the interim constitution–making process as much as possible to determine the content of the final constitution, rather than leaving this to a democratically elected constituent assembly, as the ANC had wanted. The NP's experience with regional transitions came in handy: Namibia and Zimbabwe were the precedents for mechanisms that served as guarantees in constitutional law. In the case of the former, the UN Security Council supervised the guarantees, while in Zimbabwe, the British government enforced the provisions of the Lancaster House Agreement. The ANC agreed to limitations on its future constitution-making powers in return for the NP relinquishing power[29] – a dramatic concession approved by the Western powers-that-be, who kept a close eye on proceedings. The similarity with Zimbabwe was striking, and confirmed again what kind of outcome was acceptable to the West.

The NP was remarkably successful in its bid to entrench what Corder calls 'the immutable foundation stones'[30] of the final constitution. The 1996 constitution had to be drafted in accordance with the interim document, agreed upon before 1994, and within the framework of constitutional principles accepted before the first democratic election. The principles showed the extent to which the ANC compromised, particularly with regard to the following:

- Acknowledgement and protection of the diversity of language and culture.
- Collective rights of self-determination in civil rights organisations, such as linguistic, cultural and religious associations.
- Provision for minority party participation in legislative processes.
- Three tiers of elected government at national, provincial and local level.
- Acceptance of provincial constitutions and a prohibition on national government encroachment on provincial government powers.
- An independent Reserve Bank.
- Constitutional provision of the right to self-determination on a territorial or other basis by cultural or linguistic communities, provided there was sufficient support.

These principles could not be amended 'under any condition', thereby exerting an 'external control over the Constituent Assembly [the post-1994 parliament]', Corder points out.[31] The constitutional principles represented a guarantee in constitutional law that, regardless of levels of support in the first election, 'certain structures, procedures and interests [would] be sacrosanct'.[32] In this way, South Africa's undemocratic past would continue to haunt its future.

Entrenchment of the constitutional principles was a coup for the NP that was downplayed by critics who argued that the party 'surrendered without defeat' or that the negotiations were a 'disguised surrender'.[33] Meyer agrees that the constitutional principles assured the NP of a guarantee that the democratically elected parliament would be subject to norms with which the NP concurred. In a presentation to the NP cabinet at a D'Nyala *bosberaad* in July 1993, Meyer and Fanie van der Merwe placed much emphasis on the constitutional principles, confirming the importance the NP attached to them.

Legal experts Du Plessis and Corder came to the conclusion that the ANC was 'probably the most accommodating' of negotiating parties.[34] At a glance, it was clear that the final list of rights agreed upon at Kempton Park was much more extensive than what the ANC had envisaged. The NP managed to entrench many more rights along with the constitutional principles. The trade-off was that, while the NP reached a point where it accepted that a white veto was impossible, it received liberal-democratic assurances of rights, bolstered by the global ascendance of liberal democracy at that historical juncture (the fall of communism).

In the end, acceptance of constitutionalism benefited the NP more than the ANC, because it limited the extent to which the ANC could hope to redistribute wealth – a core expectation of its constituency.

But, despite these facts, the picture looked less rosy from Delport and the other *verkramptes'* point of view. For example, while the executive's power would be held in check by making the Constitutional Court rather than parliament the highest decision-making body, the appointment of judges was a political process. But this essentially meant that the South African system worked the same as that of the US.

The internal chasm widens

The ROU ushered in a new era in the negotiations, punctuated by bitter in-fighting among NP leaders. Some within the party had not made the shift to Meyer's new paradigm. According to him, 'groups' within the leadership held on to the idea that the white minority should retain power. Such groups clung to 'ridiculous' ideas such as a rotational presidency, says Meyer.

'What was that about? To keep as much power as possible for the whites, thereby exercising a veto through a rotating presidency.' These 'groups' included Delport, Hernus Kriel and Kobie Coetsee, who hardened their stance as the negotiations proceeded, widening the chasm between themselves and the *verligtes*. The ROU in itself caused considerable friction.

Two aspects of the ROU – the ban on dangerous weapons and the fencing of hostels – came from the ANC and were directly applicable to the IFP. For Buthelezi, it was a slap in the face to suggest that the carrying of traditional weapons by IFP supporters was the cause of the violence, says Delport. It was at this point that the NP's relationship with Buthelezi finally collapsed – at least publicly.

The conservative members of cabinet blamed Meyer and Wessels for alienating Buthelezi. Wessels says he finally lost patience with the IFP leader after a hostile speech party chairperson Frank Mdlalose had made in January 1992, which he later apologetically claimed had been written by senior IFP member Walter Felgate. De Klerk met with Buthelezi on 17 September 1992, informing him fully about discussions on the ANC's three demands. On De Klerk's instructions, Meyer and Wessels held telephonic discussions with Buthelezi about the ROU. 'My general impression was that he was satisfied with [what we had explained]. But afterwards he totally denied ownership,' says Wessels. Buthelezi unexpectedly reversed his position, accusing the NP of 'ganging up' with the ANC against the IFP, Meyer recalls. This had been a problem for some time. Bilateral agreements would be reached, 'only to have the IFP return to the next meeting as though we had never spoken to each other in our lives', according to Meyer.

The NP's several efforts to placate Buthelezi after the ROU came to naught. He felt betrayed, seeing the ROU as a bilateral engagement between the NP and the ANC and showing no regard for the NP's position on bilateral meetings being the way to get the ANC back on track in the negotiations. The NP negotiators reached the point where they were tired of Buthelezi's constant antics. His timing could not have been worse. He was living up to his reputation as a renegade amid escalating political violence.

For Meyer, the IFP placed itself 'on the wrong course' when it hooked up with the Conservative Party and the governments of Bophuthatswana and Transkei to form Cosag shortly after the ROU. The IFP's response to the ROU led the *verligtes* in the NP to their decision to sacrifice the possibility of a partnership with the IFP rather than alienate the ANC. This was another layer in the foundation of the elite pact. One of the NP's considerations from the start, which built on processes commenced in the 1970s, was an elite pact with the ANC. In December 1992 and January 1993,[35] relations between the two political elites – Afrikaner and African nationalists – were further strengthened during *bosberade* at the NP cabinet's favourite haunt, D'Nyala nature reserve.

As far as Meyer is concerned, the rupture with the IFP was never mended, but not everyone in the leadership shared his and Wessels' sentiments. The Natal NP, including conservatives such as Danie Schutte and Renier Schoeman, was close to the IFP. Wessels had the impression that 'Buthelezi had his favourites in the National Party'. He got along well with two kinds of people: those who preached federalism with strong autonomous powers at regional level, and those who adopted a '*voetstoots* unqualified, suspicious attitude towards the ANC', according to Wessels.

De Klerk himself questioned whether the NP negotiators adequately conveyed to the IFP what had been discussed at a meeting with the ANC on 26 September 1992, during which the NP agreed to the release of political prisoners, irrespective of the seriousness of the crimes committed. In contrast to Wessels, De Klerk describes Buthelezi as characteristically non-committal. Delport also refutes the assertion that Buthelezi changed his positions willy-nilly. According to him, while Buthelezi was extraordinarily sensitive to criticism, he stuck to positions of principle.

Delport argues that Buthelezi deserved respect as a senior figure on South Africa's political landscape who had won international recognition for his role. Buthelezi was disillusioned to the point of declaring to Delport – who was in contact with him at the time – that he could never trust the NP again.[36]

A primary platform on which the IFP and the NP hawks met each other was regionalism. Historically, the NP leadership did not support the regional devolution of power. After all, it had presided over a strongly centralised government for more than forty years. Federalism was associated with liberal proponents in parliament. It only really entered the NP's vocabulary in the late 1980s, and then only because of political expediency. Some in the leadership – especially the regionalists – felt the NP had a chance of winning at least one province: the predominantly Afrikaans-speaking Western Cape. But even with this promise in the air, the NP leadership remained ambiguous about the issue.

Ultimately, the NP's position fell between that of the IFP, which emphasised self-determination for regional entities, and that of the ANC, which supported a united, centralised state. The NP's half-hearted case for regionalism alienated it from those that it regarded as partners earlier in the transition. Its primary haggling point with the governments of Ciskei, Bophuthatswana and KwaZulu was around this issue.

Apart from the hawks' closer relationship with the IFP and their predilection for a more iron-fisted approach to pushing the NP agenda, they were also enamoured by the idea of decentralising power to federal entities. Their position therefore differed from the mainstream position within the NP. This was illustrated after the 1994 election, when the Western Cape became the first province to write its own constitution, a move made possible by agreements reached on the eve of adoption of the interim constitution. Hardliner and subsequent Western Cape premier Hernus Kriel ensured that the Western Cape got its own constitution.

Differences on regionalism formed a major bone of contention between the *verligtes* and the *verkramptes*. Delport's suggested creation of an Afrikaans-language quasi-state was on an equal level with what Buthelezi proposed for KwaZulu and Natal: a large, 'mostly homogeneous' grouping which, for that very reason, would deserve near-autonomous powers.

Delport's justification was devolution of power to regional entities on the basis of language, resulting in a balance of power at regional level due to the size of population groups varying from one area to another. However, the proposal echoed apartheid planning, as division on the basis of language would also reflect ethnic and racial demographics. Indeed, apartheid's Bantustans were mono-lingual entities, with Venda-speaking Venda; Ndebele-speaking KwaNdebele; Tswana-speaking Bophuthatswana; and Xhosa-speaking Transkei, to name a few. The plan was nothing new.

Delport's yellow-coloured 'language map' made Wessels 'see red'. He and others strongly resisted it as 'totally unacceptable – not only for the ANC but also for us. It's not as if we capitulated to ANC thoughts. [Regional language-based entities were] not our position, it was not our policy. [Delport] was propagating a policy different to the one that we wanted. The position was not far removed from that of [FF leader] Constand Viljoen, except that Constand Viljoen did not have a map,' Wessels says.

Furthermore, the *verkrampte–verligte* split was fuelled by a fundamental disagreement about how the negotiations should proceed after De Klerk replaced Viljoen with Meyer as chief negotiator in 1992. The NP had constituted a negoti-ating committee, which included the hawks in the cabinet, but they were not among those directly involved in the day-to-day bargaining. Sheila Camerer assisted Meyer but, as deputy minister of justice, also reported to Kobie Coetsee. She would brief Coetsee on progress in the negotiations and convey his feedback to Meyer.[37] More often than not, Coetsee's proposals would clash with the NP negotiating team's efforts. His approach was 'give the ANC a bit of rope and they will hang themselves. Well, they didn't,' says Camerer. Frequently, report-back meetings would explode in acrimony, with the conservatives attacking Meyer for having gone 'past the fallback position'.[38]

Sunset escape routes

At first, De Klerk timed announcements in a gradual manner so as to keep control of the process. His approach was similar to that of other authoritarian transitions to democracy.[39] He lifted the last state of emergency regulations in October 1990, and announced the abolition of remaining apartheid measures in the statute books a year after unbanning the liberation movements. He waited another ten months before conceding the ANC's demand for an elected interim government.

This 'tardiness' changed during 1992 as a noticeable urgency took hold of the NP, as it wanted to get the ANC back to the negotiating table. In part, this could be ascribed to the success of mass action. The NP leadership found the strikes, demonstrations and public violence disconcerting. One reason was their constant emphasis on themselves as the guardians of 'orderly' change. Mass action belied the NP's insistence that it was in full command of the transition.

The ROU paved the way for an ingenious move by Joe Slovo, with the backing of some key ANC leaders. He published an article in *The African Communist* in October 1992, proposing the so-called sunset clause. This provided for a more extended transitional period – something the NP had sought from the start. Some of Slovo's proposals became basic elements of the transition: a government of national unity (GNU), and his suggestion of general amnesty in return for full disclosure of crimes. In later years, the limited five-year tenure of the GNU and the TRC would return to haunt the NP. But at the time, Slovo's package offered security to an NP entangled in the complexities of a process of which the outcome was highly uncertain.

The GNU assured NP politicians of a continued role at the highest level of political power – to say nothing of employment with concomitant salaries! Pension and employment guarantees were extended to the predominantly Afrikaner bureaucracy and security forces. At the time, Slovo was very concerned about the continued cooperation of the security forces, and these guarantees were designed to address this problem.

The ANC formally adopted Slovo's proposals in its November 1992 document called *Negotiations: A Strategic Perspective*. It was the right move, as the transitional process speeded up noticeably. By the end of November, De Klerk had committed the NP to a time frame: agreement on an interim constitution by May 1993 and conclusion of the entire process, including drafting of that document, by March or April 1994. That would be the date of the first democratic election.

With employment guarantees in hand, the NP set a pace that brooked no resistance – not from erstwhile ally the IFP or any internal faction. As the negotiators steamed ahead, individuals within the party became more anxious to secure their positions. D-Day drew closer, and members of the NP leadership scrambled to ensure their continued position in power or, at the very least, employment.

Hurtling ahead

Opaque negotiating processes kicked in after the ROU. A multiparty planning conference convened on 5 and 6 March 1993, including the CP and the PAC, which had boycotted Codesa. A committee representing all parties drew up a document detailing the agreements reached. While these were not binding, the NP was confident that the ANC's signature on the ROU would bind it to a liberal-democratic compromise.

To signify a break with the decisions taken at Codesa, the talks were called the multiparty negotiating process (MPNP), which resumed on 1 April at the World Trade Centre in Kempton Park. The NP team consisted of Meyer, Wessels, Dawie de Villiers and Fanie van der Merwe. They spent long hours in meetings with the ANC side, led by Ramaphosa.

Charisma was in short supply in the NP, compared to the urbane Ramaphosa, Valli Moosa and Mac Maharaj. Meyer was 'the discreet face of reconciliation and NP compromise', as journalist Marion Edmunds once aptly described him.[40] The one NP leader who could have lent colour to the negotiations, Pik Botha, had been sidelined. He was regarded by some as an unpredictable maverick who could change his position at any given moment.

The *verkrampte* hardliners in the NP complained about being excluded. Decisions were taken with which they disagreed. They were so insulated from the negotiation process that major policy points, such as a senate that would ensure the representation of minority interests, were 'lost somewhere along the way, never to be heard of again', says Delport. Slowly, despite the hawks' questions and resistance, the power-sharing plan was eroded.

The negotiating dynamic revolved around Meyer and Ramaphosa. The latter had decided early on that the two major forces which had to reach agreement were the NP government, the holder of state power, and the ANC, representative of the majority of the population.[41] It was of cardinal importance to create an understanding between these two on a constitution. The ANC also developed a sense of haste, especially after the abortive attempt at intimidating the Ciskei government.

While the ANC and the NP were both focused on reaching agreement through the bilateral channel between them, they were still very much aware of the smaller parties as potentially disruptive forces. On 10 April 1993, CP members were involved in the plot that killed Chris Hani, general secretary of the SACP. On 25 June, the AWB stormed and vandalised the World Trade Centre where the negotiations were taking place. Members of the PAC's Azanian People's Liberation Army killed twelve people attending a service at the St James Church, in Cape Town on 25 July, and PAC members murdered American student Amy Biehl one month later. These events, combined with the continuing decline in GNP in both 1992 and 1993, made it clear to the NP that forces had been unleashed which would be both difficult and expensive to contain through state repression. The genie could not be put back in the bottle. The NP had to forge ahead.

This dynamic made possible mutual acceptance by the ANC and the NP of the 'sufficient consensus' mechanism. The idea came from Ramaphosa, who had used it previously in labour negotiations. It was presented as an option whenever parties failed to reach general agreement. Consensus was regarded as 'sufficient' when enough parties were willing to move the process forward. The IFP and the CP in particular opposed the application of sufficient consensus, which effectively meant that decisions could be made without the concurrence of smaller parties.[42] In reality, it boiled down to the process moving forward whenever the NP and the ANC – Meyer and Ramaphosa – agreed with one another.

Theoretically, Meyer's decisions were subject to approval by the NP cabinet or De Klerk, and Ramaphosa's by the ANC's national executive committee. However, due to the speed at which negotiations proceeded in 1993, revisiting or amending agreements was virtually impossible once they were agreed.[43] Underpinning the process was a personal rapport between Ramaphosa and Meyer that had first become evident when Codesa II collapsed and they were seen 'locked in earnest and business-like conversation' while 'emotion-charged delegates vented their frustration at the lost agreement they had believed to be so near'.[44] Conspicuous one-on-one contact between the two chief negotiators took place throughout 1993, when they would be seen talking in corridors and leaving and entering rooms shortly after one another.

Apart from the Ramaphosa–Meyer channel, a subcommittee with Van der Merwe representing the government and Maharaj the ANC was intimately involved in brokering agreements whenever the chief negotiators reached a cul-de-sac on an issue. The committee was set up to draft rules for breaking deadlocks and resolving disputes, but it played an important role behind the scenes as a bargaining forum. Van der Merwe and Maharaj interacted constantly with Meyer and Ramaphosa, drafting resolutions and documents and picking up where the latter pair had reached an impasse. Their most significant con-tribution was the drafting of the interim constitution's 'postamble' (postscript) on conditional amnesty for political offences committed during the apartheid era.[45] This produced the TRC.

While these circles within circles of decision-making ensured that the process maintained impetus, they also created a lack of transparency. The system of technical committees consisting of legal experts selected by the various political parties was similarly difficult to penetrate. They were, in fact, designed to resolve disagreements before the media could report on them. This was done for good reason, namely to avoid a widening of chasms opened up at Codesa, when media reports drew attention to the differences between parties.

While the reasoning was sound, the result was even less transparency. It was thus to be expected that outsiders, including the country's citizens, would feel alienated from the process. This happened at an early stage among constituencies of both the ANC and the NP. By the end of 1990, ANC members were criticising their leaders for being too amiable with the NP, while the Potchefstroom by-election and the white referendum saw voters questioning NP politicians about what exactly the negotiations would mean. A technical committee at the MPNP expressed concern at the lack of public comprehension of the negotiations and the decisions taken.[46] Not only was this information deficit never adequately addressed, but it was, in fact, exacerbated by political posturing and propaganda in the run-up to the 1994 elections.

In June 1993, both the NP and the ANC pressed the accelerator even more. They locked themselves and the rest of the multiparty forum into hurly-burly negotiations by agreeing on a date for the first democratic elections – 27 April 1994 – leaving negotiators with less than ten months to agree on an interim constitution. Meyer wanted everything done in even less time; he was aiming for a finalised interim constitution by the end of October. On 30 June, the majority of the twenty-six delegations supported a vote instructing the technical committee on constitutional issues to draft an interim constitution. The CP was the only party to vote against the proposal, while the IFP, the KwaZulu and Ciskei governments, the PAC and the Afrikaner-Volksunie abstained. The Cosag parties walked out shortly thereafter, preferring to pursue their interests outside the negotiations.

The vexed issues of majorities and deadlock-breaking mechanisms, which had led to Codesa floundering, were given to the experts to resolve. Sensitive to criticism from the conservatives in the cabinet, Meyer and Van der Merwe made a presentation at D'Nyala in July. To allay fears that agreements clashed with NP policy positions, they presented a table comparing the NP's constitutional plan, adopted at its September 1991 federal congress, with what had been agreed upon at the negotiations. The format lent itself to some obfuscation, primarily with regard to power sharing. The negotiators indicated that they had achieved agreement on a system that would not allow 'any form of domination', and which gave 'preference to the inclusion rather than exclusion of parties and groups'.[47] They were apparently referring to the electoral system of proportional representation.

However, even this confusing rephrasing could not hide the fact that the NP's plans for veto mechanisms to prevent 'majority domination' had not come to fruition. Instead of a senate with group representation, the second house of parliament allowed for regional representation on an equal basis, and majorities were necessary for certain changes to the constitution. Therefore, parties representing minorities would be able to oppose draft legislation only if they held power in a province. Even then, they would need control of the majority of provinces in order to block laws or amendments to the constitution.

At this juncture, all the contentious issues related to the NP's core demand of power sharing were still outstanding. These included the proposal for a rotating presidency and the appointment by consensus of ministers to a multiparty cabinet. Meyer and Van der Merwe's presentation still punted these proposals as necessary for a system that 'gives preference to a multiparty government as opposed to a system where the majority party forms the executive power by itself'.[48] But by November, their scheme was off the table for good.

On a superficial level, the D'Nyala presentation was meant as a report-back by the negotiators to their colleagues. It was an opportunity for engagement, with a view to change where necessary. However, because of the speed of the negotiations and the volume of issues to consider, ministers not involved in the process were unable to catch up at the D'Nyala meeting. They were unprepared and did not feel they could tackle the myriad issues with authority. Afterwards, Delport and Coetsee raised objections.[49]

The negotiators themselves 'made plans on the run', frequently under 'pressure-cooker conditions', says Wessels. 'You could not handle [the negotiations] week by week, month by month, or from NP congress to NP congress. You had to handle it as it happened. Needless to say, the other guys [in the cabinet] were fed up with that.'

What the party's negotiators ended up with was different to what they had started out with, and what had been agreed in the cabinet. At a particularly difficult point towards the end of the negotiations, they informed De Klerk 'blow by blow' throughout the day. He witnessed how the options were shrinking away. By that evening, Wessels gave him feedback on the final decision. De Klerk gave his negotiators the nod, adding: 'I know a lot of people are going to be very sour and very bitter, but we will have to handle that at the next cabinet meeting.'[50]

Those against ...

By April 1993, the NP was letting go of the concept of itself as sovereign government. After Hani's assassination, in an effort to calm inflamed emotions, the NP proposed establishing a multiparty transitional executive council to monitor the government and ensure fair play in the run-up to the election. This came at a time when the ANC was opposed to a TEC, instead wanting an election date fixed. The NP's offer showed the depth of realisation within the party that the days of white minority rule were numbered. The journey that it had embarked upon had to be concluded swiftly.

This realisation, and the desire to partly cede power to a multiparty organ, could at least partly be attributed to the volatility of relations within the party. De Klerk, Meyer and their cohorts had not only to deal with the astuteness of a Ramaphosa, the thuggery of an AWB or the scheming of a Buthelezi in cahoots with security force elements, but also with the far-right-wing element in the NP cabinet.

Hernus Kriel attempted to tip the internal balance of power by using his position as minister of law and order to arrange raids on PAC premises and arrests of PAC members in May. He managed to create some exceedingly tense moments at the negotiations, with the PAC threatening to withdraw. De Klerk's response was to invite the opposing *verligte* and *verkrampte* factions to a pre-cabinet meeting to try to resolve their differences rather than 'take them with us into the cabinet meeting', says Wessels.

Coincidentally, they positioned themselves at the table in accordance with their loyalties: Meyer, De Villiers and Wessels were on De Klerk's left, while Kriel, Delport and Coetsee took chairs to his right. In the end, the NP allowed Kriel to be summoned before the MPNP council to explain himself. It was a drastic and unprecedented move: a government minister was forced to account to a non-governmental body. As Richard Spitz and Matthew Chaskalson noted, 'if it had indeed been [Kriel's] intention to reassert the authority of the right wing of the NP/government, [it turned out as] a miserable failure'.[51]

This was the crucial moment when the *verligtes* gained the upper hand over the *verkramptes*. It was also symbolically significant, as the *verligtes* aligned themselves with the negotiating forum. In a way, the *verligtes* used the forum to beat back internal attempts to undermine that very body. Meyer mopped up after Kriel by meeting with the PAC and arranging the release of those arrested, and the return of seized material and equipment.

The NP negotiators seem also to have used the *verligte* Afrikaans press to discipline recalcitrant cabinet members. On 1 August, *Rapport* published an article based on a leak about the 'seven anti's' in cabinet. The newspaper was jointly owned at the time by Nasionale Pers and Perskor, the former having been among the first in the Afrikaner establishment to protest aspects of apartheid that undermined capital accumulation.

'Anti's' referred to those cabinet members who opposed change. The article was aimed at intimidating the *verkramptes*, tainting them as wanting to derail the negotiations. The timing could not have been better, as the conservatives were harbouring the idea of forcing a return to the NP's federal congress. They believed that the direction taken in the negotiations would be rejected, and thus blocked by this larger NP structure.

The article prompted Rina Venter to write an angrily worded confidential letter to De Klerk, raising her concerns that such 'perceptions are being developed about members of the cabinet'. She pointed out that 'the team that is supposed to defend [the NP's] case is acting as an advocate of the [MPNP's] technical committee.

'The fact is that the process is being managed in such a way that ministers are not placed in a position to have a well-thought-out document available which produces the *NP's evaluation* of the events at Kempton Park' (Venter's emphasis).[52]

The *verligtes* thus became so deeply involved in the newly created negotiating structures that a distance developed between them and those cabinet members outside the day-to-day talks. They were so much a part of the rough and tumble of the negotiations that there seemed to have been greater loyalty towards the process than to the party. What Venter wanted – in vain – was an evaluation of progress on what the NP had set out to achieve. For the negotiators, the suspicion that marked Codesa I and II had made way for an alliance of mutual commitment to the negotiation process, but their cabinet colleagues remained distrustful of the ANC, seeing 'red lights and hidden agendas', according to Venter.

The *verligte* wing dismissed these qualms, telling the *verkramptes* 'it is not the ANC's intention to harm us'. Venter was willing to release a public statement to defend her position, but, like Delport, she was deeply conscious that the expectations of 'masses of black people' had been raised. She was worried that public comments would bring the negotiations to a standstill and precipitate a crisis for the country, and she could not bring herself to cause such a situation.

Complaints also emanated from the Broederbond, a still powerful arm of the Afrikaner establishment. Chairperson Pieter de Lange voiced his concern about Meyer – ostensibly his capabilities as a negotiator – to Venter. She duly communicated this to De Klerk, who retorted: 'Who else in the cabinet can I appoint?'[53] He had his misgivings, as illustrated by comments about his dissatisfaction with the negotiators' performance regarding the ROU,[54] but he stuck with Meyer, primarily because he remained convinced that the approach taken by the *verligtes* was the 'logical' one.

The *verligtes* believed this so firmly that Wessels told Kriel at one point it was a pity that their two positions could not be tested in public debate, as he was positive that Kriel's argument 'would not be victorious'. According to Wessels, during this period De Klerk's problem was that 'he always had to listen to a compromise position after we had wrestled it out and reached a settlement. He never got the opportunity to hear the two extreme positions; he would have been able to see the dangers if he had listened to me and to Tertius [Delport] undiluted.' This also showed that the NP remained a party steered from the very top. The *hoofleier*'s decisions continued to hold sway, even in the face of radical disagreements among the leadership.

The *verligtes* maintained their dominance, not least because, apart from the minority veto plan, the hawks had nothing else to put on the table. After 1994, they came round to accepting the constitution. Delport insists that he does not argue 'that any other constitution would have been better' than the one agreed on at the negotiations.

Another issue was the lack of unity among hardliners and the role of individual personalities. The conservative Kobie Coetsee had a longer tenure in cabinet than any of the other hawks, except for Malan. His sometimes idiosyncratic ways did not endear him to all. Wessels says of Coetsee that 'haste [was] not his companion', meaning he was chronically late. In the end, Coetsee was embittered by having been 'pushed aside'. Wessels says bluntly that while Coetsee had held crucial portfolios (being minister of justice *and* defence at one stage), he could not compete in the 'marketplace of ideas'. He had also managed to make 'a lot of enemies' in the NP, as would be seen a few years later, when he was blamed for the failure to secure a blanket amnesty agreement.

The inability to convince the ANC to accept a general amnesty for apartheid's gross human rights violators was a major source of conflict that would later turn out to be one of the nails in the NP's coffin. The issue proved especially divisive within NP ranks. Three to four days before the interim constitution was finalised in late 1993, it emerged that Coetsee had been unable to wrest from the ANC the general amnesty that the NP had sought. Even other hardliners, such as Kriel, later put the blame squarely on Coetsee.[55]

The allegation, which Coetsee refuted, was that the ANC had supported a general amnesty even before the ROU, but that he had bungled by not accepting it there and then. Meyer had to step in at the last minute and settle for what he got, according to Kriel. In fact, Fanie van der Merwe and Mac Maharaj wrote the epilogue to the interim constitution, which spelled out that amnesty would be qualified.

Agreement on this thorny question was reached only after the multiparty process had ended. Again, Meyer presented the compromise position – to which Wessels was privy – to De Klerk, who accepted it. Again, it was not what the cabinet had agreed on. And – again – the rest of the cabinet was not informed until after the agreement had been reached. At the subsequent meeting, Kriel, Delport, Coetsee, Malan and Vlok were all unhappy.

The interim constitution determined that amnesty – or indemnity from prosecution – would be subject to a public process of full disclosure to the TRC. The shocking and tragic nature of the revelations proved too much for many Afrikaners, leading to a knee-jerk rejection and an anti-TRC propaganda campaign in the Cape Town–based *Die Burger*. Both Malan and Kriel attacked Coetsee for his handling of the amnesty question, though, surprisingly, Kriel came out in defence of Meyer having to sort out the 'mess'.

This suggests that the hawks were not of one mind. Moreover, given that the securocrats had been aligned with the *verligte* agenda since Botha's time, the *verkramptes* were not sufficiently connected to the security forces that might have supplied them with the muscle needed to resist change.

For Delport, the ultimate failure of the NP negotiating team was not to have insisted on 'material agreement'. The formal agreements that were reached should have been fleshed out. The constitution contained principles that the primary parties could agree to, but how those principles would be effected was not determined.[56] Delport cites federalism and education as examples.

For Delport, the point of utmost importance was the authority that opposition parties would have in the cabinet. Since the president would be elected by parliament, the system remained a Westminster model. The majority party in parliament would elect its leader as president and they would enjoy a symbiotic relationship. Members of parliament would never vote against their leader or ministers from their party. The South African system is dominated by the cabinet, which initiates legislation, which is then channelled through parliament. Parliamentarians follow instructions and pass the legislation as required by the executive. So, for Delport, the burning question was: What comes out of the cabinet? 'If you cannot put your foot on the brake there, then you do not have authority or power.'

He points out that the original NP position had been government by consensus. One way to achieve that would have been by requiring large majorities for laws to be passed, necessitating inter-party cooperation. However, what was in the end agreed was that, even at cabinet level, the NP would have no authority to block any decisions. De Klerk and Meyer accepted the ANC position that decision-making in cabinet would be on the basis of simple majority. The best that was achieved was 'co-option', says Delport. For him, the GNU was nothing but co-option. The NP could participate in decision-making but had no final say, meaning that it could not alter decisions with which it disagreed.

The last outstanding matters on distribution of power within the GNU were resolved at a meeting between Mandela, De Klerk and Meyer the evening before the interim constitution was adopted. The next morning, De Klerk and Meyer informed their colleagues what the final decisions were. It was announced at an NP cabinet meeting that there would be no voting at cabinet level in future, but that 'a pattern of cooperation' would be established. With that, the NP proposal on a minority veto finally bit the dust.

According to De Klerk, the NP settled for the assurance of a five-year tenure in a GNU with the intention of extending the period during negotiations for a final constitution, after the first democratic election.[57] But by the time the final constitution was drafted, all power-sharing options were off the table. When the ANC insisted that the principle of a GNU would not be entrenched in the final constitution, it was clear that it wanted an ordinary majority democracy. 'The one thing said repeatedly by the NP from the start – by Mr de Klerk and other leaders – was that we would have a democracy distinguished by its own character, and never again would any one group hold all the power. [The exclusion of the GNU from the final constitution in 1996 was] when unpalatable reality hit the NP,' Delport says.

It seems unlikely that the NP could have thought the ANC would accept a longer period for the GNU once it had become the dominant party in government. After all, the ANC was resolutely against such a proposal even before it assumed power. The GNU issue was the ultimate illustration of the diminishing power of the NP in relation to the ANC during the negotiation process. In the end, it had to abandon all schemes that would have safeguarded minority political interests. It could not even secure a non-veto presence in the cabinet beyond five years.

The stomach for revolution

Ultimately, the NP could achieve nothing more than a liberal-democratic outcome, making South Africa yet another country swept along by the third wave of democratisation moving through the developing world in the early 1990s. However, this was not due to a lack of trying on the NP's part. At different levels, it did try to continue pushing the idea of a qualified democracy. It pushed that agenda as far as it would go.

The more pragmatic among the leaders – Meyer, De Villiers – realised during the middle of 1992 that the NP model was not going to fly. They were up against an ANC bolstered by international support and with the best of the local liberal classes at its disposal in terms of advice, financial assistance and ideological tweaking. The NP grasped what was available, namely the liberal-democratic model, and out of that Meyer and his colleagues extracted the best they could: a class-biased compromise, which fitted nicely with the NP's changed orientation under Botha. After all, liberal democracy 'functions primarily to elect and legitimise political elites' while failing 'to address the inequalities inherent in the capitalist economy', as former Botswanan political scientist Kenneth Good points out.[58]

The conditions had been created to extend and deracialise the ranks of the property-owning middle classes – so essential to liberal democracy – in order to further entrench non-redistributive liberal democracy. Those members of the NP executive who were more concerned about achieving a race-biased outcome and who were belligerent enough to back this effort up with firepower were outnumbered. Most importantly, De Klerk did not side with them, as his concern was re-establishment of the economy. Civil war had a much more uncertain outcome.

Initial meetings with the ANC leadership showed that a pact was possible, and that the ANC was in a better position to contain the masses than the NP. Meyer *et al.* realised that they could work with the ANC leadership. In contrast, Delport, Kriel and Coetsee still clung to a racial political model, exemplified by safeguards purportedly based on language or groups, but which in reality would have been based on race.

Continued white domination, the outcome sought by the right wing within the leadership, was one that scholars and commentators such as Hermann Giliomee and Frederik van Zyl Slabbert purport was achievable through auto-cratic means. The *verkramptes* in cabinet were intent on keeping democracy on white terms, as per the original NP plan, and using the might of the state to repress those who disagreed. They maintained this position right up to 1994, but got nowhere with their reactionary agenda, due to the momentum of the process and internal resistance from the doves/*verligtes*. The fact is, at crucial moments they backed off when they realised the options were either a violent conflagration or a transition with probable loss of power, but the potential of stability and continued white privilege. A full-on bloody confrontation to maintain white domination was possible – but no one in the NP leadership had the stomach for it.

Regarding the 'surrender without defeat' thesis, Wessels contends that it is easy to wax lyrical about optimal strategies 'if you're sitting in your study. It is not so easy if you have to make decisions on the trot, from sunrise to sunset, about whether you are going to make certain shifts, knowing full well that there are serious consequences if you do not come to a conclusion. This is why I was so grateful that FW de Klerk was the one giving instructions on that day when we negotiated the transitional council, and not Hermann Giliomee. Because he, I am convinced, would have wanted to use state power there and then, and said: "I am now halting everything and I am governing alone, with the help of the defence force and the police, until you change your position." And that would have been fatal. The difference between me and Giliomee is that he, I believe, would have gone to Kempton Park to fight for a private Afrikaner school. I went to Kempton Park to fight for a constitutional state.'

After the collapse of Codesa II, Delport did suggest a 'Plan B' to cabinet, which would have seen the NP government 'draw a line and say "forget about your mass action and come back and negotiate or you will have to bear the consequences". Some of the colleagues almost suffered apoplexy at the mere suggestion of confrontation,' Delport says with a snigger. In his opinion, the NP had entered into negotiations with one hand tied behind its back because of some ministers' dictum to 'please avoid confrontation'.

Another opportunity to prevent the transition to democracy arose the day before the last white parliament passed the interim constitution. After the final agreements had been presented to the NP cabinet, Delport considered blocking the interim constitution in parliament. To his mind, none of the mechanisms had been set in place to honour the NP's primary promise of power sharing. Delport remains convinced that he would have had enough support within the NP caucus in parliament, together with the CP, to prevent approval of the document. Sixteen NP votes would have been sufficient. The last white parliament was the only point at which the constitution could have been blocked at that stage, given that the primary negotiating parties had agreed to it.

Delport asked for a meeting with De Klerk. They had a long conversation, during which Delport was persuaded that if 'you go so far as to accept an agreement in front of the whole world and then parliament votes against it, the next day you will have a revolution in the country'. This caused him to pause and ask himself: 'Who is Ters Delport, who grew up on a farm, to carry the burden of something like that on his shoulders? It is just not thinkable.' At the caucus meeting, Delport made it clear that he found aspects of the interim constitution objectionable, but that he realised the consequences of rejecting it. 'I said I would vote for it, but that it would pose new challenges to us that we had not even thought of at that stage.'

Delport's dilemma aptly illustrates the benefit of the haste that propelled both government and ANC negotiators. One of the government's advisors summed it up as 'a settlement today is better than a settlement tomorrow'. It was for this reason that the NP agreed to an election date during 1993. This was despite the *verkrampte* position, similar to that of the CP, that the process should dictate the date, not the other way round.

Delport had a sense that the ANC was impatient to move the process along and that the NP negotiators allowed the ANC to set the pace. Therefore, the momentum was partly created by commitment to the process by moderates on both sides. It had the desired effect, as the hardliners were swept along, albeit unwillingly. They realised what was going on and objected, but to no avail.

What saved South Africa from a Chile-style Pinochet or a Paraguay-style Stroessner rising to violently suppress the movement towards democracy?

Botha, after all, had been well on his way to becoming a Bonapartist leader, clinging to the reins and ruling the country through despotic fiat. Illness stopped him. Under De Klerk, violence not only escalated, but assumed a seemingly anarchic form as unknown assailants attacked civilians.

The low-scale civil war in Natal and some Witwatersrand townships certainly held the potential for further destabilisation, creating a textbook situation into which a military leader could have stepped. But other factors saved the small country on the periphery of the capitalist world economy.

These were the first few heady years after the Cold War, when the third wave of democracy was engulfing the developing world. The developed states were promoting capitalism and democracy, and the ANC's embrace of neo-liberal economics made it unnecessary to seek another South African partner. If the Central Intelligence Agency was keeping an eye on the situation, it would have concluded that there was no need to identify and prop up a Bonaparte-style leader to steer things Washington's way, as had been its practice in strategic countries the world over. The obvious figure to don such a mantle – PW Botha – had withdrawn to his retirement home in the aptly named seaside town of Wilderness. The generals took a while to mobilise support and then suffered the public humiliation of the Bophuthatswana invasion, where the AWB's reckless and racist arrogance proved that it was an unreliable and unstrategic ally, to the point of death. The options were meagre enough for Constand Viljoen to choose the liberal-democratic route to contest power. In a final bid to win him over, Mandela conceded the principle of self-determination on the basis of language and culture and the parliamentary investigation of support for a *volkstaat* after the election.

The will of the (white) people

The NP's agenda for the negotiations is best summed up as power sharing. That was the promise to its supporters. Former NP leaders agree on this point. But, goes the argument, that was not what the white voter got in the end. Therefore, the NP had misled the white electorate.

It started with the 1992 referendum. The stakes were high. The NP had to achieve a decisive win. Questions were subsequently asked about whether or not the leadership put all its cards on the table in phrasing the referendum question. Views differ widely on whether voters were sufficiently informed and educated to understand exactly what they were letting themselves in for. Giliomee argues that the white electorate was merely asked whether the NP should continue with negotiations for a new constitution, and that the actual content of the interim document was never put to a citizens' vote.

According to Pik Botha, the referendum result gave the NP 'the green light and the authority to go ahead and negotiate power sharing and a new constitution. There was no way that we could have spelt out the details of a constitution that was still to be negotiated. What we asked was, "Do we have your support to go ahead to negotiate a new constitutional deal in which the whites would lose the power?" No voter could have claimed that he did not have an idea that we would lose political power. I, for one, made it clear in a campaign across the country that dramatic change awaited us. Power sharing would mean sharing power and it might mean losing power altogether … We felt we kept our promise to the voters who agreed with us in the 1992 referendum. By and large, we complied with their wish.'[59]

Regarding criticism that the question had been too vague, Botha argues that it had to be simple and straightforward, dealing with 'broad directions'. 'No white voter can claim that in 1992, he or she was unaware of the demands and the proposals of the ANC. They were there in the media, they were reported on. Here comes the NP and says, "We are negotiating with the ANC, we are going to enter a new constitutional phase based on power sharing, and we say to you, trust us." We could not spell out the details of the new constitution, because we still had to go and do the work.'

Thus the NP's campaign before the referendum brought no clarity about what a settlement would entail. Moreover, instead of explaining and winning support explicitly for power sharing as a future constitutional model, the concept surfaced only towards the end of the NP's campaign.[60]

Regarding accusations of poor communication with voters, Wessels argues that the negotiators were overstretched, having to handle both their ministerial duties and the talks. 'Day and night, you are talking. You are sleeping in the car. You arrive home after midnight. The next morning at five you are back. It was not possible to pamper voters. If people did not read the newspapers or watch [television] news, if they weren't curious or asking questions … we could not have done more than we did.'

Another issue is the political range of those who voted 'yes'. Among them were ANC, DP and Inkatha supporters and even far right-wingers, who may have thought no further than an end to sport sanctions. As analysts from the Centre for Policy Studies pointed out at the time, the 'ANC could conclude – as it probably did – that white voters had given unqualified endorsement to a settlement on any terms, while the NP could – and did – conclude that it now had the unqualified backing of white South Africa for a transition on its terms alone, and the ANC would have to heed this'.[61]

Delport says the phrasing of the question reflected 'an assumed knowledge and trust' in the NP to deliver on its promise. It was specifically designed to allow the party room to manoeuvre at the negotiating table. Rina Venter says significant time was spent on formulating the question so as to avoid having to present it to an NP federal congress. The argument within the party leadership was that it would be unnecessary to hold another referendum. She is highly critical of the NP's communication with the electorate at that time. According to her, voters in the Potchefstroom by-election were unclear as to what the negotiations entailed and wanted more information.

Giliomee contends that a second referendum was promised and should have been called on the content of the constitution. At the NP congress in 1990, Gerrit Viljoen had said that the NP supported the holding of a referendum to approve the result of the negotiations and lend the result democratic authority. Up to 1992, both Meyer and De Klerk made promises to the effect that a new constitutional dispensation would be put to white voters for approval. Meyer did so in 1989, and De Klerk in both 1990 and 1992.[62] Pik Botha refutes Giliomee's contention, saying he is unaware of any such promise. His denial makes sense in the light of the NP not delivering what, by his own admission, had been promised, namely power sharing.

Significantly, promises to test the constitution among voters ended in 1992 – the year of the Meyerian paradigm shift, when all the liberal elements of the NP's promises in the 1989 election and the 1992 referendum were accepted in the talks. These were above all a market economy; separation of powers for the judicial, executive and legislative arms of government; the rule of law with a constitutional court and not the democratically elected parliament as the highest authority; and proportional representation.

The latter is the optimal electoral system to ensure representivity down to the smallest parties. The apparently unforeseen drawback is that party loyalty displaces service to constituencies as the highest priority of parliamentarians. Their continued tenure depends on toeing the party line rather than on voter satisfaction with performance. This is especially problematic if the largest party's majority is such that it dominated parliament. As was seen after 1994, the party bosses in the executive arm of government could determine the level of oversight that parliament exercises via party structures. Consequently, members of parliament who went against their leaders' grain were unceremoniously yanked from their positions, as in the case of Andrew Feinstein and the arms deal scandal and Barbara Hogan's challenge to the all-powerful Treasury on its accountability to parliament.

There was a measure of devolution of power to regions, for example allowing the Western Cape to adopt its own constitution. Nevertheless, it still had to be consistent with the national constitution. Most of the health and education budgets were spent at provincial level, and the national ministers in these portfolios could request certain actions from their provincial counterparts, which the latter had a choice to apply or not.

Former members of the executive like Venter and Delport were adamant that, at the very least, the NP did not properly inform its supporters about what the deal struck with the ANC would mean in practice. For Delport, what was negotiated was 'not what we promised the people of South Africa. It is not power sharing. It is not a federal dispensation. It is not the devolution of power to lower levels. We have not protected civil society and its structures.' The guarantees that were negotiated did not go far enough for Delport. For him, what the NP delivered was not true to the people who put them in government.

The NP was rent in two by the commotion of negotiating a constitution with a long-standing foe against the backdrop of economic collapse and escalating violence. The *verligte* negotiators – Meyer, Wessels and De Villiers – accepted that events had forced a liberal-democratic outcome within which they secured the position of their constituency as best they could.

The hawkish *verkramptes*, clinging to the race paradigm, were managed in such a way that their influence was diminished. This was achieved not least by De Klerk, using his status as conservative and his unquestionable authority as *hoofleier*. State power was thus not officially made available to turn up the heat on adversaries after the breakdown of Codesa II. Delport's moment to block the interim constitution with the help of the CP passed. Crisis and bloodshed of great proportion were averted.

The ABC of elite compromise

The turmoil in ideological positioning and affiliation that was unleashed on 2 February 1990 contributed to the NP's plunging legitimacy stakes. As a result of the ANC's interactions with the West and business, it started to displace the NP as ally of capital, a position which the latter had explicitly been carving for itself since the 1970s. The NP's shifting class base placed the securing of conditions for continued capital accumulation at the top of its list of things to accomplish during the transition to democracy, next to power sharing. Business made its presence felt at the negotiations through the Business Forum, which included most of the significant organised business players, ranging from the Council of South African Bankers to the Afrikaanse Handelsinstituut and the Chamber of Mines. But the formal negotiations would be only one of a clutch of processes aimed at achieving the 'correct' economic policy outcome.

The NP was among those who ensured that the outcome would place obstacles in the way of redistribution of wealth to address the country's extreme levels of inequality.[63] Domestically, big business also worked towards this end, while internationally, the US government's extensions – the World Bank and the International Monetary Fund – played their part. This process was facilitated by the fact that the ANC lacked a detailed policy on the economy, a situation compounded by the collapsed legitimacy of socialist alternatives.

The void was filled by the NP and the other players. Within the ANC alliance, contending forces were pushing a state-centrist, socialist-inspired position against a liberal-capitalist position that reflected the ANC's historical roots as a party of middle-class intellectuals. The latter won the day. As the economic advisor in the South African presidency remarked years later: 'ANC policy had come full circle.'[64]

In 1979, the ANC's *Green Book* had elaborated on the nationalisation of mines, banks and industry, vaguely propounded in the 1955 Freedom Charter. While the *Green Book* espoused 'a revolution towards a socialist order', ANC leaders had decided at the time to downplay Marxist-Leninist convictions to avoid alienating supporters.[65]

By 1988, in a joint communiqué with the Transvaal and Natal Indian Congresses, the ANC had moved to emphasise that it was 'not a communist organisation'. Rather, it supported the eradication of social inequality on the basis of race. No reference was made to class. It foresaw a mixed economy with state, private and 'cooperative' sectors for post-apartheid South Africa.[66] Similarly, the 1988 *Constitutional Guidelines for a Democracy* included property rights.

On the NP's side, given that the power balance in the party had tipped towards the *verligtes* after Muldergate and Treurnicht's departure, the predominant feeling was that 'the economy and economic perspectives were important', says Wessels. 'PW regarded it as important; the business summits he held were important. The fear of nationalisation and expropriation of property was substantive ... In the NP it was felt that we had to speak about these things and we would have to convince the ANC otherwise.'

The NP did not set out a single strategy to convince the ANC, but connected with like-minded forces inside and outside the country. In the end, promotion of the ANC's reorientation to a neo-liberal position happened in concrete ways at several levels and in different forums that had started even before De Klerk became president. Meetings between top state officials and ANC economists had been arranged while the ANC was still in exile, the first being at a luxury location in Lausanne, Switzerland.

There, in June 1989, senior civil servants such as Jan Lombard, deputy governor of the Reserve Bank, and Estian Calitz, deputy director-general in the department of finance, engaged in lively debate with Tito Mboweni, destined to become governor of the Reserve Bank, and Maria Ramos, who became director-general of finance after 1994 and later the chief executive of Transnet, South Africa's largest parastatal.[67] Members of big business and business associations also attended.

After Mandela's release and the unbanning of the ANC, leaders were invited to international colloquia championing the economic doctrine of the moment, including gatherings of the World Economic Forum (WEF) and the World Bank. Those were the heady days of neo-liberal triumphalism, captured by Francis Fukuyama's somewhat premature announcement of the 'end of history'.[68] The zealots left few countries in transition without an invitation to the 'global casino'.[69]

Leon Wessels regards Mandela's exposure to the hegemonic paradigm at the WEF in Davos as groundbreaking. Mandela's speech contained a paragraph crafted by Mboweni that sought to reassure international power brokers that the ANC would not introduce a radical break with the past.[70] A year later, Mandela impressed upon his Davos audience that investments and white business would be safe, profits could be repatriated and inflation would be kept in check as per the dominant ideology under an ANC government.

Thus NP politicians and corporate representatives found echoes for their own thinking in what was being said by ANC leaders such as Mbeki, Mboweni, Trevor Manuel, Ramos and Saki Macozoma, as well as Mandela himself. These dynamics precipitated the ANC's movement from a leftist position espousing nationalisation to a liberal-capitalist stance with a social-democratic flavour.

By April 1990, the ANC was mostly using nationalisation as a threat to stop the NP's privatisation policy in its tracks,[71] but was increasingly stepping away from it as a policy option. An economic policy discussion document titled *ANC and COSATU Recommendations on Post-Apartheid Economic Policy*, drawn up in Harare, contained such threats. But it also revealed the extent to which the ANC and COSATU had moved ideologically.

The document propounded redistribution brought about by growth rather than the other way round – a position that was on a par with the NP's own at the time. It also prioritised fiscal conservatism; the avoidance of balance of payment problems; inflation; and competitiveness. By 1992, the ANC had been won over for the most part. Its policy document *Ready to Govern*[72] explicitly advocated a 'growth and development' path, reflecting the hegemonic position that favoured growth. Macroeconomic balance was emphasised, along with the role of a 'dynamic private sector' in job creation. Some measure of uncertainty about the role of the state was reflected by *Ready to Govern*'s qualification that state intervention should occur in accordance with the objectives of 'growth and development', and that 'flexibility' was needed in order for the state to decide on the basis of 'evidence' whether the public sector should be enlarged or reduced.

In *Ready to Govern*, the ANC committed itself to fiscal discipline as per the dominant framework, but also promised to act against monopolies in the economy and – disingenuously – to protect domestic policy formulation from IMF and World Bank interference. The document was as vague about state intervention and industrial policy – to be decided on the basis of research – as it was naive about trade policy. South Africa would participate fully in multilateral trade arrangements. and competitiveness would be improved, but the ANC also promised to prevent the destruction of local producers and job losses.

The document left the door ajar for nationalisation, but also confirmed that compensation would be paid in cases of land expropriation. These shifts eventually culminated in the ANC's editing of COSATU's welfarist Reconstruction and Development Programme (RDP) after 1994 to insert commitments to fiscal discipline, macroeconomic balance and strict monetary policies. The government White Paper on the RDP entrenched commitments to an export-led growth strategy, relaxing COSATU's original emphasis on basic needs, and stressing instead reduction of state expenditure, privatisation and the promotion of private sector expansion.[73]

According to Roelf Meyer, the NP realised that the business community was in a 'better position to inform the ANC [about economic policy] than we were'.[74] The business sector's scenario-planning exercises were a popular way to influence ANC thinkers to accept the 'inevitability' of neo-liberal capitalism. In the early 1990s, such exercises became the vogue, initiated by the big business sector, including Anglo American, Nedcor/Old Mutual and the NP's long-standing corporate ally, Sanlam.

Instead of grappling with the real conundrum of the South African situation, these moves were designed to aid deal-making in the formal forums.[75] The sessions were crucial in the process of elite pacting, as they afforded the contending players opportunities to appreciate opposing viewpoints, build trust, and enable concession and compromise. Soon, through clever public relations, what began as 'corporate survival strategy' evolved into 'social contract parable'.[76] In particular, the Mont Fleur scenario-planning exercise at a conference centre in the Cape winelands broke ground by changing key ANC role player Trevor Manuel's mind about pursuing a 'growth through redistribution' model. He was especially impressed by Derek Keys,[77] a former mining executive whom De Klerk had brought in as minister of finance.

Keys lived up to his name and became *the* key player in the NP's efforts to change the ANC's economic minds. He took the time to explain to Manuel the dangers of 'macroeconomic populism',[78] marking the start of 'a friendship and mentoring relationship across the political divide'.[79] This graphically illustrates how the transition was incorporating the black political elite into the white political and economic elite of the time.

In his autobiography, De Klerk confirmed that he had instructed Keys to engage with 'key people in the ANC'[80] to ensure that the organisation would stay the course of the NP's neo-liberal normative economic model, launched in

1993. Keys regularly reported to the cabinet on what De Klerk described as his 'wonderful work' that allowed him to 'succeed in winning the confidence of the ANC',[81] thereby playing what De Klerk regarded as a leading role in the transition.

De Klerk also drew attention to the National Economic Forum as a kind of 'economic Codesa'. The NEF was the transition's corporatist predecessor of the later Nedlac. All the major labour federations were represented: COSATU, the National Council of Trade Unions and the Federation of South African Labour Unions. Similarly, all significant business organisations took part, including the Chamber of Business, the AHI, the Chamber of Mines and the Council of South African Bankers. Delegates were addressed by a representative from the World Bank, and Keys presented the NP's Normative Economic Model to the NEF before its public release.

Among NEF priorities for policy discussion, economic growth was placed before social and developmental needs, with a focus on how to attract foreign direct investment and boost exports. While a long-term working group looked at these two issues, a short-term working group looked at job creation.

It was unclear whether the different deliberations considered these policy issues holistically, as would have been expected given the employment crisis. The NP government – Keys again – worked with big business to instil 'economic realism' in the ANC and its trade union partners, as De Klerk would have it. From business, a heavy hitter such as Bobby Godsell was involved; from the unions the future minister of trade and industry, Alec Erwin; from government, deputy director-general Calitz could continue the conversations he had previously had with the ANC in exile.

De Klerk regarded the result of the NEF deliberations as 'that the ANC accepted a broad framework of responsible economic principles, not only with regard to the first budget, but finally as the basis for its own economic Growth, Employment and Redistribution model [GEAR]',[82] which contained the same tenets as the neo-liberal RDP White Paper. It was at the NEF that COSATU sanctioned the General Agreement on Tariffs and Trade (GATT) in 1993, which translated into a job haemorrhage in the clothing industry not long afterwards – despite the issue of tariff sequencing being acknowledged as important in NEF discussions; despite having set up a special task force on the clothing sector; and despite Ebrahim Patel, general secretary of the Southern African Clothing and Textile Workers' Union, being involved in the NEF.

For several reasons, which lie beyond the scope of this book, the union members were convinced of the necessity for tariff reductions. It was at the NEF that Keys brought the ANC and COSATU economic players onto the same page as the NP, impressing upon them the vast challenges facing the country, while guiding them towards fiscal discipline and an acceptance of the dictates of neo-liberal capitalism. Keys's success could partly be attributed to him not being 'a party political animal. He enjoyed a high level of respect from both the business sector and the alternative groupings [the ANC], which indeed influenced policy,' says Wessels.

Keys had so won his way into the hearts of the ANC that they did not even bother to send one of their economic stars to accompany him to Marrakesh, where GATT was wrapped up and the World Trade Organisation came into effect as its replacement. Kader Asmal, who subsequently served as minister of water affairs and of education, went with him. Later in 1993, Sanlam's scenario planning under the academic Lawrence Schlemmer portrayed the ANC's leaders as moderate and unlikely to pursue disruptive redistributive strategies, while at the same time able to keep more radical supporters at bay. The negotiations at the NEF were highlighted as crucial, as well as strengthening 'the already ... close relationship between the ANC, the World Bank, the Development Bank of Southern Africa, the Consultative Business Movement and other organisations which painstakingly pointed out the longer run costs of many redistributive strategies'.[83] The document charted the progress made by the NP and its allies in white business and the international sphere in moving the ANC to a position more amenable to capitalist accumulation. In the person of Keys, the NP provided a meeting point for big business and the ANC.

This is the context in which the NP's role in swaying the ANC towards neo-liberalism should be seen. While the greater economic community was exerting its influence on the ANC, the NP was the 'vehicle which rounded off the final negotiations'. It did this with the assistance of its 'loyal supporters' Sanlam and Volkskas, which, according to Wessels, 'strongly pressurised the NP, saying you have to fight to the bitter end for property rights, a free market system and so forth. You have to remember that there had always been a very cosy relationship between the NP and those institutions. They used that access to exert pressure on the NP. The NP also said to them, "Don't just speak to us. Talk to the other guys." And the other guys were *willing* to speak to them.'

At one of these meetings, Danie Cronjé, a businessman and enthusiastic golfer, joked with Ramaphosa that 'if you nationalise the mines, you'll have trouble. But I have to warn you, it won't be nearly as bad as if you should decide to nationalise the golf courses.'[84] Property rights were of specific concern. Apart from private landownership being the basis of capitalism, most of the large conglomerates owned vast tracts of land that they were keen to hold on to.

Thus the NP collaborated with other forces to entrench neo-liberal policies in democratic South Africa. The NP was one of several players in a milieu of immense global pressure who ensured the ANC's capitulation in favour of a version of capitalism that failed to address the pressing needs of the bulk of its constituency. The success of the NP and its allies was a major victory for dominant white interests, as it meant in practice that white privilege not only remained largely untouched, but that the white bourgeois position became further entrenched, even as a black middle class was growing.

By the end of 1993, the ANC had agreed to the principle of an independent Reserve Bank – so crucial in the implementation of monetary policy – being entrenched in the constitution. They also agreed that Derek Keys – personifying the NP's primary contribution to ensure an elite transition – would stay on as minister of finance after the 1994 election. A multiparty team under his leadership had already begun drafting the first post-apartheid government budget by the second half of 1993. This extension of economic policy into the democratic era was the NP's greatest feat at the negotiating table.

In one of history's ironic twists, one nationalist party handed over power to another in a transition where both embraced neo-liberal capitalism and, to a qualified extent, liberal democracy. Both parties had exchanged state interventionist stances for the promise of market 'freedom'. In the NP's case, the *verligte* wing in particular had been convinced since the 1970s that class interests superseded those of race.

The entrenchment of neo-liberal capitalism during the transition translated into the continuation of apartheid and colonialism's legacy of extreme inequality. Consequently, white people could hold onto their pre-democracy gains. That was what the NP's negotiators delivered for most of its constituency – a result that contradicted subsequent Afrikaner talk of 'betrayal' by their leaders. The NP had to mostly abandon its communitarian principles in favour of a libertarian variant of liberal political values as a safeguard for white socio-economic privilege.

The outcome was predictably less favourable for the ANC's constituency, hence attempts by the post-1994 government to ameliorate the effects of neo-liberalism with panaceas such as social welfare grants and a limited public works programme. The NP lost political power, but whites held on to economic power. The ANC won political power, and a burgeoning black middle class would share in the economic spoils. Such was the shape of the elite compromise after 1990.

CHAPTER 7

The crumbling:
Without the state, we're nothing

After the election neither the National Party nor I [intend] to disappear from the scene.   – FW de Klerk, NP *hoofleier*, 2 July 1993[1]

Our people remain divided. We do not know each other. We are prevented from developing a national vision in terms of which we would see our country through the eyes of all its citizens, and not just one group or the other. We live apart, physically separated, spiritually alienated, frightened of getting too close, knowing that we have different life-chances and different views of what change means … Apartheid has left us apart.   –ANC, *Ready to Govern*, 1992

I would rather have my domestic worker belong to the NP than to the ANC.   – Female delegate at NP Free State congress in 1990, making sense of the leadership's decision to open the party's membership to all races[2]

W ITH THE NEGOTIATIONS BEHIND THEM AND AN INTERIM CON-stitution in place, the NP leadership approached the first democratic elections thinner on the ground, but confident it would do well. The party had shed many of the names from the 1980s, including those closest to PW Botha. Chris Heunis, Magnus Malan, Adriaan Vlok, Gerrit Viljoen and Barend du Plessis were all gone or on their way out by 1994.

Those who remained saw themselves playing important roles in the future government and country, based on their delivery of 'the New South Africa'. Not only had the situation not descended into anarchy, but the former political oppressor had come to embrace a liberal-democratic constitution. The NP had acceded to a constitution that ran contrary to hundreds of laws it had passed during its forty-six-year tenure.

But not all members of the leadership had made Roelf Meyer's paradigm shift. The internal rift at top level had become a vast chasm that represented fractures in the party's support base. These cracks were widened by ancient NP contradictions: lack of transparency and consultation in decision-making; the gap between the top leadership and the structures; the chasing of a class agenda that had overtaken the race agenda. The old dualism was still apparent. The NP had finally managed to shrug off group rights during the negotiations, but still projected itself as the protector of minority rights – which, in its December 1993 *National Party Policy* booklet, it misleadingly claimed to have delivered. Convolutedly, the booklet presented minority rights 'as a result' of the individual rights protected in the interim constitution. The double talk thus continued.

Johan Kilian, Gauteng NP leader in the early 2000s,[3] describes the process of propelling white voters to go along with the drastic policy changes of the early 1990s as 'an elastic band that you stretch and then shoot. You can't stretch it too far, or you'll lose the power.' Kilian argues that the party already believed under Botha that if it moved too fast, there would be no peaceful transition. While these contradictions in the NP ultimately aided a transition that stabilised the country while entrenching basic human rights and democracy – albeit of the liberal variety – the party could not survive them.

The 1994 election: Old habits, new supporters

Finally, the first democratic election arrived. The ANC and the NP scrambled to convince Buthelezi that he should participate. Last-minute mediation by the US's Henry Kissinger and Britain's Lord Carrington did not persuade the Inkatha Freedom Party leader to drop his boycott of the election, but in an unexpected turn of events, Kenyan professor Washington Okumu mediated an agreement that drew Buthelezi in.[4] Late adjustments were made to the ballot paper to include the IFP, and the historical event went ahead.

The realists in the NP went into the election believing that the party would draw up to 25 per cent of the vote. The flamboyant Pik Botha declared that a win was possible.[5] Astonishingly, indications were that his optimism was widespread within the party. As one anonymous respondent told the author: 'Some NP members felt that *as die baas praat* black people will vote for him.' The same arrogance and racism that had convinced some NP leaders that they would 'win' the negotiations, or be able to manipulate Buthelezi, raised expectations for the election. Some believed their own propaganda about the party's attraction for God-fearing, conservative black people. Others were misled by the number of blacks who attended NP gatherings in the run-up to the election. Party organisers were instructed to 'find' busloads of black people – and they did, regardless of people's real political convictions.

The voter turnout in the 1994 election was a staggering 90 per cent, with the ANC coming in at 62.65 per cent to scoop up 252 seats. The NP managed to draw more votes than at any other time in its history, clocking 20.39 per cent, with 82 seats in the national assembly. The IFP drew 10.5 per cent, or 43 seats.

Constand Viljoen's Freedom Front garnered only 2.2 per cent of the vote, or nine seats; the Democratic Party won 1.7 per cent (seven seats), and the PAC 1.2 per cent (five seats). The results showed that the ANC and the NP, communitarian parties crowding the liberal-democratic platform, had displaced the DP, which had tumbled from 20 per cent in the 1989 whites-only election.

The FF's performance was an accurate reflection of both the marginality of its concerns for a post-apartheid electorate and the fragmentary nature of the far right wing. The CP and other right-wing splinter groups boycotted the election, sapping the FF of possible support. In the first of many twists that would reflect the ANC's effective utilisation of its dominant position to gain strategic ascendance over the opposition, the FF, and particularly its leader, was assiduously wooed by the ANC, especially Mandela. At the same time, the NP, DP and IFP were regular targets of ANC attacks.

In opposition politics, a conciliatory relationship with the ruling party can be deadlier than a hostile one. Viljoen found this out as his party's fortunes waned in the second democratic election in 1999, when the FF managed to poll only 0.8 per cent, a quarter of its 1994 votes. Viljoen was eventually booted out due to perceptions that he was selling out the cause of Afrikaner self-determination through his cushy relationship with the ANC. After the 1999 election, he was replaced by Connie Mulder's sons Pieter and Corné, at the apex of an even smaller FF. Thus withered the political representation of the ideal of Afrikaner self-determination. Their *volkstaat* dreams were dashed by the FF's poor performance, which showed a lack of substantial support among white voters – the constitutional caveat that the ANC had attached to any consideration of a *volkstaat*.

In the 1994 election, the NP and the DP together drew a couple of hundred thousand votes from black people. The NP also made significant inroads among coloured and Indian voters, ironically becoming the most racially representative of all parties, since more than half of those who voted for it were black, Indian and coloured. This trend continued, and by 2003, its white support had dropped below 30 per cent.[6]

In a bitter twist, the historically white supremacist party seemed to have successfully appealed to at least some of the South Africans it had formerly oppressed. But to achieve this result, the NP reverted to its usual tricks: divide-and-rule tactics and instigating racial fears. The worst example was its *swart gevaar* disinformation campaign among coloured voters. Among this group, the party's new power base, NP 'big man' FW de Klerk was the drawcard. 'The people loved him' – to such an extent that he received a warmer ovation than Allan Hendrickse at a Labour Party meeting in the early 1990s.[7]

In the run-up to the election, the party used state patronage while it still had it. In a bid to lure more black voters, the NP equalised pension payments just before it left government. In 1991, a white pensioner received R304 per month, as opposed to R263 for coloured and R225 for black pensioners. When the coloured Labour Party pointedly raised pensions as one of the obstacles to an alliance with the NP, the latter jumped on the bandwagon, but bemoaned the sad state of the state fiscus due to sanctions, thus implicating the ANC in the inequality of pensions.[8] But it made a point of eradicating the discrimination before the election.

The NP had worked on the coloured vote since 1991, thereby addressing an issue that many *verligtes* considered long overdue. Members of the LP in the house of representatives joined the NP. Their constituencies supported the decision as, to them, the LP did not appear to have a future in a democratic country. One LP member based his decision to join the NP in 1991 on wanting to 'listen to the state president's request that a nation be built across the colour bar'.[9] Among the 'joiners' was Gerald Morkel, who later became Western Cape premier. Most LP members shared a particularly conservative variant of Christian belief, as well as pro-market economic policies, with their NP counterparts. When told about plans to merge with the NP, coloured constituents questioned their representatives 'about the NP being the party that had subjugated us', but were assured that it was 'not the same party as before'.[10]

Fault lines developed early. According to former NP provincial member Pierre-Jeanne Gerber, the Western Cape caucus split along racial lines. His involvement with issues affecting coloured voters led to white members ridiculing him with the derogatory term 'hotnotsgot' and as being part of the 'coloured caucus'.[11] The NP's appeal was among working-class coloured supporters – reflected in the support it drew in the Cape Town township of Mitchell's Plain and surrounds. Real and perceived differences in education levels between coloured and white representatives of the party caused tension on both sides, which was exacerbated by the NP leadership's unofficial internal affirmative action policy.

The NP's performance in 1994 remained unsurpassed by other opposition parties in the 1999 and 2004 elections. This was no small feat, given that as late as 1990, Gerrit Viljoen had declared the NP primarily 'the protector of the rights of the minority' (singular). Whites were still regarded as the NP's primary constituency. The 'broad partnership' that it had in mind would have worked according to the group rights principle. Parties representing different racial constituencies would have joined forces in a political movement. But as the NP's efforts at forging this movement were snubbed, it had to take what it could get.

By absorbing the LP, the NP was giving effect to thinking that had been circulating in *verligte* circles since at least the 1960s: that coloured people were part of a larger Afrikaans-speaking community. *Verligtes* had wanted to draw coloureds in before they became voting fodder for the ANC. It was this argument that was the final straw for Treurnicht in 1982, but it paid off handsomely in 1994, when the NP won the Western Cape with 53.3 per cent of the votes (twenty-three seats) against the ANC's 33 per cent (fourteen seats), the DP's 6.6 per cent (three seats), the FF's 2.1 per cent (one seat) and the African Christian Democratic Party's 1.2 per cent (one seat).

A merger with the LP was as far as the dominant grouping in the NP could go towards inclusivity. After 1994, there was resistance to cooperation with non-pliable black leaders, especially if it meant losing the NP as a separate entity. This thinking would persist throughout the 1990s, and eventually contribute to the party's downfall.

The 1994 election results sparked a debate in academic circles about whether the election was a mere 'racial census',[12] given the demographics of party support. If so, the ANC, basking in the sun of liberation, seemed set for firm entrenchment in the cushions of power for years to come. The NP was faced with the challenge of most opposition parties after 1994: how to extend its support among black people. The NP's particular weak spot in this regard was evident. As Steven Friedman put it: 'History has in fact delegitimated the NP as a contender for mass support, given its role in introducing and implementing apartheid.'[13] This reputation did not count against the party when it sought the votes of its historical support base, but it proved lethal to attempts to attract votes from the rest of the electorate. It was stuck with the conundrum of 'the post-apartheid white party': changing your message to reach a wider audience meant alienating your core base. So it happened that the NP was incongruously beating the drum of non-racialism, confusing and irritating its supporters.

The government of Nationalist disunity

After April 1994, the NP entered uncharted territory: the government of national unity (GNU). The party had managed to gain the requisite percentage to share government with the ANC, the majority party, and the IFP. But this was unfamiliar terrain for a party not only used to wielding power, but doing so in an uncompromising, mostly non-consultative way. De Klerk in particular was faced with the daunting challenge of acting as deputy president under Nelson Mandela. By that time, there was no love lost between the two.

Moreover, the NP that ventured into this alien land was even more divided than it had been in 1982. The run-up to the polls was characterised by feverish jockeying for post-election positions. The flurry was more frenetic than usual; while the NP thought it would get enough votes for some posts in the executive, it was not going to be the sole occupant of office. There would not be enough positions to go around, which raised the stakes. The dominance of the *verligtes* immediately after the election was reflected in the selection of nominees for positions.

While it was De Klerk's prerogative to choose who would fill the six available cabinet seats, Meyer – as leader of the *verligte* bloc – held considerable influence over who would be included and who would be left out. This made him the most powerful member in the party after De Klerk. His path to *hoofleierskap* was already paved, it seemed. Apart from Meyer, those who landed cabinet posts were Leon Wessels, Pik Botha, Dawie de Villiers, NP Northern Cape leader Kraai van Niekerk (reflecting the NP's good performance in that province) and Abe Williams, a nod towards the NP's coloured supporters. Derek Keys stayed on as minister of finance, as per agreement with the ANC.

The deputy ministers included rising star and De Klerk ally Chris Fismer, Tobie Meyer (Roelf's brother) and Sheila Camerer. Positions further from the core of power were used to absorb and placate the conservatives. Kobie Coetsee became head of the short-lived senate, the second house of parliament, Hernus Kriel was given the premiership of the Western Cape, and Tertius Delport occupied the agriculture and environmental affairs portfolio in the Eastern Cape's executive council. Former NP cabinet conservatives who did not make it back were Danie Schutte; André Fourie and George Bartlett. Former National Intelligence chief Niel Barnard, Meyer's sidekick throughout the negotiations, was made director-general of the Western Cape administration, where he could keep an eye on Kriel.

The immediate task at hand was to finalise the constitution. By agreement, parliament would double as a constituent assembly to write South Africa's final constitution. It would be based on the 1993 interim constitution, following the 'immutable' framework of the constitutional principles the NP had got the ANC to agree on.

Ramaphosa chaired the constituent assembly; Wessels acted as his deputy. By that time, De Klerk said in a 1997 article, the NP had come to accept that Afrikaner interests could not be promoted to the exclusion of other 'minority groups'. According to him, the NP argument was that this would position Afrikaners as an 'identifiable target for a hostile majority' – which is the same reason that former NP leader Marthinus van Schalkwyk proffered for why it was better that power sharing, as envisaged by the NP, was never included in the constitution.[14]

The concern about Afrikaners becoming 'a target' led to the NP promoting equal protection for all 'minority groups' in the final constitution. It fought with the ANC about the appointment of the judiciary, limitations on property rights and a 'super Attorney-General'. It succeeded in getting a provision for cultural councils included in the final constitution, which would allow a measure of cultural self-determination. The NP also managed to entrench the principle of mother-tongue education after negotiations deadlocked on this issue, as well as on property rights and labour provisions.

Long nights were spent on finalising the constitution by the deadline of 8 May 1996. One of the remaining obstacles was an extension of the GNU – the last vestige of the NP's original power-sharing concept. The party had agreed to an initial five-year period in 1993, planning to push the issue in the constituent assembly after the election. But Ramaphosa would not budge – partly because the ANC insisted on the basic principle of a one-person, one-vote democracy, and partly because the decisive majority it had received gave it a mandate to decide whether it wanted a GNU or not. The ANC had the weight of government behind it. Ramaphosa was immovable, despite the NP negotiators making every effort to change his mind. The ANC was in power. Why would it brook any dilution of that power? The inability to entrench even the watered-down version of power sharing – the GNU – as a principle in the final constitution gave the conservatives in the NP ammunition against remaining in the GNU. In the end, the GNU issue fuelled the NP's demise.

Tactically, the point should have been resolved while the NP was still the government, but the party had already lost the legitimacy battle by the end of 1992. A year later, NP negotiations were based on what was possible, which was a liberal-democratic outcome with a GNU for a limited period. That was what the original policy position on special protections for minorities had been whittled down to. After April 1994, there was no compelling reason for the ANC to change its stance.

De Klerk suggests that the NP could have forced a referendum by voting against the final constitution in parliament on 8 May 1996. But it did not have the stomach for such a step, fearing that it could result in the unravelling of whatever gains had been made.[15] Meyer acknowledges retrospectively that attempts to secure a second term for the GNU were misplaced, as this device was always part of an interim arrangement, designed to manage the transition. It was a compromise to compensate for the inability to entrench power sharing, 'which was part of the old paradigm. In the liberal-democratic set-up there is no space for it.'[16]

Regarding property rights, the *verligtes* were satisfied that the NP negotiators – with the help of representatives from Rembrandt, Anglo American and De Beers – had successfully safeguarded private property in the final constitution. The *verkramptes* did not regard the outcome as acceptable, as it still provided for land reform. To meet the basic imperative of adjusting South Africa's untenable racially skewed landownership patterns, the final clause in the 1996 constitution contained additional criteria – apart from market value – to be considered in cases of expropriation. But the clause was drafted in such a way that each of these criteria would be measured against the liberal standard of just and equitable (market value) compensation. The Constitutional Court would have to decide whether deviation from the requirement of market value compensation 'was justifiable and, if so, to what degree'.[17] Land reform was therefore to be tempered by the principle of 'fair' compensation. Consequently, land redistribution in post-apartheid South Africa was sluggish.

The appointment of the low-profile but highly persuasive Keys as minister of finance showed that, economically speaking, the new ruling party was on the same page as its predecessor. The budget for the first democratic government had been in the making since the second half of 1993 – drafted by a multiparty committee headed by Keys. The scene was set for a continuation of the NP's economic policies in government.

In its last years as ruler, the NP applied strict fiscal and monetary policies to lower inflation, which dropped from 25 per cent in 1986 to 13 per cent in 1990. The NP government also reduced personal tax and pushed through cutbacks to reduce state spending as a percentage of GDP. The closeness with capital was also illustrated by the appointment of prominent business figures to cabinet posts. Former Gencor executive chairperson Wim de Villiers was hand-picked to become minister of administration and privatisation in 1989. Keys similarly left his post as Gencor executive chairperson to become minister of trade, industry and economic coordination in 1991. Louis Shill, the founder of Sage, became minister of national housing and public works in 1993. Iscor, Sasol and National Sorghum Breweries were privatised, while Telkom, Transnet, the Post Office, Denel, Overvaal Resorts and others were commercialised in anticipation of privatisation.

After 1990, the NP propagated the dictum that economic growth was the best way to create wealth, and therefore effect redistribution. This was in line with its evolution into a party of the Afrikaans- and English-speaking middle and upper classes from the 1960s onwards.[18] In November 1990, Barend du Plessis observed approvingly that the ANC was reconsidering its position on wealth redistribution leading to economic growth.[19] The NP emphasised the importance of investor confidence as the only way to ensure economic growth, and monitored the country's openness. The party also explicitly distanced itself at every opportunity from 'socialism and nationalisation', committing itself to property rights and the market. NP leaders regarded the safeguarding of the Reserve Bank's independence through a constitutional clause as one of the highlights of their negotiation achievements.

Passing the economic policy baton

Concluding the final constitution was not the only task of the GNU. De Klerk describes the NP's other challenge as ensuring 'that the ANC would implement the right economic and financial policies'.[20] He tasked Keys with engaging the ANC on economic policy issues. Part of this took place in the National Economic Forum. Indeed, De Klerk regards 'the adoption of a balanced economic policy framework that would assure growth and progress and which would steer a course away from the socialist tendencies which the ANC had espoused for the whole of its existence' as the NP's 'greatest contribution in the Government of National Unity'.[21]

Much of this happened under the tutelage of Keys, who 'played a key role in changing the economic debate at the time in the Government of National Unity. He does not always receive credit for this, because he did it in a manner that didn't get people's hackles up ... he used rational persuasion to explain how we could achieve everything together, if only we developed the potential,' says Marthinus van Schalkwyk,[22] the last NP *hoofleier* (1997–2006).

The neo-liberal Growth, Employment and Redistribution economic policy was adopted while the NP was still in the GNU. De Klerk emphasised that the NP had contributed to the formulation of GEAR and supported its final approval, as it reflected NP economic thinking. In this regard, he referred to the NP's Normative Economic Model, which was released in March 1993.[23]

The model moved from a position that became popularly accepted in post-apartheid South Africa: that 'national autonomy over traditional economic policy levers are weakened as international imperatives have an increasing influence on national economic policy decisions'.[24] It identified the following structural defects in the South African economy: 'an endemic inflationary climate; excessive government claims on scarce resources; distortive and excessive protection; the dual exchange rate system [the commercial rand and the financial rand]; adversarial industrial relations; and non-competitive price determination'.

The basic tenets of the model were fiscal and monetary discipline; 'good governance' (a World Bank term); the opening up of the economy to make it internationally competitive and by boosting export-oriented manufacturing while lowering import duties; increased public spending on infrastructure; reduction of import tariffs; abolition of foreign exchange controls; containment of real wage increases; and support for small and medium enterprises and the informal sector. Fiscal discipline would be achieved by reducing government spending, including salaries and wages, while monetary discipline would be achieved through Reserve Bank interventions to keep the inflation rate low. Personal and corporate taxes would be cut, while indirect taxes such as VAT would be increased. However, import duties – another indirect tax – would be reduced.

'Good governance' meant that government should intervene less in the functioning of the 'market mechanism'. Industries would be assisted through the possible creation of export processing zones and various support measures to aid reorientation towards export production. Interestingly, the Normative Economic Model acknowledged that the envisaged restructuring of the economy would result in job losses, and proposed a transitional safety net to be instituted in a timely manner. This would have included unemployment insurance; special training; support for small entrepreneurs; and public works schemes. The influence of the World Bank in the drafting of the Normative Economic Model is visible in phrases such as 'good governance' and 'structural adjustment'.

The model was almost identical to GEAR: the emphasis on combating inflation and reducing state expenditure; improved international competitiveness and industrial reorientation towards export markets; tax reductions; boosting small business; relaxing exchange controls; and containing wage increases. The similarities in the two policies reflect yet again how the ANC and the NP's economic policy positions had converged during the transition years of 1990 to 1994, with both parties embracing neo-liberal capitalism. One difference was that the NP had started to move towards neo-liberal capitalism more than a decade earlier.

It took the whirlwind processes of transition, combined with the rise of a particular leadership corps – Thabo Mbeki, Tito Mboweni, Trevor Manuel and others – to move the ANC in the same direction. Indeed, it is conceivable that the introduction of the anti-poor VAT system by the NP, supported by the International Monetary Fund and against which COSATU rallied so strongly in 1992, would have been introduced by the ANC in government had the NP not already done so.

Final confirmation of this policy union was the signing of an IMF letter of intent in 1993 by the Transitional Executive Council, which committed the South African government to curbing inflation and state spending and to not raising taxes, in return for an $850 million loan.[25] The elite pact was in place – not just between the NP and the ANC, but between the established white elite and the incoming African nationalist elite.

The ANC's adoption of neo-liberal principles had unforeseen consequences for the NP. As the ANC moved to the centre of the ideological spectrum, the NP became increasingly redundant as a vehicle for capitalist interests. The danger that the ANC had posed to white economic interests was ebbing in capitalist minds. The ANC emerged from its pre-1990 X-factor status as a player with not only the necessary political legitimacy, but increasingly ready to promote capital. Business 'trust' in the ANC as government was yet to be demonstrated in actual investment, but capital's international partners were apparently sufficiently reassured by the sweet signals sent by the ANC's approval of the IMF letter of intent, as well as its agreement to South Africa joining the global trade game via the World Trade Organisation in 1994.

The ANC's ideological repositioning – back to its liberal middle-class roots at the beginning of the twentieth century – displaced the NP, which found itself with ever-decreasing legitimacy because of the 'party of apartheid' label, as the ANC constantly reminded voters. This developed into a crisis for the NP after the 1994 election, as it hung onto marginal state power in the GNU. Its powers of patronage, historically sought after by English and Afrikaans capital alike,[26] were drastically curtailed.

In the end, economic policy enabled the ANC's cooperation with the NP after 2001, according to Marthinus van Schalkwyk. Asked what the basis of their cooperation was, Van Schalkwyk replied: 'The greatest cornerstone for any party's policy is economic policy. It was clear that the NP and the ANC had basically exactly the same economic policy ... What always made our hackles rise about ANC policy was the old, redundant socialist policy ... nationalisation. After 1990, the ANC came with genuinely new, modern thinking, in line with world policy on this subject. The ANC came and said, we accept that redistribution can take place only against the background of enormous economic growth. Those were the things that we believed in.'[27]

Power-mongering the NP out of power

The ideological displacement at the beginning of the 1990s greatly exacerbated the trend that had begun in the NP during the mid-1980s, namely the political nightmare of having expended the options to sustain its supremacy. The *verligtes* had moved to adopt political and economic liberalism as their credo; the *verkramptes* rejected most features of the negotiated settlement, including having to cooperate with the ANC in a GNU. Where could the party position itself after 1994?

On 2 February 1996, De Klerk opened the new NP head office in Pretoria – named after him – with the announcement of a fresh vision for the party. It involved Meyer leaving cabinet and devoting himself full time to reaching out to black leaders, finding black support and building the beginnings of a new political movement. The vision floundered as the *verkramptes* went full throttle to regain control of the party. Indeed, the plan probably sparked heightened activity among them, because of its central role for Meyer.

Rather aptly, the GNU became the bone of contention. Generally speaking, participation in a GNU militated against what the party leaders were used to. The formulation of how the GNU would operate was vague – which was one of Delport's grievances. He argues that explicit mechanisms should have been agreed in terms of how cabinet decisions were to be made, particularly around majorities when voting.[28]

From a legal point of view, the agreement that the ANC and the NP governed the country 'together' meant 'nothing', he contends. The *verkramptes* wanted an unambiguous arrangement to address their fear that the NP would be overwhelmed by the ANC in government. The ANC preferred that a *modus operandus* be developed gradually. In practice, that made it difficult for junior partners in government to resist ANC decisions – which justified the *verkramptes'* concern.

Another issue was the level of influence that the NP enjoyed in the national and provincial executives. Some of them had overestimated their influence on the ANC. For example, then minister of minerals and energy Pik Botha approached deputy president Thabo Mbeki about the proposed change of name for South Africa's industrial heartland, the PWV (Pretoria-Witwatersrand-Vaal triangle).[29] Options on the table were Egoli and Gauteng, but the NP wanted to retain the name Transvaal. After what seemed to Botha like a favourable hearing from Mbeki, the name was changed to Gauteng anyway. The NP leaders were taken aback – victims, yet again, of their arrogance, naivety and incomprehension of the meaning of representivity. Some NP leaders began to feel they were merely being tolerated in the national and provincial executives. They apparently did not understand Mandela's admonition that the ANC would have to give effect to the democratic mandate of transformation it had received in the 1994 election.

But not everybody felt disaffected. Meyer does not report any difficulties in cooperating with the ANC in cabinet.[30] While he was in cabinet, he says, he exercised executive powers over his department – provincial affairs and constitutional development – without hindrance and enjoyed full cooperation from the bureaucrats.

As the ideological pendulum swung once again to the conservative side of the NP, this cooperation with the ANC provided the *verkramptes* with ammunition and, as had happened throughout the party's history, the split was reflected at provincial party level. In an echo of the 1930s, those with more progressive vision dominated the NP in the north, while the point of gravity for the retrogressive forces was in the south. This was the same division that had seen Hertzog move to the United Party with Smuts and – apart from JG Strijdom, De Klerk's uncle – caused the Transvaal NP to all but disappear. Only DF Malan's Cape NP – the die-hard Afrikaner nationalists – kept the party flag aloft.

Six decades later, the *bittereinders* were Hernus Kriel in the Western Cape and Tertius Delport in the Eastern Cape. They counted Ebbe Dommisse, editor of *Die Burger*, as an ally. At the same time, what remained of the old Afrikaner nationalist alliance was fast disappearing, as illustrated when the mother company of *Die Burger*, Nasionale Pers, broke ranks with the NP by donating money to both the ANC and the DP in 1996.[31]

With the NP's *verligte* core concentrated in the cabinet, the seventy or so MPs in the NP caucus offered fertile ground for *verkrampte* power-mongering. Relations between caucus and cabinet members ruptured. One reason was their different understanding of the NP's new role as junior partner in the executive arm of government. NP members in cabinet sometimes supported positions that caucus members were opposed to. Due to confidentiality,[32] cabinet ministers could not always fully explain decisions to the caucus.

In time, the NP found it impossible to overcome the dissonance of being the junior partner in cooperative governance. It developed a split personality, partly because the party never produced a strategy on how to operate simultaneously as part of government and as the main opposition party, says Annelizé van Wyk.[33]

This incongruity was exploited in what Roelf Meyer calls the 'revenge' of pre-1994 ministers and deputy ministers who had failed to land ministerial posts in the new dispensation. They avenged their loss of position and power by pressuring De Klerk and capitalising on the tensions of the unusual situation in which the NP found itself – rule without dominance. The mindset of party leaders remained that of 'being the head honchos'. According to an anonymous source, 'they wanted to be the top dogs and could not cope with no longer being so'.

André Fourie, Danie Schutte and Delport, led by Kriel, increasingly pressed De Klerk to leave the GNU. From outside, Dommisse – a fervent critic of the new dispensation – used *Die Burger* to egg them on. Their idea was to turn the NP into a 'pure' opposition party. But the *verligtes* felt it was possible to play the role of 'constructive opposition' while remaining in the GNU – NP members in the executive would merely have to accept that they would face critical questions from caucus colleagues at times.

De Klerk had problems of his own. His personal relations with Mandela, who treated him with disdain, were unpleasant. He thought that he was not getting the recognition he deserved as co-architect of the new South Africa, visible in the description of his experience on receiving the Nobel Peace Prize jointly with Mandela.[34] Most of all, however, he no longer had the same level of authority as before. Being the leader of the country had always accorded the NP *hoofleier* a final say over matters; being *only* the *hoofleier* did not carry the same ultimate authority at all. It was a step down in the eyes of the rest of the leadership.

Younger members who supported the move out of the GNU were Van Schalkwyk, Nic Koornhof and David Malatsi. Those serving on behalf of the

NP in the executive were mostly opposed to leaving – including Chris Fismer, who had replaced Meyer as minister of constitutional development – as were many in the caucus. The only *verligte* in the cabinet who supported De Klerk in his decision was his long-time ally, Dawie de Villiers.

In the end, the split was fifty-fifty. De Klerk's announcement that he was resigning as deputy president clinched it. The *hoofleier* still held some sway. At the end of June 1996, the NP quit the GNU. Fluctuations in the value of the rand sparked by the move showed that the party was still important to capital. The ANC was 'horrified' by the NP's departure, partly because of its abhorrence of aggressive Westminster opposition politics. But the decision was made and the deed was done.

The NP's failure to extend the lifespan of the GNU strengthened the hand of the conservatives in their withdrawal bid. In the final analysis, the departure from the GNU marked the rise of the conservatives within the party. The hand-ling of the decision also alienated the younger generation of leaders, which further weakened the party.

The decision to leave was announced before being relayed to NP represen-tatives serving at provincial level. The leader of the NP caucus in the Gauteng legislature, Olaus van Zyl, thought Annelizé van Wyk, then an NP member of the provincial legislature, was 'lying' when she informed him about the withdrawal. She had found out the news accidentally.[35]

Former leaders such as Meyer, Pik Botha and Sheila Camerer agree that the NP's exit from the GNU in June 1996 was the beginning of the party's end.[36] Botha, who opposed the withdrawal, argues that the NP gave a section of the electorate a sense of security that their interests were being represented at the highest level.[37]

Meyer believes that voters lost their trust in the party: 'With the 1994 election results, the voters showed they had enough trust in the NP for it to be part of the GNU. The results were an expression of their support for the [outcome of the] negotiations.' He believes that if the NP, or a reformed NP, had stayed the course for the full five years, it would have remained a force in South African politics. Withdrawal from the GNU constituted 'a great injustice against the white voter' in his view. Delport differs. For him and the other *verkramptes*, the time had come for the NP to become a proper opposition party.

The GNU departure led to the second major haemorrhage of leaders, as many who were not 'right' for the job of opposition (read: the *verligtes*) quit politics. Pik Botha, Fismer and De Villiers followed in the footsteps of Keys, who had seen the first budget through, then resigned to head up BHP Billiton in London.

What had been a steady flow of resignations in the early 1990s became a torrent in 1996. The energetic and astute Leon Wessels left on conclusion of the final constitution to pursue a legal career; Piet Welgemoed and Wynand Breytenbach, members of the executive under De Klerk before 1994, were next. George Bartlett quit as KwaZulu-Natal NP leader, but it was the circumstances under which deputy land affairs minister Tobie Meyer left that revealed the tumult within the party.

De Klerk decided to move Delport from his post as an Eastern Cape MEC to that of deputy minister of justice in a bid to bring him under closer control and address the division of posts among conservatives and *verligtes*. Tobie Meyer would then be moved to the Eastern Cape. *Beeld* called the ensuing internal revolt the biggest crisis in the NP since the CP's 1992 by-election victory in Potchefstroom.[38] Meyer resigned, but the machetes were out for Delport. At the 1996 Eastern Cape congress he became the first provincial leader in the history of the party to be voted out while in office.[39]

His mistake? Delport had challenged De Klerk's authority directly by inviting Kriel to address the congress in place of the *hoofleier*, as was customary. Shortly after his forced removal, he resigned and joined the DP – a harbinger of things to come, as the NP's support base moved en masse to vote for the DP in 1999. Shortly thereafter, Kriel followed Delport.

NP affirmative action and the ousting of Meyer

De Klerk's vision for the NP in opposition was laudable, if slightly hackneyed: 'A strong and vigilant opposition' to maintain and promote a 'genuine multi-party democracy'. The NP was going to play 'its full role as the main opposition party'.[40] Easier said than done.

The party had relinquished state power after forty-six years of maintaining it through an increasingly repressive system. The cake of patronage and power had shrunk dramatically, heightening the contestation of positions and ideas within party ranks. Its business allies were looking towards the NP's successor for economic advance. To top it all, the party was desperately seeking an ideology – a few within its ranks had made the move to liberal democracy, but most had not. Finally, it had just abandoned the GNU, the last drop of an already diluted promise to its constituency.

A few months after the GNU exodus, Roelf Meyer became the next victim of the rise of the right within the party. According to De Klerk, ill times befell Meyer because he had not taken the rest of the party with him in the pursuit of his assignment to transform the NP.[41] He wanted the party to be dismantled, despite not having produced 'acceptable partners' with whom the NP could create a new one. Meyer explains his point of view as follows: 'The NP, purely as the party of apartheid, could not continue to exist. It had to disappear [while] contributing towards the establishment of a party for all South Africans. I said we should make a commitment to disband. For FW, under pressure from someone like Hernus [Kriel], that was totally unacceptable.'[42]

Meyer wanted to relaunch the party with a new name and a black leader in time to campaign for the 1999 election. De Klerk and the *verkramptes* wanted the NP to be part of a new movement, but 'with the retention of its identity'. This was déjà vu. Had not the NP used similar terms when embarking on its search for black partners in 1990? And – apart from swallowing the Labour Party – had that not been an abortive quest? For a second time, the NP leadership could not let go of its 'identity': a party of and for whites. It was willing only to tweak the basics, and then only when tweaking fitted its power paradigm.

There was another dimension to the conflict. Among the rest of the leadership, it was felt that Meyer and the other *verligtes* were pushing for the 'team photo to be darker' at the cost of existing white leadership.[43] While coloured leaders appointed to high positions, such as cabinet minister Abe Williams, had to be accepted, since they represented a significant section of the party's support base, the promotion of blacks was more problematic. Unsurprisingly, the NP had an uphill battle finding black leaders who were interested in co-operation with the former whites-only party. In many cases, efforts to find such leaders seemed to deliver opportunists intent on exploiting the need for change within the party.

For some of the existing leaders, in the quest to find more representative leaders, Meyer and Pik Botha were embracing 'token leaders', who came without substantive support bases. 'We were so grateful for a black face ... when photos were taken, those guys would be put in front', says Kilian. John Gogotya and David Chuenyane seemed to have used the NP as no more than a springboard into parliament, and defected to the ANC at the first opportunity. Conservatives saw the few available posts being filled by people such as John Mavuso, who came from nowhere to land a cabinet post after April 1994. Bhadra Ranchod had barely been appointed deputy speaker of the national assembly before departing to become an ambassador – unsurprisingly, alleging racism in the party as reason.

There was a racist undertone to sentiment within the party that while black people were being placed in prominent party positions (one of the handful of Gauteng provincial posts was given to Vincent Mnisi), the white members 'were doing the work'. White Afrikaans men in the party were starting to feel threatened.[44] The backlash was evident in Delport's comment at the 1996 Eastern Cape congress that it was time for the NP to start helping 'its own people' again, namely whites.[45] In a counter-intuitive step, as part of a bid to stem the 'blackening' of the party, limits were placed on the number of branches in black residential areas to ensure that black members did not dominate the provincial structures.[46] The fear was ill founded, as such branches had nowhere near the resources of those in white areas and, in any event, black people remained aloof towards their former oppressor. Strategic decision-making and direction – the real power in the party – continued to be vested in a white male clique surrounding the internally omnipotent *hoofleier*.

Some appointments led to embarrassment that further chipped away at the party's credibility – and its attempts to 'transform'. Abe Williams was barely in his post when he was prosecuted and found guilty of corruption. David Malatsi, who became leader of the Mpumalanga NP in Fismer's stead before being pushed out by the province and becoming an MEC in the Western Cape, was also convicted of corruption after taking a bribe a few years later. His co-accused, the verbose Peter Marais, was acquitted.

The racial tensions, along with the inability to give up the party's 'identity', set the ball rolling for Meyer's departure. De Klerk dissolved the committee that Meyer had constituted to assist him in his task – a step that caught committee members unawares. Apparently, De Klerk could not follow where Meyer wanted to go. Up to that point, he had backed him. Meyer's prospects as crown prince had seemed secure. But he was going much further than De Klerk had envisaged, and this, seemingly, was where De Klerk's Afrikaner nationalist heritage finally caught up with him.

He had been a National Party cabinet member for eighteen years and was descended from a long line of Afrikaner nationalists, most of them on the hard-liner side of the party's enduring divide. He abandoned Meyer, who was left with only one choice: cling to a spent force or take a leap. It was the leap – almost as quantum as the one made in 1990 – that De Klerk could not muster.

Van Schalkwyk was at the forefront of the offensive against Meyer's initiative. He apparently used the anxieties of white middle-level leaders about their future to rally support against Meyer being De Klerk's successor. Fears were raised as to how far Meyer would drive the racial transformation of the party. According to a source that wishes to remain anonymous, he lobbied support by asking: 'Who decided that Roelf Meyer has the God-given right to become leader?'

The clashes between Meyer and Van Schalkwyk increased in frequency after Wessels, the other strong contender in the leadership stakes, left the NP at the beginning of 1996. Van Schalkwyk ascribes his tensions with Meyer to the fact that he (Van Schalkwyk) had been instructed to devise a strategy to preserve and build the party, which was at odds with Meyer's mandate. Another name that cropped up was Kriel. He was opposed to Meyer's venture and infuriated when Meyer said the Western Cape NP could follow the 'Bavarian option' and go its own way.[47] Not long afterwards, it was Meyer going his own way.

He left the NP to start the Process for a New Movement. A clampdown followed in which NP members had to sign declarations of support. Disciplinary action was taken against some, for example Annelizé van Wyk, who dared to observe out loud that the leadership had 'shot the messenger'. Various members quit to join Meyer in his uncertain venture. Discussions started with Bantu Holomisa, who had been unceremoniously kicked out of the ANC for alleging that fellow Transkeian Stella Sigcau had taken bribes while serving in the Bantustan government of Kaiser Matanzima. Holomisa had ousted Matanzima in the 1980s, and headed a military council that rejected the continued existence of the Bantustans as advocated by Bophuthatswana's Lucas Mangope and Ciskei's Oupa Gqozo. Sigcau's inaction as an ANC cabinet minister was notorious, but she loyally delivered the Pondo vote in the Eastern Cape to the ANC.

Holomisa and Meyer formed the United Democratic Movement, with Holomisa as leader and Meyer as his deputy. NP members who joined Meyer included rising stars such as Annelizé van Wyk and Gerhard Koornhof and most of the Gauteng NP Youth. Later, *verligte* old-guard member Sam de Beer followed after his bid for *hoofleierskap* failed.

'Relatively cleaner hands'

The NP was still reeling from the latest defections when De Klerk announced his retirement. It was a mere thirteen months since he had led the party out of the GNU. He acknowledged later that he 'quickly realised' after leaving the GNU that he did not have 'sufficient enthusiasm' for opposition politics.[48] Personal issues played the principal role in his retirement – including concerns raised within the party about the effect revelations about his relationship with Elita Georgiadis would have on the conservative NP vote in the next election.

It is unlikely that De Klerk's premature departure was not also influenced by the fact that, yet again, he found himself presiding over a party in disarray. Having been persuaded to follow the Meyer/Wessels approach to the negotiations, he swung the other way after 1994. In the NP, the *hoofleier*'s decision had always been the final word – something that De Klerk enjoyed despite his diminished stature after 1994. At the end of his political tether, he found it more and more difficult to balance the two opposing internal forces. With his departure went one of the NP's most powerful electoral drawcards – he was the father figure of the 'father figure NP', as political scientist Susan Booysen called the party.[49]

With De Klerk's departure, the fluidity that had marked internal relations in the party since 1994 came to an end, according to Boeije de Wet,[50] who, like Van Schalkwyk, served two terms as NP youth leader before leaving the NP for the ANC: 'Prior to 1994, you could not express your ideas inside the NP, but afterwards, you could. I think they were so confused that they simply tolerated this. This is no longer the case. Different ideas are a threat. This reflects the uncertainty in the NP. They say one thing, but mean something else. A rigidity has taken hold within the NP since FW's departure.'

Initially, rumours circulated that Hernus Kriel was gunning to replace De Klerk. This evoked strong resistance, especially among black party members. Denise Mooloo, NP member of the Gauteng provincial legislature, declared outright that black members would not support Kriel because he had a specific interest in 'Afrikanerdom', which was too narrow a constituency.[51] Moves were already afoot to replace Kriel with a coloured leader in the Western Cape.

In the end, Danie Schutte represented the conservatives. He was up against Sam de Beer, Kraai van Niekerk and Van Schalkwyk. The latter, who had arrived at parliament in 1991, was hand-picked by the Transvaal NP leadership. Interestingly, it was Pik Botha who promoted his profile when he was vying for the Randburg constituency in the early 1990s. Van Schalkwyk increasingly capitalised on the opinion that a younger leader was needed to shed the party's 'baggage from the past'. In the feud between the *verligtes* and *verkramptes*, he seemed to be the proverbial third dog that got the bone.

Optimistically, the Afrikaans press (while not explicitly pro-NP after 1994, it was still inordinately interested in 'white politics') believed that 'young blood' would bring a fresh perspective and new direction. A typical observation was that, as a 'young Nationalist', Van Schalkwyk had 'relatively cleaner' hands. And: the choice was not 'between *verlig* and conservative as it was in 1989 [when De Klerk became *hoofleier*]. It is rather a choice between the past and the future, old and young, old generation and new generation.'[52]

But the leadership pickings were slim, all the same. Those with any stature had already left; Van Niekerk's power base was too small; De Beer had a reputation of being lazy and an opportunist. Van Schalkwyk managed to muster support from KwaZulu-Natal, thanks to his ally Renier Schoeman (showing a split in conservative ranks), and pipped Van Niekerk to the post. The National Party's last *hoofleier* was elected on 9 September 1997.

For all his youthfulness, Van Schalkwyk had a conservative image. He was just old enough to have imbibed a good dollop of total strategy subterfuge: in the 1980s he launched his political career with the Military Intelligence front organisation Jeugkrag/Youth for SA, setting up opportunities for white and black youths to meet. They were exposed to the NP government's version of South African history and contemporary challenges. The events were partly funded by private corporations and aimed at creating that evasive moderate black bulwark, while offering a conservative alternative to the liberation movements – hence the 'relatively cleaner hands'.

Ideologically, Van Schalkwyk was difficult to pinpoint. He had the reputation of being a wily character, a 'shrewd operator'. In the NP, he was regarded as being unburdened by apartheid baggage because most people did not know about his MI past.[53] As the party's media director in the mid-1990s, he had used his privileged access to De Klerk to influence him. He was variously credited with both neutralising Meyer and orchestrating De Klerk's departure. He replaced Meyer as secretary general, which seemed indicative of the party's move to the right. While he supported withdrawal from the GNU, he was also the driving force behind the NP's 'cooperative opposition' stance. Another comment about Van Schalkwyk, from an anonymous source, was that he 'can fit into any space which he thinks will benefit him and with anybody who can benefit him'.

Some say Van Schalkwyk never was a conservative, but played to the conservative gallery so as to rise to power within the party. He would not be the first to have done so. Indeed, since the 1970s the NP leadership pandered predominantly to the conservatives, while pursuing *verligte* policies. But this time, without state power, there was much less room to manoeuvre. The voter – feeling insecure in the flux of change – wanted certainty, and there were viable alternatives to the NP.

These contradictions in Van Schalkwyk as *hoofleier* came to be reflected in policy flip-flops, the next important factor in the NP's demise. Van Schalkwyk's weakness was that he surrounded himself with people who would say what he wanted to hear – not unlike his ANC counterpart, Thabo Mbeki. His 'posse' included NP director Shaun Vorster, secretary general Daryl Swanepoel, MPs Renier Schoeman, Dirk Bakker, François Beukman and, to a lesser extent, André Gaum.

Symptomatic of the policy and strategy lethargy that gripped the NP, renewal under Van Schalkwyk went no further than adding the word 'New' to 'National Party' on 27 November 1998.* The designation had been a burning issue since 1990. The Labour Party's Chris April had said in no uncertain terms in 1991 that the name National Party 'disgusted' him. When he heard it, he was reminded of discrimination and apartheid.[54] Similarly, Stan Simmons feels 'the name National Party had baggage. What does it make you think of first? Oppression.' Just before the release of the party's new vision in 1996, two provincial legislature members leaked to the press that the party was considering a name change. It was popularly rejected, being such a controversial idea as to almost overshadow the new vision. White supporters made it clear that they were not ready to move on. Similarly, when Simmons proposed a further name change at the NP's Cape congress after the dismal outcome of the 1999 election, there was resistance. According to him, 'many of our people [coloured people] still like

---

* The abbreviation NP has been used hereafter to denote both the 'old' and the 'new' National Party.

the name because it is connected to FW. The people loved him. If he wanted to come back [in 2006], they would accept him back.'[55]

One result of the negotiations was the Truth and Reconciliation Commission, designed to solicit disclosure of apartheid-era human rights violations in return for amnesty. This had been one of the last-minute agreements before finalisation of the 1993 constitution, and it was one that the conservatives were especially upset about. The ensuing revelations over several months would damage the NP's image beyond repair.

Judging by letters to newspapers in that period, NP supporters were alternately beset by horror and denial, recognition and guilt as tales of murder, torture and racism filled the media day after day. The hearings led to heated public exchanges between former NP colleagues, with accusations and counter-accusations flying. The rifts among the conservatives were exposed when Hernus Kriel accused Kobie Coetsee of botching the amnesty issue and culminated in PW Botha's obstinate refusal to appear before the TRC, which he labelled a 'circus' during his subsequent court appearance. The NP made two submissions to the TRC, which are discussed in the next chapter.

The fall

The NP went into the 1999 election with Van Schalkwyk at the helm. It had to make the best of its role as official opposition in parliament. Pik Botha calls the national assembly a '*praathuis*' (chat chamber) – cabinet was where the decisions were taken. He was right. Sadly, executive dominance of the legislative arm was carried over into democracy. This was increasingly the case with the post-1994 parliament, with the ANC leadership in the executive quickly realising the benefits of proportional representation in ensuring utmost party loyalty and crushing any hint of supervision – the constitutionally assigned role of parliament.

After the arms deal scandal in the late 1990s, parliament was reduced to an irritating necessity. It was where the ANC used its majority muscle to contain opposition parties and their criticism or questions. ANC attitudes towards opposition became marked by a high level of intolerance, and parliament was sidelined in the political decision-making process. Into this terrain of diminishing importance stepped a haggard former ruling party. It had lost more leaders, such as Nic Koornhof (to the DP), Patrick McKenzie (to the ANC) and Kraai van Niekerk (to the Federal Alliance).

The worst was yet to come: the 1999 election, which was more like slaughter for the NP. It shed a massive 75 per cent of its 1994 support, tumbling from almost 4 million votes to around 1.1 million. The first reason within its control was the ill-considered departure from the GNU, which was exacerbated by derisory communication of the reasons, both within party structures and to supporters. Nothing had come of 'power sharing' – the symbol, rather than content, of the notion had been the GNU, and the NP was no longer part of it.

The second and equally important factor was the replacement of De Klerk with the lightweight Van Schalkwyk. Public communication about De Klerk's departure in the midst of the Meyer group's exodus was almost non-existent, and it was no better within the party. Even public representatives were taken aback, heightening the atmosphere of insecurity permeating the NP at the time. A senior member of the Democratic Alliance (formerly the DP), James Selfe, put his finger on the implications of De Klerk's retirement. De Klerk had done the DP 'a favour' by leaving, because his stature was 'a huge asset to the NP', making him 'virtually unassailable' in the electoral stakes.[56]

Leaving the GNU meant that the NP had lost its claim to being directly involved in government decisions: 'They walked out – they no longer played a role, could no longer say "we are working behind the scenes, we are accomplishing many things"', says Delport. The loss was compounded by the NP's confusing election messages, which reflected the split in the party between those who wanted to 'oppose' and those who wanted to be 'constructive'.

In its stronghold, the Western Cape, the party was beset with problems. During 1998, the NP invited the DP to join the executive in the provincial legislature, from which the ANC was still excluded. The ANC proposed a motion of no confidence in premier Hernus Kriel, which led to the NP ousting the ANC from all committee chairpersonships in the legislature. An obstinate Kriel was finally ejected from the premier's office in April. *The Star* succinctly observed that the 'last white male to head a cabinet anywhere in Africa has gone'.[57]

The contest for the premiership was between the seemingly pliable Gerald Morkel and the unruly Peter Marais. Morkel won, leading an angry Marais to spout vitriol while openly flirting with the ANC, until he was suspended from his position as Western Cape MEC in 2000. His perceived value as a vote magnet in the run-up to that year's local government election led to his reinstatement, but as an ordinary MPL.

According to Simmons, the party leaders 'were like chickens without heads before the 1999 election, jumping around after they had realised they were in trouble and that the voters were not going to vote for them – especially not the whites'. The leadership was anxious to hold on to its white support because, without that, the NP would become a coloured regional party, by dint of simple demographics.[58]

A survey at the time showed that white voters were partial to strongly critical opposition messages, while black voters preferred the cooperative stance.[59] To attract black voters, the NP's primary election message was that it could make benefits available to voters through its policy of cooperation with the ANC. But 'then the people could just as well vote for the ANC', says Simmons. 'We had such fights with the leader [Van Schalkwyk] over this. We were insulting the people's intelligence with this message ... People didn't want to hear such a message.' Delport says the NP in opposition was not 'pointing out what the voters were experiencing', because its leadership was too 'politically correct' and 'did not want to fight with the ANC'. For him, the NP's inability to find an effective opposition role was its death knell.

To attract white voters, the NP prevaricated from its primary election message by half-heartedly criticising negative aspects of the ANC's performance. It was both attempting to project itself as the 'constructive opposition party' – as opposed to the DP's 'negative opposition stance' – and to be critical. At the time, NP members of parliament argued in discussions with the author that their style of opposition was more 'African', while the DP's was too 'Western', and therefore alien. But, while NP leaders regarded themselves as more 'indigenous' than DP members, their messages remained muddled. Moreover, they targeted a predictable and unexciting set of issues (crime, corruption, the Zimbabwe policy). The primary message, the clumsy 'Kom ons maak Suid-Afrika werk/ Let's make South Africa work', was contradicted by its negative messaging on crime and Zimbabwe. It could not trump the DP's short, sharp 'Slaan Terug/ Fight Back', conceptualised by their strategist and confidant of DP leader Tony Leon, Ryan Coetzee. As Kilian says, 'We were everything to everyone – then we became nothing to nobody [sic].'

The NP's core constituency – the whites – identified with Leon's invective. The DP, much to its delight, added 1.2 million votes to its 1994 total of 340 000. Most of the ballots were at the NP's expense, and the DP increased its share among all Afrikaner and English-speaking white groups in urban and rural areas. By the early 2000s, the DP/DA had entrenched itself as the party of the employed and higher income groups, as well as former CP and AWB supporters among the lower classes. About 77 per cent of its supporters were white.[60] A survey found that voters categorised parties other than their own on the basis of race.[61] The class–race intersection of people's identities further accounted for the racial polarisation of politics in South Africa. The racial polarisation was indeed also a class polarisation.

The angry white man

The DP's real coup was to pick up a substantial number of Afrikaners who were disillusioned with the NP and seeking security in a country where power relations were being turned on their head in everyday social situations. According to the DA's Selfe, his party had targeted the NP's support base since 1996/7.

They had realised that the much vaunted 'checks and balances' (power sharing) were worthless. The NP had become so entangled in being part of government and then extricating itself that the new official opposition found itself sailing to the polls in 'clear blue water'.[62] All they had to do was exploit the *gatvol* factor.

The DP had realised that they could take the NP on when, in February 1997, they won a by-election in what used to be staunch NP territory: Kempton Park. Other by-elections were fought on a strategic basis to oust NP representatives, and the DP made further inroads in traditional NP strongholds such as Witbank, Boksburg, Brakpan, Orkney, Maritzburg Central and Roodepoort.

The DP's strategic move to the right emphasised the need to 'fight back' in order to 'restore moral values', which were 'crumbling', along with 'discipline'.[63] The DP promised to restore 'honesty, a work ethic and obedience to the law'; to 'nail' criminals; to oppose appointments and promotion on the basis of race, because 'too many people are getting jobs for which they are not qualified'. Appointments had to be on the basis of merit, not race. Schools were 'in chaos and hospitals … crumbling'. Of course, all of this was underpinned by the promise of lower taxes, (more) privatisation and a 'free labour market'.

In its antagonistic communications, the DP sketched a society on the verge of implosion 'since the ANC came to power', citing hundreds of thousands of rapes and murders, millions of rand lost to corruption and half a million jobs shed. Its uncompromising message was rounded off with the campaign picture of a resolute Tony Leon, arms folded and face unsmiling – the angry white man of many suburban households, blown up to billboard proportions.

This rather crude display was not unlike the *kragdadigheid* of the NP of yesteryear, except that, until 1994, its posturing had been backed up with actual *slaankrag* (strike power). Using language that most whites had historically come to identify with, the DP supplied a vent for anger and confusion at their loss of power and resultant anxiety. The party provided an anchor for conservative people who were church going, wanted to maintain standards, protect their culture and language, and who rejected poor governance.[64] This description of the DP's new breed of supporter, by Delport, echoed the profile of the old NP supporter.

But associating the first black government with destruction and decay – typical of colonial rhetoric – so soon after the advent of democracy, opened wounds that had not yet healed. The DP was subsequently rejected as racist by ANC politicians and black commentators, an accusation bolstered by its patent inability to attract votes from black South Africans. It ran up against the same conundrum as the NP in the mid-1990s: the post-apartheid white-party syndrome. Critics in the ANC reminded the DP that it was the descendant of collaborator parties in the apartheid parliament.

Political scientist Tom Lodge emphasised that the DP's move to the right was met by the Afrikaners moving to the left to meet it.[65] Delport also noticed a 'head shift' among right-wingers voting for the DP and later the DA, arguing that the party did not support policies that were constitutionally or racially comparable to apartheid. But it made the connotation: black government equals incompetence, corruption and chaos – statements so reminiscent of the centuries-old discourse that haunted South Africa. The DP/DA changed its slogan for the 2000 local government election to 'For all the people', but the racism tag stuck. The ANC made sure of that. Just as racism was a powerful mobilising force for retention of power before 1994, anti-racism served the same purpose thereafter.

Despite the DP's considerable expansion and accompanying self-congratulatory attitude, it gained only 10 per cent of the vote in 1999. Apart from the ANC flying past the DP with almost two-thirds of the vote, its harvest was half of what the NP had managed in 1994. Where had the other NP voters gone? Some had followed Meyer to the UDM. While the majority of its half-million votes were for Holomisa in the Eastern Cape, a sizeable minority, especially in Gauteng, went to Meyer's enterprise. More decisive was the rise of the missing white voter.

In the 1999 election, almost 33 per cent of eligible whites, 42 per cent of coloureds and close on 40 per cent of Indians did not even bother to register as voters. Among blacks, the figure was about 17 per cent. The NP's support base lay among the so-called minority racial groups, and it was thus the party most adversely affected by this lack of interest. In Gauteng, almost half a million white voters stayed away from the polls, while some 140 000 people who had voted NP in the Eastern Cape in 1994 and 30 000 in the Northern Province did not vote.[66] Lodge calculated that about one million white voters did not take part in the 1999 election, if the decrease in NP and FF votes were taken into account. For him, this was the election when 'traditional Afrikaner nationalism disappeared'.[67]

The stayaway vote gave cause for concern. The calculation of voter turnout (a high 89 per cent in 1999) did not include those eligible voters who chose to stay away. This was symptomatic of not only the apathy that liberal democracy engendered, but of a tendency towards self-isolation among white South Africans, especially Afrikaners. It was also a sign of the failure by not only the NP, but all political parties, to adequately represent, articulate and address the needs of certain constituencies. Across all population groups, 3.5 million eligible voters did not participate in the 1999 election. By the 2004 election, half of all eligible voters failed to exercise their franchise – more than the total who voted for the ANC. Despite this, the ANC increased its majority in the national assembly as, paradoxically, the stayaway vote boosted the party's dominance.

At provincial level, the NP was wiped out virtually everywhere except the Western Cape. Van Schalkwyk used the opportunity to move his name onto the Western Cape provincial party list to be closer to the power base. But even hopes that the NP could build itself as a regional coloured party were dashed, as it lost almost half its Cape votes from 1994 to 1999. Low levels of registration had led to a 30 per cent drop in voter turnout, and the NP suffered most.[68] The ANC captured 42 per cent of the vote against the NP's 38 per cent (down from 53 per cent). Again the class split in the coloured vote was evident, with working-class areas turning out for the NP, while middle-class areas voted ANC. The rural areas were again predominantly ANC. The DP scored white votes from the NP, and managed to almost double its support to 12 per cent. But in the coloured areas, they ran into a brick wall, says Selfe.

An alliance to 'prevent a one-party state'

The 1999 election tolled the final bell for the National Party. Van Schalkwyk ascribes the party's poor performance to 'the NP not possessing the DNA to be an opposition party … it was designed in a different time period for something different'. To hold on to power and keep the ANC out in the Western Cape, the NP entered into a coalition with the DP and the reactionary African Christian Democratic Party. A government was constituted with Gerald Morkel as premier. Cooperation between the DP and the NP had been in the offing since at least 1997. Considerable pressure was applied in the Afrikaans press – whose readers were voting for both – for the NP and DP to form a united opposition front against the ANC.

Tony Leon reported to the DP's federal council on 10 and 11 June 2000 that advisors he had consulted indicated 'that if the DP wished to pose an electoral challenge to the ANC, it could not do so if forced to fight on two fronts. It was therefore necessary to "clear the opposition decks".'[69] From the DP's point of view, it was also crucial that the Western Cape did not fall into the hands of the ANC.

The DP's federal council mandated Leon to speak to Van Schalkwyk. Both parties shared the impression that the white community wanted them to form an alliance. A 'romanticism' had been created around the idea, says Van Schalkwyk. The ball was set rolling without, yet again, proper consultation in the NP's structures.[70] The DP tried to persuade the NP to merge with it to fight the local government election – a proposal that Van Schalkwyk rejected out of hand. After initial negotiations with the DP leadership had been concluded, a memorandum of understanding was reached on 14 June 2000. At the next DP federal council meeting, Leon argued that while the alliance with the NP took people out of their 'comfort zones', it allowed the DP 'to shut down the "second front" and concentrate on a battle with the ANC'. Their memorandum of under-standing noted that both parties 'share the urgent need to consolidate opposition among like-minded voters in all communities ... and the need to consolidate democracy ... and prevent a de facto one-party state from developing'.[71]

The memorandum contained the principles of the DA, which the DP leader-ship regarded as identical to its own. These included typical liberal values such as the right to freedom of speech and association; the rule of law; separation of powers; private ownership; and 'enterprise economy'. The NP's influence was seen in principles such as the 'centrality of the family'; the acknowledgement of religious diversity and freedom of religion; and the protection of cultural values and language rights.

Instead of redistribution and redressing inequalities, the newfangled Demo-cratic Alliance stood for a liberal meritocracy in which 'economic injustices of previously disadvantaged individuals and communities' would be eradicated through human resource development, capacity building, merit and without sacrificing efficiency. Liberty was emphasised, but socio-economic equality did not feature. The only vaguely social democratic allowance was for 'minimum safety nets' for the sick, the disabled and the unemployed. The union thus gave effect to the libertarian coming together of the two parties during the negotiations.

The memorandum was tabled at the NP federal council, a body constituted on the basis of proportional representation and consisting of parliamentary and provincial members, as well as the nine provincial leaders, the *hoofleier* and Vroue-Aksie (Women's Action). The response from black members was: 'How can you put us with these people?' Marais, in particular, had been pushing for an alliance with the ANC since before the 1999 election. The discussion about the DA merger became so emotional that 'people wept'.[72] Many did not identify with the DP's emphasis on individualism, preferring the NP's communitarian emphasis. In an explanation that would have made Verwoerd proud, Simmons calls it the desire to interact in '*groepsverband*' (group regard): 'You know, a group consists of individuals, but the group is still stronger than the individual – especially when it comes to traditions and language and religion. They can say what they want, but Europe is like that. The Portuguese stay with the Portuguese and the Hollanders stay with the Hollanders. People want to stay with their own people. That is why the Zulus are living in KwaZulu-Natal, the Xhosas are living in the Eastern Cape and the Tswanas are living over there ... and the coloureds live in the Cape.' But the imperatives of political survival won out over the *groepsverband* glue: the white members persisted with their push for an alliance.

The Democratic Alliance was created, incorporating the NP, the DP and the conservative Federal Alliance of Louis Luyt, a businessman who had been involved in the Information Scandal of the late 1970s. The merger meant that the NP under Van Schalkwyk was following in the footsteps of the *verkrampte* wing. After all, both Delport and Kriel had joined the DP by 1999.

The leadership jostling of the 1990s had evicted both the *verkrampte* and *verligte* elements of the negotiation years. But shortly thereafter, Van Schalkwyk *et al.* were attaching their colours to the same mast as the *verkramptes*. With the DP under Leon having moved to the right, the conservative NP leftovers did not feel ideologically uncomfortable about their prospective home. On the DP side, the federal council was hesitant, and was convinced only after much debate. Colin Eglin and Helen Zille both predicted that the merger 'would take the enterprise forward'.[73] It did, as the DA gathered 24 per cent of the local government vote in 2000, as opposed to 16 per cent polled by the combined opposition in 1995/6. The DA also won the Cape Town unicity with 107 seats to the ANC's 77. But, as time passed, reports filtered through of liberals in the DA who felt that the party was being compromised by its conservative engorgement. After all, since the mid-1990s it had even attracted former members of the Afrikaner-Weerstandsbeweging.

The fusion was a short but rough ride, characterised by high levels of suspicion on both sides. The DP leaders wanted the NP's coloured voters and the party's decades-old infrastructure of branches and members. Shortly before the 1999 election, the NP had sported some 86 000 subscriptions in the Western Cape. The NP's leaders wanted – needed – the new political vehicle, unbesmirched by apartheid. The resultant battle degenerated into a street fight at times, with both sides taking off the gloves in their bids to gain dominance. Joint decision-making structures were created and a joint management committee was set up, with Selfe as chairperson.

After the split, one of Van Schalkwyk's acolytes, Daryl Swanepoel, accidentally gave Selfe a tape recording of an NP meeting at which Van Schalkwyk had tried to convince his highly resistant federal council to make the move to the DA.[74] According to Selfe, Van Schalkwyk pointed out that the NP had the majority of support in three provinces – Limpopo, Northern Cape and Western Cape – and that its stronger organisational structures would ensure that it recruited more members in order to take over the party when the time was ripe. To Selfe, this boiled down to 'a kind of reverse takeover'. The matter would come to a head after the 2000 local government election.

Selfe was struck by the subservience of the NP's federal council, which went along with Van Schalkwyk despite many – if not most – members objecting to the merger. Evidently, the *hoofleier's* powers remained formidable.

The DP's intentions were no purer than those of the NP. The DP had evinced an aggressive stance even while negotiating the merger. From the start the relationship was more give than take from the NP's perspective: thirty-nine local NP councillors left to join the DP in June 2000, a sensitive stage in the alliance talks. The NP threatened to reduce the DP's number of posts in the Western Cape executive, standing at four of twelve at the time. The merger was also affected by Kriel's attempted comeback while negotiations were taking place. He joined the DP after apparently trying to re-enter the NP leadership, but being blocked by Van Schalkwyk.

To concentrate all their energies on the election, the DA had suspended more contentious issues such as defining membership and drawing up a constitution. Major tensions soon arose, with the DP faction growing increasingly worried about damage to the party image by members over whom they could not exert control. The NP's effusive Peter Marais in particular was bent on doing things his way as executive mayor of Cape Town, the only metropolitan council under DA control. The debacle of streets being renamed without Marais following procedure and associated allegations of corruption led to him being disciplined and then expelled from the party. His expulsion was later overturned by the courts.

The NP used the Marais incident as an example of Leon's dictatorial leadership, accusing him of wanting 'a coloured that he could control'. This was partly due to the placement of Ryan Coetzee, first in Premier Morkel's office and then in the office of Mayor Marais – to 'help' them. The NP faction grasped the DP's 'autocracy' and 'racism' as their ticket out. The 'unholy troika' of Leon, Selfe and Douglas Gibson evoked especially strong emotions among the NP faction.

Van Schalkwyk paraded with Marais at press conferences, presenting himself as the hero who would lead the NP out of an intolerably 'racist' environment. But behind it all lay the fundamental issue of the NP's attempt to stage a coup by stealth and being caught out. According to Selfe, Van Schalkwyk produced a list of 56 000 paid-up members of whom a large number were 'sponsored'. He also insisted that such members should play the leading role in deciding representation at party congresses, which would favour the NP.

In the DP tradition, representation was based on performance, or the number of votes delivered by each constituency – which would favour the DP. The latter also became aware that the NP had brought with it large debts, which it was hoping to offload on the DA.

At the same time, the NP faction had to resist the DP faction's manoeuvres. In the middle of 2001, a laptop belonging to Ryan Coetzee was stolen. Soon afterwards, some of its contents were leaked to the press, including the 'Marthinus letter' in which Coetzee advised Leon how to manoeuvre Van Schalkwyk, then DA deputy leader, out of the party.

Van Schalkwyk was asked by the author what his strategy had been when he'd entered the alliance with the DP, and whether he thought he would have been able to take control of the party. He avoided the question by talking about the two parties' different vantage points. The NP leadership thought it could give the DA 'a more moderate face', but the opposite became clear 'early in 2001, after a very brief marriage, when one of the senior DP leaders said: What's bad for the country is good for the DA. That sparked a huge debate. Where we come from, that's not the way we see things. We wanted the country to succeed – for the sake of your own people, the country has to work.'

As part of his belated realisation that the NP did not have the 'DNA' of an opposition party, Van Schalkwyk came to see the party as 'a team player in national interest'. This does not tally with his 1996 view that the party should quit the GNU – which he admits was a mistake. Van Schalkwyk comes across as cooperative, benign. His actions gave a more accurate sense of his leadership. His power-mongering took him a long way in the struggling NP, but he came up against a different calibre of leadership when he decided to take on the DP. In the end there was not enough space in one party for both Leon and Van Schalkwyk. Somebody had to leave.

Van Schalkwyk took the decision to go, endorsed by the NP's federal council in November 2001. It was met with outright rejection by Morkel, the Western Cape premier. It seemed the DA style was not as foreign to some coloured NP members as was generally assumed. Morkel was summarily suspended from the party. DA councillors in Johannesburg also opposed the split. MPs mostly adopted a wait-and-see attitude, indicative of the volatility of political relations at the time.

'I always identified more strongly with the ANC than the DP'

To extricate itself from the DA, the NP was down to its last option: the ANC. According to Van Schalkwyk, informal discussions about collaboration had been taking place with ANC leaders for many years, while he himself had 'always' identified more strongly with the ruling party than with the DP. However, Eastern Cape NP leader Manie Schoeman had been ousted from the party, allegedly on Van Schalkwyk's instruction, for opposing the DA merger in favour of closer collaboration with the ANC.

Some ANC leaders were of the opinion that a section of the NP belonged within its ranks. ANC national chairperson Mosiuoa Lekota pursued interaction with NP members, as did former members who had joined the party during the 1990s, such as Gert Oosthuizen. It seemed the NP–ANC rapprochement was activated via the Oosthuizen–Van Schalkwyk channel. During the first floor-crossing window in 2002, Oosthuizen, who had been close to Van Schalkwyk when he was still in the NP, recruited members for the ANC.

By the end of 2001, Van Schalkwyk was meeting with ANC leaders Lekota, Steve Tshwete, Essop Pahad and Penuell Maduna to thrash out a second cross-party agreement within the space of two years. Yet again, he pursued the matter with little consultation or communication within party structures, such as the caucus.[75]

According to Simmons, 'We said: "what are you talking about with the ANC?" He responded that it was confidential and he couldn't disclose it then. He did not disclose it until the very end. And who is the one that got the post?' With the NP on the back foot, cooperation was shaped on the ANC's terms. Early in November 2001, the ANC national executive committee laid down criteria for closer cooperation with the NP. The party had to adopt the ANC's basic principles of wanting to create a democratic, non-racial, non-sexist and prosperous South Africa. The ANC accepted that although the NP was the 'chief architect of apartheid', it had gone through a process of evolution, overcome its past and was ready to make a positive contribution to the country.

The ANC saw cooperation with the NP as a way of isolating the 'confrontational' DA and winning over the coloured vote. Both were essential if the ANC was to gain control of the Western Cape, the only province apart from KwaZulu-Natal where it was not the dominant party. Cooperation could also open doors to the NP's few remaining friends in business, and thus to funding. Indeed, Mandela and De Klerk later embarked on a joint fund-raising drive for the 2004 election. But the ANC made it clear that the two parties would remain separate in programme and policy.

By the end of November 2001, a deal had been hammered out that revolved around the Western Cape. The NP and ANC would each have six seats in the provincial executive, with the premier coming from the NP. Decision-making would be on the basis of consensus, while deadlocks would be broken through national intervention. The deal included an ANC mayor for Cape Town, although the DA still held the majority until the introduction of floor-crossing legislation. Marais and Morkel played political musical chairs, with Morkel (now DA) swapping the premiership to become mayor, and Marais going from mayor to premier.

The deal also included posts in the seven provincial executives that the ANC already controlled. A forum was to be created for the two parties to engage each other on policy issues. Announcing the deal, Tshwete made it clear that the ANC was not interested in tokenism.[76] It felt closer to the NP than to any other party, and the deal was being made in the name of reconciliation, but he emphasised that it was based on cooperation and was not an alliance. He also confirmed that it was a long-term commitment, designed to stretch beyond the 2004 election.

Scandals continued to plague the beleaguered NP. Another one erupted little more than six months later, when Marais quit as premier due to recurring sexual harassment charges. In an ill-advised move, Van Schalkwyk promoted himself to the premiership in June 2002. Kilian warned him at the time that this was a strategic mistake, given the role Van Schalkwyk had played as party leader in Marais' resignation. Moreover, he was the first *hoofleier* since 1948 to hold a provincial post, signalling that the party was shrinking to regional level. It seems his decision was based on the fact that the ANC took a full year after their agreement to offer national executive posts. As it was, the two posts that President Thabo Mbeki made available in November 2002 were for deputy ministers. Van Schalkwyk rewarded his allies Renier Schoeman and, strategically, David Malatsi, the only black leader left in the NP by then.

Within three months after the appointments of the two deputy ministers, a new outrage eroded the party's credibility still further. Malatsi was forced to resign after being accused – and eventually found guilty – of accepting a R300 000 donation for the NP in return for pushing through approval of a controversial golf estate while he was Western Cape MEC for the environment. Having barely survived the sexual harassment case, Marais soon found himself facing the same charges. He was premier at the time when the bribe was paid. The proposed development at Plettenberg Bay was owned by the son of notorious Mafioso Vito Palazzolo. At the time, Marais, who was later acquitted, alleged that Van Schalkwyk had known about it, but his claims came to naught.

The abortive creation of the DA, followed by the scramble into the ANC (which it had pledged to oppose for the sake of 'democratic consolidation' a mere eighteen months before), destroyed whatever residual trust supporters still had in the NP. Van Schalkwyk was fingered as the source of the party's woes, and his popularity plummeted. A survey[77] showed that, by the end of 2002, he enjoyed the support of only 1.7 per cent of people across the political spectrum, while only 18 per cent of NP supporters still backed him, as opposed to the DA's 56 per cent support for Leon and Holomisa's 79 per cent endorsement by UDM followers. More significantly, the NP's shenanigans had compromised South Africa's electoral system. The failed union led to the DA and the NP engaging the ANC to pass legislation that would allow defectors to cross the floor, taking their parliamentary seats with them.

The law allowed local government councillors to leave the DA and return to the NP fold, but it gave rise to an untenable situation. Proportional representation is different to a constituency-based system, as the public representative gets elected to parliament on the basis of inclusion on a party list, rather than their number of votes in a particular constituency. Therefore, a seat belongs to the party to fill in accordance with its internal rules. Should an incumbent defect, the seat is transferred to another party, thus negating the outcome of the democratic process – the will of the voters – on a whim. Representatives in a proportional representation system are not directly elected and therefore do not move at the behest of constituents.

While tested and approved by the Constitutional Court in a case brought by the UDM, crossing the floor militated against the consolidation of democracy in South Africa, because it allowed for undemocratic changes to election results. All three major parties – the ANC, the NP and the DP – supported the law, but the ANC benefited most from it. The rules prescribed a threshold of 10 per cent of any party's representatives for floor crossing to take place. Thus one person could easily decide to leave if a party had ten or fewer representatives, but it would have been well nigh impossible to persuade twenty-six of the ANC's 266 representatives to change sides after the 1999 election. Floor crossing wrought havoc in smaller parties. For example, the UDM lost almost half of its seats in one fell swoop in 2002.

When first introduced, there were questions about why floor crossing was also to be allowed at national and provincial level, given that its purpose at the time was to disentangle the NP and the DA at local level. Nevertheless, the legislation was made applicable at all levels of government, and both the ANC and the DA used it to maximum advantage. Floor crossing served to further erode confidence in the system as power changed hands without voters' say-so. This caused the DA to lose control of Cape Town at local government level in October 2002 after just two years. Twenty-seven of its members went back to the NP and forged a new alliance with the ANC to form a majority, while forty-three others remained with the DA. The DA merger demolished the wall that the DP had run into in the 1999 election, as a substantial segment of the NP's coloured support base switched to the DA. The NP lost a sizeable chunk of its representatives, who stayed behind in the DA at all three government levels.

Interviews by the author[78] with three NP members who left the party for the DA in 2003 shed further light on its inability to hold on to old and new constituents alike. Frik van Deventer, who started out as part of the group of PW Botha party organisers and rose through the ranks to become an MP, was the traditional face of the party. An Afrikaner and active member of the NP since the age of sixteen, he came from a family that served the party as volunteers for eighty-eight years. The NP's Prieska branch was founded on his grandfather's farm in 1915. He quit the NP because he felt betrayed and had come to believe that the DA was more likely to counter abuse of power by the ANC.

Sheila Camerer, an MP and the most senior woman in the NP, was an English-speaking *verligte* and proponent of Willem de Klerk's ideas. She quit because the party had been supposed to fight for 'minority rights' from within the GNU.

The cooperation model found few takers among the electorate, disqualifying it as an option. Charles Redcliffe, a founding member of the Labour Party who had participated in apartheid's coloured representative structures but was also locked up and tortured for participating in the 1976 uprising, defected because Van Schalkwyk was pursuing 'the politics of co-optation' by cooperating with the ANC.

A high-level meeting with Mbeki, Lekota and ANC secretary general Kgalema Motlanthe on the one side, Van Schalkwyk, Northern Cape NP leader PW Saaiman and Gauteng NP leader Kilian on the other, took place on 27 April 2003 in Pretoria. Despite Mbeki declaring that the parties would not enter the 2004 election as opponents, both remained vague about the nature of their relationship. Nothing came of the posts promised at provincial level, or of the policy forum. There were indications that Lekota had run up against intractable resistance within the ANC. The argument – quite rightly – was: Why throw the mortally wounded party of apartheid a lifeline? In true realpolitik style, collaboration happened only in those areas where the NP still held power, so with the exception of the Western Cape, the agreement never got off the ground.

The ANC held back on the appointment of the two NP deputy ministers until it was sure that enough members would cross the floor back to the NP for their coalition to gain control of Cape Town. In the run-up to the 2004 national election, the ANC rejected a pact to first see how the NP would fare by itself. ANC Western Cape leader Ebrahim Rasool also made it clear that there would be no agreement to the NP retaining the premiership.

For the election, the NP reverted yet again to its failed pre-1999 messages, promising to advocate the case of minority voters 'within government' through its tatty cooperation agreement with the ANC. Van Schalkwyk assured voters that the NP was their 'voice in government'. At the same time, the ANC was unapologetically campaigning against the NP, with Mbeki referring to it as one of the 'silly parties' that people should not vote for; blaming De Klerk along with Verwoerd for unemployment, and dismissing parties 'that have been in power before'.[79] His comments were made even as the joint De Klerk–Mandela fund-raising campaign was under way.

Public perception got the better of the NP. Floor crossing had filled the media with quotations from disgruntled former NP representatives, and the dominant image was of a party in collapse. In a sense, the NP was trying to squirm its way back into the GNU, but voters would have none of it. The NP could garner no more than 1.65 per cent of the vote, with the DA picking up most of the previous NP support. With the slogan 'South Africa deserves better', Leon's party gained twelve new parliamentary seats, giving it a total of fifty, reflecting 1 931 201 votes, or 12.37 per cent of the total. But this was well short of the DA's

30 per cent target. Its 'coalition for change' with the IFP had not attracted popular support.

The IFP itself drew about 7 per cent, or one million votes. The *volkstaat* cause received a brief flicker of interest, with the FF+ gaining a seat, though this could probably be attributed to the disappearance of the Afrikaner-Eenheidsbeweging, which lost the single seat it had won in 1999. The UDM's representation fell from fourteen to nine seats, reflecting the departure of Roelf Meyer and other former NP members. Patricia de Lille's newly formed Independent Democrats picked up UDM and NP votes from coloured and white people in both the Western and Northern Cape, to take seven seats, the same number as the NP. But what was a sterling performance for De Lille, coming from nowhere, signalled the end for the NP. The ANC added only about 280 000 votes to its 10.6 million in 1999, but, due to the high number of eligible voters who did not even bother to register, it ended up holding 70 per cent of seats in the national assembly.

In the Western Cape, with a 71 per cent turnout, the ANC failed to achieve an absolute majority (coming in at 45 per cent of the vote, which was up from 42 per cent in 1999 and 33 per cent in 1994). It thus had to govern with the NP, despite the latter having dropped 27 per cent since 1999 to achieve about 11 per cent of the vote in 2004. Compared to 1994, the party had shed a massive 42 per cent of its voting support in the Western Cape. The DA came in at 27 per cent in 2004. This again showed its success in winning over coloured voters through its short-lived merger with the NP.

Overall, the performance of opposition parties was dismal. While 2004 firmly established the DA as the official opposition, it had little prospect of ever forming a government. Once again the DA had run a fear-mongering campaign that asked questions such as: Would the ANC use its dominance to change the constitution? Would Mbeki stay on for an unconstitutional third term? But it also showed a change of tack. Amid claims by Ryan Coetzee that the party had not departed from its liberal roots but had merely moved closer to social-democratic principles, the DA had uncharacteristically come out in support of a basic income grant (BIG). The BIG had previously been promoted by COSATU, the South African Council of Churches and other civil society organisations as a safety net for the eight million unemployed South Africans ineligible for existing social security measures, because they were aged between fourteen and sixty. The DA also supported the free distribution of antiretrovirals to an estimated five million HIV-positive South Africans. The ANC, by contrast, opposed both free ARVs and a BIG, despite the social-democratic undertone of its neo-liberal policy stance.

The slow-down in the DA's growth showed that attempts to sit on two policy chairs and appeal to both poor black people and well-off (resentful) white people were not nearly as fruitful as Leon *et al.* had hoped. Some interpreted the DA slogan of 'South Africa deserves better' as ridiculing efforts of the ANC (the party that delivered 'liberation') to improve people's lives.[80] Political scientists Adam Habib and Sanusha Naidu suggest that the DA's strategy of 'frightening minorities into voting for it' so constrained the party by race that it could not play the electoral game on the basis of policies and principles, and therefore could not reach out to the broad population.[81]

An Afrobarometer public attitude survey[82] conducted after the 2004 election spelt out the complexity of post-apartheid politics. The majority of white respondents scored apartheid almost equally with the post-1994 democratic system when asked to identify the 'best form of governing the country'. Black respondents unequivocally selected apartheid as the worst and democracy as the best form of governance. They also believed that governance would improve even more over the next decade, while whites mostly thought it would remain at the same level of efficiency as in 2004 or under apartheid.

Among white respondents, 21 per cent were not sure if they supported a return to apartheid (along with 10 per cent of black respondents), while 19 per cent approved or strongly approved of the idea, as did a surprisingly high 18 per cent of blacks. The majority of white participants (66 per cent) said their lives were the same or worse than during apartheid, while the majority of black participants (65 per cent) felt the opposite was true about their lives. Despite improvement in the socio-economic status of whites since 1994, the majority felt that their situation had deteriorated in the year preceding the survey. A staggering 44 per cent said their living conditions were the same as those of other South Africans, while only 32 per cent could bring themselves to acknowledge they were better off. The socio-economic indicators in the study showed that about 80 per cent of white respondents had never experienced hardships such as not having food to eat or being able to afford basic amenities, as opposed to 50 per cent of black respondents. These were the contradictory experiences and attitudes that political parties were trying to translate into votes.

The NP's catastrophic performance in 2004 forced its leaders to take whatever the ANC was willing to offer. Lekota told the NP caucus that cooperation would not extend any special privileges to NP members. Furthermore, they would have to become registered ANC members and work their way up through party structures. After this, Van Schalkwyk finally abandoned any pretence at representing Afrikaner interests: 'There are people who expect us to be a pressure group for Afrikaners [in the ANC] … We are not a torch-bearer for Afrikaner minority interests.'

The South African Communist Party, an ANC alliance partner, remained unconvinced that the NP was not a Trojan Horse that would try to insinuate right-wing ideas into the ANC and undermine policies on the poor.

The ANC was willing to offer one senior window-dressing post – its gesture of 'reconciliation' – which went to Van Schalkwyk. In return, he ceded the post of Western Cape premier in April 2004 to the ANC's Ebrahim Rasool. All that remained of the NP caucus in the national assembly was Van Schalkwyk's inner circle, bar Stan Simmons.

Four more tortuous months were to pass before the ANC finally swallowed the last shreds of its decimated former foe. Meanwhile, the NP went far 'beyond hoisting the white flag', adopting the ANC's Freedom Charter in the middle of 2004 in a 'shamelessly public display of a bare-faced, last-ditch attempt at securing the political careers of individual politicians'.[83]

On 8 August 2004, ninety years and seven months after the party was founded by JBM Hertzog, Van Schalkwyk announced the steps that would be taken to bury what remained of the longest ruling party in South Africa's history. NP representatives at all government levels would be 'encouraged' to take up ANC membership. They would then cross the floor during the next window period. Van Schalkwyk lost his poise and blushed when reporters asked when he himself would join the ANC, then admitted this would happen within weeks.[84]

In the Western Cape local government elections, NP members stood for the ANC in white-dominated wards, but mostly failed to get in. 'The ANC thought it could grow its majority this way, and then it didn't happen,' says Simmons. But Van Schalkwyk had his cabinet post – as minister of environmental affairs and tourism.

The final decision to disband was taken at a federal congress meeting on 9 and 10 April 2005, attended by a paltry eighty-eight delegates – a far cry indeed from the approximately 2 000 at congresses in the past.[85] Two people voted against the proposal and three abstained. Johan Rademeyer, from the Northern Cape, was one of the two 'nay' voters. He told Beeld's Liezel de Lange[86] that the party leadership had failed supporters yet again, leading them to think that cooperation with the ANC would remain just that – cooperation. 'Our people believed us. I defended the party to the last; I am a disgrace in my community.' FW de Klerk, who had supported cooperation with the ANC, renounced Van Schalkwyk's latest move and resigned from the party. By unceremoniously bowing out, the NP had left a void and weakened the opposition, he said. The DA noted that about 257 000 people had still voted for the NP in 2004.[87]

But realising that the chances of individual survival had dwindled to 'now or never', the leadership remnants had become utterly divorced from their handful of supporters. Without an identity, the writing was on the wall. As Dan O'Meara put it: 'The NP long ago gave up being an ethnic party. It could never translate itself into a purely class party. Throughout the 1990s it tried to be both an ethnic and class party and fell between two stools. No longer the master of the politics of racial identity, it was unable to find an identity post-1994.[88]

Its voluntary dissolution into the ANC was an appropriate ending to almost three decades of manoeuvres to find the ideal black partner. While the NP had succeeded in entrenching white privilege, its fantasies about holding onto political power had evaporated. Instead of the black partner fitting in with its plans, the NP was forced to disappear into the ANC. African nationalism absorbed Afrikaner nationalism.

In broad society, the NP's demise barely caused a stir. Some South Africans were engrossed in the latest set of nationalist elites fighting for domination in the ruling party, but most were simply battling to stay afloat in the morass of iniquity that the National Party had bequeathed them.

CHAPTER 8

The globalisation of the Afrikaner

*Finding a real Panama [hat] in South Africa has always been a huge
struggle. There is nothing worse than imitation Panama – rather no hat
at all ... My next buy is going to be a classic Humphrey Bogart-style
fedora. I just can't decide between grey and black.*
　　　　　　　　　　　　– Dan Roodt, self-declared '*volk* leader', 2006[1]

*My past has ... disappeared. These words and sentences
　I inherited from somewhere,
but the language that I speak, died long ago.
One day, I forgot where I came from,
where my home is, my country is, or the sound of my name.*
　　　　　– From a song by Brixton Moord en Roof Orkes, 2006[2]

Our leaders never told us.
　　　　　– Historian Hermann Giliomee on
　　　　　the 'lament of the *verligtes*', 1999[3]

A S THE NATIONAL PARTY HAEMORRHAGED SUPPORT AFTER 1994,
its leaders sensed that white voters wanted to put as much distance between
themselves and the party of apartheid as possible.[4] Revelations at the Truth and
Reconciliation Commission reinforced this tendency.

Debates raged in the Afrikaans press about denial and deception, guilt
and forgiveness, and commentators identified a scapegoat mentality among
Afrikaners. The debates were ultimately about identity. The 'Afrikaner' had
been conceived in nationalism and gestated by apartheid, with the NP as the
midwife. The question was whether a new Afrikaner identity could be created
by reinterpreting history, or whether the Afrikaner should discard all and be
submerged in nation building under an ANC government.

An unprecedented level of soul-searching took place among Afrikaans-
speaking whites after 1994. It manifested in diverse modes of expression –
music, writing, sculpture, performance art. All the while, attempts continued by
some latter-day neo-Afrikaner nationalists to resuscitate the ethnic chauvinism
of yesteryear. But efforts to reawaken Afrikaner nationalism proved largely
fruitless. The end of apartheid – and with it, state-enforced racial identities –

unleashed an explosion of activity as Afrikaners sought to make sense of themselves and their changing environment.

From the 1950s onwards, as apartheid grew ever more ignominious in global eyes, Afrikaans-speakers became more defensive, withdrawing into isolation and parochialism. Insulation was a feature of Afrikaner nationalism. The unskilled, illiterate *plaasjapies* (country bumpkins) who flocked to the cities after the South African War of 1899 to 1902 met up with black people in similar circumstances. Cross-racial contact was inevitable, and it was this that awakened fear among the *dominees*, teachers, journalists, lawyers and traders that their 'market' of Afrikaans-speaking whites would be anglicised and subsumed by racial intermingling. From the 1930s on, this middle-class grouping self-consciously propounded an exclusive Afrikaner nationalist identity based on insularity.

While boosted by outside influences, the dynamics of Afrikaner nationalism promoted an inward-looking orientation characterised by powerful us-and-them themes. In the broader context, this was facilitated by South Africa's geographical isolation from global intellectual circuits. Closer to home, it reflected the Afrikaner nationalist self-conception of a minority group under threat of *swart oorstroming* and communist *gelykstelling*, the influence of Calvinist norms of authority and duty,[5] and the alienating effects of the ideology of racism during the colonial and apartheid eras. As the political vehicle for Afrikaner nationalism, the NP actively contributed to insulation, not least through efforts to control the flow of information, and thus the level of ignorance.

The *volksbeweging* led by the NP had its own media – Nasionale Pers, owner of several influential newspapers and magazines. In the 1960s, the NP banned some 16 000 works by authors ranging from Sartre to Voltaire, and efforts were made to have Ingrid Jonker's poem 'The child who was shot dead by soldiers at Nyanga' excised from her second book, *Rook en Oker*. HF Verwoerd vehemently opposed the introduction of television, which was not allowed until the mid-1970s, and then only because the NP was sure it could be controlled, as was especially evident under PW Botha. Party leaders had become unhappy with the Afrikaans media's pursuit of commercial interests, which led to the 'press war' between the Cape and Transvaal from the 1960s onwards.

But despite the NP's best efforts, growing affluence from the late 1950s exposed Afrikaners to different influences. Middle-class status came with individualism, which undermined Afrikaner nationalist collectivism, while the capitalist class became unwilling to place ethnic affinity ahead of profit, as the press war showed. The cohesion wrought by Afrikaner nationalism fractured as the realisation slowly set in that apartheid – its primary mantra – was unworkable, both economically and in practice, quite apart from being morally reprehensible. The tumult that followed the 1976 student uprising accelerated the fragmentation, as white South Africans were confronted with the fragility of their elevated position.

During the 1980s, whites developed a siege mentality, in step with studies that show group cohesion increases in the face of competition and conflict with outsiders.[6] However, when failure looms, group cohesion breaks down and resentment increases, as happened when the white minority lost political domination in 1994.

The advent of democracy reconnected South Africa to the world. Strikingly, it also marked the start of the Afrikaner's globalisation. Apartheid allowed Afrikaners to attain far higher levels of education than before. After 1994, many became globally mobile, escaping the strictures of insulation that aided the growth of reactionary ideologies. By 2007, an estimated 500 000 white South Africans, including many Afrikaners, had emigrated, and through them relatives became connected to the global society. With this came anglicisation and exposure to global liberal values that were embraced by many, even if they continued to live in South Africa.

The global maxims of materialism and consumerism offered safety valves for frustrated Afrikaner ambition, and the 1990s and 2000s saw an explosion in expressive self-exploration. Were Afrikaners Africans, as Thabo Mbeki and various NP leaders declared? Or Euro-Africans? Or just plain settlers, with everything that implied? Or were they colonialists 'of a special kind' because they stayed, while those in many other countries returned to the lands from whence they or their ancestors originally hailed? At the bottom of these searing explorations of identity lay memory – which in itself was a contested terrain.

Many Afrikaners – both leaders and followers – pleaded ignorance. As the TRC process unfolded, 'we did not know about the violations perpetrated in our name' became a stock response. Was this protestation merely the result of denial induced by the loss of political hegemony? Or were the Afrikaners who had supported the National Party – in other words, the majority of them – deceived into doing so by their leaders?

While grappling with their disappointment in the NP, Afrikaners were also trying to get to grips with what it meant to live in a human rights–based democracy. Resentment, which seemed to be the overriding emotion, was captured by popular musician Karen Zoid in a satirical song called 'Danville Diva', released in 2003. The end of publicly sanctioned racism forced confrontation with hitherto hidden dimensions of Afrikanerhood, with Afrikaners not knowing 'what to do with the anger when you're not allowed to hate anyone any more'. Zoid described young Afrikaners' state of mind as depressed to the point of suicide due to the feeling of having lost 'everything'. They were confused about their identity, as democracy had brought an end to the ideological construction of Afrikaners as 'the chosen ones'. Reading anti-establishment authors such as Jeanne Goosen (who wrote the 1990 book *Ons Is Nie Almal So Nie* (We Are Not All Like That)) gave hope in the beginning years of the transition, but provided no antidote against the growing resentment, according to Zoid's description.

In their search for meaning, people could no longer cling to the past – it was contaminating everything that 'the Afrikaner' purportedly stood for. Tim du Plessis, editor of *Rapport*, articulated these fears as follows in 2006: '[Y]oung white Afrikaners ... are fed up with being demonised as nasty racists who have done nothing right, while consistently being reminded of their "shameful" history ...'[8] In 2007, an Afrikaans reader wrote to the *Mail & Guardian*: 'The perception among many Afrikaners is that they will never be forgiven; that their history is irrelevant; that they are condemned to be permanent whipping boys for all the nation's ills; that their skills and energies are not wanted and that they are interlopers in the land to which they have given their hearts, because they are whites and therefore cannot be true Africans.'[9]

Sociologist Melissa Steyn described the phenomenon as 'acute dislocation', causing Afrikaners to engage in 'profound existential work' to redefine 'us' and 'them', and to 'rehabilitate' and repackage Afrikanerness in ways that are compatible with the ideals of democratic South Africa.[10] As the 2000s progressed, the Afrikaner clamour for rehabilitation became more openly defiant. 'Ek sal nie langer jammer sê nie' (I won't say sorry any more) declared the title of a song by the band Klopjag (Raid), played incessantly in 2007 on Tuks FM, a radio station linked to the University of Pretoria. An attempt by the department of public service and administration to initiate an investigation of corruption by the apartheid administration was dismissed by *Beeld* in a sub-headline on the front page as a 'Nuwe soort WVK'[11] (New form of TRC). This was unusual in a newspaper that habitually restricted editorial comment to the leader page. But the main headline revealed the internal conflict behind the sub-heading: 'Ou skandes spook' (Haunted by old scandals).

Eventually, public expression and sentiment travelled to a time before apartheid, before the NP, to the very fountainhead of Afrikaner nationalist myth-making: the South African War. Pop singer Bok van Blerk gave expression to the *volk*'s confusion and nostalgia in his quadruple-platinum-selling song called 'De La Rey'. Its catchy chorus had even black talk show host Redi Direko of 702/Cape Talk Radio admitting that she and her colleagues hummed along to the tune, despite the Afrikaner-specific nature of the lyrics:

De La Rey, De La Rey
Sal jy die Boere kom lei [Will you come to lead the Boers]?
De La Rey, De La Rey

Generaal, Generaal
Soos een man sal ons om jou val [As one man we'll fall around you]
Generaal De La Rey

The song, which ended with the promise that 'the nation will rise up again', was embraced with a fervour – bought, sung and played wherever Afrikaners congregated – that made the entire country sit up and take note. The overwhelming response catapulted the issue of Afrikaner disquiet onto radio talk shows and into statements from the ministry of arts and culture. Was the spectre of Afrikaner nationalism re-emerging? Despite arts and culture minister Pallo Jordan's conviction that only 'a minority of right-wingers' were attempting to hijack 'De La Rey' as a 'struggle song', he still found it necessary to warn that 'taking up arms against a democratically elected government ... is a crime and a grave one at that'. Given the right to political freedom, 'it would be a terrible shame if a handful of misguided individuals hope to use an innocent song as a rallying point for treason'.[12] Jordan admonished fans to express their support within the ambit of the country's constitution and laws.

Jordan was correct in concluding that conservatives and far right-wingers were trying to capitalise on the nostalgia that some purveyors of culture were peddling. Tim du Plessis warned that 'De La Rey' was tapping into a rising discontent among young Afrikaners, but blamed elements in the ANC government who were 'hell-bent on taunting' Afrikaners by 'demonising' them and their history.[13] The trade union Solidarity (previously the Afrikaner nationalist whites-only Mine Workers' Union) opportunistically pointed out that 'something is brewing among the young people', and conducted focus group research among young Afrikaans 'leaders' (165 head prefects at Afrikaans schools).[14] The organisation hoped to pinpoint the 'ideas of the De La Rey generation', evidently to gauge the potential of a future constituency.

Solidarity's deputy chief executive Dirk Hermann claimed in *Rapport* that the youth were handling political transition better than their parents. For him, the proof lay in how they approached the raging debate about complicity with the apartheid system. He quoted one respondent as saying: 'We don't wrestle day in and day out with a guilt complex. We don't feel we have to confess all day long. I know my father, sir. He is not a criminal as the propaganda would have us believe. We know who and what we are.'[15]

The Freedom Front Plus joined Solidarity in gratefully seizing on the youthful malcontents in the hope of replenishing its stagnant support base. Leader Pieter Mulder – son of Connie, who was defeated by PW Botha in the NP *hoofleierskap* race of the late 1970s after being implicated in the Information Scandal – used the opportunity to define the 'De La Rey generation'.

According to Mulder, the typical member was excluded from opportunities due to affirmative action; 'he' was 'discriminated' against for being white and an Afrikaner; and 'his' history had been erased from the official version. Notably, the De La Rey generation believed it was 'the government and the authorities that were pushing them into the laager with their racist measures'.[16] Melissa Steyn's analysis seems apt: 'white talk undertakes ideological work to minimise damage to "white" privilege and maximise group advantage'[17] – and political advantage, in the case of Mulder and Solidarity.

Similarly, Dirk Hermann quoted one of his focus group respondents as saying: 'Us young people are not moving away from identity, we are seeking it. Bok van Blerk has given substance to that identity. When Bok sang that we are Boers, we ourselves realised that we are Boers. I have to admit, it's rather liberating to be someone.'[18] Such is the stuff of which nationalism is constructed.

Conservatives were appropriating the mass appeal of the song for their own political ends – it opened a door to mobilising the younger generation. Apart from Solidarity and the FF+ – relatively benign twenty-first-century *bittereinders* – Lets Pretorius, a member of the Boeremag who was on trial for plotting to overthrow the government, approached Van Blerk to sing 'De La Rey' during a protest march to the Union Buildings in Pretoria. Van Blerk refused, but the protestors nevertheless played a recording of his song.[19] Similarly ominous was the financial support to the singer by anonymous 'older fans who feel strongly about The Cause',[20] as a *Rapport* journalist put it in an interview with Van Blerk (real name Louis Pepler).

Nasionale Pers–owned *Rapport*, the largest Afrikaans newspaper in the country, had been repositioned as a mouthpiece for Afrikaner dissatisfaction about perceived exclusion and discrimination. In this role, the newspaper seemingly promoted Van Blerk as a 'leader', along with bestselling pop singer Steve Hofmeyr, who had reinvented himself as an activist, rallying Afrikaners around issues such as crime. *Rapport* also gave generous publicity to Solidarity's attempts to mobilise discontented Afrikaners, as with Hermann's article on 'young leaders'. Just as had happened under apartheid, some Afrikaans media were trying yet again to cultivate a consciousness predicated on the ideological construction of Afrikaner victimhood.

Along with other organisations, the media was also seeking to fill the leadership vacuum left by the NP's 'betrayal', and Van Blerk's hit song reflected these sentiments. Not only had former leaders been disgraced, they had also left their *volk* in the lurch. Not surprisingly, former law and order minister Adriaan Vlok's washing of apartheid victims' feet was met with scepticism and suspicion.

In August 2006, Vlok made an appointment with Frank Chikane, director-general in the presidency, and insisted on washing his feet as a gesture of contrition for security police attempts to poison Chikane in the 1980s, when he was head of the South African Council of Churches. Vlok went on to wash the feet of nine women in the Pretoria township of Mamelodi as an act of atonement for the deaths of the 'Mamelodi 10', orchestrated by Vlakplaas operative Joe Mamasela. Newspaper editorials pointed out that while Vlok had gone further than any other apartheid leader in humbling himself, the 'truth and reconciliation' contract between South Africans demanded full disclosure before amnesty from prosecution could be granted. Vlok duly undertook to comply with this demand, and within months Chikane was furnished with full details of his attempted assassination. However, Vlok continued to deny any knowledge of the Vlakplaas death squads or cross-border police raids.[21]

In February 2007, the National Prosecuting Authority indicated that it would charge three retired security police officers for the Chikane plot, thereby paving the way for prosecution of both Vlok and former police chief Johan van der Merwe. Instead of backing Vlok's belated penitence, the response from former NP supporters revealed a sense of having been personally wronged by their leaders. As one put it in a letter to *Beeld*:

> Why did he wait so long to do this, or has he only just woken up to the consequences of the NP cabinet's actions? While he's washing feet, what about the feet of the young policemen of all races who were maimed, the feet of the parents of those [policemen] who died and those [policemen] who gave their all in that conflict? These true South Africans were used as pawns in the dirty political game of the now dead NP cabinet. Go and wash the filth that clings to that cabinet from the feet of those innocent victims.[22]

Another letter-writer in *Beeld* acknowledged what Vlok's action meant for 'our fellow citizens', but wanted more:

> Like many of our national servicemen, Adriaan Vlok and Magnus Malan and PW Botha and many others knew only too well what injustices they were perpetrating against our fellow citizens. I am convinced that Vlok's quest for forgiveness is a noble and an honourable gesture, but it's one that needs to be displayed closer to home as well. The big guns in the old government, defence force and State Security Council ought perhaps to take note of the following people, who are also trying to wash their own feet: the thousands of conscripts who were abused daily as worthless scum, or worse, by hungover permanent force members ...[23]

Antjie Krog, author of *Country of My Skull*, commented on the significance of Vlok's deed:

Since the TRC started its work, there has been a need for a white man to respond adequately to the convincing reconciliation gestures of people like Mandela and Tutu. Because of them, every South African has in his or her head a picture of a powerful black man reaching out to whites on behalf of blacks ... [I]n a patriarchal society such as ours, a 'white prince of reconciliation' was needed ... In his way, Vlok did what De Klerk could not ... He is the first once-powerful, guilty white male to make an act of contrition that had nothing to do with an amnesty application or a TRC submission ...[24]

White masculinity, as represented by the leader, the 'father of the *volk*', was assuming a hitherto unknown form: the repentant father. Vlok confirmed this when he addressed a Gauteng church congregation, using a traditional Afrikaans song's tribute to a 'real' man as illustration: 'If you have come here today to listen to the story of a strong man – with an eye that doesn't flinch, a look that can crack something, an arm that can strike a blow and a will as steady as a rock – then you will be disappointed.'[25] Many Afrikaners *were* disappointed. They would not be following Vlok on his newfound path of honesty, humility and responsibility any more than they would follow former NP leader Marthinus van Schalkwyk – dismissed as a 'weakling'[26] – into the ANC.

In stark contrast to the flurry of activity around 'De La Rey', Afrikaans civil society made no effort to mobilise the *volk* around Vlok's new and humble version of leadership. They were seeking what they had come to know during decades of NP rule, as the fantasy of 'De La Rey' showed: the resurrection of a leader with a steady gaze and an arm that could strike a blow – the militarised Afrikaner male who would show the way out of the confusion that was a democratising country. It seemed the disillusion expressed by journalist Chris Louw in *Boetman is die bliksem in*, his retrospective denouncement of military service in an open letter, was not shared by all Afrikaners. For many, the identity was too ingrained to imagine differently. Louis Esterhuizen captured this identity in his poem 'Patria' in 2000:

Father,
when I was still in your house
a little child and the world was big
and knuckled like a fist
I always believed that one day you would lead
the avenging commando
against our enemies.
And I, the page on horseback
at your side would bear the family standard

high: with blazing trumpets
proclaim your fame to all.
But now the world has become small
and crumpled, now the members
of our triumphant commando
have deserted.
The door to the house stands open, the weeds
run rampant and I
wander with bloodshot eyes
thirstily through the city bars
banners
cover my nakedness
thoughts of revenge
overwhelm
me.
You owe me a battle, Father.
A holy war.[27]

The poem shows how anger manifests in a militarist reflex, which becomes an end in itself. The underlying plea was seemingly: Where is The Father, where is The General to take back 'what is ours'? In the public debate about the 'De La Rey' phenomenon, commentators emphasised that the real General Koos de la Rey was a peacemaker, given his initial opposition to war against the British. However, far from selecting De la Rey as their ideal leader, Bok van Blerk's song-writer merely chose a name that rhymed with *lei* (lead). What was needed was a leader.

Where were the *verligtes* in all of this? The difference between the Afrikaans business elite's engagement with post-apartheid South Africa and that of civil society is perhaps best summed up by Sanlam chief executive Johan van Zyl's reaction to the media frenzy about Bok van Blerk and his perceived 'hidden agenda': 'I have never heard "De La Rey" and anyway, I come from an apolitical family.'[28] The *verligtes* did not have to excavate fallen heroes to achieve their goals.

Denial and/or deception?

Historically, the relationship between the NP leadership and supporters reflected that of the Afrikaner family patriarch and offspring. The oft-repeated notion that children 'should be seen and not heard' was embraced in Afrikaner public life. BJ Vorster exhorted the *volk* to trust their leaders to know what was best for them. *Verligte* opinion-maker Willem de Klerk saw it as a conformist group discipline dictating that you 'kept your trap shut' when the leaders-with-a-capital-L gave instructions.[29] NP policy-making was top-down and characterised by fanciful theories, such as Verwoerd's grand apartheid and Botha's total strategy.

The NP's massive clampdown on alternative ideologies in the 1950s, combined with a propaganda campaign through its civil society extensions, silenced most opposition. Bram Fischer's statement from the dock fell on closed ears: '[W]hen the laws themselves become immoral, and require the citizen to take part in an organised system of oppression – if only by his silence and his apathy – then I believe a higher duty arises. This compels one to refuse such laws.' Not even his quoting of Paul Kruger in the statement – 'Freedom shall rise in Africa like the sun from the morning clouds'[30] – stirred opposition. Only in literary circles – Ingrid Jonker, Etienne Leroux, Breyten Breytenbach – was there some criticism of the system. Within party ranks, questioning of apartheid policy amounted to 'treason' up to the end of the 1970s, according to former finance minister Barend du Plessis.[31] Conformism was highly valued in the Afrikaner community, while dissent led to pariahdom and prosecution, as most infamously demonstrated by the cases of Breytenbach and Fischer, or public rejection and humiliation, as in Jonker's experience with her father, NP MP Abraham Jonker.

For at least three decades, the vast majority of NP supporters never challenged their leaders over policy. They supported apartheid – or separate development, as it was renamed in a transparent bid to stem international condemnation. This adherence involved a convoluted interaction between denial and justification, as described by popular Afrikaans fiction writer WA de Klerk[32] in 1979.

According to him, most Afrikaners historically believed that the NP government needed 'to impose its will, by violent means if necessary. The ideal, after all, is the health, wealth and happiness of all. Some may have to suffer in the process, but as the ideal is slowly realised and the vision becomes incarnate, the harshness will disappear.' Over the course of time, some Afrikaners became aware of the 'bizarre', 'cold-hearted' and 'cruel' outcomes of attempts to separate the races, particularly the forced removals from District Six and the story of Sandra Laing, a child rejected by her community and even her 'white' parents because she looked 'coloured'. Such results 'had never properly been allowed for in the radical dream of the builders of the new society'. Nonetheless, De Klerk said, '[e]ven when the signs were there for all to see, a great many still believed that all the hardships, all the inhumanities were but temporary discomforts; that once the new society had been properly realised all would be well, even for those who had borne the brunt of the restructuring of the human polity'.

But an apparently unforeseen factor reared its head: an increasingly authoritarian NP. Quoting Calvin's *Institutes*, WA de Klerk resorted to Christian parlance to criticise the government for exercising absolute power over people's lives, while pretending that it possessed 'all knowledge of good and evil' and a 'final answer to man's earthly happiness'. He ended his essay with a plea for Afrikaners to return to the 'basic moral minimum of equity, reason and charity'. Only when Afrikaners returned to the 'Christian precept of humility' would they experience 'true renewal'.

Willem de Klerk made similar appeals, asking Afrikaners to step away from their arrogance, self-exoneration and the mentality of *alleenreg* (monopoly). In an argument similar to WA de Klerk's, he explained that the 1976 uprising had 'destroyed the dream that blacks would tolerate the apartheid policy – it would allegedly just be a question of time before they become converted as they taste the fruits of Utopia'.[33]

It strikes the observer as improbable that supporters of apartheid never realised that all those suffering 'the brunt of the restructuring of the human polity' were black, while all the beneficiaries were white, or that they could truly believe that black people were on their way to tasting the 'fruits of Utopia'. Afrikaners such as Beyers Naudé and Bram Fischer did not think that apartheid promised Utopia to black people. A collective and widely sanctioned denial existed among white people, the functionality of which was obvious. While partly reaffirming the denialist stance, WA de Klerk's essay was an example of moral doubt about the true implications of apartheid emerging among the Afrikaner intelligentsia and middle classes.

In certain quarters, Afrikaner nationalist fervour and wilful ignorance gradually made way for confrontation with the realities of apartheid social engineering. The 1970s marked the beginning of a heightened sensitivity about the human cost of the system, as demonstrated in Afrikaans literature of the time, such as Elsa Joubert's *Die Swerfjare van Poppie Nongena*. The pro-NP media became concerned that the daily 'small' humiliations suffered by black people were sowing the seeds of resistance against apartheid. Influential philosopher Johan Degenaar of Stellenbosch University was gaining support for the idea of a 'morally critical Afrikaner' who wanted to be part of a new nation, free from classifications of race and colour.[34] WA de Klerk's attack on the government showed a shift in the previously blind support afforded Afrikaner leaders. The change was further influenced by the Information Scandal, which forced Afrikaners to face the fact that their leaders could be dishonest and corrupt.

Realisation that the 'blind support of leaders can be a deadly danger'[35] began to dawn in the wake of the white miners' strike in the late 1970s, when the NP displayed its new class colours by supporting management against the workers. With the formation of the Conservative Party in 1982, blue-collar workers abandoned the party of their parents. By 1984, Willem de Klerk was arguing that the relationship between leader and follower was changing.

The changing mood demanded responses. From the *verligte* side of the NP,

Pik Botha warned BJ Vorster about the international ramifications of Jimmy Kruger's dismissive comment at a party congress in 1977 about Steve Biko's death in detention. An NP pamphlet released in 1982 or 1983 to promote the tricameral parliament stressed that not only was the plan 'Safe!' and 'Logical!' but also 'Just!' in an effort to address growing concern about the morality of apartheid. This gradual awakening might have been instrumental in the Botha securocrats opting to cloak excessive acts of state repression in secrecy, thus sidestepping to some extent even the limited accountability to white voters. State actions increased in severity and went underground by the early 1980s, when the Vlakplaas police unit was first used for illegal operations.

Instead of the promised Utopia for 'everybody' that Afrikaners apparently believed in, the 1983 constitution dictated the concentration of power in the state president's hands. At the time, Frederik van Zyl Slabbert, leader of the official opposition Progressive Federal Party, warned parliament that the constitution in fact represented the opposite of power-sharing, as suggested by the NP, since it 'compounded, nourished and entrenched' the government's power, moving the country towards dictatorial rule.[36] By the mid-1980s, gags on the relatively mildly critical media under the state of emergency confirmed that South Africa had entered an era of shadowy and sinister activity.

The distraction of the far right wing

Apart from the class fracture in 1982 when Andries Treurnicht broke away from the NP, the questioning of leadership had not yet translated into a breach of the laager. The business elite and upper middle class stayed the course with the party as Afrikaners became embroiled in an internal class conflict, though it was not presented as such. The NP equated the far-right-wing threat with halting or even reversing 'progress', which was understood in capitalist terms. The party and its allies spent an inordinate amount of energy undercutting the CP and other groupings, to the exclusion of serious public engagement about the full spectrum of consequences of enforced minority domination. The rhetoric of the time showed a preoccupation with the possibility of losing votes to the right, which was also reflected in the propaganda war waged by NP-aligned newspapers against the Herstigte Nasionale Party, the CP and its leader.

Cartoons in Afrikaans newspapers showed HNP leader Jaap Marais wearing dark glasses, to emphasise his lack of vision. The HNP increased its share of the vote in NP constituencies from 8 per cent in 1977 to 29 per cent in 1981, but still could not manage to win a parliamentary seat. The NP nevertheless launched counter-attacks, for example proclaiming its commitment to separate states and group areas in a 1981 pamphlet.[37] In the same tract, the NP denied HNP charges that 'everything is being done for the blackman [*sic*] with whiteman's [*sic*] money'; that the government was 'selling out the White'; that it was preparing to integrate schools and residential areas; and that it was 'pumping money' into African states and thereby cultivating terrorists in its search for allies on the rest of the continent. On the contrary, the pamphlet boasted, 317 000 people ('about 51 000 families') had been forcibly removed from 'wrongly situated areas and Black spots', and the government had ended the earlier *deurmekaarwonery*' (ill-assorted living) by proclaiming 761 862 hectares as white areas, 92 294 hectares as Indian areas, and 45 001 hectares as coloured areas between 1950 and 1979 (note the racial disparities in these land allocations).

Treurnicht was depicted in newspaper cartoons as a tortoise – a reference to the Skilpadsaal in Pretoria where the CP had been founded, but also to emphasise his retrogressiveness. Five years after its formation, the CP became the official opposition, but with only 26 per cent of the white vote, against the NP's 52 per cent. In 1989, the CP pushed its share up to 31 per cent, with the NP, at 48 per cent, dipping below the halfway mark for the first time since 1958. But electoral support for the far-right-wing agenda stagnated at around 30 per cent, as was confirmed in the 1992 referendum.

NP negotiator and former deputy minister of law and order Leon Wessels concedes that efforts to combat the CP in the 1980s were disproportionate,[38] while Barend du Plessis says that the NP expended so much energy on the 'right-wing threat that it could not tackle the political problems of the time'. In retrospect, the aspirations of black people were not given enough priority, he says.

Given the injustice unfolding in black areas, the attention devoted to the far right was indeed excessive. This was partly because white politics was regarded as more important than black politics. Black people's lives were not of much concern to the vast majority of white South Africans in their 'white South Africa'. But Treurnicht, Marais and the AWB's Eugene Terre'Blanche also offered a distraction from the real political challenge. The far right, donning the mantle of a neo-Verwoerdian nationalism, charged the NP with 'betraying' the Afrikaner, and the NP went all out to disprove this.

Another effect of the NP's fixation on the CP and continuing efforts to woo far-right-wing voters was the counteracting of the few liberalising tendencies within the party. To stem the mostly imagined haemorrhage of white votes to the right, a heady concoction of colonial and Cold War discourses was continually stirred up in NP rhetoric during the 1980s. Supporters dutifully swallowed in a demonstration of their agreement with the NP's version of the world.

How *verlig* were the *verligtes*?

In the 1980s, an opinion-maker like Willem de Klerk was writing about and hoping for a more critical Afrikaner (within limits, of course). Those questioning

NP leadership and policies were concentrated among the far right wing outside the party and the *verligte* insiders. The latter were pushing away the historical Afrikaner nationalist class base to steer the party in a direction that served their own class interests more directly. The *verligtes* gathered in a few hallowed forums and included academics, journalists, members of the business community and politicians. The far right was predominantly to be found in the ranks of the CP, AWB and HNP. The right-wing bogeyman came in handy as a powerful force to unite white 'moderates' – including English-speakers – behind the NP. Exactly how moderate they were becomes clear when one casts a discerning eye over the writings of the ostensibly enlightened wing of the NP at the time. For all their talk, not even the *verligtes* could envisage more than a revised form of apartheid.

As late as 1984, Willem de Klerk, primary proponent of the *verligte* position, was unable to let go of certain apartheid precepts. These included the accommodation of a black franchise in a confederation that would have included the Bantustans, and principles such as 'differentiation', 'separation' and 'spatial ordering'[39] (another name for the Bantustan policy). The title of his book, *Die Tweede (R)evolusie*, showed that he was on the same page as business leaders who were declaring at the time that (unsurprisingly) they supported evolution rather than revolution. He questioned the NP emphasis on ethnicity, but declared in the same breath, with reference to other African states, that 'the African style' of black solidarity lasted only to the point of political victory, after which it was replaced by the domination of one group over another.[40] De Klerk's 'new politics of compromise' involved the retention of ethnicity as a political category and territorial division with 'group' autonomy over 'own affairs'.[41] He dubbed these recycled apartheid ideas the Afrikaners' 'second (r)evolution', the first being the 'radical restructuring' wrought through apartheid.

In other words, Willem de Klerk was in step with none other than PW Botha himself, despite the personal animosity between the two. The most noticeable difference between Willem de Klerk's 1984 position and that of Botha in the mid-1980s was that De Klerk argued that a new political settlement should be acceptable to black people, rather than being imposed upon them, as had historically been the case. The NP would move to this position only at the end of the 1980s.

Former deputy minister of justice Sheila Camerer confirms that the *verligtes* could not think beyond the concept of groups.[42] She was one of a paltry six female members in the 166-seat parliament by the late 1980s, of which four of the six were NP. She was also one of the 'Parktown Nats', a group of *verligte* English-speaking NP members who regarded Willem de Klerk as their 'elder statesman'. She believed, as did most *verligtes*, that the NP's seemingly unassailable hold on political power meant a change in the system could be initiated only from within the party. Botha's open invitation to English-speakers and English-speaking business to participate in reforms opened the door to such change, she believed.

However, she could not bring herself to serve in a party with the likes of Treurnicht, and thus did not stand as an NP candidate until after the 1982 split, when she won a predominantly English-speaking Johannesburg constituency. Camerer believed that the 1983 constitution should have accommodated black political aspirations in a fourth chamber of parliament, alongside those of whites, coloureds and Indians.

Denis Worrall, the most prominent English-speaking NP politician during the late 1970s and early 1980s, was a *verligte* who headed the commission that recommended creation of the tricameral parliament. Yet again, this confirms that the *verligtes* were stuck in the rut of groupthink, aimed at protecting the white minority against *swart oorstroming*. Former health minister Rina Venter explains it as 'the unthinkability of *not* fearing a black majority'[43] in power.

Former deputy minister of justice Tertius Delport points out that Afrikaners who were opposed to apartheid, such as Beyers Naudé, were not regarded as *verligtes*. 'Within Afrikaner ranks, the *verligte–verkrampte* division was not about being against or for apartheid. It was about variations within a broad spectrum [of thinking about apartheid]. *Verlig* was about a softer approach, maybe open sport, open access to facilities, but not one man, one vote – it was not about totally doing away with apartheid within the constitutional framework. The group within the NP that believed [apartheid should be done away with] was very small.'[44]

Nevertheless, while the *verligtes* remained trapped in racial and racist thinking, their advent opened some room within the NP for the exploration of policy alternatives. From the 1970s, their numbers grew to the extent that they could challenge the ideological calcification in the party, says *verligte* Barend du Plessis. The *verligtes* became willing to acknowledge that the 'Afrikaner ideal of liberation clashed with black people's ideal of liberation and that it had become politically, socially and economically unsustainable, while the *verkramptes* saw it as a struggle unto death', explains former minister of constitutional development Roelf Meyer.

The *verligtes* became increasingly aware of the injustices and absurdities of apartheid, as described by both WA and Willem de Klerk. More significantly, they were deeply conscious that apartheid had become economically unsustainable, says Du Plessis. The differences between the *verligtes* and *verkramptes* 'culminated' in their disagreements about the economic viability of apartheid, says Meyer.[45] The rise of the *verligtes* paralleled the rise of the Afrikaner middle class and reflected the changing class base of the NP. Du Plessis quotes Nic

Diederichs, first appointed to the cabinet by Verwoerd and who was pivotal in the development of apartheid policies, as saying that, if needs be, 'we will bend the economy until it makes apartheid work'.

For the generation of NP leaders who entered politics in the 1970s and 1980s – Pik Botha, Du Plessis, Wessels, Meyer, Camerer – the opposite held true. Delport traces the disagreement on economic policy back to the 'Verwoerd versus Anton Rupert' approach within NP ranks. Rupert maintained that the Bantustans could not develop without a 'partnership' with white business. Verwoerd insisted that this would amount to a form of 'economic colonialism', says Delport, and that the black states should be totally independent of white capital. These fault lines ran through the Afrikaner nationalist ruling establishment even after the rupture in 1982.

For the *verligtes*, the differences in principle between the NP and the CP hinged on three issues, all of which were about the economy. According to Willem de Klerk, the first was race, including the workplace, which the CP insisted should remain strictly segregated, with white job reservation. The second was capital. The CP sought disengagement between Afrikaner capital on the one hand and English-speaking and international capital on the other, as these *geldmagte* (financial forces) undermined apartheid. The third was disengagement from the outside world. CP foolhardiness held that the apartheid state did not need to pay international sanctions any heed, as it would survive them.[46] These positions were perceived by the *verligtes* to fly in the face of their concerns about the lack of skilled labour as a result of apartheid rigidities, the crisis of accumulation exacerbated by the lack of access to other markets and the economic stagnation government policy had necessarily created in its bid to deal with the debt crisis in the 1980s.

By the latter years of that decade, several factors had infused the *verligtes* with a sense of urgency, a desire for 'drastic change', says Barend du Plessis: the cost of security involved in maintaining white domination in its old-style apartheid or Botha-esque form; disinvestment and the inability to access international credit; and the realisation that South Africa's worst ever recession would not end while the political dispensation remained unchanged. The battle with Treurnicht *et al.* was about how to retain state power while adjusting to the changed class interests of a significant segment of the NP leadership and support base.

Delport estimates that at the beginning of the 1980s, at least 80 per cent of white voters supported some form of apartheid, either as *verkrampte* Verwoerdians or from the *verligte* power-sharing camp. When the CP broke away, the majority of white voters stuck with the NP. Shared class interests ensured a peculiar consensus about relations between whites and the rest of the population, as well as with the international community. This was the basis for adherence to the NP dictum that the leaders were not to be challenged.

Docility or agreement?

Docility persisted, both between leaders and followers and within NP structures. Critics frequently accused Afrikaners of 'herd-like behaviour', an insult that acted as an excuse. The docility reflected agreement with the NP policies of the day. The NP's vast organisational machinery made provision for a high degree of accountability by parliamentarians to their constituents. Every MP was subject to the rigours of the constituency system – a system associated with a high degree of direct accountability to voters, as election to parliament is based on service delivery to a particular group or area. At its height, the NP had more than a thousand branches – between fifteen and twenty per parliamentary ward – across the country. NP branch executives determined the composition of management committees (*afdelingsbesture*) in the Transvaal and district councils (*distriksrade*) in the Cape, which nominated candidates for national election. Prospective parliamentarians had to first win the support of the majority of branches in a constituency in order to be endorsed by the *afdelingsbestuur*. The latter had the power to make or break an NP politician's career. The chairperson, in particular, determined the continuation of the incumbent's career in parliament.

At least once a year, members of parliament had to report back to their constituency, and they would also arrange for cabinet ministers to address their voters. The branches were a crucial rung on the party leadership ladder. They had the power to nominate more progressive candidates for public office, but they did not. The concurrence between what their public representatives stood for and what NP members and supporters believed in translated into a lack of critical inquiry, which, in turn, allowed avoidance of responsibility. Voters left the details to the politicians, and the NP caucus left decisions to the executive arm of government. The flow of information was also controlled in a way that entrenched the leaders. They would inform the caucus of policy decisions after the fact, and caucus members informed branches on a feedback basis. There was no discussion or consultation with branches before caucus decisions were taken.[47]

Beyond the parliamentarian–voter relationship, accountability was dissipated. Political parties are typically hierarchical in structure, and the NP was no different. Its configuration was federal, which meant that the four provincial arms of the party functioned as autonomous 'mini-parties'. This allowed the largest of the four, the Cape and the Transvaal, to be the king-making centres of power.

The provincial structure made the NP as a whole more hierarchical. Protocol dictated that an MP from the Transvaal, for example, could not broach a matter of national importance with the *hoofleier* directly, but had to consult with the

Transvaal leader. Branch delegates attended the annual provincial congresses, where cabinet ministers would respond to *besprekingspunte* (points of discussion) that had been submitted in advance, as well as to follow-up questions. However, despite the appearance of democracy in action, the format made it nigh impossible to effect policy change through the congresses.[48] Delegates aired grievances, ministers trotted out the party position and, for the most part, that was where it ended.

However, the four annual congresses did offer opportunities for personal contact between party leaders and members, since ministers could always be waylaid in the corridors. From the 1960s onwards, the predominance of ministers reflected the shift away from the party structures to the bureaucratic state as power base, which further diluted accountability. After 1994 the party structure was changed to correspond with the nine new provinces. The federal council was the party's highest national body outside of the federal congresses. Congresses continued to be managed in a top-down fashion, with party leaders deciding beforehand who would speak and on what topic, as well as assigning delegates to propose motions. By the early 1990s, branches were highly efficient administrative structures, but remained politically impotent.[49]

Ignorance lubricated the ideological project. After Jimmy Kruger's comment on Biko's death, groups of delegates at the NP congress were abuzz with the question: 'Who is Steve Biko?'[50] They had not heard of him. Throughout the 1980s, it remained a feature of NP gatherings that politically active whites did not exercise an ability to introduce critical and open debate.[51] Former Transvaal NP leader Barend du Plessis says that internal debate was in an 'ideological stranglehold'. The pervasive atmosphere of concurrence at congresses reflected the confluence in thinking between NP leaders and the rank and file. The format of the congresses may also explain why the party's top leadership did not discuss the decision to open the NP to all races with management structures in the early 1990s, but went straight to the congresses with what was effectively a *fait accompli*. The very structure of the congresses was such that compliance was far more of a certainty than might have been the case if the issue was first put to the caucus or the provincial structures.

Leon Wessels sums up the ubiquitous relationship between leader and follower as: 'People tend to let themselves be led.' At the same time, 'people tell leaders what they think they want to hear'. The unquestioning stance towards the NP leadership, and especially the *hoofleier*, became worse during PW Botha's tenure. Former members of the executive reported that the tone in cabinet was such that ministers dared not ask questions, as Botha did not tolerate opposition. Only under FW de Klerk did the atmosphere change to accommodate debate.

PW Botha: NP denialism at its peak

Final decision-making power in the NP was vested in the *hoofleier*, elected by the caucus. He (and it was always a he) was the final arbiter over how policy would be interpreted. The *hoofleier* enforced party discipline and was untouchable. This is why FW de Klerk was able to ensure the ultimate success of constitutional negotiations, despite the *verkrampte* onslaught within leadership ranks. It is also why, once he had decided to quit the GNU, the move went ahead, despite substantial resistance. Ultimately, *hoofleier* status allowed Marthinus van Schalkwyk to push through the alliance with the DP; the withdrawal from that alliance; cooperation with the ANC; and even the demise of the NP. The *hoofleier* called the shots.

The position was further bolstered by the *hoofleier's* ascendance to the most powerful office in the country, which had become even more commanding under the technocrat PW Botha. Like HF Verwoerd before him, PW exhibited a high degree of contempt for those who differed from him and for notions of governmental accountability. He personified the NP denialism of the time, reinforced as it was by sophistry and superciliousness. This was abundantly clear from his official interpretations of the reasons for the countrywide uprisings and the appropriate responses.

By 1984, Pretoria faced a rising tide of discontent born of and exacerbated by desperate socio-economic conditions that had been generated by a system in which the colour of your skin dictated an existence of toil and frustrated potential. Addressing parliament in January 1985, then national (white) education minister FW de Klerk explained the NP's reading of the situation as follows: 'The whites call for the effective protection of their lawfully obtained freedom, the assurance of the preservation of their established rights, the assurance that they will be able to preserve their lifestyle and their values ... The black people and the black communities make the demand for full democratic rights. For the sake of South Africa, these demands must be reconciled with each other ... Everyone knows the time has come to start writing the next chapter ... If fruitful progress does not come now, we are playing into the hands of the radicals inside and outside South Africa.'[52] His assessment acknowledged that the uprisings were about denying black people the franchise, yet he continued to denounce pro-democracy activists as 'radicals'. It was a reflection of the NP's conviction that Pretoria would be the sole determinant of which demands were legitimate, and which were not.

A few months later, PW Botha further demarcated black people's room to manoeuvre, adding a twist of cynicism. He assured parliament of his commitment to 'a programme of reform to broaden democracy and improve the living conditions of all South Africans regardless of race, colour or creed' (note the

Beaufrean inclusion of the welfare dimension). Then, in a perverse refusal of reality, Botha said: 'We have some very fine traditions in this country which virtually no other country in Africa has. One is that all people, regardless of race, colour or creed, are free to hold, pursue and promote their political views without interference from government. The only condition is that the pursuit of political objectives be done in a peaceful and civilised way. The maintenance of law, order and stability is crucial to the attainment of these objectives.'[53]

In other words, black people were free to express their political persuasions, as long as they did so on the government's terms. In NP parlance, they had to be 'responsible South Africans' who rejected 'revolutionary activities and outside interference' while cooperating with and accepting Botha's commitment – 'gallantly' made on their behalf – 'to a process of positive reform'.[54]

In the same address, Botha denied the popular nature of the nationwide uprising, preferring to pin it on 'people of ill will [who] instigate demonstrations and marches which result in arson, violence and death'. In an apparent reference to religious leaders such as Beyers Naudé and Allan Boesak, he disparaged 'certain people [who] under the guise of morality and religious conviction ... take the lead in fomenting disobedience, violence and destruction'. Revealing the paranoid undertone of his understanding, Botha imagined that such people sought 'South Africa's destruction'; they wanted to bring 'South Africa to its knees'; they wanted 'chaos to reign'. He depicted these aims as part of the Soviet plan for world domination: 'they have embarked upon this course at the behest of foreign powers'. And, lest there be any doubt which side he was on, he threw in some Cold War 'good versus evil' rhetoric, typecasting his opponents as 'diabolical' before defiantly vowing: 'I want to state clearly and categorically here today that they will not succeed ... I am committed to maintaining law and order and stability in our country. I have already given instructions for appropriate steps to be taken to restore and maintain law and order.'

What it took 'not to know': The NP caucus

Botha's speech was made on 21 March 1985, six days after the police had killed nineteen protestors and wounded another thirty-five at Langa, outside Uitenhage. The immediate response – and lack of it – in parliament offered an illuminating insight into the apartheid process of silencing and denial. The Langa massacre was one of many instances in which the versions of eye-witnesses and victims differed markedly from those tendered by the police and NP politicians. Helen Suzman, long the sole voice of liberalism in parliament, pointed out this discrepancy in many addresses, as did the Black Sash, an organisation of concerned white, middle-class, English-speaking women. Botha, followed by the rest of the NP parliamentarians, refrained from expounding on the Langa shootings, ostensibly because appointment of a commission of inquiry precluded public discussion. Suzman, however, pointed out that the matter was not *sub judice*, and proceeded to inform the house what she and other MPs from the PFP had found on a fact-finding mission to the township.[55]

Despite interjections by both FW de Klerk and then justice minister Kobie Coetsee aimed at silencing her, Suzman forged ahead. She pointed out that notwithstanding police commissioner Johann Coetzee's assurance that the SAP would use live ammunition only as a last resort, there was 'no evidence of any crowd control methods being used'. The SAP had fired live rounds at unarmed people.

Affidavits collected by the Black Sash confirmed eyewitness accounts made to Suzman. Police officers had ordered a large crowd of funeral-goers out of the vehicles they were travelling in and, without provocation, opened fire indiscriminately. Afterwards, police officers placed stones at the scene that were photographed, according to one affidavit.[56] Langa and several other incidents led the Black Sash to conclude in a March 1985 memorandum on police conduct in the Eastern Cape that 'the abuse of power appears to be part of a strategy which is being used to crush opposition'.

Similarly, the South African Catholic Bishops Conference (SACBC) released a report on police conduct characterised by 'wanton violence' on the Witwatersrand from August to November 1984. The SACBC came to the conclusion that 'the police behaviour in the townships resembled that of an occupying foreign army controlling enemy territory by force without regard to the civilian population and, it appears, without regard to the law'.[57]

The Black Sash concluded that events created 'the overwhelming impression ... that the police are unaccountable' and operating with the government's tacit consent. 'This must be assumed unless there are strong indications from those in authority that such [brutality] is considered totally reprehensible through the taking of firm and visible action against those in the police force responsible for such behaviour. To date such action has been conspicuous [by] its absence.'[58] The Black Sash also pointed to a pattern of similar police action from Sebokeng to Crossroads.

Suzman came to similar conclusions, as she told parliament: 'It seems to me the police in South Africa have reached the point where their attitude is "we have stood enough from these blacks. Now let's show them once and for all who is boss." I for one have an uncomfortable feeling that this attitude is condoned from the top. There is [another] explanation and that is that the police have become a law unto themselves. We know that the reckless use of firepower occurred not only at Langa but also at Addo, Cradock, Kimberley, Kroonstad and Cookhouse – practically across the map of South Africa. The minister responsible ... for law and order in this country is the man, it seems to me, who is responsible for the breakdown of law and order.'[59]

Suzman and others voiced concern about excessive state force as far back as 1984 – long before many of the atrocities revealed at the TRC hearings had even been perpetrated. But she was paid no heed by her co-parliamentarians in the NP benches – the same people who would later allege that they 'did not know'. Strangely, *she* knew.

After Suzman made her points, the parliamentary session degenerated into an argument between NP and CP members over 'own affairs' issues. The lack of engagement from the NP benches was so stark that FJ le Roux (CP) remarked that 'the NP is not prepared to enter the fray with the member from Houghton [Suzman]', and then, in an intimidatory tactic, proceeded to implicate 'a white woman' in the instigation of stone-throwing in the Eastern Cape.[60]

This parliamentary interaction is one example of how elected NP representatives avoided dealing with the human cost of maintaining white domination. A line could be drawn to the subsequent white insistence that 'we did not know', repeated ad nauseam during the latter half of the 1990s, when the TRC hearings were taking place.

The subservience of the caucus was a feature of NP rule from the start. DF Malan made it clear that the role of the caucus was not to question the executive, but to advance the NP position in parliament vis-à-vis other parties. BJ Vorster reiterated this stance. During the 1980s, control of the caucus was reinforced by 'spies' who would report any subversive sounds to PW Botha. Rina Venter recalls how Botha bragged to the caucus about his handling of a meeting in his office with Anglican Archbishop Desmond Tutu. Tutu asked whether he had a toilet, to which Botha replied, 'Yes Tutu, even *I* use the toilet'. The almost all-male caucus burst out laughing. When Venter, not yet a cabinet member, commented to a colleague that Botha's behaviour was 'un-statesmanlike', she was warned that one of Botha's informants ('Oom Koot') would be relaying her insubordinate remark.[61] Apart from illustrating the atmosphere of bombast and hero worship in the caucus, this anecdote also exemplifies the clampdown on independent thinking.

Thus, when it was proposed that the NP caucus meet with Ciskei Bantustan leader Lennox Sebe, who by the mid-1980s had adopted positions unacceptable to the regime, the members declined. As representatives of *white* people, they were concerned only with 'white affairs'. In their world, a meeting with a black leader seemed irrelevant. Their counter-proposal was that some of the ministers should meet with Sebe and inform them afterwards about the outcome.

'Not knowing' was sometimes accompanied by much bluster, derived from the party leaders' position as controllers of state power. An example was the response of NP caucus members at a meeting with business leaders in January 1978, where the consequences of Biko's murder on South Africa's international standing were raised. Wessels summarises the attitude of NP members at the time as: 'We hear what you are saying, but we choose to ignore it. *We* will dictate the development of events. We will not allow others [to do so] – whether [they be] black activists, the business community, the international business community or the international diplomatic community.' There was 'an absolute unwillingness to understand what was going on in the country', he says. Former foreign affairs minister Pik Botha contends that the branches and the caucus 'held the party prisoner. The common denominator was usually the most conservative attitude, seeking security through the wrong means – through repressive laws – and not realising the true challenges that faced the country.'[62]

What it took 'not to know':
The executive and the security forces

In their 1986 report, the Commonwealth Eminent Persons Group noted that 'even the more enlightened ministers whom we met seemed out of touch with the mood in the black townships'.[63] When repression increased in the 1980s, NP politicians asked few questions. Leon Wessels was one of a handful who publicly searched his soul about events of the time. In a remarkably candid submission to the TRC, he said the following: 'I further do not believe that the political defence of "I did not know" is available to me, because in many respects I believe I did not *want* to know. In my own way I had my suspicions of things that had caused discomfort in official circles, but because I did not have the facts to substantiate my suspicions or I lacked the courage to shout from the rooftops, I have to confess that I only whispered in the corridors ... We simply did not, and I did not, confront the reports of injustices head-on. It may be blunt but I have to say it. Since the days of the Biko tragedy right up to the days of hostel atrocities in the late, late eighties, as we moved towards the record of understanding, the National Party did not have an inquisitive mindset. The National Party did not have an inquiring mind about these matters.'[64] He argues that 'an entanglement exists between what you know, what you don't know and what you want to know'.[65]

Wessels insists that former law and order minister Louis le Grange 'was indeed not informed about every raid, every knock on every door. The fact is, we created the atmosphere that we did not *want* to know. This had been the case for many years. I still think about my submission to the TRC almost ten years ago, and I still stick to what I said there: the explanation that we did not know is not acceptable. It doesn't go down. We did everything to keep ourselves from any information that reached us via non-official channels, or from putting our fingers into the wounds around us. We were also guilty when we were castigated by Helen Suzman and others who were saying that the security forces had become a law unto themselves. We said: you are talking rubbish, we are in control, we are the political heads, we created the policy framework, we supervise. You have to ask, did we supervise?'

Craig Williamson, a former member of Military Intelligence, testified to the TRC that members of the executive deliberately kept themselves at arm's length from knowledge about the violent and unlawful 'remedies' that formed part of 'the arsenal of combating counter-revolutionary onslaught'.[66] If they had wanted to know, they could have, as they were furnished with intelligence reports on a daily basis, according to Williamson. However, they never queried the methods outlined in the reports.

Following his act of contrition in 2006, Vlok made a qualified admission: 'As [former police chief] General Johan van der Merwe has often told me, maybe we also closed our eyes against the practices. You must remember, you are busy with a war. If you can get info from a guy and you can use that info to stop the explosion of a limpet mine, or a car bomb – if you can stop it, we said thank you, and that was wrong.'[67]

While security report-backs were accepted without question, most other sources were dismissed out of hand. In the mid-1980s, Wessels met activist Gugile Nkwinti, who would later become the speaker in the Eastern Cape legislature. He asked Wessels whether he knew what was taking place on the ground. Wessels replied that a minister would not know how every police officer behaved when arresting someone – 'it was impossible to know'. Shortly there-after, Nkwinti's movements were restricted and then he was detained. His circumstances were dire, leading Albert Wessels and Konrad Strauss of the Standard Bank to appeal directly to Wessels to intervene. He took the matter to Louis le Grange on an official basis. 'Minister le Grange called me in and said: "Leon, you have a very good image among the police. Do not spoil it with your appeals on behalf of these pink liberals." He accepted as alpha and omega what the police told him. The fact that the minister did not know was indeed possible, but it does not excuse us or him, because we had access to *Vrye Weekblad*, *Weekly Mail*, Helen Suzman's speeches – but we chose to dismiss them as alarmist, exaggerated and coming from people who did not have good intentions.' Vlok also said that, at first, he dismissed reports of police torture as propaganda.

The relationship between the politicians and the militarists added a layer of opacity to governance. Wessels argues that NP politicians hid behind the argument that PW Botha let himself be influenced by the securocrats. He agrees that Botha's close relationship with the military over many years had fostered a mutual trust between him and the generals. Even in his office, Botha surrounded himself with militarists. 'They sketched a picture of the world and the environment within which he had to operate. But I refuse to accept that his policies – the constellation of states, the relationship with the business community, his attitude towards hurtful apartheid measures – [were formed by the militarists]. Those [policies] were exclusively the domain of the politicians which [the militarists] did not enter.' According to Wessels, the political sphere still held sway over the military rather than the other way around. He 'never met an SADF general who believed the conflict could be resolved militarily. They said it time and again: we can help you to win time, to develop initiatives, but it cannot be won on military grounds.'

Wessels argues that Botha and his ministers took political policy decisions. The failure was on the side of the rest of the collective NP – leaders and followers – who offered no viable alternatives to military solutions. He remembers a significant moment when Botha acknowledged that the security option had not delivered the desired result.

A spate of prison hunger strikes in late 1988 could not be resolved, and Wessels was asked to investigate. He spoke to inmates at a prison in his constituency, Krugersdorp, and their version of why they were being detained differed substantially from the official one. He relayed this to Botha and Vlok. According to Wessels, Botha's response was: 'We embarked upon this [counter-revolutionary] campaign and we have resolved nothing.'

'He let himself be led by the necessity of introducing a state of emergency, the measures that he had promulgated. He acknowledged that it had failed and we – the NP collective, the corps of supporters – did not assist him with an alternative. That was not the security forces' problem. That failure is for our account. It must be for our account.'

Nevertheless, the security measures of the time constrained even politicians' movements. Wessels was detained together with a film crew for entering a township without permission from the police. Helen Suzman spoke about the difficulty of having to get a permit from the police before being able to enter Langa in March 1985. Wessels ran up against a brick wall when he tried to pursue reports of human rights violations. He took up the case of white men in balaclavas assaulting a grandmother and her grandchild in Kagiso on the West Rand. They were attacked while on their way to take a bus after the police had ordered people to stay off the streets. The matter was investigated, but then the case disappeared without trace.

Wessels went to Kagiso and Swanieville after the IFP attacked residents on 12 May 1991. 'I was at the scene where those people were murdered. If you look at those tragic events, it was a military operation.' He concluded that the security forces played a significant role in the incident. The officer who was supposed to patrol the area had left his post around 3 a.m. to seek treatment at a hospital for 'a stomach cramp'. In his absence, an impi moved from the hostel in an 'extremely ingenious' way and systematically mowed down residents of the township. Civilian sources in Kagiso informed Wessels that the perpetrators were strangers – 'even those sitting on the Casspirs were strangers'. This pointed to the violence being 'instigated'. 'By who, by what?' asked Wessels. He pursued the issue, but never got satisfactory answers from the police. His efforts to find answers stonewalled, he told then president FW de Klerk what he had found out. Nelson Mandela also spoke to De Klerk.

According to Wessels, there were 'all these conversations about a third force and people playing roles and we don't know who is giving them the mandate. All these things have not been unravelled. What did the minister know? PW's argument was that if I had suspected these things and I was in a position of authority, why did I not run with it? A position of authority meant that if you weren't in the executive, the one place you could speak was in the caucus. I spoke in the caucus, but I also spoke to him. If you're a member of the executive, you have your line function, but you also participate in cabinet meetings. [For example] foreign affairs did not have all the information, but I got the information. You spoke to the number one in the country [Botha] and, despite that, guys succeeded in scaling down and reducing your suspicions to nothing serious.'

Part of the problem was institutional. 'My experience in the State Security Council was that when a presentation had been made by a minister about his line function, or there was a briefing by the secretariat of the council and Mr Botha agreed with it, it was very difficult to go against that grain. The questions that were asked were frequently not answered very politely. You had to have very strong *other* information to change the course of events.' Moreover, 'within a line function of a department there are many grey areas for the interpretation of policy'. Wessels points out that decisions taken at the many different levels of bureaucracy would not necessarily have been known to the head of a particular structure. Even in democratic South Africa, misappropriation would only be discovered by the Auditor-General – when it was too late.

Rina Venter tells a tale that further beggars understanding. After she became an MP in the mid-1980s, a group of concerned Afrikaner women in the former Transvaal brought her into contact with a group of black women. She was surprised to discover that they were neither communists nor atheists. Rather, the leader of the group told her 'to dress like Sarah in the Bible' and to go tell 'their father' in the government – PW Botha – that 'his children' were suffering. Venter did not know what to do, given that NP protocol dictated that she would first have to approach FW de Klerk as provincial leader to get permission to speak to Botha. She told a cabinet minister of her dilemma and, soon afterwards, learnt that the leader of the women's group had been arrested under the laws allowing detention without trial. Venter spoke to another cabinet minister to find out what was going on. A while later she was called from the national assembly by a cabinet minister who admonished her for 'interfering in things that you don't understand'. The woman was released after being held for several weeks. Strikingly, this incident seemed to confirm a direct link between at least a small clique at cabinet level and police action aimed at individuals at local level.

But Wessels rejects suggestions 'that Louis le Grange as minister of law and order and a member of the State Security Council would allow Steve Biko to be transported naked in a bakkie from Port Elizabeth to Johannesburg. I refuse to believe that.' And, he says, there is not the slightest doubt in his mind 'that the State Security Council of which PW Botha was the chairman and on which Pik Botha served, Chris Heunis served, would never, never have given permission for a police general to make a false statement under oath in court to cover up a death that happened during torture ... Another example would be Eugene de Kock, braaing meat and drinking for hours next to a corpse that they had set on fire ... I deny that this ever would have enjoyed the sanction of any security council, whether under PW or FW. The core question is, how did this happen, and the only conclusion that I could come to is that we created a culture of "we do not want to know". It started in Vorster's time [when he said] trust the leaders ... from the minister to the commissioner or to the general, to the commander to the bottom. Here is your budget and here at the top we are making big statements ... we are not going to hand over to the terrorists. We will fight to the last man.'

Born of this culture was Connie Mulder's declaration during the Information Scandal, which later became an NP idiom: 'When the future of my *volk* is under threat, rules do not apply.' Wessels contends that 'all this rhetoric was absorbed. You have security people sitting in the State Security Council and they are listening to what the politicians are saying and they interpret their mandate. The question is, what does it mean to remove somebody from society? Does it mean you should limit his movements or shoot him dead ... what does it mean? And all these grey areas play themselves out between us.'

An example was the Khotso House bombing. Vlok did not have an SSC resolution instructing the police to blow up the building. 'What he brought was his interpretation of debates ... [It was being said that] there is an increasing infiltration of people who are guilty of violent crimes. They are given safe haven by church organisations in Khotso House. Can't you stop this thing? What are you doing to stop it?' There was an arsenal of security legislation available to arrest people, limit their movements, interrogate them and revoke passports, but Wessels argues that Vlok 'would have interpreted PW's irritation and anger as that he had to do something. He believed he was acting with a political mandate.' According to Vlok, Botha had instructed him to stay behind after a meeting of the cabinet or the SSC and issued an instruction that led to the Khotso House bombing.[68]

From the side of the ministers not responsible for security, Barend du Plessis blames the civil servants in the SSC's secretariat, as they controlled the information flow. 'Gruweldade' (atrocities) were never discussed at SSC meetings, he says. Action was taken after 1990 to make secret projects more transparent, and this was successful, to some extent, regarding the defence force, but not the police, according to Du Plessis. However, some SADF projects remained under wraps – it was the prerogative of the minister of defence and the generals to decide what needed to be known, and by whom. It was part of the NP culture not to question cabinet colleagues, but to accept their integrity, says Du Plessis.

What it took 'not to know': The NP's official explanation

The National Party government's submissions to the TRC claimed that it did, indeed, supervise the security forces. In August 1996,[69] De Klerk emphasised that he had appointed commissions while he was president and was 'acutely aware of the difficulty of establishing what exactly happened during past conflict'. Referring to Botha's reforms and his own scrapping of apartheid laws, De Klerk insisted that it would be incorrect to call his or Botha's administrations 'apartheid governments'. He saw reform as the period during which apartheid was dismantled while the government still had to defend South Africa 'against those who planned to seize power by violent and unconstitutional means'. His view of the NP post-1990 was that it had played a 'leading role' in helping to create the 'non-racial democracy' of 'the New South Africa'. De Klerk reiterated his apology on behalf of the NP for the 'pain and suffering caused by former policies'.

He argued before the TRC that the NP government had regarded the ANC as a communist, revolutionary organisation that had worked towards a violent insurrection since the 1960s. The ANC's relationship with the Soviet Union and the United Nations' support for its cause had led the NP government to 'believe ... that it was being confronted by a total onslaught'. Thus, the 'revolutionary strategies adopted by the government's opponents blurred traditional distinctions between combatants and non-combatants; between legitimate and illegitimate targets; and between acceptable and unacceptable methods ... Consequently, the then government began to make use of unconventional strategies which, of necessity, had to be planned and implemented on a "need to know" basis.' However, these strategies never included assassination, murder, torture, rape or assault, De Klerk stated categorically. Neither he nor any other members of the cabinet, the SSC or any committee 'authoris[ed] or instruct[ed] the commission of such gross violations of human rights', nor did they 'directly or indirectly ever suggest, order or authorise any such action'.

He did, however, indicate that the changes he had brought about had not been supported by 'some elements' in the security forces: 'My colleagues and I were accused along the grapevine of being "soft" and of being traitors. I suspect that many of the unauthorised actions that are now coming to light were at the time directed as much against the transformation process as against the revolutionary threat. It has now become clear that certain elements misused state funds and were involved in unauthorised operations leading to abuses and violation of human rights.'

In his second submission on behalf of the NP, De Klerk acknowledged that covert operations had been carried out on a 'need to know' basis, and said, '[e]vidently, those with knowledge of such actions sometimes consciously failed to inform their superiors of them, in terms of the doctrine of "plausible denial" (despite the rejection of this doctrine in terms of cabinet guidelines) ... [T]he possibility must also be accepted that some elements of the security forces might have been following their own agenda and were actively working against the transformation process. For obvious reasons such elements would not have informed their superiors of their activities.' He made a distinction between support for organisations such as the IFP and the fomenting of 'black-on-black violence', saying it would be 'ludicrous' to suggest that such actions were the primary or even the major cause of the violence between the ANC and the IFP.

Ultimately, De Klerk declared that the NP was willing to accept responsibility for the policies it had adopted and the actions of its office bearers in implementing them. But it was '*not* prepared to accept responsibility for the criminal actions of a handful of operatives of the security forces of which the party was not aware and which it would never have condoned. Neither is it prepared to accept responsibility for the actions of any office bearer who might have acted outside the mandate given him by the party.' Vlakplaas and the CCB acted outside the law, and such actions were never approved by the cabinet or the SSC. Former police commissioner General Johan van der Merwe and other senior police officers had also assured De Klerk that they were unaware of such actions. De Klerk became aware of the CCB only when its activities were publicly exposed. No one in the SADF ever approached any organ of the government to gain authorisation for a CCB-type structure after 1990. According to De Klerk, he would have stopped such an attempt if it had come to his knowledge, as 'it would have been irreconcilable with everything that I was trying to achieve in the negotiation sphere'. The CCB was shut down when he found out about it. Its dismantling was delayed because the advocate general had to be called in to resolve the legal wrangling. De Klerk did not comment on the paradox of a legally constituted organisation that 'no one' knew of. The SSC secretariat destroyed surplus documents, but De Klerk was unaware of any originals being destroyed.

The TRC was not impressed. Alex Boraine called the first submission 'in many ways a damp squib'.[70] De Klerk was on the offensive with the second submission in May 1997[71] in response to questions posed by the TRC. The commission, he said, was losing its credibility because it was concentrating on 'only one side of the former conflict', namely the version of the ANC and its allies. 'The overwhelming majority of the members of our party have been horrified by the revelations of abuse that have come to light as a result of the activities of the commission and other investigations that preceded it. [...] They also want to know how these abuses could have happened and why they were not detected long before their public exposure.' Untested allegations were being made at TRC hearings that were then reported as truth, resulting in 'trial by media'. Several sections of the NP submission were used to detail gross human rights violations committed by the ANC and the Mass Democratic Movement – De Klerk's response to the ANC's submission on government abuse.

He bemoaned the lack of representations from the government's side by comparison with testimony from 'the other side'. He reminded the commission that 'many of those involved were fighting for the preservation of their historic right to national self-determination; many were carrying out their duty to maintain law and order and to defend a duly constituted and internationally recognised state from armed insurrection; many others felt it their duty to defend their country and their region from the threat of international communist expansion'.

In answer to the TRC's question about whether the struggle against apartheid could be equated with the struggle to defend it, he argued that those who acted on behalf of the government were not 'morally inferior' to those involved in the liberation struggle. De Klerk pointed out that 'the question also assumes, quite incorrectly, that all those who fought on the government side were doing so in defence of "apartheid". Very few of those involved were fighting to repress fellow South Africans or to maintain the segregated facilities associated with apartheid.'

Asked by deputy TRC chairperson Boraine whether he should not apply for amnesty – as Pik Botha had suggested to him – De Klerk answered that since he was not guilty of any crime, there was no reason to seek amnesty. At a subsequent news conference, the head of the TRC, Archbishop Desmond Tutu, expressed his dismay at De Klerk's testimony, not least because he had visited De Klerk in the 1980s to tell him what was going on, and found his 'apparent amnesia' saddening.[72] The NP then brought a lawsuit against the TRC, demanding an apology and Boraine's resignation. In the end, an agreement was reached in which Boraine and Tutu apologised for criticising De Klerk's testimony. The TRC found that the NP government was to blame for human rights violations; that torture was officially sanctioned; and that the security ministers and police commissioners were directly accountable for deaths in detention while the NP cabinet was indirectly responsible. Similarly, the president, security ministers, minister of foreign affairs and all heads of the security structures were found to be accountable for extra-judicial killings, while members of the cabinet and the SSC were found to be indirectly accountable.

The failure of De Klerk and other NP leaders to take responsibility for apartheid security force actions had a direct influence on the party's support base. This was articulated by younger NP leaders Pierre-Jeanne Gerber and Boeije de Wet, who had left the party and joined the ANC by 1999. While still in the NP, De Wet had tried to release a statement saying that Botha should take responsibility, but it was blocked by the powers that be in the Eastern Cape.

What it took 'not to know': The supporters

Pik Botha argues that speedier change would have been possible if voters could have elected the executive head of government directly. His claim is based on a national survey conducted by the Argus group of newspapers in the early 1980s, which found that more than 80 per cent of respondents would have voted for him if they'd had the choice. Pik was the most prominent *verligte* in the party – in the mid-1980s, PW Botha almost expelled him for saying he would serve under a black president. He saw the survey as proof that white voters were 'far in advance of the caucus and the thinking within the traditional structures of the National Party.'

Other former NP leaders also contend that opinion polls at the time showed that white voters were more progressive than the party, but this was not borne out by election results during the 1980s, when the liberal vote shrank and white support was concentrated in the NP and the CP. Nor does it explain why the NP leadership devoted an inordinate amount of attention to preventing the far right wing from attracting votes, or address the fact that among ordinary party members, the level of discussion displayed obliviousness to the reality of white domination. One factor was ignorance.

According to the Commonwealth Eminent Persons Group in 1986, only about 10 per cent of the white population had first-hand knowledge of living conditions in black townships. State control over black people's movements and the spatial arrangement of apartheid – literally 'apartness' – rendered them invisible. Townships were hidden behind mine dumps or set kilometres away from 'white' towns. In the absence of personal experience, apartheid enabled white people to indulge in constructed images of black people.[73] 'Good blacks' were traditional and law-abiding, while 'bad blacks' were terrorists or communists.

Through separate areas and manufactured images, the true effects of apartheid were obscured. The power of this manipulation manifested in all Afrikaner nationalist spheres, including the church. As Fritz Gaum, ex-editor of the DRC's *Die Kerkbode*, said in 2006: 'The church examined the issue [apartheid] theoretically, said that it was in order if separate development was implemented consistently and that every *volk* in the end has its own country. But the official church kept itself blind and deaf to the misery and destruction that apartheid caused in practice in people's lives. Because it mostly happened far away from most NG Kerk people in desperate townships and homelands.'[74]

Another factor inhibiting the desire 'to know' was fear, which escalated during the siege years of the 1980s, but had always been there. Cape liberal Jan Hofmeyr, a member of Jan Smuts's last UP cabinet, spelt out some of the typical white fears (and his own) in 1931. He spoke about the fear that development of black people would cause 'the white man' to be submerged in a 'black ocean'. Then he asked: 'Will the blacks not avenge themselves? Will the black man who was forced into subjection by the white man not one day harm the white man?'[75]

Steve Biko addressed the same issues forty years later. 'There is an obvious aura of immorality and naked cruelty in all that is done in the name of white people that no black man, no matter how intimidated, can ever be made to respect white society. However, in spite of their obvious contempt for the values cherished by whites and the price at which white comfort is purchased, blacks seem to me to have been successfully cowed down by the … brutality … The claim by whites of a monopoly on comfort and security has always been so exclusive that blacks see whites as the major obstacle in their progress towards peace, prosperity and a sane society … blacks envy white society for the comfort it has usurped and at the centre of this envy is the wish – nay, the secret determination – in the innermost of most blacks who think like this, to kick whites off those comfortable garden chairs that one sees as he rides on a bus, out of town, and to claim them for themselves.'[76] In the face of this resentment, 'there are those whites who will completely disclaim responsibility for the country's inhumanity to the black man. These are the people who are governed by logic four and a half years [between elections] but by fear at election time … All whites recognise in [the NP] a strong bastion against the highly played-up *swart gevaar*. One must not underestimate the deeply embedded fear of the black man so prevalent in white society. Whites know only too well what they have been doing to blacks and logically find reason for the black man to be angry. Their state of insecurity however does not outweigh their greed for power and wealth, hence they brace themselves to react against this rage rather than to dispel it with open-mindedness and fair play. This interaction between fear and reaction then sets on a vicious cycle that multiplies both the fear and the reaction.'[77]

Biko's words echoed sentiments from an unexpected source. *Die Burger*'s political columnist, Dawie, wrote in 1962: 'Because of excessive fear, a good piece of construction is discredited by some as appeasement, liberalism, fatal leniency and who knows what else, and then to refute the charge, we feel obliged to put down a destructive foot somewhere in the name of steadfastness and firm principle.'[78]

Such observations showed the cycle of repression, anger and fear – fuelled, as Biko pointed out, by the NP's *swart gevaar* rhetoric. This was sometimes spiced with self-righteousness. Gerrit Viljoen, the *verligte* Broederbond chairman from 1974 to 1979 who was regarded as an intellectual in the NP, stated in 1979 that the Afrikaner's humanity 'stands in sharp contrast to the cold-blooded cruelty that marks so much of the history of Africa. This humane attitude pervades a broad spectrum of life; it manifests itself in a fundamental respect for another's life ... but it also shows in a spirit of live and let live so far as other communities, races and national groups are concerned. It is because of this attitude that the Afrikaner need not face his neighbours in the world with a burden of historical guilt or a troubled national conscience.'[79]

The unmistakeable sense of moral superiority was belied by the policies and known state actions of the time. Indeed, the SADF's attack on Cassinga and Chetequera camps in Angola took place less than a year before Viljoen's tract was published. In that attack alone, 1200 people died, many of them civilians. Soldiers had been ordered, 'where possible', not to shoot women and children. Despite the knowledge that civilians were present, fragmentation bombs – known to kill and maim indiscriminately – were used.[80] In 1990, a decade and many more murders later, Viljoen was still caught in the same mindset, insisting that 'history proves that the whites are democrats'.[81]

FW de Klerk argued before the TRC that truth was 'elusive ... in an historical or political context. Perceptions of what is true vary from time to time, from place to place and from party to party according to the affiliations and convictions of those involved.' Viljoen's sentiments would probably be seen as an example of the relativity of 'truth', but what they showed was the way ideology could be used to justify the unjustifiable. In a 1987 survey that asked whites what would happen if South Africa had a black government, between 78 and 91 per cent of Afrikaners and 70 to 78 per cent of English-speakers answered yes to the following questions:

- Would blacks discriminate against whites?
- Would communist policies be implemented?
- Would black men 'molest' white women?
- Would white living standards decline?
- Would the physical safety of whites be threatened?[82]

The NP played an essential role in the development of such attitudes, partly because it 'perfected the art of saying two things, neither of them clearly', according to Rina Venter. Barend du Plessis calls it the Connie Mulder strategy: 'praat *verkramp*, doen *verlig*' (talk conservative, act enlightened).

The NP government thus applied the opposite of what would win votes in post-apartheid South Africa, where the ANC would 'talk left, walk right'. The NP constantly exploited right-wing concerns – not only to stave off the CP, but also to maintain white support. After all, racism had paid off well in putting the party into government and holding on to state power, and the strategy continued.

From the Vorster era onwards, the power bases within the NP shifted beyond the grasp of party structures, to government. In the 1970s and 1980s, the circle became even smaller. The decisions to invade Angola in 1975, to bomb neighbouring countries in 1986 and to blow up Khotso House were taken by the president alone or in conjunction with the ministers responsible for security. The move towards state terrorism under Botha meant a deepening duplicity on the side of NP leaders towards their constituency. Even party members were unsure about the need for change. At the 1990 Transvaal NP congress after De Klerk's 2 February announcements, two questions were posed to Viljoen: Why a new constitution had to be drafted, and what would be the implications of opening party membership and seeking alliances? The first reflected a low level of political communication. The second suggested white anxiety.

How much responsibility should individual whites therefore take for a system drenched in total strategy duplicity and maintained through ideological manipulation? These questions fed white consternation about the TRC. FW de Klerk argued that the SABC used 'every opportunity to cast a pall of collective guilt over anyone associated with the former government or with our party. Whole classes of decent people and communities are being associated in the public perception with the criminal actions of a few individuals, of which they were not aware and which they would not have condoned had they known of them.' The NP's supporters, who voted for reforms in 1987, 1989 and 1992, were feeling 'alienated and victimised'.

However, Wessels sees a convergence in the denial of apartheid's effects with the anger about power loss: 'The voters who said they were not informed when they said "yes" in the 1992 referendum are the same voters who in 1978 asked, "Who is Steve Biko?" These are the same people who participated in the 1983 referendum. They could hardly not have known [the way things were going]. This thing of "we didn't know" is said by the same people. Antjie Krog puts it brilliantly: "The day you woke up and you heard that Dulcie September had been murdered, what did you think?" These are the same people who said they didn't know. What did they want to know? FW de Klerk stumbled into Krugersdorp – tired, exhausted – to give an audience, which I had arranged, the opportunity to ask him questions before the referendum in 1992. Do you know what they asked him? That evening the guys asked him about crime. Can you believe it? I remember it like yesterday. They got up and they asked him about crime.'

Memory and forgetting – and capitalism

Milan Kundera says 'the struggle of man is the struggle of memory against forgetting'. Making sense of what had happened in the name of Afrikaners – building an understanding individually and collectively – would to a great extent determine Afrikaners' participation as citizens in a country grappling with democratic consolidation. The majority of Afrikaners rejected 'self-determination' as a political goal, seen in the far right wing's low polling figures. They also rejected the party of Afrikaner nationalism – the National Party. Yet many of them voted for a fear-mongering DA that had combined minimum liberal values with the rhetoric of self-righteousness and denial.

Even more worrying was the growing stayaway vote in 1999 and thereafter, including more than one million whites. While illegal activities aimed at promoting white supremacy were limited to small groups such as the Boeremag, the non-participation of white people in legitimate processes did not augur well. Nevertheless, in the first half of the 2000s a few transparent efforts to reactivate Afrikaner nationalism failed, most notably Dan Roodt's Pro-Afrikaanse Aksiegroep (PRAAG) and the Groep van 63.

Roodt hoped to utilise *Die Taal* to catapult himself into a *volksleier* position. His ideas, throwbacks to nineteenth-century 'science of race' delusions, alienated all but the extreme far-right fringe. Similarly, the Groep van 63 never took off. One of its main proponents, Johann Rossouw, was hoping to tap into communitarian sentiments reacting against the universalising forces of globalisation. The Groep van 63 floundered when prominent Afrikaner intellectuals withdrew as they realised its nationalist aims. Rossouw and his ally, academic Danie Goosen, then staged a takeover of the Federasie van Afrikaanse Kultuurverenigings

(FAK), the old Broederbond front organisation, which they appropriated in a search for a revamped Afrikaner nationalism. Rossouw's FAK publication *Die Vrye Afrikaan* adopted a critical position towards neo-liberal globalisation. Both PRAAG and the FAK/*Vrye Afrikaan* initiative attempted to capitalise on perceptions of white embattlement in a democratic South Africa. However, the DA was already tapping into this emotion and providing a political outlet. The trade union Solidarity had also offered more by providing a vehicle for white workers' interests. Moreover, Rossouw's ideological position contradicted that of the majority of middle-class Afrikaners. As the miniscule interest in far-right-wing parties or the secessionist settlement of Orania showed, Afrikaners were not attracted by promises of isolation from Western decadence and black people. Rather, they embraced global values such as materialism and consumerism with abandon.

Indeed, such capitalist values proved far more attractive to Afrikaners riding, as most of them were, on an ANC-sponsored wave of increased affluence. The rise of the middle class unstitched the multi-classed Afrikaner nationalist alliance. This was the legacy of the *verligtes*. Attempts by PRAAG, the Groep van 63 and the FAK to reactivate the old machine could not trump the security and headiness of increased wealth and material success. In a sense, the ANC's adoption of a predominantly neo-liberal economic policy framework was the best possible antidote to Afrikaner ethnic mobilisation. As a disgruntled resident from Orania wrote in a letter to *Rapport*:

> In South Africa today, Afrikaners suffer daily under race-based transformation and affirmative action, farm murders, high crime rates, an education system that alienates Afrikaans children from their own culture as if it is a plague, harsh, race-based land reform and black economic empowerment, race-based sport administration, blatant disarming, changes to Afrikaans place names, phasing out of the Afrikaans language in state departments and institutions funded by the state, and so on. But we do not complain. We are enjoying economic prosperity and our welfare allows us to endure the punches and slaps.[83]

While the Afrikaner middle class, among others, reaped the benefits of finance minister Trevor Manuel's neo-liberal tax cuts and the increasing ability to move ever-larger sums of capital out of the country, the Afrikaner and English-speaking capitalist classes went from strength to strength. Long gone were the days of an economy stunted by isolation and apartheid-imposed domestic market limitations. Companies were allowed to move their headquarters abroad and corporate taxes were lowered while disinvestment continued, sometimes facilitated by government approval of deals or restructuring.[84]

The ANC government's economic policy addressed the crisis in capital accumulation. After excruciatingly slow average economic growth of 2.77 per cent between 1990 and 2003 – in contrast to the government's GEAR prediction of 6 per cent – the property, construction, media, financial services and retail sectors were booming in the mid-2000s. In spite of the ANC's original intention in *Ready to Govern* to 'curb monopolies [and] the continued domination of the economy by a minority within the white minority',[85] ANC government decisions in the banking, fisheries, retail clothing, diamond and retail pharmaceutical sectors entrenched the power of large companies to the detriment of small players. Despite the continuing dearth of skilled labour, economic growth levels squeezed past 5 per cent by the second half of the 2000s and the country enjoyed its longest economic growth period since the Second World War. The Johannesburg Stock Exchange's share index rose to record-breaking levels.

No longer the pariah, South Africa also benefited from access to the rest of the continent. The New Partnership for Africa's Development, a continent-wide structural adjustment programme piloted by President Thabo Mbeki, was criticised by academics from the rest of Africa as a transparent attempt at 'economic imperialism'. This described the reach of South African companies into the continent. Afrikaner capital in particular benefited from these developments as Naspers, Shoprite and Pepkor moved into African states and across the world. By the late 1990s, the highest growth in shares on the JSE was among those in Afrikaner, not black, hands.

The ANC's economic policies continued the patterns created under the NP in its last years of rule. The emphasis remained on a capital-intensive growth path, and economic policies exacerbated unemployment rather than mitigating it. Unemployment had become structural – 72 per cent of those without jobs in 2002 were under the age of 35.[86] Unemployment reached 40 per cent in the 2000s, according to Statistics South Africa's expanded definition, which included jobless people who had stopped looking for work. The ANC expanded social grants and instituted a public works programme but, in adherence to the neo-liberal dictum, remained hostile to a basic income grant. By the beginning of the 2000s, according to the Human Sciences Research Council, 57 per cent of South Africans were still living below the poverty line of R1 290 per family of four per month. Indeed, by 2000 the richest 20 per cent of the population was receiving 65 per cent of the national income, compared to the poorest 50 per cent of the population, receiving 9.7 per cent. The income of the poorest 60 per cent of the population dropped by 15 per cent between 1995 and 2000.[87] One result was that the prevalence of undernourished children grew from 9.3 per cent to 10.3 per cent during the late 1990s, while stunted growth in children aged from one to six remained at more than 22 per cent between 1994 and 1999.[88] In 2002, 30 per cent of households reported that children were receiving inadequate nutrition because of a lack of food.[89] As one might expect, these figures had a distinct racial dimension. By 2000, according to Statistics SA, the average black household income had dropped by 19 per cent since 1995, while that of whites had increased by 15 per cent. A study by economist Servaas van den Bergh at the University of Stellenbosch showed that, in 2000, the average white South African still earned eight times more than his or her black counterpart.[90]

But, due to the bias in ANC government economic policies, the elite and upper middle classes had been deracialised. The upper classes became increasingly racially representative, while intra-racial inequality worsened. The white proportion of the top income group moved from 73 per cent in 1995 to between 61 and 55 per cent in 2000, while the black component increased from 18 per cent in 1995 to 31 per cent in 2000. In the second highest income group, blacks accounted for 61 per cent by 2000, up from 46 per cent in 1995. Whites had moved from 38 to 17 per cent over the same period.[91] Overall, inequality worsened, especially within racial groups, as opposed to between white and black. This trend of deracialising the upper echelons had started under the NP, as the white population's share of national income dropped from 71 per cent in 1970 to 52 per cent in 1996.[92] These shifts were the result of the NP's attempts to create a co-opted black middle class and working class and thereby obviate the need for a transfer of power. The process of creating a black middle class accelerated under the ANC, with the eager assistance of white capital.

Class convergence was particularly noticeable at the elite level, as deracialisation of the apex of the class structure picked up after 1994.[93] The *verligte* agenda came to fruition. Sanlam, the NP's primary capital partner since the 1910s, activated the first black economic empowerment (BEE) deal in 1993 through which New Africa Investment Limited was created. In its submission to the TRC in 1997, Sanlam acknowledged its 'special relationship' with the NP government. In answer to a question, managing director Desmond Smith admitted that Sanlam had the 'best of both worlds' – apartheid South Africa and democratic South Africa. 'I really am delighted that we have been able also with the new ANC government to establish a very warm relationship,' he said.[94]

The NP's other staunch traditional ally, Nasionale Pers, was the largest media company on the African continent by the 2000s. It had extended its interests to China, India, Brazil, Greece, Cyprus, the Netherlands, South Korea, Singapore, Thailand and the US. Its annual revenues were R14 billion, while the market capitalisation of the group's network of companies stood at more than R34 billion in 2005. Group MD Koos Bekker's shareholding was valued at almost half a billion rand in 2007.[95]

And, as a final symbol that the goal of the second Ekonomiese Volkskongres of October 1950 – consolidation of Afrikaner big business – had been achieved, Sanlam's small mining subsidiary, Federale Mynbou, which was boosted by Anglo American's gift of General Mining in 1964, had grown to become Gencor in the 1980s and BHP Billiton by the 2000s – the largest mining company in the world.

The Ruperts of Remgro and Richemont (Rembrandt) had by the mid-1990s been included on the Forbes list of the 500 richest people in the world. They were the second wealthiest South African family after the Oppenheimers (and the fifth wealthiest family in Switzerland). The Ruperts had slightly narrowed the gap between themselves and the Oppenheimers, jumping from $1.6 billion in assets in 1996 to $4.3 billion in 2007, compared to the Oppenheimers' $2.5 billion in 1996 and $5 billion in 2007.[96]

The total market capitalisation of companies in which the Ruperts held shares was $14 billion by 2002, in sectors ranging from luxury goods, tobacco and wine to gold mining, banks and telecommunications. By 2006, the Rupert family empire spanned thirty-five countries on six continents. When family patriarch Anton Rupert died that same year, Thabo Mbeki 'hailed' him not only as a great Afrikaner, but 'a great South African'. It demonstrated the coming together of the black political elite with the Afrikaner economic elite.

Rupert had publicly stated during the apartheid era that continued white prosperity was in danger while black people struggled at a subsistence level,[97] but he had also 'managed to avoid confrontations [with the NP government] that may have threatened his business interests'.

In the political heat of the late 1980s, the Ruperts – somewhat unpatriotically – created Richemont in the financial haven of Geneva as an 'overseas investment vehicle'.[98] In other words, the Ruperts behaved like many other pre-1994 South African capitalists. But Mbeki stressed Rupert's role in 'supporting and initiating significant transformation of South Africa's business'.[99]

With the ANC's political and legislative BEE efforts, business transformation was at the top of its government agenda. Capital played its role by selling shares to black companies through empowerment deals with special provisions built in. While some of the deals contained 'broad-based' aspects that included employees or communities, the largest chunks went to the same names. Most of these multiple BEE beneficiaries were ANC-connected, and by the second half of the 2000s, Patrice Motsepe had moved into fourth place on the *Who Owns Whom?* list of richest company directors, partly thanks to a Sanlam empowerment deal. Ahead of him were London-based Lakshmi Mittal of Mittal Steel South Africa (formerly Iscor until the NP privatised it), Anglo American's Nicky Oppenheimer and Rembrandt's Johann Rupert. In 2007, two new names were added to the list: Liberty Group/Standard Bank non-executive director Saki

Macozoma, and Shanduka chairperson and former ANC chief negotiator Cyril Ramaphosa, both members of the ANC's national executive council. Tokyo Sexwale, a former NEC member and erstwhile Gauteng premier, was already on the list.[100]

In another initiative, academic Willie Esterhuyse, who was involved in the initial brokering of contact between the National Intelligence Service and Thabo Mbeki in the late 1980s, had set up a group of Afrikaans business representatives and academics who regularly met with Mbeki for discussions, details of which remained largely undisclosed. Members included Ton Vosloo (Naspers); Christo Wiese (Pepkor); Thys du Toit (Coronation Fund); GT Ferreira and Laurie Dippenaar (Rand Merchant Bank).[101] One result was a pilot project to support emergent black farmers in the northern Free State.

After 1994, *verligte* notions about coloured Afrikaans-speakers found support in the Afrikaans media's promotion of so-called 'Afrikaanses', meaning all who speak Afrikaans, as opposed to 'Afrikaners'. The drive even included coloured leaders who had made their name in the ANC, such as Jakes Gerwel and Franklin Sonn. The former was made a Naspers director and began writing a regular column in *Rapport*, while the latter became head of the overhauled business association, the Afrikaanse Handelsinstituut. While to some extent the inclusion of coloureds in Afrikaner ranks was the result of duress imposed by laws such as those on affirmative action, it also seems to have been part of a calculated attempt to boost both Afrikaner demographics and political clout.

Verligte politicians such as Pik Botha and Roelf Meyer had joined the ANC by 2000 and 2006 respectively. In a further strengthening of cross-elite alliances, Meyer's association with his former ANC negotiating counterpart, Cyril Ramaphosa, deepened as he was made a director in a global management consultancy co-owned by Ramaphosa's Shanduka and AT Kearny.[102]

While those of *verligte* ilk embraced ANC capitalists and spread their corporate wings across the globe, a closing of the Afrikaner mind could be detected by the mid-2000s. After the fluidity of thought and expression brought about by the relatively peaceful dawn of democracy, there was a backlash. The socioeconomic inheritance of apartheid seemed insurmountable to many, but most Afrikaners could financially afford to insulate themselves from these bitter facts. Making sense of the social destabilisation wrought by political change proved daunting. Poet Herman Engelbrecht captured the feeling of alienation:

> One door after another that slams in your face.
> A country full of nowhere to go.
> Here it feels as if not even God
> wants to understand Afrikaans any longer.[103]

Despite *verligte* godfather and Afrikaner intellectual Willem de Klerk's pleas to the contrary,[104] parochialism, saturated with indignation and even self-pity, became evident. In many cases this was accompanied by privatisation of a rabid (even by apartheid standards) form of racism in homes and the workplace, which sometimes resulted in criminal prosecution and thus reached the public domain. The likes of Willem de Klerk became the target of resentment, as in the *Boetman is die bliksem in* open letter by former anti-apartheid journalist Chris Louw. Another father figure was given the boot. As a result, De Klerk's introspective discoveries, which had led to his final letting go of apartheid in all its permutations, as seen in his 2000 book *Afrikaners – Kroes, Kras, Kordaat*, were disqualified as a possible new direction.

In the book, De Klerk attempted to propound a revised Afrikanerness that acknowledged guilt over apartheid, but also accepted *saambestaan* (co-existence), inclusiveness and colour blindness. He argued that 'if we can triumph over the offensiveness of our exclusivity, we will become part of the greater whole, without losing or having to give up our identity. Then there will not be a demand that Afrikanership has to be sacrificed.' But, he admitted, most Afrikaners would reject his suggestion. For De Klerk, Afrikaner identity meant that 'you are at the same time African, South African, Afrikaner and an Afrikaans person, who is part of the Afrikaans community. Instead of one excluding the other, they complement one another.'[105]

Could Afrikaners be all these identities and *also* Afrikaners? The 'De La Rey' phenomenon provided some clues. It reinforced attempts by neo-Afrikaner nationalist groupings to mobilise Afrikaners on an ethnic basis. By the mid-2000s, the ground seemed more fertile for these moves than when PRAAG and the Groep van 63 appeared on the scene. Superficial individualism oiled by rampant materialism and consumerism seemed to provide only a temporary panacea. The heightened civil society activity around 'De La Rey', led by Solidarity and spurred on by *Rapport*, along with pop singer Steve Hofmeyr's new incarnation as an 'activist' fighting for Afrikaner interests, signalled another phase in the search for a legitimate Afrikaner identity.

De Klerk's call for an inclusive identity incorporating both African-ness and Afrikaner-ness suggested how complicated the process of rehabilitating Afrikaner identity could be. Statements by 'De La Rey' singer Bok van Blerk highlighted some of the contradictions inherent in the process. According to him, 'You say "Boer" and everyone immediately asks, "who are you talking about?" People form ideas and pictures in their heads … that a Boer is a far right-winger in khaki clothes who wants to murder black people.' His words held the promise of a renewal of Afrikaner identity that accepted the legal limits of democracy, while rejecting the extreme racist abuse of the past. Van Blerk expressed his opposition to the use of apartheid or old Afrikaner nationalist symbols such as the *Oranje-blanje-blou* and *Vierkleur* flags, or the singing of the old anthem 'Die Stem', but added: 'We are one of those rainbow colours [of the rainbow nation]. When you sit around a table with a Zulu, Xhosa and Englishman, you have to know who you are.'

Van Blerk was thus holding on to apartheid's ethnic divisions as a basis for an Afrikaner identity. While the persistence of Afrikaner group consciousness was to be expected, Afrikaner history offered little to draw on ideologically that could enrich it. The NP had successfully extinguished ideological alternatives among white people. The clampdown on communism and liberalism in the 1950s and 1960s was so thorough that it had created an Afrikaner nationalist ideological hegemony by the mid-1960s. While the capitalist drive necessitated ideological change within the NP, capitalism is not synonymous with democracy. The most obvious examples of this in the 1990s and 2000s were China and the mass disengagement of voters in the so-called mature liberal democracy of the United States.

In the realm of ideas, Afrikaners were left with a meagre inheritance. As political scientist André du Toit wrote in 1985: 'as is well known, there is ... no strong liberal tradition in Afrikaner history and politics – to say nothing of an Afrikaner socialist tradition ...'[106] Thus Afrikaners have almost no tradition of philosophical commitment to equality or social justice. Indeed, some opinion-makers were still unable to distinguish between social democracy and socialism by the 2000s. Former *Die Burger* editor Ebbe Dommisse and Mbeki ally Willie Esterhuyse slated 'increasingly socialist' Stellenbosch economist Sampie Terre-blanche in their 2005 biography of Anton Rupert. They condemned Terreblanche for shedding Afrikaner nationalism and criticising the ANC for 'not doing enough for the poor' in his 2002 book.[107] In fact, while employing a class analysis, Terreblanche was contrasting the liberal capitalism of Britain and the US with the social-democratic capitalism of Western Europe, advocating pursuance of the latter by South Africa to address inequality. For him, that translated into a thriving private sector, and even partnerships between the state and business, but also state intervention to correct market outcomes detrimentally affecting social welfare[108] – a far cry from socialism. What seemingly irked Dommisse and Esterhuyse was Terreblanche's suggestion that 'market forces' not be left to their own devices.

The paucity of ideas did not bode well for a group in the throes of an identity crisis in a country where the extreme disparity in wealth represented a volcano on the verge of eruption. Relative to where South Africans had come from, a number of enormous, essential and life-changing steps had been taken. But to entrench democracy, all South Africans – including Afrikaners – had to actively claim their rights as citizens. The transition was a state of grace – assumptions were dangerous. Would Afrikaners have the courage to understand and to act accordingly? Could they imagine themselves differently?

Notes and references

INTRODUCTION

1 Leon Wessels, interview, 17 August 2006. Unless otherwise indicated, direct and indirect quotes attributed to the following individuals throughout this book emanate from interviews conducted by the author with them between 12 April 2006 and 23 January 2007: Wessels, Barend du Plessis, Sheila Camerer, Rina Venter, Roelf Meyer, Pik Botha, Tertius Delport, Johan Kilian, Annelizé van Wyk, Stan Simmons, Marthinus van Schalkwyk and James Selfe.

2 Thabo Mbeki, 'Letter from the President', *ANC Today*, Vol. 6 No. 5, 10–16 February 2006; 'Letter from the President', *ANC Today*, Vol. 6 No. 43, 3–9 November 2006.

3 Heribert Adam and Hermann Giliomee, *Ethnic Power Mobilized. Can South Africa Change?* New Haven: Yale University Press, 1979, pp. 154–8.

4 Hermann Giliomee, 'Herontdekking en herverbeelding van die Afrikaners in 'n nuwe Suid-Afrika. Outobiografiese aantekeninge oor die skryf van 'n ongewone biografie' in *Fragmente. Tydskrif vir Filosofie en Taalkritiek*, No. 14/15, 2005, p. 26.

5 Benedict Anderson, *Imagined Communities. Reflections on the Origin and Spread of Nationalism*, revised edition. London: Verso, 1991 (1983), p. 7.

6 Gerrit Viljoen, 'An Afrikaner looks ahead' in Edwin S Munger (ed.), *The Afrikaners*. Cape Town: Tafelberg, 1979, p. 173.

7 Allan Bloom, *The Closing of the American Mind*. New York: Simon & Schuster, 1987.

8 Jeremy Seekings and Nicoli Nattrass, *Class, Race and Inequality in South Africa*. Scottsville: University of KwaZulu-Natal Press, 2005.

9 Willem de Klerk, *Afrikaners – Kroes, Kras, Kordaat*. Cape Town: Human & Rousseau, 2000, p. 52.

10 In Daniel Hugo, Leon Rousseau and Phil du Plessis (compilers), *Nuwe Verset*. Pretoria: Protea Boekhuis, 2000, p. 78.

CHAPTER 1

1 JJ Lubbe, 'A tale of fear and faith'. In '1948 Plus 50 Years. Theology, apartheid and church – past, present and future', WJ Hofmeyr, CJS Lombaard, PJ Maritz (eds), *Perspectives on Christianity*, Series 5 Vol. 1, University of Pretoria Printers, 2001, p. 49.

2 James Barber, *South Africa in the Twentieth Century*. Oxford: Blackwell, 1999, p. 20.

3 FA van Jaarsveld, *Die Evolusie van Apartheid*. Cape Town: Tafelberg, 1979, pp. 6–7.

4 This paragraph is partly based on discussions with Prof Sheila Meintjes, February 2007.

5 André du Toit, 'Puritans in Africa? Afrikaner "Calvinism" and Kuyperian neo-Calvinism in late nineteenth-century South Africa'. In *Comparative Studies in Society and History*, Vol. 27 No. 2, April 1985, pp. 218, 231.

6 *Ibid*.

7 Nigel Worden, *The Making of Modern South Africa. Conquest, Segregation and Apartheid*. Oxford: Blackwell, 1994, p. 72.

8 *Ibid*, p. 71.

9 *Ibid*, pp. 72, 73.

10 Barber, p. 24; Hermann Giliomee, *Die Afrikaners. 'n Biografie*. Cape Town: Tafelberg, 2004, p. 216.

11 Barber, p. 41.

12 Peter Fryer, *Black People in the British Empire. An Introduction.* London: Pluto Press, 1988, p. 71.

13 Barber, p. 43.

14 Le May, 1965, in *ibid.*

15 Giliomee, 2004, p. 217.

16 Sampie Terreblanche, *A history of inequality in South Africa 1652–2002.* Sandton: KMM Publishing Company/ Pietermaritzburg: University of Natal Press, 2002, p. 233.

17 Barber, p. 18.

18 Nancy L Clark and William H Worger, *South Africa. The Rise and Fall of Apartheid.* Harlow: Pearson Education Ltd, 2004, p. 16.

19 Giliomee, 2004, p. 216.

20 Barber, p. 24.

21 *Ibid*, p. 43.

22 Pyrah, 1955, in Barber, p. 40.

23 Marks and Trapido, 1987, in Barber, p. 44.

24 Marks, 1986, in Worden, p. 23.

25 *Ibid.*

26 *Ibid*, p. 25.

27 Barber, p. 42.

28 D Yudelman, 1983, in Terreblanche, p. 247.

29 Terreblanche, pp. 68–9.

30 Karis and Carter, 1972, in Barber, p. 41.

31 Published in *Umteteli wa Bantu,* 29 November 1924. Quoted in Tim Couzens, 'Introduction', in Sol T Plaatje, *Mhudi.* Oxford: Heinemann, 1978 (1930), p. 17.

32 William Beinart, *Twentieth Century South Africa.* Oxford: Oxford University Press, 2001 (1994), p. 93.

33 Clark and Worger, p. 19.

34 J van Melle, *Bart Nel.* Cape Town: Tafelberg, 2004 (1942).

35 Worden, p. 52.

36 Hancock, 1968, in Barber, pp. 89–90.

37 Adam and Giliomee, p. 150; Giliomee, 2004, p. 286.

38 Giliomee, 1987, in Barber, p. 90.

39 Worden, p. 71.

40 *Ibid*, pp. 71, 72, 75.

41 DF Malan, *Afrikaner-Volkseenheid en my ervarings op die pad daarheen.* Cape Town/Bloemfontein/Johannesburg: Nasionale Boekhandel Beperk, 1961, pp. 239–40.

42 *Ibid.*

43 DF Malan, 'Boodskap van sy hoogedele Dr DF Malan'. In DP Goosen (ed.), *Die Triomf van Nasionalisme in Suid-Afrika (1910–1953).* Johannesburg: Impala Opvoedkundige Diens Edms Bpk, 1953, p. 9.

44 DF Malan, 'Vaderskap en broederskap'. Address to Christian university students in the Cape province, 1923. In SW Pienaar with JJJ Scholtz (eds), *Glo in U Volk – DF Malan as Redenaar 1908–1954.* Cape Town: Tafelberg, 1964, pp. 186–193.

45 Beinart, pp. 92, 102–6; Clark and Worger, pp. 23–6.

46 Malan, 1961, pp. 46–7.

47 *Ibid*, p. 98.

48 *Ibid*, pp. 213–4.

49 *Ibid*, p. 51.

50 *Ibid*, pp. 49–50.

51 DW Krüger, *The making of a nation. A history of the Union of South Africa 1910–1961.* Johannesburg/London: Macmillan, 1977 (1969), p. 205.

52 *Ibid*, p. 207.

53 Dan O'Meara, *Volkskapitalisme: Class, Capital and Ideology in the Development of Afrikaner Nationalism.* Cambridge: Cambridge University Press, 1983, pp. 6–7.

54 Giliomee in Adam and Giliomee, pp. 156–7.

55 O'Meara, p. 16. The next section draws on O'Meara, pp. 51–6.

56 Barber, p. 108.

57 Piet Cillié, 'Pers en Party'. In Beukes, WD (ed.), *Oor Grense Heen: Op Pad na 'n Nasionale Pers 1948–1990.* Cape Town: Nasionale Boekhandel, 1992, p. 459.

58 Nic Diederichs, 1934, in O'Meara, p. 50.

59 In O'Meara, pp. 51, 151.

60 Malan, 1961, p. 98.

61 O'Meara, p. 50.

62 AJ Bosman, 'Die Sakewêreld – 'n Halfeeu opkoms en groei'. In Goosen, p. 716.

63 *Volkshandel*, 1950, quoted in *ibid*, p. 717.

64 *Ibid*, p. 716.

65 PJ Furlong, *Between Crown and Swastika: The Impact of the Radical Right on the Afrikaner Nationalist Movement in the Fascist Era*. Johannesburg: Witwatersrand University Press, 1991, p. 144.

66 Barber, p. 108.

67 O'Meara, pp. 86–9.

68 *Ibid*, pp. 88, 163.

69 Bosman, p. 716.

70 O'Meara, pp. 154–5.

71 Adam and Giliomee, p. 157.

72 *Ibid*.

73 O'Meara, p. 176.

74 *Ibid*, pp. 218–9.

75 Bosman, p. 717.

76 TRC, transcript of Sanlam testimony, 13 November 1997, www.doj.gov.za/trc.

77 Adam and Giliomee, pp. 163–5.

78 Du Toit, p. 219.

79 O'Meara.

80 Furlong, p. 140.

81 *Ibid*, pp. 201, 300.

82 Ivor Wilkins and Hans Strydom, *The Super-Afrikaners. Inside the Afrikaner Broederbond*. Johannesburg: Jonathan Ball, 1980, p. 108.

83 Malan, 1961, p. 188.

84 Furlong, p. 192.

85 Malan, 1961, pp. 97–8.

86 *Ibid*, p. 189.

87 Wilkins and Strydom, pp. 107–8.

88 Malan, 1961, p. 216.

89 Furlong, pp. 162, 172–4, 262; Barber, p. 17.

90 Furlong, p. 218; Wilkins and Strydom, p. 109.

91 Furlong, p. 209.

92 *Ibid*.

93 Margaret Ballinger, *From Union to Apartheid. A Trek to Isolation*. Cape Town/Johannesburg/Wynberg: Juta, 1969, p. 223.

94 Hermann Giliomee, 'The Leader and the Citizenry'. In Robert Schrire (ed.), *Leadership in the Apartheid State. From Malan to De Klerk*. Oxford: Oxford University Press, 1994, p. 104.

95 Leonard Thompson, *A History of South Africa*. Johannesburg and Cape Town: Jonathan Ball, 2006 (2001), p. 148.

96 Van Jaarsveld, p. 9.

97 Furlong, p. 253.

98 Beinart, p. 156.

99 Giliomee in Schrire, p. 114.

100 Springbok Legion, *Will we be banned for this?* Archive for Contemporary Affairs, University of the Free State, Bloemfontein, ca 1950.

101 Giliomee in Schrire, p. 113.

102 Cillie quoted in David Welsh, 'The Executive and the African Population – 1948 to the Present'. In Schrire, pp. 139–40.

103 Ballinger, pp. 227–8.

104 *Hansard*, 25 April 1954.

105 Beukes, p. 56.

106 Ballinger, p. 467.

107 *Ibid*, p. 467.

108 Beukes, pp. 62, 64; Ballinger, p. 436.

109 Van Jaarsveld, pp. 13, 14.

110 Giliomee in Schrire, pp. 115–6.

111 Ballinger, p. 233.

112 Van Jaarsveld, p. 7.

113 Furlong, p. 264.

114 Beinart, p. 130.

115 Welsh in Schrire, p. 149.

116 NP, '[Kongres] Beskrywingspunte aan hoofbestuur', 7 March 1952. Archive for Contemporary Affairs, UOFS, Bloemfontein. Translated from Afrikaans.

117 NP, '[Kongres] Beskrywingspunte aan hoofbestuur', 2 August 1950. Archive for Contemporary Affairs, UOFS, Bloemfontein. Translated from Afrikaans.

118 NP, 'Politieke regte van die kleurlinge in die Volksraad' [Political rights of the coloureds in the National Assembly], ca 1964. Marais Viljoen Collection (1961–1974), Archive for Contemporary Affairs, UOFS, Bloemfontein. Translated from Afrikaans.

119 Krüger, pp. 252, 262–94; Ballinger, pp. 259–309.
120 Ballinger, p. 257.
121 Gerrit Viljoen in Munger, p. 177.
122 Krüger, pp. 262–6.
123 Ballinger, pp. 276–7.
124 *Ibid*, p. 278.
125 *Ibid*, p. 276.
126 *Ibid*, p. 278.
127 Krüger, p. 277.
128 Ballinger, 1969, p. 305.
129 *Ibid*, p. 308.
130 NP, 'NP beleid ten opsigte van kleurling', *Die Kruithoring*, Cape, June 1961.
131 *Hansard*, 17 June 1965.
132 NP, Minutes of federal council meeting, Cape Town, 17 May 1968. Marais Viljoen Collection, Archive for Contemporary Affairs, UOFS, Bloemfontein. Translated from Afrikaans.
133 Beukes, p. 81; A van Wyk, *The birth of a new Afrikaner*. Cape Town: Human & Rousseau, 1991.
134 NP Federal Information Service, July 1971. Marais Viljoen Collection, Archive for Contemporary Affairs, UOFS, Bloemfontein. Translated from Afrikaans.
135 GJ Rossouw, 'Essentials of apartheid' in Hofmeyr, Lombaard and Maritz, p. 97.
136 *Ibid*, p. 100.
137 *Ibid*, p. 102.
138 Giliomee, 2004, p. 425.
139 Lubbe in Hofmeyr, Lombaard and Maritz, p. 32.
140 *Ibid*, p. 29.
141 *Ibid*.
142 *Ibid*, p. 30.
143 Rossouw in *ibid*, pp. 102–3.
144 Giliomee, 1994, p. 108.
145 Lubbe in Hofmeyr, Lombaard and Maritz, p. 38.
146 *Ibid*, p. 39.
147 Schrire; Ebbe Dommisse and Willie Esterhuyse, *Anton Rupert. 'n Lewensverhaal*. Cape Town: Tafelberg, 2005.
148 George M Fredrickson, *White Supremacy. A Comparative Study in American and South African History*. New York, Oxford: Oxford University Press, 1981, p. xix.
149 Krüger, p. 11.
150 Du Toit, pp. 218–9.
151 *Ibid*.
152 Apartheid Museum, Johannesburg.
153 Gerrit Viljoen in Munger, p. 174.
154 This section draws mostly on Jan Nederveen Pieterse, *White on Black. Images of Africa and Blacks in Western Popular Culture*. New Haven and London: Yale University Press, 1992, pp. 32–51.
155 Malan, 1961, pp. 46–7.
156 Elsabé Brink, 'Man-made women: Gender, class and the ideology of the volksmoeder'. In Cherryl Walker (ed.), *Women and Gender in Southern Africa to 1945*. Claremont (Cape Town): David Philip, 1990, p. 287.
157 NP, 'NP beleid ten opsigte van kleurling'.
158 Hermann Giliomee, 'The development of the Afrikaner's self-concept'. In Hendrik W van der Merwe (ed.), *Looking at the Afrikaner today. Views of Compatriots and Foreigners*. Cape Town: Tafelberg, 1975, p. 6.
159 Fryer, p. 67.
160 Pieterse, p. 42.
161 DF Malan, 'Beleidstoespraak, Stellenbosch', 5 March 1953, in Goosen, p. 89.
162 In Thompson, p. 88.
163 Giliomee, 1975, p. 13.
164 Krüger, p. 10.
165 O'Meara.
166 Welsh in Schrire, p. 148.
167 Krüger, p. 290.
168 Beinart, p. 163.
169 Giliomee, p. 11.
170 Pieterse, p. 223.
171 Melissa Steyn, 'Rehybridising the Creole'. In Natasha Distiller and Melissa Steyn (eds), *Under Construction: 'Race' and Identity in South Africa Today*. Sandton: Heinemann, 2004, p. 70.
172 *Ibid*, p. 51.

173 Rotberg in Barber, p. 27.
174 Fryer, pp. 67, 75.
175 Pieterse, p. 104.
176 Fryer, pp. 67–8.
177 *Ibid*, pp. 78–9.
178 Apartheid Museum, Johannesburg.
179 Fredrickson, p. 36.
180 Pieterse, p. 104.
181 *Ibid*.
182 Giliomee, 2004, p. 150.
183 Barber, p. 18.
184 Nancy CJ Charton, 'Afrikaners as viewed by English-speaking compatriots'. In Hendrik W van der Merwe (ed.), *Looking at the Afrikaner today. Views of Compatriots and Foreigners*. Cape Town: Tafelberg, 1975.
185 *Beeld*, 6 September 1990.
186 Fredrickson, p. 36.
187 Charton in Van der Merwe, p. 47.
188 Fredrickson, pp. 108–24.
189 *Ibid*, p. 120.

CHAPTER 2

1 *Die Kerkbode*, 13 April 1960, quoted in Lubbe, in Hofmeyr, Lombaard and Maritz, p. 38.
2 Dan O'Meara, *Forty Lost Years: The Apartheid State and the Politics of the National Party 1948–1994*. Athens: Ohio University Press, 1996, p. 154.
3 http://www.anc.org.za. Historical documents.
4 André Brink, *Mapmakers. Writing in a State of Siege*. London/Boston: Faber & Faber, 1983, p. 17.
5 Furlong, p. 210.
6 Ballinger, p. 475.
7 Stephen Gelb (ed.), *South Africa's Economic Crisis*. Cape Town: David Philip; London and New Jersey: Zed Books, 1991, p. 2; Charles H Feinstein, *An Economic History of South Africa. Conquest, Discrimination and Development*. Cambridge: Cambridge University Press, 2005, pp. 108–12; O'Meara, 1996, p. 173.
8 Pienaar and Scholtz, p. 41.
9 DF Malan, p. 98.
10 *Ibid*, p. 97.
11 Adam and Giliomee, p. 161.
12 *Ibid*, pp. 161–2.
13 Hein Marais, *Limits to Change. The Political Economy of Transition*. Cape Town: University of Cape Town Press, 1998, p. 19.
14 *Ibid*.
15 Seekings and Nattrass, p. 140.
16 O'Meara, 1996, p. 143.
17 Louwrens Pretorius, 'The head of government and organized business'. In Schrire, pp. 217–8.
18 *Ibid*, p. 218.
19 *Ibid*.
20 Barend du Plessis, interview, 16 August 2006.
21 Barber, p. 143.
22 O'Meara, 1996, p. 141.
23 Dommisse and Esterhuyse, pp. 175–6.
24 O'Meara, 1996, p. 142.
25 Marais, p. 18.
26 O'Meara, 1996, p. 15.
27 Ballinger, p. 231.
28 John D'Oliveira, *Vorster die Mens*. Johannesburg: Perskor, 1977, p. 216.
29 Krüger, p. 257.
30 *Ibid*.
31 *Ibid*, pp. 282–3.
32 Clark and Worger, p. 51.
33 Mongane Wally Serote, 'City Johannesburg' in Denis Hirson (ed.), *The Lava of this Land*. UNESCO/TriQuarterly Books/Northwestern University; Cape Town: David Philip, 1997 (1971).
34 Stephen Clingman, *Bram Fischer. Afrikaner Revolutionary*. Claremont: David Philip, 2005, p. 193.
35 Beinart, p. 134.
36 Barber, p. 132.
37 Nelson Mandela, *Long Walk to Freedom. The autobiography of Nelson Mandela*. Randburg: Macdonald Purnell, 1995 (1994), p. 128.
38 *Ibid*, p. 130.
39 Barber, pp. 146–7.
40 Mandela, p. 130.
41 Barber, p. 150.

42 Giliomee, 2004, p. 449.
43 Springbok Legion, ca 1948, *To Cape Corps Voters/Aan gekleurde kiesers*. Abraham Jonker Collection, Archive for Contemporary Affairs, UOFS, Bloemfontein.
44 Springbok Legion, ca 1950, *Will we be banned for this?*
45 Krüger, p. 264.
46 Springbok Legion, 1951, *Action Stations! A Crisis Call! From the Springbok Legion*. Abraham Jonker Collection, Archive for Contemporary Affairs, UOFS, Bloemfontein.
47 Krüger, p. 272.
48 Clingman, pp. 192, 193, 233.
49 Hugh Lewin, *Bandiet. Out of Jail*. Johannesburg: Random House, 2002, p. 6.
50 http://www.anc.org.za. Historical documents.
51 Abraham Jonker Collection, Archive for Contemporary Affairs, UOFS, Bloemfontein.
52 Worden, p. 105.
53 Abraham Jonker Collection.
54 Apartheid Museum, Johannesburg.
55 Ingrid Jonker, *Selected Poems*, translated by Jack Cope and William Plomer. Cape Town: Human & Rousseau, 2001 (1988).
56 Breyten Breytenbach, *The True Confessions of an Albino Terrorist*. London: Faber & Faber, 1989 (1984), p. 31.
57 Beinart, pp. 158–9.
58 *Ibid*, p. 159.
59 Steve Biko, *I Write What I Like*. London: Heinemann, 1982, p. 75.
60 Clingman, p. 263.
61 *Ibid*, pp. 274–5.
62 *Ibid*, p. 356.
63 *Ibid*, p. 419.
64 Lewin, p. 175.
65 *Ibid*, p. 176.
66 Brink, pp. 17, 19.
67 Furlong, p. 263.
68 Springbok Legion, *Will we be banned for this?*
69 Van Jaarsveld, p. 12.
70 South African Press Association, 25 May 1955.
71 Beukes, p. 63.
72 *Ibid*, pp. 54–5.
73 Giliomee, 2004, p. 436.
74 *Ibid*, p. 435; Van Jaarsveld, p. 12.
75 Giliomee, 2004, pp. 427–8; Van Jaarsveld, p. 12.
76 Welsh, p. 159; A van Wyk, *The Birth of a New Afrikaner*. Cape Town: Human & Rousseau, 1991.
77 Giliomee, 2004, p. 382.
78 Dirk Richard, 1985, in Welsh, p. 165.
79 O'Meara, 1996, p. 157.
80 Willem de Klerk, 'The concepts verkramp and verlig' in N Rhoodie (ed.), *South African Dialogue: Contrasts in South African Thinking on Basic Race Issues*. Johannesburg: McGraw Hill, 1972.
81 D'Oliveira, pp. 225–6.
82 Marais Viljoen Collection, Archive for Contemporary Affairs, UOFS, Bloemfontein. Translated from Afrikaans.
83 NP Secretariat, 'Verslag oor probleme, klagtes en griewe van die kiesafdelings Christiana en Wolmaransstad' [Report on the problems, complaints and grievances of the electoral wards Christiana and Wolmaransstad], March 1972. Archive for Contemporary Affairs, UOFS, Bloemfontein. Translated from Afrikaans.
84 Marais Viljoen Collection. Translated from Afrikaans.
85 D'Oliveira, 'Foreword'.
86 Laurence Boulle, 'The Head of Government and the Constitution'. In Schrire, p. 22.
87 *Ibid*.
88 D'Oliveira, p. 212.
89 The next section draws on O'Meara, 1996.
90 *Ibid*, pp. 136–7.
91 Steenekamp in Seekings and Nattrass, p. 137.
92 Beinart, p. 181.
93 O'Meara, 1996, pp. 140–1.

94 TRC, Sanlam testimony.
95 Patrick Bond, *Elite Transition. From Apartheid to Neo-liberalism in South Africa*. Pietermaritzburg: University of Natal Press/London: Pluto Press, 2000, p. 25.
96 Feinstein, p. 179.
97 O'Meara, 1996, p. 141.
98 *Ibid*.
99 *Ibid*, p. 142.
100 *Ibid*, p. 143.
101 *Ibid*, p. 144.
102 Giliomee in Schrire, pp. 112–3, 122.
103 D'Oliveira, p. 125.
104 *Ibid*, p. 124.
105 George Bizos, *No one to Blame? In Pursuit of Justice in South Africa*. Claremont: David Philip/Bellville: Mayibuye Books, 2000 (1998).
106 TRC Report Vol. 2. Cape Town: CTP Book Printers, October 1998, p. 198.
107 D'Oliveira, pp. 133–4.
108 TRC Report Vol. 2, p. 200.
109 Beinart, pp. 186–7.
110 McGrath in Seekings and Nattrass, p. 137.
111 Barber, p. 185.
112 *Ibid*.
113 Ballinger, p. 233.
114 Worden, p. 111.
115 Beinart, p. 214.
116 Beinart in Seekings and Nattrass, p. 96.
117 *Ibid*, pp. 95–6.
118 Simkins in Seekings and Nattrass, p. 95.
119 *Ibid*.
120 Jeremy Seekings, 'Political mobilization in the black townships of the Transvaal'. In Philip Frankel, Noam Pines and Mark Swilling (eds), *State, Resistance and Change in South Africa*. New York: Croom Helm, 1988, p. 200.
121 Beinart, p. 203.
122 *Ibid*, pp. 202, 353.
123 *Rand Daily Mail*, May 1976.
124 Photographed by Peter Magubane in Soweto.
125 Worden, p. 119.
126 Biko in Worden, p. 117.
127 Inquest into the death of Steven Bantu Biko, 11 November 1977. Campbell Collection, University of KwaZulu-Natal.
128 TRC Report Vol. 2, p. 16.
129 D'Oliveira, p. 211.
130 *Ibid*, p. 212.
131 Magnus Malan, *My Lewe met die Weermag*. Pretoria: Protea Boekhuis, 2006, p. 120.
132 Constand Viljoen, TRC testimony, 8 October 1997, http://www.justice.gov.za/trc.
133 SANDF submission to the TRC, 1997.
134 Deon Geldenhuys, 'South Africa's foreign relations'. In Schrire (ed.), p. 272.
135 Welsh in Schrire (ed.), p. 174.
136 Mervyn Rees and Chris Day, *Muldergate. The Story of the Info Scandal*. Johannesburg: Macmillan, 1980.

CHAPTER 3

1 Magnus Malan, speech delivered on 24 September 1981 and included in his submission to the TRC, 1997, http://www.doj.gov.za/trc.
2 Koos Kombuis, 'Swart September', *Niemandsland en beyond*. Shifty Music, 1994.
3 Worden, p. 119.
4 Charles Rukuni, 'Who started the war?' In Mothobi Mutloatse (ed.), *Africa South. Contemporary Writings*. London: Heinemann, 1980.
5 Pierre du Toit, *Power Plays. Bargaining Tactics for Transforming South Africa*. Halfway House: Southern Book Publishers, 1991, pp. 22–4.
6 Sheila Camerer, interview, 27 September 2006.
7 Leon Wessels interview.
8 André du Toit, p. 238.
9 Teivo Teivainen, *Enter Economism, Exit Politics. Experts, Economic Policy and the Damage to Democracy*. London/New York: Zed Books, 2002, p. 1.
10 Gelb, p. 2.
11 Adam and Giliomee, p. 164.
12 *Ibid*, p. 163.

13 Worden, p. 122.

14 O'Meara, 1996, pp. 136–7.

15 Lipton, 1985, in Feinstein, p. 179.

16 Hermann Giliomee, 'Surrender Without Defeat. Afrikaners and the South African "miracle"', In *Daedalus, Journal of the American Academy of Arts and Science,* Vol. 126 No. 2, 1997, p. 114.

17 Heribert Adam, 'Interests behind Afrikaner power'. In Adam and Giliomee, pp. 178–80.

18 *Ibid,* p. 178.

19 Beinart, pp. 256–7.

20 Kneifel, Leatt and Nurnberger, p. 82.

21 Terreblanche, p. 73.

22 O'Meara, 1996, p. 188.

23 Pretorius in Schrire, p. 213.

24 O'Meara, 1996, pp. 184–5.

25 Adam, pp. 189–90.

26 O'Meara, 1996, p. 184.

27 *Beeld,* 2 February 1978, in Adam, pp. 178, 189–90.

28 Beinart, p. 245.

29 Pretorius, p. 226.

30 Michael Mann, 'The giant stirs: South African business in the age of reform'. In Frankel, Pines and Swilling, p. 69.

31 O'Meara, 1996, p. 186.

32 Giliomee, 1997, p. 134.

33 Mann, p. 59.

34 Terreblanche, p. 75.

35 *Ibid.*

36 *Sunday Times,* 9 April 2006.

37 O'Meara, 1996, p. 301.

38 Alf Ries and Ebbe Dommisse, *Broedertwis.* Cape Town: Tafelberg, 1982, p. 123.

39 O'Meara, 1996, p. 316.

40 Hermann Giliomee, 'The communal nature of the South African conflict'. In Hermann Giliomee and Lawrence Schlemmer (eds), *Negotiating South Africa's Future.* Halfway House: Southern Book Publishers, 1989, p. 120.

41 O'Meara, 1996, p. 312.

42 Mann, pp. 60–1.

43 *Ibid,* p. 54.

44 Barend du Plessis interview.

45 Leon Wessels interview.

46 *Ibid.*

47 Terreblanche, p. 73.

48 Adam, p. 187.

49 Philip Frankel in O'Meara, 1996, p. 228.

50 *Ibid,* p. 226.

51 O'Meara, 1996, p. 227.

52 Mann, p. 54.

53 O'Meara, 1996, p. 225.

54 *Ibid.*

55 Pretorius, p. 231.

56 *Ibid,* p. 232.

57 Terreblanche, p. 74.

58 Gerrit Viljoen in Munger, p. 173.

59 *White Paper on Defence,* 1977, in SANDF submission to TRC, 7–10 October 1997, http://www.doj.gov.za/trc.

60 P Eric Louw, *The Rise, Fall and Legacy of Apartheid.* Westport/London: Praeger, 2004, pp. 88–93.

61 *Ibid,* p. 91.

62 TRC Report Vol. 2, p. 16.

63 First SANDF submission to the TRC, 1997.

64 Deon Geldenhuys, 'The head of government and South Africa's foreign relations' in Schrire, p. 280.

65 *Ibid,* p. 281.

66 First SANDF submission to the TRC.

67 TRC Report Vol. 2, pp. 27–8.

68 Christi van der Westhuizen, 'Bom in apartheidstaat se hart knypdraai reus se neus'. In *Beeld,* 20 May 2003.

69 Boulle in Schrire, p. 35.

70 *Ibid,* p. 29.

71 *Ibid,* p. 20.

72 *Ibid,* p. 28.

73 Annette Seegers, 'The head of government and the executive' in Schrire, pp. 60–1.

74 Boulle, p. 24.

75 *Ibid,* p. 31.

76 *Ibid,* p. 21.

77 Michel Albeldas and Alan Fischer, *A Question of Survival. Conversation with Key South Africans.* Johannesburg: Jonathan Ball, 1987, p. 491.

78 Boulle, p. 20.

79 TRC Report Vol. 2, p. 540.

80 *Ibid.*

81 Mahmood Mamdani, *Citizen and Subject. Contemporary Africa and the Legacy of Late Colonialism.* Princeton (NJ): Princeton University Press, 1996.

82 FW de Klerk, *The Autobiography. The Last Trek: A New Beginning.* London: Macmillan, 1998, p. 191.

83 Albeldas and Fischer, p. 485.

84 Thompson, p. 220.

85 NP, ca 1982, *Die NP se plan vir SA* (pamphlet).

86 Thompson, p. 219.

87 Hennie Kotzé, 'The Stakeholders' in Pierre du Toit and Willie Esterhuyse (eds), *The Myth Makers. The Elusive Bargain for South Africa's Future.* Halfway House: Southern Book Publishers, 1990, p. 40.

88 James Leatt, Theo Kneifel and Klaus Nürnberger (eds), *Contending Ideologies in South Africa.* Grand Rapids: Wm B Eerdmans/Cape Town: David Philip, 1986.

89 Jeremy Grest, 1988, 'The Crisis of Local Government in South Africa'. In Frankel, Pines and Swilling, p. 103.

90 Seekings in Beinart, p. 255.

91 Grest, p. 95.

92 Seekings in Beinart, p. 204.

93 Grest, p. 98.

94 *Ibid.*

95 *Ibid*, p. 103.

96 *Ibid*, p. 104.

97 William Cobbett, Daryl Glaser, Doug Hindson and Mark Swilling, 'A Critical Analysis of the South African State's Reform Strategies in the 1980s'. In Frankel, Pines and Swilling, pp. 30–6.

98 Grest, pp. 92–3.

99 *Ibid*, pp. 98–101.

100 Thompson, p. 219.

101 TRC Report Vol. 2, p. 204.

102 Thompson, p. 222.

103 Clark and Worger, p. 96.

104 Louw, p. 91.

105 *Ibid*, pp. 90–1.

106 Seegers, p. 62.

107 Wessels interview.

108 CJ Joubert and D Jooste, *Geskiedenis vir St 7. Volgens die nuwe kernsillabus.* Johannesburg: Perskor, 1984 (1974), p. 96.

109 Kotzé, p. 41.

110 *Ibid*, p. 43.

111 TRC Report Vol. 2, p. 218.

112 *Ibid*, p. 226.

113 *Ibid.*

114 *Ibid*, p. 228.

115 *Ibid*, pp. 231–2.

116 Barber, p. 261.

117 Wessels interview.

118 Du Plessis interview.

119 Feinstein, p. 227.

120 Du Plessis interview.

121 Martin Murray, *South Africa. Time of Agony, Time of Destiny. The Upsurge of Popular Protest.* London: Verso, 1987.

122 Feinstein, p. 225.

123 *Ibid*, p. 230.

124 Du Plessis interview.

125 *Ibid*; Wessels interview.

126 NP, *Die Nasionalis/The Nationalist*, Vol. 3 No. 3, March 1985.

127 Du Plessis interview.

128 Murray, p. 370.

129 *Mail & Guardian*, 11 October 1996.

130 PGJ Meiring, 'Faith communities face their apartheid past'. In Hofmeyr, Lombaard and Maritz, p. 109.

131 Lubbe in *ibid*, p. 45.

132 Esterhuyse, quoted in Lubbe, *ibid*, p. 46.

133 *Ibid*, p. 47.

134 *Ibid.*

CHAPTER 4

1 Major General Joep Joubert, TRC testimony, 8 October 1997, http://www.doj.gov.za/trc.

2 From the song 'Hou my vas korporaal', Bernoldus Niemand (translated from Afrikaans lyrics). James Phillips and Carl Raubenheimer, *Wie is Bernoldus Niemand?* Shifty Music, 1984.

3 TRC Report Vol. 2, p. 34.

4 Clark and Worger, p. 96.

5   Magnus Malan, written submission to TRC, 1997, http://www.doj.gov.za/trc.

6   TRC Report Vol. 2, p. 204.

7   Beinart, p. 265.

8   Clarke and Worger, pp. 94–6.

9   *Ibid.*

10 Thompson, p. 261.

11 Worden, p. 134.

12 Beinart, p. 263.

13 *Ibid*, p. 264.

14 Adrian Guelke, 'Southern Africa and the Superpowers' in Stephen Chan, *Exporting Apartheid. Foreign Policies in Southern Africa 1978–1988.* London and Basingstoke: Macmillan, 1990, p. 232.

15 Stephen Chan, 'Foreign Policies in Southern Africa: The History of an Epoch'. *Ibid*, p. 21.

16 Rob Davies and Dan O'Meara, 'Total strategy in Southern Africa – An analysis of South African regional policy since 1978'. *Ibid*, pp. 196–7.

17 Pik Botha, verbatim transcript of TRC testimony, 14 October 1997, http://www.doj.gov.za/trc.

18 Magnus Malan, verbatim transcript of TRC testimony, 4–5 December 1997, http://www.doj.gov.za/trc.

19 Barber, p. 263.

20 Barend du Plessis interview.

21 Davies and O'Meara in Chan, p. 198.

22 TRC Report Vol. 2, p. 88.

23 *Ibid*, pp. 79–80.

24 Robert M Price, 'Pretoria's Southern African Strategy' in Chan, p. 153.

25 TRC Report Vol. 2, p. 56.

26 *Ibid*, p. 60.

27 *Ibid*, pp. 93–4; Price, pp. 153–4.

28 TRC Report Vol. 2, p. 94.

29 *Ibid*, p. 74.

30 *Ibid*, p. 77.

31 Chan, p. 25.

32 TRC Report Vol. 2, pp. 43–4.

33 *Ibid*, p. 454.

34 Barber, pp. 239–41.

35 International Defence and Aid Fund for Southern Africa, 'The Natal Violence. South Africa's Killing Fields'. *IDAF Information Notes and Briefings*, No. 90, 4 August 1990.

36 TRC Report Vol. 2, pp. 457–8.

37 IDAF, p. 2.

38 TRC Report Vol 2, p. 627.

39 *Ibid*, p. 463.

40 FW de Klerk, p. 208.

41 TRC Report Vol. 2, p. 186.

42 FW de Klerk, p. 208.

43 Mangosuthu Buthelezi, press statement: 'The training of 150 Zulus in VIP protection services', Ulundi, 13 August 1991. Campbell Collection, University of KwaZulu-Natal, Durban.

44 TRC Report Vol. 2, p. 464.

45 *Ibid*, p. 631.

46 Black Sash, Affidavit No. KLM 01/1/237/01. Campbell Collection, University of KwaZulu-Natal, Durban.

47 TRC Report Vol. 2, p. 606.

48 Black Sash, Affidavit No. KLM 01/1/237/04. Campbell Collection, University of KwaZulu-Natal, Durban.

49 IDAF, p. 3.

50 TRC Report Vol 2, p. 468.

51 *Ibid*, p. 231.

52 *Ibid*, p. 273.

53 *Ibid.*

54 *Ibid*, p. 274.

55 Adriaan Vlok, verbatim transcript of TRC testimony, 14 October 1997, http://www.doj.gov.za/trc.

56 TRC Report Vol. 2, p. 218.

57 *Beeld*, 9 October 1997; 7 April 1999; 24 May 1999.

58 TRC Report Vol. 2, p. 322.

59 Joep Joubert, verbatim transcript of TRC testimony.

60 Chan, p. 15.

61 *Beeld*, 7 April 1999.

62 *Beeld*, 9 April 1999.

63 Joep Joubert, TRC testimony.

64 TRC Report Vol. 2, pp. 231–2.

65 Malan, TRC written submission.

66 *Ibid.*

67 TRC Report Vol. 2, p. 274.

68 *Ibid.*

69 *Ibid.*

70 Vlok, TRC testimony.

71 *Ibid.*

72 Malan, TRC written submission.

73 TRC Report Vol. 2, p. 273.

74 *Ibid*, p. 219.

75 *Ibid*, p. 221.

76 *Ibid*, pp. 261–3.

77 *Ibid*, pp. 259–61.

78 *Ibid*, p. 239.

79 *Ibid*, p. 293.

80 Johannes Kerkorrel and the Gereformeerde Blues Band, 'Energie'. *Eet Kreef!*, ca 1990. Translated from Afrikaans.

81 Terreblanche, pp. 75–7.

82 Robert W Cox, *Production, Power and World Order. Social Forces in the Making of History*. New York: Columbia University Press, 1988, p. 187.

83 FW de Klerk, p. 138.

84 Cox, p. 190.

85 Deborah Posel, 'The case for a welfare state: Poverty and the politics of the urban African family in the 1930s and 1940s'. In Saul Dubow and Alan Jeeves (eds), *South Africa's 1940s. Worlds of Possibilities*. Cape Town: Double Storey Books, 2005, p. 66; Cox, p. 189.

86 FW de Klerk, p. 139.

87 Cox, p. 190.

88 In Mann, p. 52.

89 Timothy Scarnecchia, 'The "Fascist Cycle" in Zimbabwe, 2000–2005'. *Journal of Southern African Studies*, Vol. 32 No. 2, June 2006.

90 Pretorius in Schrire, p. 233.

91 Murray, p. 361.

92 Beinart, p. 260.

93 Murray, p. 371.

94 Bond, pp. 158–9.

95 Vishnu Padayachee, 'The politics of South Africa's international financial relations, 1970–1990'. In Gelb, pp. 89–90, 91–2.

96 *Ibid*, p. 93.

97 *Ibid.*

98 FW de Klerk, p. 189.

99 Marais, p. 101.

100 Bond, p. 159.

101 NP, *Die Nasionalis/The Nationalist*, Vol. 3 No. 3, March 1985.

102 Du Plessis interview.

CHAPTER 5

1 *Business International*, 1980, in O'Meara, 1996, p. 187.

2 Roelf Meyer interview, 15 September 2006.

3 Bond, *Elite Transition*.

4 Christi van der Westhuizen, 'FW de Klerk: Prototipe van die Suid-Afrikaner'. In *Beeld*, 5 February 1999.

5 Giliomee, 1997, p. 117.

6 Hermann Giliomee, ''n Leier wat sy volgelinge nie vertel het nie' [A leader who did not tell his followers]. *Boekewêreld*. Supplement in Nasionale Pers newspapers, 2 March 1999.

7 Giliomee, 1997, p. 130.

8 Robert Schrire in Giliomee, *Boekewêreld*; James Hamill, 'A disguised surrender? South Africa's negotiated settlement and the politics of conflict resolution'. In *Diplomacy and Statecraft*, Vol. 14 No. 3, September 2003.

9 In *Rapport*, 9 February 1997.

10 *Ibid*; *Boekewêreld*.

11 Johannes Kerkorrel and the Gereformeerde Blues Band, 'BMW', *Eet Kreef!*, Shifty Music, 2002. Originally released ca 1990.

12 O'Meara, 1996, p. 391.

13 NP, *Die Realis/The Realist*. Supplement in *Rekord*, Pretoria, 6 September 1989.

14 NP, full-page advertisement, *Beeld*, 3 July 1989.

15 NP, 'Federal Congress. Agenda and resolutions', 1989.

16 NP, 'KP Leuens'. In *Die Realis/ The Realist*.

17 Du Toit, p. 29.

18 NP, 'Zach de Beer forecasts an ANC government'. In *Die Realis/The Realist*.

19 Janis Grobbelaar, 'Afrikaner nationalism: The end of a dream?'. In Abebe Zegeye (ed.), *Social Identities in the New South Africa. After Apartheid*, Vol. 1. Roggebaai/Maroelana: Kwela

Books; SA History Online, 2001,
pp. 307–8.

20 Willem de Klerk in O'Meara, 1996,
p. 404.

21 *Beeld*, 3 July 1989.

22 *Ibid.*

23 Van der Westhuizen in *Beeld*.

24 Rina Venter interview, 29 August 2006.

25 Dave Steward, 'Sommige herskep die
geskiedenis, ander maak dit'. In *Rapport*,
27 August 2006.

26 Willie Esterhuyse, *Die Burger*,
15 August 2006.

27 *Ibid.*

28 Steward in *Rapport*.

29 Thabo Mbeki, 'Letter from the
President', *ANC Today*, www. anc.org.za,
Vol. 6 No. 43, 3–9 November 2006.

30 Tom Lodge, 'The African National
Congress in the 1990s'. In Glenn Moss
and Ingrid Obery (eds), *South African
Review 6. From 'Red Friday' to Codesa*.
Johannesburg: Ravan Press, 1992, p. 50.

31 *Ibid.*

32 TRC Report Vol. 2, p. 37.

33 *Beeld*, 3 July 1989.

34 Van der Westhuizen in *Beeld*.

35 Sheila Camerer interview,
27 September 2006.

36 Giliomee, 1997, pp. 134–5.

37 Meyer interview.

38 De Klerk, 1998, p. 134.

39 Pik Botha interview, 12 April 2006.

40 Barend du Plessis interview.

41 De Klerk, 1990, from *Hansard Debates
of Parliament*, quoted in Clark and
Worger, p. 147.

42 Venter interview.

43 De Klerk, 1998, p. 148.

44 *Ibid*, p. 165.

45 Meyer interview.

46 Camerer interview.

47 Venter interview.

48 Leon Wessels interview.

49 Pik Botha interview.

50 De Klerk in Clark and Worger, p. 147.

51 O'Meara, 1996, p. 405.

52 NP, *Die Nasionalis/The Nationalist*,
June 1990.

53 Barber, p. 277.

54 Johannes Rantete and Hermann
Giliomee, 'Transition to democracy
through transaction? Bilateral
negotiations between the ANC and
the NP in South Africa'. In *African
Affairs*, Vol. 91, 1992, p. 523.

55 NP, *Die Nasionalis/The Nationalist*,
June 1990.

56 Thompson, p. 245.

57 Rantete and Giliomee, p. 523.

58 De Klerk, 1998, p. 162.

59 NP, *Congress Minutes*, 1990.

60 O'Meara, 1996, p. 405.

61 *Ibid.*

62 Friedman in Giliomee, 1997, p. 139.

63 ANC, 'Response by Nelson Mandela,
president of the African National
Congress, to the speech by the state
president FW de Klerk at the first
session of CODESA'. World Trade
Centre, Kempton Park,
20 December 1991.

64 Venter interview.

65 Rantete and Giliomee, p. 525.

66 Nicholas Haysom, 'Negotiating a
political settlement in South Africa'.
In Moss and Obery, p. 42.

67 Chris April, in *Beeld*, 24 June 1991.

68 Barber, p. 292.

69 Wessels, Meyer, Delport, Venter
interviews.

70 Venter interview.

71 Magnus Malan, 2006, p. 383.

72 De Klerk, 1998, p. 208.

73 *Ibid*, pp. 208–9.

74 TRC Report Vol. 2, pp. 465–6.

75 De Klerk, 1998, p. 214.

76 TRC Report Vol. 2, p. 630.

77 Magnus Malan, 2006, pp. 383, 393.

78 Joanne Collinge, 'Launched on a bloody
tide' in Moss and Obery, p. 12.

79 *Ibid*, p. 6.

80 Wessels interview.

81 De Klerk, 1998, p. 222.

82 Richard Spitz and Matthew Chaskalson,
*The Politics of Transition. A Hidden
History of South Africa's Negotiated
Settlement*. Johannesburg:

Witwatersrand University Press,
2001 (2000), p. 21.

83 Collinge in Moss and Obery, p. 15.
84 Tertius Delport interview,
28 August 2006.
85 Steven Friedman (ed.) *The Long
Journey. South Africa's quest for a
negotiated settlement*. Johannesburg:
Ravan Press, 1993, p. 39.
86 *Ibid*, p. 42.
87 *Ibid*, pp. 70–1.
88 *Ibid*, p. 67.
89 Spitz and Chaskalson, p. 23.
90 *ANC Negotiations Bulletin*, No. 10,
18 May 1992. Quoted in speech by
Tertius Delport, 'The new South Africa:
Creating the confidence to make it
work', 3 August 1992.
91 This paragraph is based on Spitz and
Chaskalson, pp. 21–5.
92 Friedman, p. 64.
93 This paragraph is based on Friedman,
pp. 70–85.
94 Delport interview; Wessels interview.
95 Friedman, p. 82.
96 *Ibid*.
97 *Ibid*, p. 81.
98 Delport speech.
99 Delport interview.
100 Friedman, p. 40.
101 *Ibid*, p. 41.
102 Alex Boraine, *A Country Unmasked.
Inside South Africa's Truth and
Reconciliation Commission*. Cape Town:
Oxford University Press, 2000, p. 154.
103 TRC Report Vol. 2, p. 584.
104 SA Institute of Race Relations,
submission to conference on violence
and intimidation, Pretoria,
24–25 May 1991. Black Sash
collection, Campbell Collection,
University of KwaZulu-Natal, Durban.
105 TRC Report Vol. 2, p. 630.
106 International Defence and Aid Fund for
Southern Africa, 'Information Notes
and Briefings', No. 91/1, January 1991.
Black Sash collection, Campbell
Collection, University of
KwaZulu-Natal, Durban.

107 Chan, p. 15.
108 De Klerk, 1998, pp. 202–3.
109 *Ibid*, p. 210.
110 Chan, p. 16.
111 *Ibid*.
112 Magnus Malan, 2006, pp. 362–4.
113 Annelizé van Wyk interview,
19 June 2006.
114 Frederik van Zyl Slabbert, *The Other
Side of History. An Anecdotal Reflection
on Political Transition in South Africa*.
Johannesburg and Cape Town: Jonathan
Ball, 2006, p. 17.
115 De Klerk, 1998, p. 201.
116 *Ibid*, p. 265.
117 NP, press statement by Fanus Schoeman,
16 January 1997.
118 IDAF, 1991.
119 De Klerk, 1998, p. 286.
120 TRC Report Vol. 2, p. 601.
121 Goldstone Commission,
in IDAF, 1991.
122 IDAF, 1991.
123 De Klerk, 1998, p. 199.
124 TRC Report Vol. 2, pp. 645–8.
125 Van Zyl Slabbert, p. 17.
126 *Beeld*, 9 September 1993.
127 Grobbelaar, in Zegeye.
128 TRC Report Vol. 2, pp. 611–3.
129 IDAF, 1991.
130 TRC Report Vol. 2, p. 625.
131 *Ibid*, p. 630.
132 *Ibid*, p. 606.
133 *Ibid*, p. 608.
134 *Ibid*, p. 603.
135 *Ibid*, pp. 648–51.

CHAPTER 6

1 Antjie Krog, *A Change of Tongue*.
Parktown: Random House, 2003.
2 *Beeld*, 'Wil die WVK sê al die mense lieg
oor Boipatong?', 25 November 2000.
3 Hein Marais, pp. 102–3.
4 Friedman, p. 81.
5 *Ibid*, p. 42.
6 Rina Venter interview.
7 Leon Wessels interview.
8 *Sunday Times*, 20 September 1992;
Rapport, 13 August 1995.

9   Coetsee in *Rapport*, 13 August 1995.

10 De Klerk, 1998, pp. 250–4.

11 Coetsee in *Rapport*.

12 De Klerk, 1998, p. 252.

13 Pik Botha interview; *Star*,
    1 November 2006.

14 Sheila Camerer interview.

15 De Klerk, 1998, p. 256.

16 Mandela, p. 596.

17 De Klerk, 1998, p. 252;
    Thompson, p. 247.

18 Waldmeir, 1997, in Barber, p. 295.

19 Roelf Meyer interview.

20 Organisation for African Unity,
    'Declaration of the OAU Ad Hoc
    Committee on Southern Africa on
    the Question of South Africa', Harare,
    21 August 1990. Confirmed as ANC
    policy at consultative conference,
    December 1990.

21 ANC, National Consultative Conference,
    'Resolutions for the coming year',
    December 1990, www.saha.org.za.

22 ANC, *Ready to Govern*. Policy
    guidelines for a democratic South
    Africa adopted at national conference,
    28–31 May 1992.

23 Lourens du Plessis and Hugh Corder,
    *Understanding South Africa's
    transitional bill of rights*. Cape Town:
    Juta & Co Ltd, 1994, p. 31.

24 *Ibid*, p. 32.

25 Hermann Giliomee, 'The Leader and
    the Citizenry'. In Schrire, p. 122.

26 Du Plessis and Corder, pp. 23, 26, 27.

27 *Ibid*, p. 26.

28 *Ibid*, p. 32.

29 Hugh Corder, 'Towards a South African
    Constitution'. In *The Modern Law
    Review*, Vol. 57 No. 4, July 1994, p. 515.

30 *Ibid*, p. 491.

31 *Ibid*, p. 515.

32 *Ibid*.

33 Hermann Giliomee, 1997; Hamill, 2003.

34 Du Plessis and Corder, p. 45.

35 Spitz and Chaskalson, pp. 31–2.

36 Tertius Delport interview.

37 Sheila Camerer interview.

38 Rina Venter interview.

39 As described in Rantete and Giliomee,
    p. 524.

40 *Mail & Guardian*, 11 October 1996.

41 Spitz and Chaskalson, p. 57.

42 *Ibid*, pp. 58–9.

43 *Ibid*, pp. 56, 58.

44 Friedman, p. 85.

45 Spitz and Chaskalson, pp. 51–2.

46 *Ibid*, p. 55.

47 NP, 'Comparative study of framework
    for a new constitutional dispensation
    as approved by federal congress,
    September 1991 and already approved in
    constitutional principles or proposed
    in draft constitution', July 1993.

48 *Ibid*.

49 Venter interview.

50 Wessels interview.

51 Spitz and Chaskalson, p. 39.

52 Rina Venter, letter to President
    FW de Klerk, 2 August 1993.

53 Venter interview.

54 De Klerk, 1998.

55 *Beeld*, 10 February 1997.

56 Delport interview.

57 De Klerk, 1998, p. 257.

58 Kenneth Good, 'Democracy and the
    control of elites'. In Henning Melber
    (ed.) *Limits to liberation in Southern
    Africa. The unfinished business of
    democratic consolidation*. Cape Town:
    Human Sciences Research Council/
    Grahamstown: *Journal of Contemporary
    African Studies*, 2003.

59 Pik Botha interview.

60 Friedman, p. 41.

61 *Ibid*, p. 42.

62 Giliomee, 2004.

63 Bond; Marais.

64 Alan Hirsch, *A Season of Hope. Economic
    Reform under Mandela and Mbeki*.
    University of KwaZulu-Natal Press/
    IDRC, 2005.

65 *Ibid*.

66 ANC, joint communiqué of ANC, Natal
    Indian Congress, Transvaal Indian
    Congress and members of the Indian
    community of South Africa, Lusaka,
    10 October 1988, www.anc.org.za.

67 Allister Sparks, *Beyond the miracle. Inside the new South Africa.* Johannesburg and Cape Town: Jonathan Ball, 2003, p. 180.
68 Francis Fukuyama, *The End of History and the Last Man.* New York: Free Press, 1992.
69 Susan Strange, *Casino Capitalism.* New York: Basil Blackwell, 1986.
70 Hirsch.
71 *Ibid.*
72 ANC, *Ready to Govern*, ANC policy guidelines for a democratic South Africa, 1992.
73 Edward Webster and Glenn Adler, 'Towards a class compromise in South Africa's "double transition": Bargained liberalization and the consolidation of democracy'. In *Politics and Society*, Vol. 27 No. 3, Sage Publications, 1999, p. 365.
74 Meyer interview.
75 Bond, p. 57.
76 *Ibid*, pp. 56–7.
77 Sparks, pp. 181–2.
78 *Ibid*, p. 182.
79 *Ibid.*
80 De Klerk, 1998, p. 345.
81 *Ibid.*
82 De Klerk, 1998, p. 345.
83 Bond, p. 64.
84 Wessels interview.

CHAPTER 7

1 De Klerk, 1998, p. 279.
2 *Beeld*, 6 September 1990.
3 Johan Kilian interview, 23 January 2007.
4 Deon Geldenhuys, 'International involvement in South Africa's political transformation'. In W Carlsnaes and M Muller (eds), *Change and South Africa's external relations.* Johannesburg: International Thompson Publishing, 1997, p. 40.
5 *Die Suid-Afrikaan*, February/March 1993.
6 Human Sciences Research Council, South Africa Social Attitudes Survey, 2003.
7 Stan Simmons interview, 11 December 2006.

8 Barend du Plessis in *Beeld*, 9 August 1991.
9 *Beeld*, 25 May 1991.
10 Simmons interview.
11 In *Beeld*, 19 May 1999.
12 See for example Maxine Reitzes (ed.), *Election Synopsis*, Vol. 1 No. 2, HSRC/CPS, 2004; Sidney Letsholo, 'How the ANC won the 2004 election: Perspectives on voting behaviour in South Africa'. *Electoral Institute for Southern Africa*, Occasional Paper No. 31, April 2005; Pierre du Toit, 'The South African voter and the racial census, c 1994'. In *Politeia*, Vol. 18 No. 2, 1999.
13 Steven Friedman, 'No easy stroll to dominance: Party dominance, opposition and civil society in South Africa'. In Hermann Giliomee and Charles Simkins (eds), *The awkward embrace: One-party domination and democracy.* Cape Town: Tafelberg, 1999, p. 110.
14 Marthinus van Schalkwyk interview, 2 November 2006.
15 De Klerk, 1998, pp. 359–60.
16 Meyer interview.
17 Theunis Roux, 'Property'. In Dennis Davis, Halton Cheadle, Nicholas Haysom (eds), *Fundamental rights in the constitution. Commentary and cases.* Centre for Applied Legal Studies/Juta & Co Ltd, 1997, p. 250.
18 Dan O'Meara, correspondence with the author, 29 January 2007.
19 *Beeld*, 14 November 1990.
20 De Klerk, 1998, pp. 344–5.
21 *Ibid*, p. 345.
22 Van Schalkwyk interview.
23 De Klerk, 1998, p. 344.
24 NP, 'Normative Economic Model', March 1993.
25 Webster and Adler, p. 364.
26 Adam, pp. 177–95.
27 Van Schalkwyk interview.
28 Delport interview.
29 Kilian interview.
30 Meyer interview.

31 *Argus*, 10 December 1996.
32 Van Schalkwyk interview.
33 Annelizé van Wyk interview.
34 De Klerk, 1998, pp. 297–99.
35 Van Wyk interview.
36 Meyer, Botha, Camerer interviews.
37 Botha interview.
38 *Beeld*, 13 February 1996.
39 *Beeld*, 17 October 1996.
40 De Klerk, 1998, p. 362.
41 *Ibid*, p. 363.
42 Meyer interview.
43 Kilian interview.
44 *Ibid*.
45 *Beeld*, 17 October 1996.
46 Van Wyk interview.
47 *The Star*, 22 April 1998.
48 De Klerk, 1998, pp. 362–3.
49 *Beeld*, 7 June 1999.
50 *Beeld*, 19 May 1999.
51 *Beeld*, 27 August 1997.
52 Arrie Rossouw in *Beeld*,
     9 September 1997.
53 Simmons interview.
54 *Beeld*, 24 June 1991.
55 Simmons interview.
56 James Selfe interview,
     13 September 2006.
57 *The Star*, 22 April 1998.
58 Christi van der Westhuizen,
     'Opposisie woel op oorlogspad … en
     bring woedespasmas'. In *Beeld*,
     20 June 2000.
59 *Beeld*, 7 June 1999.
60 HSRC, South Africa Social Attitudes
     Survey, 2003.
61 Institute for Democracy in South
     Africa (IDASA), political information
     and monitoring service, 'Party support
     in SA's third democratic election'.
     No date.
62 Kilian interview.
63 Democratic Party, 'Die moed om terug
     te slaan/The guts to fight back', 1999.
     The quotes that follow are from the
     same pamphlet.
64 *Beeld*, 8 April 2003.
65 Tom Lodge, *Consolidating democracy.
     South Africa's second popular election.*

     Johannesburg: Wits University Press,
     1999, p. 183.
66 *Ibid*, pp. 168, 170, 173.
67 *Ibid*, p. 183.
68 *Ibid*, pp. 176–7.
69 DP, Federal Council minutes,
     10–11 June 2000.
70 Simmons interview.
71 DP/NP, 'Outline agreement between the
     Democratic Party and the New National
     Party', 24 June 2000.
72 Kilian interview.
73 Selfe interview.
74 *Ibid*.
75 Charles Redcliffe in *Beeld*, 21 June 2002.
76 *Independent Online*, 27 November 2001.
77 In *Beeld*, 8 April 2003.
78 In *Beeld*, 28 March 2003.
79 *ThisDay*, 12 April 2004.
80 Letsholo, p. 12.
81 Adam Habib and Sanusha Naidu,
     'Are SA's elections a racial census?' in
     Reitzes, p. 7.
82 Robert Mattes, Annie Barbara
     Chikwanha and Alex Magezi,
     *Afrobarometer. South Africa: A decade
     of democracy.* IDASA/Ghana Centre for
     Democratic Development/Michigan
     University, 2004.
83 Christi van der Westhuizen,
     'Bittereinders they ain't'. *Wide Angle*
     column in *ThisDay*, 10 June 2004.
84 *Beeld*, 9 August 2004.
85 *Beeld*, 11 April 2005.
86 'Net 100 daar toe NNP ontbind'. In
     Beeld, 11 April 2005.
87 *Guardian Weekly*, 15–21 April 2005.
88 Dan O'Meara, correspondence with
     the author, 29 January 2007.

CHAPTER 8

1 *Sunday Times Lifestyle*, 29 January 2006.
2 Brixton Moord en Roof Orkes,
    'Fortuinverteller', from the CD *Terug in
    Skubbe*. Lyrics by Roof Bezuidenhout,
    2005.
3 *Boekewêreld*, 3 March 1999.
4 Johan Kilian interview.
5 Willem de Klerk, *Die Tweede (R)evolusie.*

Afrikanerdom en die Identiteitskrisis.
Johannesburg: Jonathan Ball, 1984, p. 8.

6   Rupert Brown, *Group Processes.*
    Dynamics Within and Between Groups.
    Oxford: Basil Blackwell, 1989,
    pp. 200–03.

7   Karen Zoid, 'Danville Diva' on *Chasing
    the Sun.* EMI Music, 2003.

8   *Business Day,* 3 October 2006.

9   *Mail & Guardian* letters page, 23
    February–1 March 2007.

10 Steyn in Distiller and Steyn, p. 70.

11 *Beeld,* 9 December 2005.

12 Ministry of Arts and Culture, 'Bok
    van Blerks's [*sic*] supposed Afrikaans
    "struggle song," [*sic*] De La Rey and
    its coded message to fermenting
    [*sic*] revolutionary sentiments.'
    Press statement, 5 February 2007.

13 *Business Day,* 3 October 2006.

14 *Rapport,* 28 January 2007.

15 *Ibid.*

16 *Beeld,* 7 February 2007.

17 Steyn in Distiller and Steyn, p. 70.

18 *Rapport,* 28 January 2007.

19 *Ibid.*

20 *Ibid.*

21 *Mail & Guardian,* 8–14 September 2006.

22 *Beeld,* letters page, 28 August 2006.

23 *Beeld,* letters page, 27 September 2006.

24 *Mail & Guardian,* 15–21 September 2006.

25 *Beeld,* 2 October 2006.

26 *Beeld,* 30 September 2006.

27 Louis Esterhuizen, 2000, 'Patria' in
    Hugo, Rousseau and Du Plessis, p. 78.
    Translated from Afrikaans.

28 *Sunday Times,* 11 March 2007.

29 Willem de Klerk, 1984, p. 11.

30 Clingman, p. 415.

31 Barend du Plessis interview.

32 WA de Klerk, 'An Afrikaner revolution'
    in Munger, pp. 63–71.

33 Willem de Klerk, 1984, p. 23.

34 *Ibid,* p. 11.

35 *Ibid,* p. 23.

36 Barber, p. 236.

37 NP pamphlet, 1981.

38 Leon Wessels interview.

39 Willem de Klerk, 1984, p. 26.

40 *Ibid,* p. 35.

41 *Ibid,* p. 41.

42 Sheila Camerer interview.

43 Rina Venter interview.

44 Tertius Delport interview.

45 Roelf Meyer interview.

46 Willem de Klerk, 1984, pp. 32–3.

47 Annelizé van Wyk interview.

48 Wessels interview, Du Plessis interview.

49 Van Wyk interview.

50 Wessels interview.

51 *Ibid.*

52 *Hansard,* 30 January 1985.

53 *Hansard,* 27 March 1985.

54 *Hansard,* Vol. 3 Col. 2826, 1985.

55 *Hansard,* 27 March 1985.

56 Black Sash, Memorandum on police
    conduct in the Eastern Cape, March
    1985. Campbell Collection, University
    of KwaZulu-Natal, Durban.

57 *Hansard,* 29 January 1985.

58 *Ibid.*

59 Suzman in *Hansard,* 27 March 1985.

60 FJ le Roux in *ibid.*

61 Venter interview.

62 Pik Botha interview.

63 EPG report, 7 June 1986, p. 65, quoted in
    Leon Wessels' submission to the TRC,
    15 October 1997.

64 Wessels evidence to TRC.

65 Wessels interview.

66 Verbatim transcript of TRC hearing,
    5 December 1997, www.doj.gov.za/trc.

67 *Mail & Guardian,* 8–14 September 2006.

68 *Ibid.*

69 NP submission to TRC by FW de Klerk,
    August 1996, www.doj.gov.za/trc.

70 Boraine, p. 155.

71 Second NP submission to TRC,
    May 1997, www.doj.gov.za/trc.

72 Boraine, p. 161.

73 Pieterse, pp. 105–7.

74 *Beeld,* 2 December 2006.

75 Giliomee, 2004, pp. 355–6.

76 Biko, pp. 76–7.

77 *Ibid,* p. 77

78 Beukes, p. 62.

79 Gerrit Viljoen in Munger, p. 179.

80 TRC Report Vol. 2, p. 53.

81 NP, Congress Minutes, 1990.
82 Pierre, 1988, in Clark and Worger, p. 101.
83 'Afrikaners soos vrou wie se man haar slaan'. *Rapport* letters page, 26 November 2005.
84 Bond, pp. 24–9.
85 ANC, *Ready to Govern*.
86 Altman, 2003, in Benjamin Roberts, 'Empty stomachs, empty pockets: Poverty and inequality in post-apartheid South Africa'. In John Daniel, Roger Southall and Jessica Lutchman (eds), *State of the Nation South Africa 2004–2005*. Cape Town: HSRC Press, 2005, p. 488.
87 Statistics SA, 2002, in Christi van der Westhuizen, 'Gety moet nog draai vir die armes'. In *Beeld*, 26 February 2003.
88 Bradshaw, Masiteng and Nannan in Roberts, p. 491.
89 *Ibid.*
90 Seekings and Natrass, pp. 341, 352.
91 *Ibid*, p. 306.
92 Whiteford and Van Seventer in *ibid*, p. 304.
93 Roberts.
94 Sanlam hearing, TRC, www.doj.gov.za/trc.
95 *Financial Mail*, 16 December 2005; *Business Report*, 11 March 2007.
96 *fin24.com*, 22 January 2006; *Sunday Independent*, 11 March 2007.
97 Dommisse and Esterhuyse, p. 217.
98 *Business Report*, 5 March 2007.
99 Thabo Mbeki, 'Apartheid is dead! Hail the spirit of Anton Rupert!' Letter from the President, *ANC Today*, Vol. 6 No. 5, 10–16 February 2006; www.mg.co.za, 19 January 2006.
100 *Business Report*, 11 March 2007.
101 *Business Day*, 12 May 2006.
102 *Business Day*, 3 May 2007.
103 Herman Engelbrecht, 2000, 'Waarheen?' in Hugo, Rousseau and Du Plessis, p. 15. Translated from Afrikaans.
104 Willem de Klerk, *Afrikaners – Kroes, Kras, Kordaat*.
105 *Ibid*, pp. 20–1, 95.
106 Du Toit, p. 238.
107 Dommisse and Esterhuyse, p. 231.
108 Terreblanche, pp. 439–49.

Index

Do you have any comments, suggestions or
feedback about this book or any other Zebra Press titles?
Contact us at talkback@zebrapress.co.za

8